A Year Ago Today

– GRAHAM HAITCH –

Printed and bound in England by www.printondemand-worldwide.com

http://www.fast-print.net/bookshop

A Year Ago Today
Copyright © Graham Haitch 2018

ISBN: 978-178456-600-5

First published 2018 by
FASTPRINT PUBLISHING
Peterborough, England.

A Year Ago Today
A self published novel by
Graham Haitch
For more information
ayearagotoday@icloud.com

Prologue

It started like any other day in early February. The skies were overcast. The winds were picking up and it looked like rain. As normal for weekends over these last few months, I had preempted the event the previous evening by compiling a list of things to do. I found it easier to face the weekend knowing in advance the options that were out there. Knowing and then realising I would feel like an audience of one trying to adapt to my surroundings. It is difficult to understand one's feelings when every thought is of Anna. My every waking moment is another moment filled with those thoughts. A herd of buffalo could be rampaging through the streets and rather than diving for cover, my last thought would be, "Anna?".

Heading into town early on Saturday morning, avoiding the hustle and bustle of daily road rage that's customary in this part of France, I managed to park without incident. Buy a copy of The Times. Sit with coffee in hand while watching the world go by. The rain was holding off. My thoughts drifted away to happier times. Happier times that coincidentally started a year ago today.

A Year Ago Today

Chapter One

My mood was ambivalent, it was a Friday evening. I should go out. Sitting by the fire, the temptation receded. Turning to my computer seemed the better option and why not see who's out there. My mood lightened as I trawled through many a pretty face. Now I'm not saying I had an epiphany as the picture was of no real consequence and I could have easily passed it by but the more I gazed, the more intrigued I became about this woman. A casual setting which was obvious by the background and yet, there she was, pearl neckless with matching earrings and that yellow dress. Holding a flute of champagne with such an endearing smile. With eyes that reminded me of the Mona Lisa. No matter from which direction I viewed, the eyes followed. Nothing to lose and the lady had asked for more than the standard reply of, "Hello. My name is …… Lets chat." Perfect! As it was all about getting her interest. Ladies love humour and it just so happened to be one of the few qualities I possessed. She looked an intelligent, well groomed woman easily put off by flippant nonsensical remarks. That cut down my options. Something simple and to the point.

Hi Anna, I didn't want to write twenty pages of interesting dialogue only to find it trashed out of hand. Consider this a connection being made, albeit by a slim thread, a connection never the less. The next step is yours and being the intelligent woman I take you to be, I shouldn't have long to wait. Yours Chris. (I had to call myself something)

I wasn't expecting a response as to expect can often lead to disappointment. Having moved on temporarily to browse through more faces I received a message. Barely fifteen minutes had passed, it was Anna.

Yes, you have made a connection and yes, by a slim thread. Other than your good looks and obvious humour, do you posses depth of personality?

Now, I have been on and off web sites for a number of years but this was a first. A question with implications and a compliment in a matter of but a few words. Who was this woman? What should I reply? I read and reread that short message trying to imagine her thoughts as she wrote. What was she thinking at that moment? Could the reply shift the balance in my favour? Deviate from the normal response was my first thought. Keep it light. Try and show intelligence, reason, taste and discretion befitting a mature gentleman such as I. No chance. Sooner or later she would see through that facade. I was not saying I didn't possess those qualities, but "mon talent caché" had always been humour. The message board remained blank. Come on James, think of something.

What to say? She had remarked on my photo? Depth of personality. Mmmmm, let me think about that. Depth as in, out of mine! What happened to the, "Nice to meet you. What are your hobbies"? I stared at the screen trying to pick that relevant thought I knew was flying around inside my head. It was locating that thought, that was my problem. Decision made. It had to be witty. Could I do intelligent witty?

Hi Anna, thank you for such a prompt reply. I'm sorry to disappoint you but that photo was taken when I was twenty. Photoshopped to make me look older and more, "Windswept & Interesting." I have pondered over your question asked for some time and that in itself must render a clue to my depth. A shallow man would find no need to ponder.

I pressed send.

A laughing face was the response. I waited. Twenty minutes passed and my vigilance pays off.

Why have I not received a reply?

So I sent a smiley face back. Three smiley faces returned. This couldn't continue. She was gauging my responses. Had to be proactive. How did that work again? I think it went something like, "A picture is worth a thousand words." Who ever said that had never tried communicating on a date site where icons are in abundance but mostly, irrelevant!.

This was it James, your chance to show that depth. That proactive depth. Don't blow it now!

You are teasing me Anna. Waiting for some substance. Making it worth your while to reply, sans icons. Sorry to disappoint you once again Anna but if you require anything more than casual banter at this point in our fragile communication, you will have to do better than <u>iconic</u> replies.

An intelligent and humorous response so far.

The fragile communication, hanging by a thread, now depends on your response Anna. You are no doubt by now, considering this. You might be

2

wavering between reply or reject. The pendulum swings. Perhaps I can help tip the balance in my favour. You look most divine in your yellow dress and pearls.
I sat back to await a reply. Immediate response! I was found to be amusing and for some unknown reason, still considered intelligent. The yellow dress compliment went down well. Worn at a Polo match in Hollywood. Friday evening was picking up.

Messages passed back and forth but I wasn't going to be drawn into believing it might go further. (I don't do disappointment very well.) Her messages became of a more positive nature. Liking what I wrote and responding in kind. An astute woman writing in the manner of someone knowing what she wanted and directing her questions accordingly. I rode the wave for the next few days.

Anna suggested we get off the site and continue via email. Preempting any possibility for discussion, Anna's' email address was included. A capital, YES PLEASE when replying, this time via email, was my first thought. Too simple. To easy.

Upgrade our relationship Anna?   I have contemplated this suggestion and taking into consideration the potential and possible downsides to this upgrade, I feel the benefits far out-way the deficits. I therefore conclude your idea to be based on sound judgement. Yours James.
My decision not to follow up with a heavily underlined, large capitals "yes please", played on my conscience. Would the undercurrent of humour show through? Was I assuming too much of Anna? Had I opened myself up to ridicule? After all, it was only a, That's a good idea Anna. Email supplied. Sort of message she required.

It was late but I waited. Then I waited some more until finally, accepting the inevitable, I went to bed.

A cold Sunday morning. Put the porridge to soak. Kettle on for tea and now, a shower. Tea made, I reached for my phone. An email from Anna!

I don't know you, but I appreciate your contemplation.
Don't know you? We'd been messaging for days? I was confused? While suffering the indignation of being confused a follow-up message arrived.

Oh, it's sweetie Chris!!! I see. So it's James now. Thank you for your email. What are you apart from good looks and the only person I know that writes a paragraph just to say Yes.
How did she do that? It threw me off balance. Who asked, What are you? What do you do. I understood? What was your stand on the wider implications surrounding the political upheaval in Afghanistan? What is your zodiac sign? Those I could handle. Admittedly I might struggle on upheaval, political or otherwise but "What are you"?

Digression was the only possible answer. Digression and humour. A powerful combination. Thoughts of digression. Thoughts of humour were in free fall. I waited for them to collide.

3

Hi Anna. As an intelligent woman it will not be beyond your capabilities to do the maths. If I write a paragraph where yes would have sufficed, can you imagine how many paragraphs it would require for me to answer the question, "What are you?" In all probability, you'll have lost the will to live, well before the end of the debacle. While you ponder that thought may I suggest a more direct line of enquiry?"

Being well aware Anna had used the, good looks, remark on more than one occasion, I decided to send a photo. Not so easy. What photo? The one I Photoshopped. Combining four of me dressed differently. Ok, that worked. Now for the content to compliment the pic?

Meanwhile Anna, I am going to refer to the idea of the "What are you?" question, pictorially. I am who you see. A complex character who can adapt to his surroundings. Multi tasking by times four. Surely that would encompass any and all needs of an interested party?

Maybe not digression but certainly avoidance. How else could I keep her interested? Send and see. Her reply was almost instantaneous.

Ha-ha-ha, Dear James, not just good looks times four but an intellectual fellow. Typing on my phone which is difficult, especially with these long manicured nails. Let me get hold of my pc to answer fully.

I took fifteen minutes to compose the previous response. Should I wait for the pc or perhaps a short reply which, to be honest, was almost irresistible. I replied!

You mention, those nails Anna? Are they the nails of some third party? Getting hold of your pc. Is it avoiding you? I am confused? I'll get hold of a shower and maybe all will become apparent.

An immediate response.

Having a shower James? Do you sing? My nails are my own, like most of the rest. Still from my phone.

Once again. Answers but also questions.

After many years of listening to my father singing My Way in the shower, let me just say Anna, it dampened my enthusiasm to continue with this family trait. You say, "Most of the rest"? Does this mean you have parts belonging to someone else?

Maybe not the perfect response but hey, I was under pressure but I think it worked! I got a pc answer an hour later, post shower.

Sorry couldn't get back earlier James, I was involved in a dinner engagement with friends. (Have to keep up appearances.) I've now had time to peruse previous messages. Yes, I am proactive unless there is someone worth submitting to. Finding the right man would be the priority. Thus allowing me to concentrate on those now, notorious nails, if the situation permits. But with whom? When and Where? That is the question.

You asked me to ask questions. How about these?

Why are you always on the move when writing messages? Hyperactive?

Why do you find the need to weave the laces of enigmatic phrases, unclear hints and beautiful words just to impress an unknown woman in a yellow dress? Don't get me wrong, I really do appreciate your efforts but why do you not talk about, What you do? Where you live? Hobbies? What are you looking for in a woman? I guess your occupation as …… a lawyer. A screen writer. A teacher. Do you like sport? Are you fit and slim. Of course you are! I've seen your times four photo. (I like the way you combined the four photos of you. Photoshop?) Musical likes? I'm assuming you are single. What I don't understand, is why? Children? Need I say more?

I was getting the idea Anna said what was on her mind. If only I had the answers.

I'm going to have to sleep on your questions Anna as it's too much to assimilate this late in the evening. Other than to say, I might have preferred you when you just had a nail problem to distract you.

Bon Nuit Anna,

I liked this woman. I liked how she thought.

I was brought up, third in line with three sisters. I had to deal with girls throughout my adolescence. Watch them grow into teenagers. To young adults before, one after the other, they flew the nest. I had confrontations with all during our early years together. Not being singled out as the only male but included as any child would include another. Not by sex nor race but through natural hierarchy. I learnt to fit in. To play the game. Not realising nor appreciating at the time that these well learnt lessons of my earlier years with three sisters would stand me in such good stead. I was not saying I fully understood the ways of women but it surely helped.

I received a reply.

Good Night James. I'm sorry if my questions seem intrusive. It wasn't exactly what I wanted to do but you did say, Ask. It is only because I need to start to trust you, at least a little bit. It will allow me to open up. Don't worry if it is a problem at this time. Just wanted to know you better.

Sweet Dreams,

Anna.

Early the next morning I read through Anna's last emails. It would seem Anna was interested. Why else would she ask so many questions? Possibly because I encouraged her? I thought about how I might answer. It had just become personal. Maybe there was more riding on this reply than I realised. That was being a little naive James. Surely you realised there was a lot riding on every reply? Anna was interested, just hold that interest. Easy for me to say.

Good Morning Anna, I regard it as an inquisitive mind rather than an intrusive one. I asked for questions and you've kindly supplied. I will do my very best to give honest and unbiased answers. (I think that rules out the possibility of being a lawyer.) Always on the move? Actually no. My computer is upstairs. Therefore simpler to email on the phone. So to answer that question Anna, it would be no, I'm not on the move. Just on my mobile. Where do I live? An easy one. I live in Antibes. Hobbies? What flashed through my mind was asking whether playing darts and drinking myself into oblivion on a Friday night, constituted a hobby? I decided against it.

Hobbies. I enjoy walking in the rain on a wind free day with a good umbrella. I find the persistent, gentle tapping of the rain soothing. Reading. Tennis, yes. I love it. I go to Roland Garros every year ...... to watch! I have also been known, in my limited capacity, to enjoy skiing. Fit? Slim? Of course I am. (Reminder to myself. Must cut out that wine of a lunchtime.) *What am I looking for in a woman? Obedience with that feeling of a preordained destiny of being semi permanently tied, metaphorically speaking, to the kitchen sink when not satisfying my every desire.*

Taking a risk with that one. It could end in one of two ways. I'd be deleted immediately or I'd found my ideal woman. Or possibly, she had a keen sense of humour and would be laughing in the aisle.

My musical tastes are wide and varied. Time for discovery in the future while spending those, soon to be, wonderful times together. (Always good to be positive and maybe even romantically put?) *Children. Yes I have two. One of each. She is thirty something and lives in London. He is also thirty something and lives in Houston.*

Work, yes. But you are way off the mark. But talking of lawyers. Do you know what five hundred lawyers at the bottom of the sea constitute? A Good Start! I am going to be "Glass Half Full" here Anna and say, I do believe we have that good start. I told my daughter that joke, who was a lawyer at the time. She didn't think it was funny? I wondered why?

You asked why I find the need to be enigmatic, with the Lady in the yellow dress. And oh so pretty in her yellow dress. I'm thinking Anna, that through the many conversations we will have (and I know we will), you'll discover more about my mystifying ways first hand, than from any questions I might answer. You are a clever and intuitive woman. Give it time. I believe you will enjoy the journey.

Most questions answered and I have two for you.

What nationality are you and if I may be so bold as to ask, how old are you? Forty seven I noticed on the website but surely not a day over forty two?

Later Anna, James x

It was just after nine in the morning when I sent that email. I had work to do. I was involved in a discussion on our future logistics. My area of expertise. Needed to concentrate. The thought process was interrupted by the message ping. It was barely ten minutes since I sent my message! I had to ignore it. The time ticked by. The conversations flowed. Points noted. Decisions made. Time to escape the office. Phone in hand I set off, only to be waylaid by Stuart, the floor manager.

6

I will need the drawings of that reception desk James as soon as you can. I've Philo standing by to start. Oh and can you take a look at the delivery that came in earlier?

Off to the loading bay where a new consignment of laminates and wood sat. More time. There would be time to read Anna's email later. It was well after lunch before I found that time.

Good Morning James, This is just to express my surprise and pleasure to have received such an early and again elaborate message. I am on the move at the moment, typing at the red traffic lights. Will come back to you later with your questions answered. (maybe). Meanwhile have a fulfilling day, À bientot! Anna

Maybe not the answer I was hoping for but positive enough all the same. I could but wait until later. The day moved uneventfully forward. Once home, in my room upstairs, sat in front of a blank screen. I knew I should wait. Wait for that promised email to arrive. Could I mail before receiving that reply? I didn't want to appear too keen. It was the way the game was played. Trying to establish a rapport without seeming needy. I couldn't just sit there waiting. I needed a subject as I already knew I was going to reply.

Hi Anna, While waiting with undisguised relish for your up and coming mail, I decided to preempt the moment and throw a couple of photos your way. If I don't hear back I will certainly blame my lack of photogenic ability or not having had the forethought to give them a severe case of Photoshop before sending.

Talking of preempting and while in the mood to "open up", as seen in the photos of James close up! I am now about to bore you with the abridged story of my life. Born in the SW of England, had a good time then got married. Not saying the good times stopped at marriage, it just gives me the possibility of expanding on my earlier years, at a later date. Where was I? Oh yes, married. A son was born. We moved to London. Shortly after, blessed with a daughter. Started a business with a close friend. Car Buffs Valeting Service. It is quite amazing how profitable such a venture can become in just a few years. Separated and was soon advised by a good friend, who had connections, that a stay in Kitzbuhel might be what I needed. Closed the company. Two years passed in Austria then I moved to Holland. Having met a Dutch girl on her annual ski holiday the season before. We lived happily in Dordrecht for seven years until Josey's desire to live in France, coinciding with an offer I had of employment near Cannes. She has now become my future ex wife. Future in so much as we have been separated for eight years yet not divorced. I once remarked to a friend that all women are potential future ex's. It didn't go down well. Possibly because he was recently married. And that Anna brings you up to date on the abridged version of my life.

Anna's reply came within the hour.

You're a funny Brit! It's good to hear from you despite the pics. Only kidding. No worries James. You're fine. I think I've figured out your age. Two children in their thirty somethings. (I hope you know their exact age and birthdays?) You must be in your mid to late fifties?

Thank you for your openness this time. I really appreciate that.

I don't know where to start. How about. If texting at the red lights constitutes multi tasking then I'm definitely good at multi tasking. (I knew a woman who could breast feed while driving)

What did you say about your expectations of a woman? Obedient creature confined to the kitchen. Cooking and .....? Are you a direct descendant of the Ottoman Sultan? Not impossible, knowing your countries imperial past. You Brits were everywhere. Never mind, it might be interesting to put to the test. Never say never! Did I say I was widowed? It was last year. Before that sad event I used to be a solid and established Madame. Pampered and protected. Loved and cared for. It was tough in the beginning but time heals. The page has turned. (Don't worry, I won't ask you to look at pictures of my late husbands gravestone.) I have two beautiful daughters. One living in Switzerland, the other is hoping to go to uni in England in the fall. My ambition in life is quite simple. To fall in love again. The rest? I have it, or can have it, if I wish.

A practical thought. I am going to Courmayeur a week on Sunday. Do you want me to invite you for drinks before I go or after? Or do you want to invite me? Or no chance, forget it?

ps: These photos are of me on my way to play tennis this morning. (I took them especially for you) Unfortunately, I lost. Which is a pity as I'm a bad loser!

So much to think about. Never say never? A veiled implication? Pampered and protected? Do we pamper our women? I was not sure if I did. Wasn't that just a nice way of saying, spoil our women? Mmmmm

Invited for drinks! It did not go unnoticed Anna was taking control. But with a certain amount of confidence lacking, when saying, "Or no chance, forget it". My chance to regain her confidence. But first a comment on the photos.

Hello Anna, It is my turn to thank you for such enlightenment. I do have to admit, it did take me some time before I'd actually read a single word. (Distracted by your photos could have had something to do with it.). Off to play tennis, and you think of me. There is bad news. Since estimating my age to be in the mid fifties, it would be bad form on my part to go out with someone who is obviously twenty years younger. That's my way of saying, No Worries Anna. You're Fine. I find my version to be more eloquent and flattering. Don't you agree? I immediately understood your problem when you said you'd lost. Look at the photos. I'm surprised you haven't realised it your self. It's those nails! As beautifully long and crimson red they might be, hardly ideal for playing tennis? Take my advice .... stop playing tennis.

Not sure why Anna's nails have become so relevant to our conversations? A point of mutual "Safe ground" perhaps?

What nationality are you? Your command of the English language is good. (I was going to say exceptional but a little too early to be praising ones future ex wife.) I'm assuming French as you said you were taking your parents out, so they must live nearby and therefore French. How am I doing?

I'm sorry to hear about your loss but you are right I might not be interested in looking at the gravestone photo. Albeit potentially more agreeable than a pic of my ex wife. And she is still alive! I think that might be in the category of bad taste and I do apologise Anna but it serves two purposes. To gauge your sense of humour (obviously being aware us Brits are known for it) but also to have a dig at the ex wife without retaliation. Perhaps I should add, we are good friends and I'm sure if she read this it would be with a wry smile. I mention sense of humour Anna because mine has a tendency to be, a little dry. You have been warned. On a more pleasant and concluding note.

Drinks. I look forward to it.

James.

ps: Please Don't Reply While Driving

The next morning I got a reply.

Hi Brit. Driving again. Personal chauffeur to my daughter. You make me laugh and I like it. Texting at the red lights. Speak to you later.

One word from me Anna and you do the opposite. I am very flattered by this attention but am also concerned for your safety.

Later that evening I was rewarded, if that be the right word, with paragraphs from Anna but maybe not so rewarding, as I was hoping for that drink.

No, I am not French although Je parle francais tres bien. We are in France. We have to. "Do in Rome as Romans do." (Almost right Anna) I say it just to show off even though I think its not correct. (Right that time Anna.) Rebel? Me? No way. I am the most conservative shallow-minded bourgeois woman I know. And I know a lot! My expertise is housekeeping. How to look good and please a husband. Make sure the children are fed. Dinners-invitations-charity, all that stuff. But indeed, deep inside there is a little devil.

Tonight it is dinner with my parents. (Just escaped to mail you.) Drinks? Here come the excuses. I'm panicking obviously. I'm too pale. Need a ski complexion on my cheeks. An evening with my daughter in Beausoleil early next week. On the Friday, seeing my lawyer. Saturday packing with last instructions to the service. Early start Sunday as it's a five hour drive. Please say you understand my lame excuses although I do have one valid reason for not seeing you before. If we meet now and by chance have the complicity combined with a perfect understanding, I will feel terribly guilty while flirting with gorgeous Italian ski instructors. I need to feel free from moral obligations for that week. (Just to say something funny. I am not that liberal. Honest!)

I suppose it is better to keep the wine maturing for sometime and wait until the nightingales start to sing in the gardens. (I speak of our future rendezvous. I

9

return on the twenty eighth.) Even if you never have the courage to admit it, I know my English is exceptional. Yes, I have an education. As I am sure you do. Higher education or you wouldn't be such a mentalist! Finally,

Tell me something nice James, before we call it a day.

Concentrate on the something nice James. Just that. The rest can follow.

Nice is not something I just switch on and off Anna. It has a tendency towards hypocritical. Have a nice day. What does that mean? Oh, she's nice. What a nice hat. See where I'm going with this Anna? So rather than disappoint you. I will tell you a joke.

Two Goldfish in a bowl.

First Goldfish says, "It's great being a Goldfish".

Second Goldfish says, "Yes but it's a shame about our three second memory span".

First Goldfish says, ... "It's great being a Goldfish."

Pleasant Dreams Anna,

The following morning I had time to think of a suitable reply to that previous mail. There were a few comments made that confused. Instructions to the service. Dinners, invitations, charities. It was not a world I lived in. Perhaps comments on those particular subjects should be avoided, for the time being? Reading through the last email supplied me with adequate resources for a fun packed reply. No need to venture into the unknown. Save "the service" for another time.

Dear Anna, having read and reread your email I have come to a variety of conclusions. Your sincerity has been brought into question. No, you didn't know I was going to look at your nails closely. Unless you are hyper conscious about them? Meaning perhaps, you regard your nails as an important part of who you are? So which is it Anna? Lacking in sincerity or extremely shallow?

I was comfortable with that reply. I had accepted this was a woman of strong character. She knew who she was. She would see the truth in my remarks and laugh at my attempt to enrage her. At least that was the theory. Keep up the pressure. If I was wrong. Bye bye Anna. If I was right. See you soon Anna. I continued.

I do believe Anna, a few emails ago, you asked if I would like a drink prior to your departure. And now you change your mind? For the moment I will accept it is all about nervous tension which I can understand. Meeting someone such as I could be a daunting task. Do not fear. You will find me to be a pleasant distraction from the hectic social functions you endure in your life.

With the thought of sincerity still ringing in my ears, I'd like to draw your attention to another valid point. My intentions have always been honourable and am now lead to believe you go to have fun with Italian ski instructors. I am not worried nor jealous Anna. I think it's understandable you would want to have some fun before settling down with your true love. It is fortunate for you I'm a tolerant

10

person who understands the ways of women and their need to discover said love in their own sweet time. But Italian ski instructors?

Btw, I'm going to a divorce party the Saturday evening before you depart on your ski trip, held by Cristina a woman I know. She is a bit "wacky". An artist. Need I say more. I've decided to go for a suit, back tie and shirt. Not quite sure what to expect but she is rather sexy. And single! But don't worry Anna, my intentions, as I said, are honourable. I do believe my earlier uncontainable desire to supply you with subtle misgivings regarding your character might back-fire on me. I could delete the entire mail and start again but I had too much fun writing it. Dilemma! Obviously I've gone against my better judgement and have decided to send but before doing so I'd like to add, something as they say, totally different. I've been giving some thought to your nationality. Dinner with your parents, so they are local French! The only other possibility available is that you are Welsh! Please don't be embarrassed to admit this. As heavy a burden it might be to carry. I promise to be the one who doesn't curl up in laughter the moment you speak. Don't you just love that accent? If you have other Welsh friends then I sincerely apologise unless they are, very small or very old. (A good chance I could beat them in an unfair fight.)

Enjoy your Day Anna,

James x

How many times had I read that message? It was not my style to be so cutting. Then why was I? It was Anna. I thought of her as a woman who was used to getting her own way. I wasn't saying it was a bad thing, it was just that my intuition drove me to be ...... somebody I wasn't? That, I was afraid could not be prevented. Certainly not before we meet. Hang in there James. If it was going to happen. It would. I received a reply.

"OMG James. HOW FUNNY!!! "

Nothing more? I waited. Five minutes later, I responded.

You might think it funny Anna but don't think I haven't noticed your avoidance of the subject matter." Wait a minute? You are Welsh!

An immediate response.

Funny for several reasons James.

1. The moment you sent me the last message I was rereading and savouring the one before. waiting at the red light, of course. What timing!

2. Welsh! How funny. Beautiful as Wales is, you are nowhere near.

3. And being a hopelessly positive person, I'm just laughing cause the morning is fantastic!.

BTW, I'm not religious. (ref OMG!)

I felt compiled to respond even knowing it wasn't necessary.

Nor I Anna. My father who was an atheist, insisted at the age of eight I went to Sunday school. I didn't understand his reasoning but a few years later, when I

11

quit he said, "Now wasn't that a waste of your time"? And that, as God is my witness, is how I view religion.

Think I might go to Isola next weekend. I hear the snow is good and it's under two hours away. Check out the female ski instructors. Perhaps we can compare notes on your return. Assuming of course, I haven't been snapped up by a ravishing blonde instructor. Or possibly, dark & sultry. I'm not fussy when it comes to ski instructors.

Ah well. Lunch is concluded. Coffee drunk. Back to work

James

I'm funny. That was what Anna said. There was no denying it, I was flattered by that remark. Content. My day was complete and it was barely three o'clock! What I needed to do, was keep it in perspective. Those were emails. Conversations passing to and fro. Of no substance in the real world. Although? I felt our messages were, gathering substance. Those thoughts that filled my head were real. Accept it James, you're captivated by your own creation. The time to meet will come and then we will see.

Anna did not take long to reply.

I cannot believe my James is jealous already. How wonderful. (Only a jealous man would try to make another like himself.) Do you really believe you could possibly be more successful with ski instructors than I?

If you are really intrigued as to my nationality, may I suggest the following. Make up some posters with the top line in large red font saying WANTED. Next line. €1000 reward for any information concerning the woman in the photo below. Don't forget your contact details. Now all you need to do is fly around Antibes (at 3 a.m.) throwing posters as you go and then wait for the calls to come rolling in. Sorry this was stupid. Your Goldfish joke was better!

I've pondered over my reply Anna. Having read your message earlier, I was tempted to reply immediately. Then I thought, never answer a mail in anger.

So, I'm now calm. What do you mean, jealous!!! I'll have you know, I don't have a jealous bone in my body. I remember the time I found myself in the fraught position of having three girlfriends at the same time. There was never a moment I was jealous of any of them. QED

I feel better now, having got that off my chest. My Yin has now realigned with my Yang. (Does that make any sense?)

I thought your idea would work. So I had a thousand posters made up. Employed five people to post them around the town (self adhesive backs) ……….. then read the rest of your message. "Sorry, this was stupid". I've paid the five and threw the posters in the bin. In the normal scheme of things, women cost after meeting. This is a first for me. 1285:73 Euro's so far……….and I haven't even met you! Stay calm James. I've decided on plan B. Knowing your destination for the coming week, I've hired a couple of unscrupulous characters who will break *into your room, photograph your Passport and, et voila! Total to date, 2885:73 Euro's*

So, you liked the goldfish joke. It's the only one I have. Don't do jokes. Can't see why people get so excited about humour. What they need is a cold shower and a couple of years in the army. That will bring them to their senses. Bad moods and a cantankerous nature is far more practical. You know where you are with this kind of attitude. Everything "pisses you off", no surprises. Perfect! I'm sorry, I think I lost my thread of conversation. My Yin is obviously not as inline with my Yang as I thought. That calm exterior must be cracking? But then it's got every reason to be. 2885:73 good reasons!

Two Hours later I return to this message.

So where was I? Oh yes. Discussing that positive effect you seem to have on me. I've decided to say no more on that subject but leave it open to be discussed at a later date. In person. I will now deviate by asking, apart from being the perfect role model to your daughters. How do you fill your day? I can't imagine you have a job. Surely, with all the tea parties, charity work and the odd jumble sale to organise, you must be terribly busy. (I bet that doesn't get me a straight answer.) God knows where the last three and half hours have gone? Oh, and my Italian burglars asked if you have a better photo. You know, as you would normally look....... Smug with a slight touch of mischievous devilment!

Your ever, increasingly appreciative friend,

James.

It was late when I finally sent that message so not expecting a reply, I went to bed. It wasn't until late the following evening did I receive that long awaited reply but I think it was worth the wait.

Dear anti-jealous James (only with your permission can I say dear?) It's unbelievable. How do you do it? I had a totally sleepless night! My day is ruined....even driving+texting is now impossible. You keep me thrilled and wanting to read more. The more the better. The story of the posters is fascinating! And the style with the well-measured sense of humour! The deep economic analysis of the possible project "glue the poster" leaves no doubt we are dealing with the profoundly knowledgeable expert here. Have you ever written anything like Jerome K Jerome short stories? Are you Jerome K Jerome? If not, you should write! You might become rich, if you sell a million.

Only one remark. What is QED? We, the Welsh, don't use such abbreviation. Is it something to do with Al-Qaeda? Are you threatening me for misbehaviour? And only for texting at the red light? On comparing ski instructors. I will definitely beat you in this competition for a very simple reason. Where have you seen smashingly attractive female ski instructors? They are as rare as smashingly attractive female IT administrators (according to my observations, also attractive males in this domain are a rarity).

Girlfriends issue. How many are presently left out of the three? (Sorry for such indiscreet question, but I really need to know if you are free!)
Unscrupulous characters breaking in, while I am peacefully enjoying my nights dreams. May I advise you on hiring those Italian (male please!) ski instructors for this job? - please don't be jealous again!!!
Sweet night to you, dear James do not drink too much, please. Spare your liver. And please, do not fall easily into the trap of the freshly divorced female friend! I am sure she is waiting for this Saturday party to seduce you! (I have not a pinch of jealousy in me either)
Now take or leave it, I am of Russian origin. Home town, Moscow. Citizen of Holland (don't ask why, too long of a story) Not quite Welsh! Good Night Dear James!

Anna caught the mood of my messages perfectly. Note James, the usage of the word dear. Are we becoming more familiar? Barriers breaking down. I would like to think so. Don't let my enthusiasm get the better of me. What confused was her reasons for believing I had the capability of writing anything? Who is Jerome K Jerome anyway? So Anna is Russian (I think I read the book?) With a Dutch passport. Why did I think it was going to be simple? My joke about three girlfriends brought forth the serious side of her. Asking the question. "Are you free"? It was certainly obvious to me that she was considering these mails to be a potential start of something. We were going to meet. One day soon, we were going to meet.

Hi Anna, I was just off to bed but having read your mail I thought I should not avail you of any possibility of more sleepless nights. The three girls disappeared a very long time ago. Hope that news helps you secure a good nights sleep?
Bonne Nuit Anna
ps. QED - Quod Erat Demonstrandum. Loosely translated. That which was to be demonstrated. Usually found at the end of a mathematical proof to indicate that the proof is complete. You did ask.

Anna's reply arrived the next morning. Too late for the school run. I therefore concluded, not written at the lights.

Dear James, didn't you know that money politics and religion are taboo subjects at social encounters? In fact, we've touched on all three of them, breaking the odds. Sorry, need to recharge my batteries now. My computer refuses to function. And I need him (or her?) for the days to come!!! Have got tons of things to do before leaving to meet my ski instructors. I give you the wishes of a wonderful and almost Spring day.
ps: Another small portion of information about myself (if you are still interested, of course): I studied Anglo - American Philosophy in my home town university for 5 years. But please don't ask me to quote Charles Dickens, I simply don't remember! This explains my English proficiency, and one of my present

weaknesses. A genuine interest in one English gentleman (btw, never dated an Englishman in my life!!!) And you? I bet engineering? As of "QED", Anna

Well Anna, I've just read your mail. No time for too many words. (Work calls) I just thought I would say, "That's amazing! We already have something in common. I've never dated an Englishman either!"

Three tearfully laughing icons was Anna's reply.

"Work calls". I was wondering why I said that? Was it her earlier reference to charities and functions? Her day filled and no time to fit in employment. It was more likely I was reading too much into my "throw-away" comments.

The following afternoon and half way through lunch I decided to message Anna. Never send under the influence of alcohol! I broke the golden rule.

"I love you & I want to have your babies!" Let me explain Anna.

This is what happens when my boss decides, it's his birthday and lunch today, is on him. Personally I prefer a jog along the beach followed up with a lettuce and carrot cocktail. So ...... unaccustomed as I am to alcohol, I find myself in a confused state of mind. It's ok Anna. The term, "I want to have your babies", as I'm sure you're aware, is a male impossibility. As such, you don't have to worry. I am having such an enjoyable lunch I thought it only right and proper to include you. And lucky you, another pic of me to follow.

Until later,

James (as in, Your Dear......)

I received an immediate reply.

Oh, aren't you a darling, Jimmy! Thinking of me even when having lunch with his boss! Or while pretending that he's working?

I replied later that day, wrongly assuming I was no longer under the influence.

"Jimmy", Anna? I can see that smile on your face as you wrote that. You are wondering if I will, "Rise To The Bait". (Fishing terminology. Not that I'm into fishing, you understand. To be honest, never did understand that one. Fishing, that is.) But I digress, as usual. (You can't protect an Empire for years by being direct.) You Anna, can call me what you like. What ever name inspires and I will read into that, what I will.

I was sat in front of the computer that evening, rereading what I'd previously sent that afternoon. Not good. My dilemma at that moment? I felt I needed to redeem myself. Unfortunately I was still under the influence of the extremely extended lunch.

I've just reread my afternoon intro. I'm now wondering, what category those paragraphs fell into? Utter nonsense, I think. I apologise. Now here, I digress for a moment. Analysing My Thought Process.

I sit in front of the screen, with not a thought in my head. I will read the previous few mails. Mine & yours. This will set my mood. Allowing the words to flow. They are words in my head. I wait awhile. The words in my head are in "free fall". They need a nucleus to converge upon. Now this is where it gets interesting. I will be controversial. I will definitely be mildly sarcastic and hopefully humorous. This creates not one, but many nuclei. Feelings and words, in free fall. Occasionally, (Occasionally. Who am I kidding?) I get impulsive in my writing. This impulsiveness is directly related to the person I'm mailing. The next bit is the important bit.

It seems, what I am trying to say, and this is a kind of, ... Maybe James needs help? Like serious help. I would ask, "Do you really want to be involved with someone who is clearly unhinged". You might think it so but it won't stop you reading. Then why? Because, at the very least it brings a smile to your face, at the traffic lights. At the very best. Well that's easy. It makes your day. The conclusion therefore is..........Another lot of, Utter Nonsense. Underpinned by the typical Englishman's curse.......the inability to come to the point. To be discussed at a later date.

Moving swiftly on. ..... All packed? Tank full of fuel? (Always useful to know. It's expensive in Italy) Skies? Boots? Socks? Poles? Dutch passport? Sun Cream? Credit Card? Italian Phrase book telling you a hundred and one ways to say "No", to ski instructors? Wooly Hat? Music? Pack of Playing Cards? (Necessary once you've become proficient in saying, No). A thought worth mentioning. In my vast experience of working in ski bars. I would suggest you avoid them. (Full of old men, smoking pipes and playing cards.)

I would advise a late breakfast to avoid the queues. Followed by an early night to recapture the energy needed to restart the next days wonderful skiing. Have a healthy holiday avoiding those smokey bars.

Enjoy! James

Now that turned into a long email. Not much substance I agree but I was convinced it wasn't too important. When Anna wanted substance Anna would get substance. My concern was not about producing substance to any question she might ask, it was being of substance when we met. Getting ahead of myself there. You're doing just fine James. Keep it up.

Reading, and re reading, and re reading. And enjoying. Thank you James. Just going to a function in Monaco so I asked my daughter to take this photo. (Just for you.) We returned from the function which is when I realised I hadn't pressed send earlier. So I finish by saying, Monaco was a tad boring. Anna

ps. We leave on Sunday, not tomorrow.

I needed to reply. Thinking she was leaving tomorrow. That was a mistake. Did I know it was Sunday? I kept it short.

1st Point Anna, It pleases me that it pleases you. (My subservient side.)

2nd Point. (Where am I picking this up from? I don't do points?)

You look.........sensational. No sideways compliment there.

3rd Point. Sorry to hear the evening was, but a tad, boring.

4th Point. You leave on Sunday.

Did I mention you look sensational?

16

Pleasant Dreams Anna,
Seemingly, not to be outdone, a follow up message.
Sweet Dreams, James, but before I go, I need to ask you. How tall are you?
Now you can ask me about my age, and we'll be even. I need to know so I can
calibrate the heels for our forthcoming encounter. Once again, Sweet dreams
…….. to my addiction.
Her addiction? "Addicted To You". A song by Avicii came to mind. That had my
head spinning. Our forthcoming encounter? Anna was going to the mountains,
skiing and yet she was asking about such details? That had to tell me something
about Anna apart from the obvious conclusion that she wasn't short. I was
wondering why I was having the feeling Anna had already covered most
possibilities for the forthcoming encounter? Dress according to shoes
possibilities? A woman who paid a lot of attention to details? A considerate
woman, wanting to avoid any possible embarrassment on my part? I was going
to have to sleep on that but knowing full well it might be sometime before my
mind allowed me that indulgence.
OMG Anna, you are two metres tall! Maybe it should be me who wears the
heels? How tall am I? About five centimetres taller than my sister. I'll call her
and ask her then I can calculate my height. Just realised, I don't have to do that.
I stood against the wall, marked it and measured. Clever, Yes? 1778 (Give or
take a millimetre.) Having answered your question as honestly as my
calculations have allowed, I'm now supposed to ask you about your age. Is it
nice being your age?
I hope you don't read this while driving.
Take Care Anna
James xx (a kiss for each cheek. When in France………)
You have your morning prize James, for such honesty and diligence. There are
fresh golden - crusted pancakes I've just made and I will save one for you.
Unfortunately I now see, having already indulged myself, along with the rest of
the household there doesn't seem to be any left? Very nice with some honey
and freshly ground coffee. You feel the aroma? I can share the recipe if you wish
or better still, I will make some for you when you visit. Bisous You know what?
Forget about the heels... shame though - I just bought a pair of gorgeous
Ferragamo's. (I am exactly the same height, minus a centimetre.) See you on
my return.
Ferragamo's? Google it James.
The thought crossed my mind, I'd never been out with someone my height. I
could remember many years ago, I was with a friend discussing a couple of girls
across the way. "So which do you prefer", he asked. "Not really my type", I
answered. "What is your type", he questioned. I couldn't answer. I was twenty
two years old, what did I know. Girlfriends came and went. Never thought of
analysing why there was a particular interest in one over the other. It wasn't until

many years, and two wives later that I was able to look back and see similarities comparable to "my type". One particular similarity. They were all a lot shorter than I. So it would be a first! As a man who was always willing to accept change, I ventured out into the unknown. I liked that. Venture out into the unknown. Total disregard of preconceptions. ..... Only one centimetre shorter!

Shame about the shoes Anna. Crusted pancakes? I don't need the recipe. I'll look forward to savouring yours. ..... For breakfast one day. (Now I am getting ahead of myself. It's a nice thought though.) To be honest, I'm not sure I would want ground coffee on mine. Just the Honey will do. (It's ok. I know what you mean. The coffee is separate.)

The emails were now flowing back and forth with barely a minute between.

Yes James, I understood what you meant. Perhaps getting to know you? The pancakes are special. Once tasted it is an addiction for life. Think carefully before you decide to savour.

I was not sure I wanted to go there. I changed the subject.

I was watching the French news earlier and when you see queues of cars heading to the mountains, it is easy to understand the motorists frustration. Hope you're as pleased as I am you're not amongst them! You didn't answer the question that you ask me, to ask you. So I've decided to work it out for myself. Two daughters. Eldest living in Geneva. I think? (It's that goldfish problem rearing its ugly head.) At a guess, I would say she is twenty five? You were a child bride. Pregnant almost immediately after the marriage, I have to come to the conclusion that you must have been eighteen when you gave birth. How am I doing? Close, Yes? You sent me a pic, (while looking sensational) before going to your "function". So in return, I will send you a pic of me, all dressed up for the divorce party.

An immediate response.

Remember what I said James about the wickedness of freshly divorced middle aged women! Yes, I am pleased we leave tomorrow but I have the sniffles and sneezing every thirty seconds. My daughter is looking at me with worried contempt, daring me to cancel the holiday but as she has just brought me a bowl of hot soup, I forgive her.

What was she saying? Why did she bring this up now? I was going to a divorce party and she was concerned about me being seduced? Was she saying anything? Other than being amusing? Was I trying to read too much into those few words? Let it pass James. She was being amusing. Or maybe not? Let it pass.

Don't worry, Anna. I'm a grown man, capable of making grown up decisions. I mean, she from Argentina. (Isn't that the origin of Latin Lovers?) Ok. She has legs that go on forever. Effervescent. Charismatic. Oozing sensuality. .... On second thoughts Anna. .... I'd worry if I was you. I do hope you are feeling better for the drive tomorrow.

My age apart James, I have three dogs and no sisters or brothers. All dogs are alive. Never kept any goldfish. What else is relevant?   Oh yes …….. I hate Cristina!! Big Kiss. (Now you have my bug.)

No, she was not being jealous. She was playing the game and enjoying it. My enthusiasm in this woman built. Short and sweet, throwing out irrelevant details disguised as relevant and almost as an afterthought, Cristina. I love it!

Three dogs! Somehow I can't imagine you walking the streets of Cannes, with lots of little plastic bags. Amusing as that thought might be. Still avoiding the age thing I see, thus remaining a Woman of Mystery. So what is your age Anna? It's just that I feel you need to tell me. Don't be concerned about this. It's normal for women to conceal. And you seem to be excelling in that. Therefore, I was thinking of setting out a questionnaire of simple questions avoiding age. What's your favourite colour? Do you like ice cream? What music do you prefer? How many pairs of shoes do you buy in a year? Do you like cute furry animals? Do you sunbathe nude? Where do you buy your vegetables? Nothing controversial there. One word answers will suffice. I look forward to your reply. In order to facilitate this move towards a more open dialogue please allow me to initiate this discussion with a few basic facts. I have three sisters. (ref your no sisters or brothers. An only child? Something worth noting.) I used to have a cat but he died. My favourite colour is blue. You could follow up with something equally uncontroversial. For example. You could give me intimate details of your needs and desires. On second thoughts, forget that one. I think I know the answer. It begins with "s" and ends in "hoes".

I don't like ice cream James. Also, I have a drop of Jewish blood in me. Seriously! My question. What is your age, Lady Lover?

Again! Unbelievable! Ice Cream! That's her answer? Where did the Jewish blood come from? I could play that game. Be an equally evasive James.

I am amusing, as I think you've already discovered Anna. I'm also sarcastic. I think you've got that one to. What you don't know, is why? It is a defence mechanism I developed at an early age to hide an underlying problem that I've battled my entire life to overcome. Notice how I manage to deflect the question of age by applying that well used male tactic. A well kept secret. A well kept secret never fails. It becomes a need-to-know distraction. Now, What were you saying?

Where is the promised photo James? Two hours have expired.

That was it? Where was the photo? Anna wasn't going to fall into the trap of asking about my well kept secret. Short and sweet. Ok I could play that game.

You will receive the anticlimactic pic around 19:15........I think?
My sincere apologies for the delay.

It was seven thirty before I sent. Just before leaving. Not a bad photo I thought. Seven hundred pound suit (bought in an Oxfam shop), black shirt and Converse

All Stars. Finished off with a white rose in the lapel, stem uppermost. I do believe I even looked younger than my years.

Hippy chic à la Rod Stewart! Love the rose James. Enjoy the party with that horrible woman but behave. I will be watching you. Ferragamo shoe in my right hand.

Just leaving Anna. I'll be looking out for that shoe.

Sunday morning. Keep the reply light. Well said James! I kept it light.

I don't know if you have left. Are on route. Or have arrived at your destination. If still on route. Bon courage. If you have arrived, remember what I said about those smoke filled bars. Better to be avoided. I hope every day is a Blue Sky Day.

Anna, please......Rod Stewart! I think I'll wear that suit at our first meeting. Or maybe I'll just throw it in the bin and arrive in a Track Suit. (Three white stripes down the leg with a prominent logo.) You will be pleased to know, I escaped unscathed from the party. Stayed the night in Cannes at a friends place then back home to enjoy the sunshine. Sat on my patio reading a good book. A personal detail. (Not relevant to books but entertaining all the same.) I can get emotional when watching sad movies. If I see Lassie caught in barbed wire one more time .... Suffice it to say, A box of tissues are considered a must. Hope the drive is going well. How is the cold? Catch up later.

(Are you a Rod Stewart fan?)

James xxx's (isn't it three kisses in Italy?)

Not expecting a reply as I thought Anna would still be driving and I was right, it arrived the next day.

Sorry, my dear James, nothing to report. I have a terrible flu. Arrived in pieces. I don't know how I managed to drive almost five hundred kilometres. I'm now in bed with a fever. Your emails help. x

Anna was unwell. Dead on her feet arriving in Courmayeur and now in bed with a high fever. Therefore I was grateful and understandably relieved she managed messaging at all. My dear James would almost have been enough. I needed to respond.

Oh Poor You. Hopefully Elena appreciated the sacrifice you made. Driving when feeling unwell is not on my list of, Must Do. My only practical suggestion would be plenty of fluids, keeping warm and sleep. A final suggestion. Turn your phone off. I left that one until last knowing it's the hard one. Turn your phone off and no more messages from James! I know. I did say it was the hard one. Do it Anna. Switch it off and get as much sleep as possible. I will email you tomorrow morning. Your concerned, Dear friend James. Switch it off Anna.

I am doing as told. Thank you for your concern James. I look forward to your email tomorrow. Phone off.

It was now seven thirty and time to visit friends next door for early evening drinks. I'd known Paul and Chiara for over thirty years. First meeting Paul when living in Plymouth. Later meeting Chiara, his Italian, soon to become, wife. Although living next door and sharing the same driveway, it was on rare occasions we met. Early evening drinks allowed for catch-up time. I walked next door to find Paul in a jubilant mood, thus setting the scene for what turned out to be a couple of hours full of amusing repartee. Of course, I couldn't resist telling them about my "Woman in a Yellow Dress". (Where have I heard that or something similar before?) I have been composing lyrical verse to someone, I told them. "Does it start, Roses are Red", asked Paul? No, said I. In a feigned tone of indignation. (I saw where that was going) "Tell me more", Chiara asked. I could always count on Chiara to dampen Paul's enthusiasm in giving me a hard time. So I told all. Embellishing the story with my own take on high points that had not yet happened but were not outside the realms of possibility. It was only a matter of time before they became reality, I was thinking, thus alleviating myself of any guilty feelings I might have had. My story over. Questions answered. I felt it time to make my exit. Wishing them a goodnight, I left in an upbeat mood. More so having had the last say in the latest banter of words with Paul.

The following morning I emailed Anna.

How are you today Anna? Hopefully not too sick. You can't disappoint those ever so sweet instructors. So pull yourself together and get out there. I know, easy for me to say. Actually it was. Easy to say, that is. Better soon I hope, and to hell with infection. I do hope that, optimistic, glass half full approach is not in vain. A Big Sympathetic Hug from Me!

Anna got back later that day.

So sweet of you, darling James, to have sent me A Big Hug. That's exactly what I need right now. The last thing I would be interested in is the macho ski instructors. (I should have invited you.) Hugs & Sympathy. Oh and a little self indulgence on my part. I'm not good at being ill and need someone to cater for my every whim. Could you do that James? How about you? How's today treating you? A Big Hug returns to you.

Replying to the idea of catering for Anna's every whim, I was thinking of taking a few days off. Driving to Courmayeur and doing exactly that. No you were not, James! Yes I was! No you weren't. It's a wonderful idea which presented itself with untold "brownie points" or a missed opportunity. Anna was being flippant. Not in a negative way and yet with a certain, off-handedness, believed to be part of her nature. Or was that nurture? Was "darling James" an upgrade from "dear"? I decided not to reply immediately. A couple of hours later, I did.

I think it seems very unlikely, you were, "out & about" today Anna.

What a pity you aren't at home. I would have taken the day off work, to supply you with a constant flow of tissues. Therapeutic drinks. Sympathetic attitude and as many hugs, poor sick you requires. All carried out under the strict guidelines

of, "Looking after poor sick girl with a Dutch passport who may, or may not have, originated from Moscow". Is that "whim catering enough" for you?
How was my day? You ask Anna. In a word, Uneventful. Just how I like them. I say that because as the days role by and the work load increases there will be a period of about a month (starting mid March) where one has to accept, a certain lack of weekends. Putting it another way. Anything up to forty days with no days off. On the up side, this allows me to have two months off in the summer and the same in the winter. Take note Anna. Ask me about work at any time you need light relief from.......... My inane trivia, incomprehensible sentence construction or pics of, Rod Stewart look-a-likes. Question. Do you always wear your hair tied back? I'm in two minds as to whether I should sign off now. Allowing you to slip away into a peaceful slumber or, inundate you with more.....well.....more inane trivia. Talking of trivia. A topical Italian joke. I know, I said I only knew one joke. I forgot, I know two. (It's the Goldfish in me.)
An Italian man emigrates to the United States of America and moves in with some distant relatives in New Jersey. They tell him he should apply for citizenship and they will help him study for the test. They go over all the U.S. history from the Revolutionary war to present day. Finally, he feels he has enough knowledge to pass the test so he sets an appointment. He walks into the testing room and the agent giving the test thought he would have a bit of fun, so he said to the man "We have a very simple test for you today. If you can use three English words in one sentence, you will be granted citizenship! The words are green, pink and yellow". The Italian man thought for several minutes and finally said "O.K., I think I can do that". He said "I hearda the telephona goa green, green, green, so I-a pink it upa, an I a saya, "Yellow, ou isa thisah"?
Perhaps not so good but still topical.
A remedy a friend gave me for flu. Eat lots of crushed raw garlic and carrot. Also, cold followed by hot showers. Personally I'd stick to the whisky, lemon etc. remedy. Your choice. I have to go to bed early tonight. I'm getting up at four to take a friend & her daughters to the airport. It's a hard life when one is so amenable. Lots & lots of Gentle Hugs,
James x
It was early the following evening when I received a reply.
Hello all-caring sweetheart James,
Your trivia is fine. Amusing time and again. So don't hesitate to dwell upon your yin-yang endless stories. (Do I need to repeat that I really enjoy reading your compositions?)
Despite my miserable general state after the feverish night, and having stuffed my organism with paracetamol and Nurofen, I ventured to the slopes this morning (prepaid, all inclusive vacation!) Just to find out, shortly after setting off on the first run, I find the dizziness might drive me to the next abyss of Mont Blanc. So, I had to ski down to the hotel, noticing with my trained eyes, that at

22

least ninety nine percent of local ski instructors look rather like mountain dwarfs. Totally disillusioned!!! Another observation. The resort is full of your compatriots and well bred Frenchies. Seems to be posh. I like it!

Had a great massage and hammam at the spa, plenty of lemon-honey tea, so surely tomorrow my powerful Russian organisms will win a complete and undisputed victory over the nasty French virus. I will then be in shape to carry on with the wording duel with you! Sleep well. Thank you for thinking of me. Going for a, hopefully delicious Italian dinner now, Bisous

I had another hour before early bedtime. I replied.

DO NOT READ THIS MESSAGE IN COMPANY.

Now that has your attention. Don't deny it Anna.

What were you thinking? You were thinking. OMG, James is going to divulge his inner most thoughts of adoration, only tempered by his inability, as an Englishman, to over come that, "Stiff Upper Lip", annoying habit they have. Well, no. That's not the reason. I know, you are disappointed. Actually, to digress for a moment although remaining true to the current subject of disappointment. (Is it possible to digress without changing the subject?) Anyway, disappointment. If I was to divulge my inner most thoughts so early in our "relationship" what would you have to look forward to?

No. The real reason is ..... Don't you find it annoying if someone decides to read their messages while in your company? Therefore, by putting the opening sentence into capitals, I've helped you avoid annoying your companions. Now isn't that thoughtful of me? The real reason for replying before bedtime? I enjoyed your mail, so had to respond. (Compliments flowing back and forth. We should stop that or we are in danger of becoming narcissistic.)

The dwarf instructors. Perspective can play tricks. Seen from below, they would look taller. Not that I'm suggesting you should try this. I'm happy to know you believe they are all dwarfs. Seems to be posh. Two thoughts here. Do you know what "posh" stands for? Second thought. You like posh? .... Ah well James. Never mind. Better luck next time.

Wording Duel? I don't know what you mean Anna. I have but spoken the truth. Never deviating from my true passion that honesty has its place on the right side of God.............knows what. Talking of God. I must lend you a book called, The Second Coming. It's not what you think. All I can say is, after reading this book, I could whole heartedly believe in the God portrayed. BTW, it's a comedy. Again, thanks for the interesting and amusing mail. Even in sickness she rises to the occasion. Hope you enjoy your evening.

Have fun tomorrow,

James x

I did not expect a reply as I assumed Anna would be by now, on her way to dinner, if not already seated and tucking into her .... Spaghetti? But to my surprise, that is exactly what I got.

My thought for the evening James.
"The Second Coming".

Turning and turning in the widening gyre
The falcon cannot hear the falconer;
Things fall apart; the centre cannot hold;
Mere anarchy is loosed upon the world,
The blood-dimmed tide is loosed, and everywhere
The ceremony of innocence is drowned;
The best lack all conviction, while the worst
Are full of passionate intensity.
Surely some revelation is at hand;
Surely the Second Coming is at hand.
The Second Coming! Hardly are those words out
When a vast image out of Spiritus Mundi
Troubles my sight: somewhere in sands of the desert
A shape with lion body and the head of a man,
A Garye blank and pitiless as the sun,
Is moving its slow thighs, while all about it
Reel shadows of the indignant desert birds.
The darkness drops again; but now I know
That twenty centuries of stony sleep
Were vexed to nightmare by a rocking cradle,
And what rough beast, its hour come round at last,
Slouches towards Bethlehem to be born?
Ps: It's now definitely a Good Night, Sweet James

Wow! I was impressed. Did I know The Second Coming was a poem? Of course not. Anna did! She reads poetry. What else, in the depths of this woman, would surprise me? Why did I use the word depth? Subconsciously aware I was out of mine? A thought that seemed to recur.

Not at all swayed by Anna's ps, I left it until the next morning to reply.

The Second Coming where God blames Moses for a lot of today's problems. God asks Moses to go up to the mountain and write one thing. BE NICE. What does Moses do? Comes down the mountain with Ten Bloody Commandments! I will admit, the intensity of the poem sits in balance with the humour of my Second Coming. Or maybe not. Well done Anna for introducing me to such as this. Posh. Port out, Starboard home. Something about the rich having the cabins that faced the sun. A fallacy I know but a good story.
Enjoy the skiing Anna.

Anna's reply came later that day.

So this James, is when people with money, willing to cross the Atlantic went on board the Titanic? Is that what you mean James?
PS: What a cruelty to say, "Enjoy your skiing", when you know I am not.

Looked like I had landed myself in something and it wasn't good, whatever it was? Not sure I was getting on with those ps's. Was that petulant Anna seeking attention? If it was, I could play that game. Worth a try.

My initial response would be one of apology Anna. I thought you were hitting the slopes today? How can you possibly forgive me for such insensitive cruelty. Possibly more hugs could be the answer? More. Many more Hugs, But wait just one minute? Reason for assuming (one should never assume, I know), that you would be fit for the slopes today. "Had a great massage and hammam at the spa, plenty of lemon-honey tea, so surely tomorrow my powerful Russian organism will win a complete and undisputed victory over the nasty French virus". So, I ask myself. Is the apology necessary? Far be it from me to rescind my apology. (Girls always prefer a man who is willing to admit he is wrong.) Just trying to point out, in as delicate a way as possible, that there is substance to my claim.

Covered all bases there. Apologised for my insensitivity while giving a point of view that can't possibly be misinterpreted. Remembering that theory to be based on many a year living with three sisters. Perhaps not a comparison that holds water? But surely it was significantly more than the outlook of an only child? Getting too deep James. Return to what I do best. What I do best? I put words together? It reminded me of an interview with David Bowie, who was asked how he compiled his lyrics. His reply. "I write down sentences. Cut them out with a pair of scissors into individual words and move those words around. No thought process." (I apologise to David Bowie for paraphrasing.) It was how my head worked. Words tumbled out. I had but a millisecond to put them into sentences. Back to what I do best, I continued.

No work talk today Anna. Not that is was a bad day. There is the danger I'd become boring. I'll reserve further talk of work until you need a good nights sleep. A guaranteed recipe for instant slumber. To be able to talk a women into bed. An amazing gift. Although when she falls straight to sleep, maybe not such a gift? I prefer the scenario of the two of us walking off hand in hand into the sunset. Does this vision indicate that I'm romantic or just naive to the ways of the world? Or more precisely, to the ways of women? TBD

Lingering for a while on the above paragraph. One should never leap into a relationship based on a first date. It could be a roaring success. Two or three dates later I might discover you have a particular party piece you like to perform, usually in public, that has you farting to the tune of, The Star Spangled Banner. Perhaps I should apologise for using that particular analogy but it just seemed more dramatic. Call it, Poetic License. You might perform your rendition with such aptitude and panache that I am won over and insist you perform on a regular basis. I think I'm becoming somewhat surreal. I'll stop. So how was your day Anna? Wrapped up with a hot water bottle? Or enjoying the après ski? I do hope, the latter.

If wrapped up. A big hug from me. If après ski......avoid the dwarfs! Be well,
James
I heard from Anna an hour or so later.
Dear James, You have me giggling like a school girl! You are the tonic I need. And subservient! (That was just for fun. No need for paragraphs on my petulant nature.) I will come back to you as soon as I can, as I am having a night out with my two lovely girls. The elder drove over from Geneva, such a rare opportunity for me to spend a happy hour with both. I am not yet perfectly well, but I have managed to be on my feet. Thank you for your caring thoughts.
Hugs and see you very soon,
Anna
I gave Anna a quick reply.
Rare opportunities should be taken Anna. Enjoy your evening with the girls. I'm off to bed. Up at four doing another airport run.
I will wish you and your daughters an entertaining evening.
Pleasant Dreams
Glass half full ...... On the slopes tomorrow?
James x
Good Morning, Dear James, this is just to say Good Morning.
Had a VERY long soirée yesterday. Went to the Courmayeur village centre, boring. In fact dead! Came back to our hotel at a very reasonable hour, with the innocent intention of falling into the arms of Morpheus early enough for a good nights sleep but met a group of American extreme skiers in the lobby. A heated political dispute ensued, "Putin vs Obama" until three in the morning, complimented by a generous supply of good whisky. Suffering a headache this morning. But the virus is dead! As is the village of Courmayeur.
Big hug
Anna
Hi Anna, there I was concerned. Thinking, I haven't heard from Anna. The poor girl must still be suffering with the deadly virus. But no. She is out, getting totally wasted. Hopefully you had plenty of pain killers. Talking of killers, (not necessarily in the literal sense) how did the Putin-Obama discussion conclude? Enjoy your days on the slopes.
Kisses, James
James, Dear (decided to switch the word order to make it more emphatic)! How I missed my intelligent, educated and enlightened, analytical - minded, eloquent, modest, well-informed friend (you of course) in this unfriendly lengthy dispute with the flock of American polar wolves....who tried to corner me with their overwhelming number (seven vs me and my daughters) with their utter ignorance, total absence of critical thinking and inability to listen! What do they study at schools in the USA, I wonder? Just the legends of the first pilgrims and the ever - lasting wisdoms of George Washington? Amazing degree of

brainwash. The legends of Lenin of my sweet childhood is nothing compared to this. Sorry, no more politics. It was just an amusing country study accompanied with some scotch on the rocks. Wish you were here. The slopes were fantastic today.

Anna x

I didn't hear from Anna during that next day but knowing that, hadn't stopped me before. I reached for the On button. The computer came to life.

This is an interesting moment for me Anna. I've been staring at the screen for five minutes. Nothing. I think the problem lies in the fact, I am torn between writing something sensible (James, writing something sensible? I hear you say) or continuing in that never ending deluge of really interesting yet lacking depth, humour.

I've decided to go make a coffee and wait for inspiration. I'm sure I have plenty of time. You're most likely in the hotel bar getting drunk with some crazy Americans. Me! Jealous? Never.

I'm going sensible. At least for the moment. I was thinking. What do we know about each other? My conclusion, as I think you will agree, is not much! Then I asked my self, "Is that a bad thing".? Answer. Not really. There will come a time.......when you return from drinking? Sorry, skiing?.........we will meet. Possibly you will be, lets say, disappointed. I could be devoid of any emotional attachment. (It's possible! I could have hit the male menopause. What exactly does that do? Assuming we have one.) Then again maybe it's me wondering how long is an acceptable time before saying, "Oh shit! Is that the time. I have to hurry if I want to catch the last bus".

How am I doing so far? On the Sensible Conversation front. I've thought of something else sensible. We don't know what we sound like. Tell me you don't have a high pitch squeaky voice. Do you like to talk? (I can be a good listener. Well, at least for the first five years.) I think you like to talk. Do you consider the application of makeup based on, necessity or on what you might be doing at the time? For example. Off to one of those many celebrity functions, one would assume, full impact necessary. Hours spent in front of the mirror. Or, having a few whiskys with lets say...........a crowd of American skiers, for example. I would think on this occasion, not wanting to draw too much attention to yourself, it will be low key makeup? By saying, "not wanting to draw........attention", I mean NO attention. I might be getting into this. Sensible conversation is the way forward. No more of that shallow humour! I think I'll close here Anna. Already so many questions for you to digest and reply. I'm being thoughtful. Have a Pleasant, American free evening Anna,

James xxxxxxxxxxxxxxxxxxxxx (unlikely any Americans can beat THAT?)

Anna's reply? Ten smily faces. Once again leaving me wanting more. I knew I was being selfish and it had to stop. Anna was on holiday with her daughter,

now daughters. Not a lot of time on her own. Allowing for my wisdom and understanding to acknowledge this. We were getting on just fine.
Don't ask me why Anna. I was looking, on a whim, through some old pics. So I'm sending you one. Not exactly, the rugged sailer. (Note the umbrella. As if you could miss it!) Taken three hundred years ago while playing Captain, barging around the canals of London. Not literally barging. You don't barge around in a barge. (Seems like an inappropriate name, when you think about it?) No. One sedately ambles, at five miles an hour. Life slows down. One of the best holidays I've had. And that includes the time I back-packed around the world always in the company of beautiful women, fast cars, waterfalls of champagne and being seen in all the best places. Yes. Better than that! (Actually, thats not true. But I did once have a weekend in Brighton. And the barge trip was definitely better.)
I'm going now, Anna Dear.
My first thought James. (Excusez-moi, l'anglais n'est pas ma langue maternelle) barges are rather used to transport loose gravel, or sand, or cement, or what else? Timber! But not good-looking young male passengers with female umbrellas! I didn't miss the umbrella, impossible. And you really dreamt (and it never came true?) of traveling the world in a company of a gorgeous woman in a fast car sipping Veuve Cliquot on the way? Come and join me in my Aston Martin on a trip to Monte Carlo? Wouldn't that be the simplest solution to catching a glimpse of what you missed in Brighton? Champagne is on you.
Was she serious? Not the barge part, no. That was well put.
Anna didn't have dreams. She had moments when she would like to have. Would like to do. Would like to go. And so she did. For her it was as simple as that. No, the serious part was the Aston Martin?
Good Morning Anna.
Hope it's a blue sky day. No hangover. And lots of skiing.
Technically speaking it's known as a Narrow Boat but it's still a barge. Aston Martin? Can I drive? Enjoy your day Anna, With thoughts of much fondness, and Hugs, James xxx
Hello James. In the absence of red traffic lights and while standing gracefully on the sunny slope of Courmayeur, I thought that I missed something yesterday. Yes, I forgot to ask. How come that in just three hundred years you so dramatically changed the hair colour?
Aston Martin - wishful thinking. Champagne - quite realistic.
I wish you a wonderful working day (One of the forty you will be doing in series. Said with compassion. Not as a gloat) Kisses from the sunny slopes.
How does one "stand gracefully", Anna? I thought the idea was to ski gracefully? Ok. Let me try something easy. In three hundred years dramatic change in hair colour. I'm just pleased after three hundred years, I have any!

Aston Martin. Wishful thinking as in, you will not let me drive, or you don't have one, or perhaps it's in the garage and you can't afford the repairs? I was thinking of going back through all the emails and creating a list of, Not answered questions. Is there a limit to how many pages one is allowed to email? Fortunately for You, I don't have the time tonight. Nothing for you to worry about. Just meeting up with a crowd of Party Girls who seemed particularly interested in my company. OK. Thats not quite true. Going next door for dinner with Paul and Chiara. Tonight I thought I would have your pic on screen (after tennis, without sunglasses.) as it might inspire me. I'm not sure if its going to help. My eyes keep drifting towards your.............wait for it...........nails. I'd like to point out, this is not your problem. I'm sure my "interest" in your nails is not something you should be concerned about. In fact, I think your view would be more along the lines of, "Love me, Love my nails". And I would whole heartedly agree. Which leaves me trying to understand my interest in said nails. Oh...be aware, this "nail thing" I've adopted is not a negative interest. Imagine, first date. You are going to be wondering why I seem to be intrigued by your hands and not listening to you. You might start feeling uncomfortable. Knowing in advance will enable you to compose yourself for this potentially foreboding experience. Wear gloves! Why didn't I think of that before. Problem solved. Phew! Time is catching up on me Anna. Expected next door in twenty minutes and I haven't yet showered.

Still looking at your pic. You have a nice smile. As you know, I really don't like to use the word nice, too overused. In this case, the word nice was created, for your smile. Got to go Anna, Hope you enjoyed your day. James xxx

ps: When DO you get back? And if you answer that one, perhaps, if you're bored, you can check out the other thirty six unanswered questions.

Dear James, You will not believe it! I read your last letter to my daughter. Sorry for breaking the vow of disclosure, but I was so delighted to have read it the first time to myself I decided to share it! She will understand. Plus I thought, it will set up an example for the future life of a young woman when she has to choose boyfriends. That's the kind of letters you should be looking for, I said. Someone with an intelligent humour. Learn by example and set your own standards. Teaching her to ski today and she is becoming very proficient. I told her so adding, I was pleased to find her standards were obviously high. Her reply? "Like mother, like daughter". Sorry, I drifted away from my main topic. Yet to be discussed. Gloves. Yes, I love wearing gloves and will do so. You can listen to my "high pitch piercing voice" telling you stories of my past lovers and late husband. Instead of staring at my sexy red nails. Ok. Stop now. It's only because I am under the treacherous influence of the local Italian alpine digestive plant-based liquor (I am sure it has got hallucinogenic properties), I am writing all this rubbish. Please forgive me if you can! I want to talk to you! Do you want my number?

Good Night, Dear James

Ps: What exactly did you ask me about? If I wear my hair always tied up? No, not always, although I prefer it that way. More practical, and I think it suits my Slavic looks
Pps: I think I mentioned I return on the twenty eighth.
"Do you want my number"? That obviously wasn't a question as her number was provided. Read my letter to her daughter. What did I make of that? I couldn't decide. I could only think of Anna's last remark. Once again, taking the initiative! Exchanging numbers. I was thinking on her return would have been soon enough but no, evidently not soon enough for Anna. I'll leave it for later. No, it was getting late. Time enough tomorrow.
I managed to get the day off to a good start. Always questions to be answered. Jobs to be assigned but by nine things were running along smoothly. I got a mail.
I gave you my number. OMG - OMG - OMG!!! What if you find me speaking with a horrible accent? Ah well, what can I do …….. Coming back on Sunday".
What could I do but reply.
You read my letter to your daughter!
I immediately reread my mail searching for any indiscretions. Fortunately found none. It would not have been a good start, having read my letter to your daughter, for her to have an immediate dislike to this ranting Englishman. So much enjoyed your, "under the influence of a woman eating, a drunken plant". That was what you said, wasn't it? I'm always interested in hearing about past lovers and if you could supply me with a few of their phone numbers ………. Always useful to have some background information. Not that I want to be forever discussing your nails but did I say anything about, sexy nails? I do remember a certain, shall we say, bordering on compulsive desire to talk about your nails but I don't believe, correct me if I'm wrong, I mentioned anything about sexy. Interesting! Perhaps be more careful what you say Anna, I have a very analytical mind. Not that it really serves to any advantage when trying to analyse your mind. In fact, ignore that analytical mind thing. It rarely works out that I've got it right. My last point of interest for the evening. Phone numbers.
It would seem churlish if not to say, unacceptable to refuse such a kind offer of exchange. I had thought about it. Yes, I had! Part of my reason for asking you, "When do you return", would have been followed up with a, "It might be a good idea to exchange numbers in case we miss each other at our forthcoming meeting". But Oh No. Anna takes the initiative. So if you are returning on Sunday, that evening would have been my first suggestion of a meet but knowing you have a five hour journey ahead, I feel it only proper I give you twenty four hours to recuperate and look your most radiant. I will call you this evening, when home.
I called Anna that evening. No answer. I had five seconds of Anna's recorded message. Relation of the queen, I thought. What an accent. Dumb struck by her

voice wasn't helping to formulate words. Words I would need unless I wanted to sound as dumb as I felt. I muttered something which I instantly regretted. I hung up and sent an email. Just one paragraph of amusement with no content, trying to disguise my apology for such an inept message.

Thanks for the email James, enjoyed it as usual. I will answer to that later, going to the slopes now, it's the last day of skiing. American? No, long gone. Norway - just arrived! Helsinki group. Had fun last night which is why I missed your call. Your voice.... are you a professional seducer? Is that what you do for a living? Consider it a compliment.

Blowing you kisses from the summit of Mont Blanc, XXX

I've heard your voice Anna! Albeit a voice message. Ok, you've now heard mine. I can't comment on your thoughts but mine, well........so positive. I bet, and I'm sure I'm right, you've never been complimented on your tone of voice. Can't really imagine the situation where you are talking to some gentlemen and he turns to you and says, "We have only just met but I must say, You have a beautiful tone of voice". Not happened, has it? Well......it has now! Do you think it possible we never meet, just talk? With you sending me the odd photo. Preferable just prior to a tennis match. Do you see the position you now put me in Anna? Infatuation takes on a new meaning. I'm not sure if I can take this to the next level of actually meeting you. I will be stunned to silence. You will be considering the possibility that this is not James. He has sent an imbecile in his place. "But why", I hear you think. (ok, I can't actually hear what you are thinking but give me a break on that one.) No. it's not an imbecile, it's me! I therefore suggest, and this is important so don't just skirt over it looking for the more interesting bits. What was I suggesting? Oh yes, I suggest........be gentle with me. I will snap out of my imbecilic ways. I will realise I do have a part to play in this, this the first, and oh so important meeting. It's almost a certainty that I will spill my coffee. Hopefully over myself rather than you.

Lets analyse that last paragraph.

"Just talk. While I sit, dumbfounded" .... *Obviously psychotic.*

"Consideration of being imbecilic" ....*Unable to come to terms with the interaction necessary in creating a long term relationship.*

"Fragmented mind"? …. Doesn't look good for me. If I were you. … Before continuing. I've often pondered that remark. "If I were you". I mean, what does that MEAN? If I were you, I would do exactly what you would do. Isn't that so? Therefore, who ever was to be you, would be you. QED That said. If I was you. I'd run a mile. No way would I be considering meeting someone such as I. Personally, I can't wait to meet you! Last day on the slopes tomorrow. Blue skies. No hangover. Hopefully a good day for all. Enjoy, Just for a moment, I will jump out of the imbecilic mode and say, What ever happens from here on in. If it's as enjoyable as our correspondence, then it will be a delight. Kisses, James

Anna's voicemail. She was Russian? Then why or perhaps how, did she manage The Queens English? It was unusual for me to be face to face with English spoken in such a refined and rarefied manner. Got to lose those Devonian "a",s. In thirty six hours! Speak slowly and carefully James, then she was sure to believe you an imbecile. Oh Great! Hey, it was not that bad. It was a first date and if it didn't pan out, so be it. Who am I kidding! Tomorrow, her last day skiing. Home Sunday evening. Dinner Monday. Dinner! Where? It was winter and most restaurants were closed. My thoughts turned to the problem of where, which as it turned out was not a bad thing. It helped detract from the problem of what I was going to say. I could have taken that positive thought one step further realising if I didn't find a where, there would be no problem about what to say. Positive thought. That was all it took! I put that aside for the moment. Placed it in the "too hard to think of box". Send a message James. Far easier.

Last day of skiing. Up early the next morning. Five hour drive.
Back in time for afternoon coffee. Perfect. See you then. Wishful thinking on my part Anna. Take no notice. Enjoy, James xxx
ps: Don't get too drunk with the Norwegians tonight. Remember, it's an early start tomorrow.

I set to doing those things reserved for weekends. Shopping. Washing. Cleaning. The joy of weekends! I received a message from Anna's mobile, mid afternoon. The first message. Was this the end of emails, I wondered?

We didn't ski today James. On our way home. Tired but almost there. Decided this morning that we have skied more than enough and it's time to return. Will call you tomorrow.

I messaged back. At the same time, wondering if this truly was the end of an era. Emails, a thing of the past.

You cut your ski holiday short for me Anna? Drove through the night so you might spend more time with me. Another possibility. The hotel threw you out. Too many crazy late evening parties in the Hotel bar. I prefer version one. Hear from you tomorrow. In your own dear sweet time. (No sarcasm intended.)

Anna was almost home! We will talk tomorrow. Got to get a good nights sleep James, was the thought in my head. I looked at the clock. Was five thirty too early? Calm down James, Anna's calling tomorrow, was my next thought. That helped.

It was seven thirty, breakfast time. Carry on as normal and hope Anna felt my pain. The inescapable pain of waiting. I waited. Actually, I had work to fill the space so no problem, my day was full. Then why did I check my phone every five minutes? Seven minutes past eleven she called.

Hello Anna. Yes I'm fine. How was your trip?" (This was going nowhere! Our very first conversation and it was going nowhere! Give her something to laugh about. Ease the tension.)

I was thinking of you earlier Anna. A small item in The Times caught my attention. A rich Russian lady walked into her pre booked five star hotel, skies in tow, asking if the hotel was far from the ski station.

Why did that catch your attention, James?

Maybe something to do with the fact the hotel was in Amsterdam! Not a Dutch relative perchance Anna? I quizzically asked. It had the desired effect.

So, that's what Anna sounds like when laughing like a schoolgirl.

More giggles. The ice was definitely broken. We talked. I got down to practicalities. Practicalities as in, the unfortunate situation of little to choose from, reference restaurants. It was winter! She understood, having been in the same situation. I suggested an Italian place, well regarded by Paul and Chiara. (She is Italian after all.) It can be cosy, with its own family run appeal. So it was decided. I offered to pick her up.

Sorry, magnanimous offer not accepted. I don't want to abuse your kindness.

What did that mean! No thanks, I'll make my own way. That I understood. Does Anna really use such terminology in every day speech. She just had! Let it pass. We decided on eight. I would text her the name and address.

"*Don't forget the gloves*", I said as a parting remark.

"*Be careful James or I might decide to arrive in heels*". She laughed.

I received a text minutes later. Before I could send the address. That was quick.

You know, James, to call you this late morning was a much delayed decision. Delayed until it wasn't possible to wait any longer. And then, ….. the decision was made. As in, "Shutting my eyes and jumping". Did I sound as nervous as that or was it a well - disguised casual "normality"? If it was normality, that was down to you. You make conversation easy and something to enjoy. Something to savour. Anyway, more stress coming this evening!!! (Please don't read the stress thing the wrong way. I might be right in suggesting you are feeling it also?)

I sent the address. Mentioning I'd arrive just before eight. Also mentioning I too, felt the stress and adding, was there such a situation where stress could be something to look forward to?

You're so understanding James, thank you! Looking forward to the historical meeting, which is taking place after just one hundred and one emails!

Dalmatians came to my mind.

Chapter Two

I had plenty of time, it was barely one. Time for some lunch. A baguette. A couple of boiled eggs and finely chopped tomatoes. A few mixed herbs. Shake or two of pepper and et voilà!

Working it backwards is how I did it. Arrival, seven fifty in the car park, giving plenty of time to walk the ten metres to the front door. Anything could happen in ten metres! Probably not but it was my way. Didn't like to be late. There was I, so caught up in working it back when I had another thought. What shall I wear! Not that I was particularly accustomed to first date nerves. You have to have that first date before being able to become accustomed. My nerves had just taken a trip to a whole new dimension, explicitly there to enhance my anxiety. What the hell do I wear! She obviously had a thing about shoes. Not sure the All Stars would work. Timberland deck shoes? I dug out a pair of Clark's brogues. A bit dusty but they would clean up. What next. I started to despair. I was thinking coat. I have two. One being corduroy that my daughter, on a recent visit, condemned in a way, when heard from my daughters lips, one shuddered, "Oh Dad, you're not still wearing that thing, are you? Tim has one you can borrow while you're here. Haven't you Tim?" The other, a dark blue Nike jacket. Dark blue Nike and black shoes. Just the middle bit to go. The shirt was no problem. I have a full range of blue shirts. The new black jumper. This was coming together. I toyed with the idea of Levis only to dismiss as too casual. I forgot to remind myself, this was who I was. It was whom I'd been since I can remember knowing me. Casual. I remembered the trousers I bought when visiting my son in Houston. Good quality. American made. I continued counting back. I had four hours before it would be time to shower, get dressed and leave. Paul called asking for help to load the TVR onto the trailer. "Sure", said I. "See you out front in five." A perfect distraction. Once at Paul's workshop we realised this would be no easy matter. With the trailer hooked up the problem was obvious. "First time on this trailer," said Paul. It was too high off the ground. Unachievable for the TVR. We spent an hour or so in the construction of ramps. Satisfied, we put them to the test. Not the easiest of beasts that TVR, to guide onto the ramps. Delicate clutch work needed. Third attempt. Task accomplished. I then asked the question, that was always regretted but it was part of the, "being interested in Paul's love of racing" routine. "So where are you off this time?" The Nuremberg Ring, was the reply.

Hey that's in Germany. I've seen the episode on Top Gear. Do that in under six minutes forty seven seconds and you've got a world record.

Paul looked at me, not impressed. To understand that expression Paul had given me would take the thirty five or so years we'd know each other to explain. Suffice it to say, my automatic response to said look was ....

You didn't know that? But you do know it's in Germany?

Paul knew to avoid that one. "Come on, it's getting dark, let's head back."

It was six o'clock when I walked in the door. Plenty of time but needed to be used wisely. Beer from the fridge. Roll a cigarette. Anna was down as a non smoker. No problem. Cigarette outside. Maybe two with a second beer? Wash hair in the shower and emerge squeaky clean.

I parked easily. Plenty of spaces. Seven forty five. Too soon to go in so I walked to the sea front. A few hundred metres there. The same back. Eight minutes to and I entered the restaurant to be warmly greeted by the owner who surprisingly remembered me from visits with Paul and Chiara. I had a choice of tables as it wasn't busy. I ordered a beer and waited. Expecting Anna to approach from the main entrance, I sat myself appropriately positioned for a view of said entrance. One of those thoughts that seem to come from nowhere, came from nowhere. I was drinking beer? I didn't think Anna would drink beer. I gulped down the remainder and checked the wine list while surreptitiously placing my empty beer glass on the accompanying table. I continued perusing said list, while having one eye locked on the entrance. There was a tap on my shoulder. Anna! She came in the side door. Later to discover, she had ignored my directions to the car park. Parking where, in my many years of visiting this establishment I'd never seen an empty space, she found one. Hence the side entrance.

Hello James.

I'd been here for twenty minutes. I was the only single male in the place. Anna must have realised that and I was now wondering if my photos were perhaps a shade too, complimentary? Was she instantly disappointed or was this her normal approach, in a situation such as this? Anna was standing over me. Get up James. I took a brief few seconds to compose myself as I closed the menu. I rose reaching for her open hand. It was a firm grip while making eye contact. This was my first view of Anna. Eye to eye contact. I was hoping for the luxury of seeing her approach. That bloody empty parking space! French custom when

35

meeting someone for the first time. A handshake was sufficient. This was different? A hundred emails had past between us. We knew each other. Initiate James! I reach forward and we kissed cheeks. I instigated that and Anna followed through. I surprised myself when realising I was assisting Anna in removing her coat. The placement of her chair was typical Cary Grant. Cary Grant? Was I that old? Go James. I sat. Another moment of eye contact. She didn't look as I'd imagined? I cast that thought aside as the waiter approached. We decided on an aperitif of red wine. When deciding on a wine, my rule of thumb had always been, pick the second cheapest. For no other reason than all should be palatable. I picked the fifth! Anna was nervous and it showed. I needed to put Anna at ease. My chance for proactivity.

Well Anna, I am going to take this opportunity to talk. You might be wondering why opportunity was my choice of word. Let me explain. We have corresponded for a month. I know you are an intelligent woman capable of keeping me enthralled for hours while captivating me with your tales of the Russian, with a Dutch Passport.

Anna laughed.

This was easier than I'd thought. Anna was attentive and happy listening to me but most importantly she laughed at my humour. Knowing Anna as I now do, it would have come as a surprise to see her sat being so attentively silent. I continued in a light hearted manner until our pizzas arrived. Anna seemed more relaxed as she talked about her past. Leaving her first husband with the clothes on her back and a two year old daughter. This was not the woman I saw sat before me. Her posture. Her presence. These were not qualities you learn overnight. And that voice. Our conversation never faltered. I watched Anna talk. Yes, watched. Listening to her voice, not really taking in the words. Her movements of expression. The calming, almost hypnotic effect was my indulgence. Then she stopped. She was watching me. I realised, I had absolutely no idea what she was previously talking about. Looking straight at me she said, "*What?*"

It was the first of many times to follow that Anna would say that. My response that very first time was a smile. Hopefully a smile that would see me through my ignorance of the previous conversation without betrayal. Never again would I be expected to answer the, "What" question. It was a moment I would recognise in the future. It wasn't intended to be answered. In that brief moment of thought, I realised Anna was still watching me. (Fortunately not aware that there was a good possibility, I wasn't listening, just in a state of pure infatuation.) But I digress, I get ahead of myself. Reassured by my smile, she continued.

Through the course of the next three hours I had many an occasion to study this lady before me. I must profess my knowledge of the finer things in life could not be mistaken. I didn't have one. This was not to say I didn't notice the labels attached to her every item of clothing. Were those real diamonds on her watch?

My first impressions of Anna were so removed from the reality. First impression was one of mixed feelings. Perhaps that first smile was a little too forced giving her a slightly austere look. Admittedly her height was intimidating, not being used to eye level contact. I thought, this was going to be hard work. Continual conversation on my part with little in response. I'd seen it before when women expect to be entertained, thinking their very presence is enough contribution on their part. I was so wrong! There she sat, casually waving her glass, with a nonchalant, carefree manner. imparting enthusiasm on the topic of tennis. Anna played tennis. She played tennis, a lot. I daren't probe too deeply. "So you don't work then?" Might not be the ideal question. I didn't ask. She admitted to being a bad loser but getting some satisfaction from the age old tradition of the winner buying the drinks.

So what do you do James?

(Me? I work for an exhibition company, spending most of my day figuring out how to put bits of various shaped wood, onto a pallet.) I don't think so.

I'm under contract to an American Design Company who have a base in Cannes. Dealing mostly in Logistics. It keeps me occupied for a good part of the year.

Don't get carried away James. Let's change the subject.

You have two daughters don't you. One in Geneva. The other has you as personal chauffeur. Have I got that right?

Correct! Ferrying between school, ballet classes and social engagements, she does keep me busy. She's decided on an English university starting in September. The dilemma lies in choosing the right university. Aim too high and not get the expected results could be disastrous.

(I nod, knowingly?)

Seriously thinking of Leeds. We are going to take a look in a couple of weeks. Should be fun!

No forced smiles present. This was Anna. Relaxed and exuding confidence. I asked her about her Dutch passport. I asked her where she learnt such precise English. We spoke about my early years living in Plymouth. Intentionally leaving out any reference of the time I was a long haired hippie. Sex and drugs and rock & roll! Not that Plymouth saw much of that. But I forget The Van Dyke. I would defy anyone to name a band not seen at the Van Dyke relevant to the era. Bearing in mind, that often used phrase of the seventies, "If you remember the sixties, you weren't there!

Was I guilty of nostalgia? The sixties. The nineties. That I understood. The eighteens? Was that what the twenty first century had to offer us? "Hey remember that thing going about in the twenty thirds?" "Yeh but we in the twenty sixths, know better!

"Good luck with that one," I thought.

We were talking about my first wife. It was one of the Golden Rules. Don't discuss the ex but Anna was interested. I could see that. What I didn't understand was why. I told her about the time Susan and I spent four months travelling around Europe in our VW van.

"I would love to do that", said Anna.

Then you could be lucky Anna. In the next couple of years I want to buy an American RV and travel the States for six months. Anna looks at me, puzzled? *RV. Recreational Vehicle. Ten metres of luxury travel. I can put you on the list of possibilities if you'd like?*

"You would be so lucky"! Was her immediate response. We laughed.

It was getting late and I was thinking how to bring the evening to a close. Anna, the evening is coming to a close but before time overtakes us I would like to ……. I would like to…… (I don't know why but for some unexplainable reason the words in my head couldn't be placed into an understandable phrase?) Anna was watching me.

"What"? She said.

It was the first time I'd noticed, Anna was shielding her eyes. Or maybe I had noticed it but had put it down to nervousness.

Anna, do you have a headache. I only ask because you are constantly, rubbing your brow.

Anna laughed.

No James, it is the light in the ceiling. It is in my eyes.

You should have said earlier Anna. We could have moved.

It is okay James. After all, I've just proved I can suffer in silence.

I smiled looking around at the now empty restaurant.

Perhaps the staff would appreciate our departure and you might appreciate the return of your eye sight.

No possibility to mention anything about, "I would like to ….", as Anna was half way out of her seat. Amazingly, thoughts of Cary Grant sprang to mind. I helped Anna with her coat.

Once outside Anna pointed to her car.

The blue one is mine. Where are you parked?

Pointing vaguely towards my Figaro realising this was the final moments of the evening, I turned to face her.

Anna, It was an absolute delight and my only regret? Time has tricked me into believing three hours to be but three minutes.

Did you just make that up James, or have you been thinking about your concluding remark all evening?

Why did she ask that? Even admitting to it being more than partially true. She was waiting for my response. Do I try to explain my previous remark? We're stood on the street and I am unsure. I smile. I now saw Anna was laughing.

Drive safely Anna, ask me the next time.

I leant forward to kiss her cheeks. Anna responded in a way I could only describe as, with warmth. She stepped back. Smiled while turning and crossed the road. I watched her drive away.

It was a ten minute drive home. Plenty of time to assess the evening. Way out of my league but so what! Had I not always said, Making a connection is justifiably dependent on circumstance. The circumstance that drew us together became more justifiable as the evening matured. We affirmed that original connection via email. My assessment was now concluded!

I arrived home. Made a coffee. I had to text.

Not going to be able to go to bed until putting pen to paper Anna. Expect an email in an hour or two. Don't wait up, it might take awhile. Having told you not to wait up ….…. You don't strike me as a, "Do as you're told", kinda woman. My advice. Don't wait up!

Jx

It took me two hours before I was satisfied with my email.

Well Anna,

First night nerves over. I'm going to try to remember those first minutes. I think it highly unlikely I will see you in such an uncharacteristically "vulnerable" position again. I know, it would be easy for me to say it was down to my effervescent wit & charm that warmed you to me, thus setting you at ease. So as its easy to say so, lets accept that it was so. You warmed, as I to you.

What conclusion have I drawn from our evening together? Neither of us find pizzas particularly interesting. See how I start? Find common ground "On a First Date is one common interest enough"? I ask myself? Which, with the utilisation of my third, and yes final joke in my repertoire, I can answer.

What are Five hundred lawyers at the bottom of the sea?

A Good Start! And I think that is what we had Anna. A good start.

I told that joke to my daughter when she finished Law School. She didn't think it was funny. I still don't understand why?

"This is all very well James", I hear you say. "But what about ME"! What do you think of ME"? After our initial but acceptable, shaky start Anna, I can honestly say, (Yes James.......get on with it!)

I like You. (Define "like", James.) Have I got that right so far Anna?

There is so much I find interesting about you. Not a sort of earth shattering opening line but it gets better. You have elegance, finesse and obvious intelligence and yet remain totally approachable. That I find enchanting. Actually, watching you, indifferent to the bright light in face situation you found yourself, I was captivated. Now don't read too much into that Anna. The wine could be playing its part. Do you notice what I just did? Put you on a pedestal and then pulled the rug out from beneath your feet.

You are special though Anna. Whether we have a long and fruitful relationship, or it stumbles at the first hurdle, You are definitely special. Oh and I almost

forgot.......Radiant. I think you're back on that pedestal. So when reading this tomorrow morning, hopefully not at at the red light, please feel free to immerse yourself in a warm glow of contentment.
Good Night/Morning Anna
Thank You ..... for such a Pleasant Evening
James x

I switched off the phone and went to bed. The obvious first thoughts of the morning were of Anna. Yes, an interesting woman exuding self confidence. Interestingly amiss in the opening half hour of our first meeting? How much of a cover was that self confidence? If given the chance, time would tell. It was a work morning and as usual I arrived early. My first thought was to text Anna. I texted last night. And sent an email. Let's not seem too interested. Whenever did I take any notice of what I thought?

Good Morning Anna. What a lovely day it is. Or is that just my mood? Either way, it's a fantastic day!
Enjoy yours, James. x

Not the most intelligent thing you'd ever done James but you know what? I didn't care. Anna was a wonderful lady and I felt good knowing her. It was a first date. Just keep it in perspective. If only Anna knew. This last month of emails and now meeting had, in some way, helped lay to rest the love I still felt for Emanuela. My Italian girlfriend from Torino. I believed Anna started as a distraction. One that I had grown fond of. Was it possible to inversely like someone and at the same time have an equal yet opposite reaction to the other? The more I thought of Anna, the less I thought of Emanuela. I was on the rebound. Not necessarily a good thing. Confusion of loyalties sprang to mind. What if Emanuela decided she'd made a mistake and wanted me back? Highly unlikely and anyway, I'd cross that bridge, if it ever got built. Back to my wonderful and hopefully not fleeting, distraction. A reasonably uneventful day with other distractions to keep my mind on the job rather than Anna. It helped remind me of an earlier thought. Keep it in perspective.

Arriving home I proceeded to fall into my usual routine. Settling in front of the computer, it didn't take long before anxiety reared it's ugly head. Why had she not called? Emailed? Texted? Just to say thanks, would have been enough.

Anna, please excuse this relentless invasion of your privacy via all media possibilities known to man while trying to get your attention. I do have a last resort but that incorporates the use of less scrupulous means. A helicopter, eleven highly trained men, a whole heap of cash transferred into the local Police Chiefs private account and even then you might just say No. You can lead a horse to water ......
Knowing how you like lists I've complied a few options for you to consider.
a) Lost your phone.
b) Lost for words.

c) Lost your tennis balls and need to find them.
d) Lost the will to live after 101 messages.
e) Lost interest.
I'll leave you to ponder.
For Now, James. x
I was happy with that but would Anna think the same? More importantly, would she reply? She did. An hour later.
Dear James,
Thank you for the pleasant evening and the pizza, of course! I like pizza, by the way. It is not the food I would eat every day, but if I have good company, why not? (And the company was good!)
A résumé of the evening. Lovely! Thank you for keeping me on a pedestal at least for a while before you pulled that rug. At least for a few moments I thought I was a queen. You were extremely caring and delicate, yet genuinely curious about me, and I was flattered by this attitude. Sorry I did not answer right away, my day has been really hectic. After the week-long absence I had a pile of correspondence to deal with, plus the school, tennis tournament, car problems - had to go to the Mercedes service centre.
I'll come back to you by tomorrow with more details about my life and sentiments but right now my Mother is calling for dinner!
Take good care of yourself and speak to you soon,
Anna
I sent a brief reply.
My thought for the evening Anna. Anna does not have to robotically answer all messages. I think I might have been subjecting you to a minor form of school boy adolescence. Mmmm, I might have to think about that. Adolescence v's Maturity.
The approach could be deemed, curious innocence. Always in search of something new. No matter how small the detail the fascination never wavers. Maturity breeds the cynic within us. More wary. Less accepting of new ideas. So schoolboy adolescence it will be. I was going to apologise for my subliminal petulant behaviour having realised I was pressuring you for a reply. Instead I will admit to having adolescent tendencies. Don't be misled here Anna. This is not a twelve year old adolescence. This is Mature schoolboy adolescence. There is a big difference. I can use longer words. Better terminology. Sentence construction like no twelve year old could imagine. And yet...... sounding equally ridiculous.
I'm tired Anna and if I continue, the fine thread of reality I'm holding onto will snap. And believe me when I say, if you find this message a little obscure.........
I do apologise.
I wish you Pleasant Dreams
James xx (delicately placed on each cheek)

The day came to a close. I pondered Anna's reply. Flat, was my first thought. My reply was unnecessary. Perhaps not the perfect end to the day I imagined it would be.

It was eight fifteen. Wednesday morning. "Brown Eyed Girl" ringtone! It was Anna.

Oh James, I must stop reading your messages at the lights. Giggling School Girls find it difficult to drive. I have a match in fifteen minutes. Wish me luck.

And she was gone. ……. Good Luck Anna ….. I said to myself.

I made that mental note of including spontaneous to the list of Anna adjectives. I imagined Anna rushing to her tennis match and finding time to call. Wondering if that also allowed her to tick that box. "I've called James. Taken the dog to the vet. Daughter at school. Now tennis." How does she fill her day? With that diminishing thought, I headed for the office already aware it was going to be one of those days. It was mid afternoon when I received a message.

Can I call you this evening James? BTW, I lost the match!

Of course Anna. I look forward to it. Talk to you later and my commiseration on the outcome of the match.

I should have said, "I'll call you". I knew it would leave me, pacing the floor for hours on end waiting for the call. No matter. The day was shaping up ready to administer a prolonged and hard fought battle. I'd be bouncing off those ropes for some hours to come. It was seven thirty before the day ended. The one advantage of leaving work later was the lack of traffic. Twenty minutes and I was throwing my coat aside while aiming my keys at the bowl. Both landed with perfection. For the first time, as far as I could remember. Was that a good sign? Opened iTunes, selected random play and hit the button. Off for a shower. Anna could call at any moment, so no time for the, pre drink and cigarette.

I didn't have to wait too long.

Hello James, how are you?

Hi Anna, sorry to hear about the match today. Was it important or just a friendly? Do you do friendlies? Something tells me, every match is important to you. Competitive spirit, is my guess.

You are right James, I am a bad loser but only annoyed at myself. I've got no animosity towards my fellow competitors. Although it's particularly frustrating when I know I could have won. On this occasion lets just say, it was close. I do play in a league and that match is tomorrow. Today was the warm-up.

I let Anna talk. She liked talking but to her credit, she was also a good listener. Now was not her, good listener moment.

If I win tomorrow I will have the opportunity of playing someone on Saturday who is a higher ranking than I. Win or lose, it will help my rankings. Preferably a win as that should place me in the next category.

Was I suppose to understand this or was it assumed I knew what Anna was talking about? Categories? Rankings? I would have to get an explanation one day as I was sure it would please her to impart the knowledge she had on the subject. Until such time? Wing it!

I am sorry James, I'm rambling on about my concern for ratings and you're likely to have no idea what its all about. (She'd understood that.) *Even I'm not totally sure where I would stand if I win on Saturday. Assuming I win tomorrow. Glass half full, I always say.*

No need to apologise Anna, even if I have absolutely no idea what you are talking about, which I would never admit to. It doesn't matter! I am surrounded by the sound of your voice. I find it captivating. What were you talking about?

How do you do that James? You've admitted not listening to a single word I've said and wrapped up your reply in an obvious "gooey" concoction of literal nonsense, and I find it endearing?

Will you be my boyfriend?

I let that remark pass, for the moment. Fairly sure it was a throw away remark.

What can I say Anna. Gooey it may have been but nonsense, I think not? Perhaps past compliments you've received came under the category of nonsense but I assure you when I give compliments, believe them. In fact, treasure them. Note them down. I'm not saying I hand them out rarely but certainly not liberally.

I receive a noncommittal Mmmmm, as a reply.

"Anna", I said, laughing. *Concern yourself not! I've already stockpiled enough compliments from our first meeting to last me well into our third year of marriage. On the basis we're assuming a short engagement.*

I think two hundred for the wedding James. Honeymoon in the Seychelles. You will have to give up your job. Perhaps we could buy a place in England? Find a place here and flit between the two. So many things to plan.

Would it be ok if I talk to my broker before we get too carried away Anna. You know what it's like. A matter of moving ones acquisitions around to free up monies for said venture.

You have a broker James and you are considering our future life together as a venture?

I'm not sure to continue or to reassert reality. We were having fun.

No on two accounts. The first being an admission of inadequate wording. For venture read adventure. Our adventure together down the ions of time. Where the universe revolves around the love and affection we have for each other.

Oh James, how wonderfully sweet you are!

I know! And the other admission, No, I don't have a broker! A broker! The very word terrifies me. Unless I have it wrong? Isn't a broker someone who contrives to make one broke?"

I think you and I should sit down one day and I will try to explain the ways of the financial world James. Perhaps after my big match on Saturday, (glass half full as I've already won the match tomorrow.) we can discuss the effects a preempted Bullish market will have on worldwide economies in the longer term. I can suggest sites that will be beneficial and give you a layman's perspective. Oh what fun we will have on Saturday afternoon!

She was good! I could tell she was holding back on the laughter from my previous remark but not to be outdone, back she came. I could almost feel her gearing up to my next response. I had no idea what that might be. No thoughts bubbling under. It was easier when face to face. A smile of acknowledgement on her retort thus giving me that vital moment to respond. It was normally all I needed. I had spent my entire life refining that ability. Yes, ability. The ability to hide, who I am. We all do it. In my case it was the battle I had yet to win but I hid it well.

I tell you what Anna, You win on Saturday, we won't be studying economics, we'll be celebrating. My favourite girl has just upped her ranking. Lunch is on me. And if you don't win? We'll celebrate anyway and lunch is still on me. The thought of a pleasant lunch with someone such as I, post match will be just what you need.

I think that was holding out a blanket of comfort as only James knows how to. And yes, whether I win or lose we will have a pleasant lunch. I did tell you I am a bad loser, didn't I?

Now she was laughing.

I am looking forward already. Must go now. Talk to you after my match tomorrow. Bye for now James.

Good luck for tomorrow Anna. ... but she had already disappeared?

I had to say, I believed that went well. I reflected on the call. Actually no. Not just the call but all that had gone before. A hundred emails. Dinner and those few conversations. I had to be careful not to hold too much credence in the emails. If there was a relationship to be had, it would be the mutual feelings when together that captured the essence and less so what went before. It was early days James. Let us not read too much into it. I allowed myself a smile and headed for bed. I set the alarm earlier for the next day.

Sat in the office a good hour before anybody was due, gave me plenty of time to write a message.

Good Morning Anna, My very first thought when I awoke? "Will you be my boyfriend". I must have been tired yesterday to have let that revelation pass me by. I will not dwell on this point because as you know, it could take me paragraphs before I finally said Yes. Easier just to assume it so, don't you agree?

I doubted I would get a straight answer on that. I would be more inclined to believe Anna will ignore it.

OK, big match today. Your incentive to win is? Keep knocking them out until Saturday and I will be there to watch. Alternatively, lose if you think it would add undue pressure on you if I came. You now have a dilemma. Win because you would really, really like me to come. Win because as we know, you are too competitive to throw a match. So you are going for a win! As Saturday approaches and you're still winning.........do you want me there? "Of course", you say. Then I will be. Feeling that pressure? Will there be a lot watching?

Next Date. It has been shortened to next date over the years of usage. Strictly speaking, one should say, For the next time we meet. I do realise you are a very busy Lady who has daily commitments. Unlike myself who just has a paying job to occupy my time. (That's veering on the side of sarcasm.)

Options:

Early evening drink allowing you to get back for dinner. Which Mother would prepare on this particular evening.

An all night rave. Getting you home in time to take your daughter to school.

06:00 breakfast. (A continuation of option two.)

My place for a sentimental movie to see who cries the most.

My place? I would need to organise for the place to be painted. Buy that new rug I've been promising myself. Find somewhere to "hide" the many framed pictures of previous lady friends. (Maybe shouldn't have added that one?) Not forgetting to borrow some food from next door to fill the fridge. Thus giving the impression of healthy eating. You know what? I think it would be easier if we just forget this option.

Saturday. All Day!!! I would, "clear my desk" for the day if there was the possibility of seeing you albeit for but a brief moment. (Do you think I overdid that a little?) Definitely lunch.

Good Luck today Anna, and may your day be full of love. Forty love .... to You!

James.

Hello James, sorry if I keep this short. Just taking my daughter to school. Then have to drop the car off at the Mercedes garage, again! Someone is picking me up then on to the court. The last sounds good but without you watching me. I will get too nervous and lose concentration. The rest to be said by phone later. Thank you for the love times forty! Anna.

It did make one feel somewhat restricted knowing people exist who spend their day, filling their day. Filling it in a manner befitting someone who has no restrictions on what the day had to offer. I wondered why I thought that. Anna obviously doesn't work in the true sense of the word but didn't she mention something about organising functions on our first meeting? Although I didn't get the idea this was a job. I returned to my day. Returning from lunch I sent a message.

Hi Anna, I have been wondering all day. Did she win? Normally, No news is Good news. I am now wondering if this is the case? I'll give you a call tonight. Your concerned friend, James.

As usual Anna seemed to be on her own agenda. She called.

Hello James, I hope you don't mind me calling? Are you still at work? You are. Ok, Yes I lost but it was so close. Nothing in it so although I lost, I came away feeling positive. I'll call you this evening. Bye for now.
She had managed to turn it around, yet again. I was going to call her this evening now she was calling me? It was a petty thing I know but why did she do that? Was it control? Not necessarily a control of me just control of her own life. Open her agenda and fit James in nicely between taking delivery of the new garden furniture and calling her daughter in Geneva? Or perhaps to have the time to eject her present lover? The strange thing was, I believed all to be possible. I'm not a jealous type. Never have been. If my girl preferred someone over me, so be it. It was not to say I didn't suffer the emotions of separation any more or less than others. Jealousy was sending useless love messages to someone who didn't care. Who gained? No matter how painful, move on. Why was I thinking this way? I'd keep it as an interesting thought and perhaps relate back after future meetings. Future meetings? Anna had me thinking glass half full. The drive home gave its usual tribulations. Middle lane drivers. So much better if we adopted American motorway driving. The locals would love that. No indication necessary. An English friend of mine once asked his French wife why she didn't indicate when exiting the motorway. Her reply? "Why? Everybody knows where I'm going". "They do now!" Was his reply.
A relaxing shower lightened my mood. First cigarette of the day with a cold beer and surrounded by silence. There were times I would switch on the radio the moment I walked in. This was not one of those moments. I had a couple of emails to write but decided to savour the beer and cigarette, prior to computer time. Reply to my sister who sent me a mail yesterday. Stuck in her apartment in Sass Fee, watching the heavy snow descend. It often happened that way. Lucy was bored. Derek as usual, didn't care about the White Out. He was out there. So Lucy sends James an email. I wondered to mention about Anna but decided against it. Lucy would want to know all the details. I sympathised with her situation. Stuck in their holiday apartment with only lunch and Apres Ski to look forward to, until Derek returned. "Such a hard life you have Lucy." I was being unfair, Lucy worked very hard at fitting four or five holidays a year into her hectic social life. Did this sound familiar? Perhaps it was not such a bad idea to discuss Anna? But not now. I round up the mail mentioning my busy work schedule over the next six weeks then, Kisses James.
I had received an email from Nadine. We became friends via some website and had met on several occasions. I would put off a reply for the time being. Needing to be in a different frame of mind to answer. The mind set necessary for such a mail was not there. My mind set was Anna. No matter. Another evening soon will do. I was closing down Safari when Anna's ringtone interrupted the process.
Hello James.

I didn't know why but I now had an image of new garden furniture. Adorned by her latest lover who was sprawled across the sofa eating grapes from Anna's hand. I laughed!

What is so funny James? I only said Hello.

Dropped yourself in it now James.

Don't take this the wrong way Anna but as you said Hello James, I felt a slight, almost undetectable condescending manner. I'm sure it wasn't intentional assuming it was there at all, I just found it amusing. Now if you were to ask me why I found it amusing, that might be more difficult to answer so lets change the subject and talk about your almost victory today.

I think I'd thrown out enough confusion to have emerged unscathed from that faux pas.

The match. It was really testing for both of us. Sarah is forty eight I think? Yes, I remember her saying she is a year younger than me. Oh Dear, I've just told you my age. All I can say in my defence is the website never updated my age. Anyway, it went to the third set with almost every game reaching deuce. Very thrilling and nerve racking with the adrenaline still pumping long after my Gin and Tonic consolation prize had been drained. How was your day? Not too demanding I hope.

No Anna, my day was fine in fact one could almost say, boring. Boring days are to be cherished as they are so few and far between particularly this close to a major event. More importantly, I was thinking about this up and coming weekend. What if we ......

Actually James I wanted to talk about that. Can we make it Friday evening as Saturday might become a little unpredictable.

She paused. I knew it to be pointless to question the unpredictability of her day. I knew, "Sure, no problem Anna, I understand." Should have been the answer. Followed up with a discussion about what time and where. But there was a part of me. A part of me that wanted to question the reason why I couldn't be included in that unpredictable day. I settled for the understanding approach.

Friday evening? That will be fine Anna. I know a family run Italian restaurant near the market in Antibes. We could meet in Latino's for a cocktail beforehand. Do you know Latino's? No. Ok I'll text you the address.

Can we make it early James, as I have a practice match at ten on Saturday?

Eight?

That's perfect James. See you there at eight.

I didn't try to reply. Why would I? She had already hung up.

I spent twenty years living with a Dutch girl. Living and loving, I might add. Some consider the Dutch too direct. Say what has to be said and nothing more. I think about the time Josey's mother asked me if I would like tea or coffee. My answer was typically English. "I don't mind." Wrong answer! "James, you seem to have missed the point of the question. Do you want tea or coffee?" I got the point.

"Tea please." I became used to this direct form of conversation. Anna and her form of abrupt conversation was something new. Her English was perfection and yet the Russian loitered beneath.

"Good Morning Anna", I text. What a beautiful day. Arrived early at work and decided to enjoy a croissant and coffee on le bord de mer. Did you know, the Austrians invented the croissant?

I received an immediate response.

You can guess where I am James. Yes, sat at the red lights, taking my daughter to school. So, The Early Bird catches the Worm and some Austrian invented croissants? I am jealous about the coffee and intrigued at the amount of wonderful irrelevant knowledge you possess.

I was not going to bombard Anna with messages today. It was not the time to be overly familiar. Ok, I admit it. I'd got feelings of dismissal. Big match Saturday and win or lose, I was not included. I was thinking, Anna didn't know how Saturday would pan out but wanted to keep her options open with the obvious exclusion of "moi"! Being over sensitive? After all, wasn't it what I would have done in her place. Fortunately work took precedence over my oversensitivity as the day was taking a turn for the worse. In this business of design and build of exhibition stands, deadlines are all important. The word for deadlines in French is délais. You pronounce that word with a silent "s" and what do you have? Need I say more. Two local suppliers had let us down with materials promised. It was not unusual so there was always a Plan B, and C. Plan B involved sourcing the goods and sending someone from the company to collect. Normally a four to eight hour round trip. Plan C was ordering through the parent company in New York and the goods would arrive in three days! Plan C was so much easier but it was Plan C for a reason. To avoid the indignation from the parent company who really did not understand the continual frustration we suffered when proposing deadlines only to later realise the reality of such a proposal to be meaningless, we preferred Plan B. Lunchtime! Thank goodness. It was usual for a small group to head to a local restaurant which we'd frequented on a daily basis for the last seven years. Needless to say, one knew the staff and owner. Today was no exception as five headed for lunch. A three course lunch and coffee. All for fifteen Euros. With the added bonus of all you could drink. I say bonus with a reflected mood of yesterday year. It was too enticing. How could one resist a carafe of rosé included in the meal? Occasionally more. For the majority of the time I could resist that temptation. A small beer and Badoit controlled any spontaneous urge to rebel. The wine seemed to be flowing as we offloaded the mornings frustrations. It was a stressful industry one worked in and as we all knew, stress manifests itself into many forms of self denial. That day, I had two glasses of wine and a message from Anna mid lunch.

Hello James, how goes your day? Mine has turned into a complete disaster. A sudden downpour cancelled my practice and while sat in the club house I had a call from Marta. The electricity has failed. Eight people are coming for lunch. Damn! Now waiting for the electrician who promised to be here thirty minutes ago. Sorry, I just needed to vent. Please, tell me something funny.

I was reading Anna's message while sat in the office. I had a moment or two to digest the information. Who was Marta? Oh Dear, cancelled lunch and you've only been waiting thirty minutes, for a local electrician. Do Anna's days normally flow uninterrupted by such inappropriate interruptions? The day was spoilt and the petulant child needed distraction? Maybe there was another side to Anna's strong character? Something funny was what she wanted. Who was I to disappoint. It just so happened my graphics friend Chris, mailed me a couple of jokes the other day. Try one of those as I'd no time for spontaneity

Ok Anna. A personalised joke while considering your predicament.

I came home from work and the wife had left me a message on the fridge. "This isn't working. I'm going to stay with my mother".

I opened the fridge door. The light came on. The beer was cold. No idea what she was talking about?

I'm sure the electrician will be along soon to turn on YOUR fridge.

You are a tonic James! Your perception is uncanny. Let's talk about YOUR day soon. x

Soon? I think that was sometime in the future and when that future came it would be so far removed as to become irrelevant. So much for my day but it didn't matter as there would be an update of Anna's day later and I had to admit, I liked to hear her talk. Excuse me James but could we take this one step at a time? Yeh, got that, I told myself.

Time to be homeward bound.

Night James, see you tomorrow, said Will.

Uh, yes, see you tomorrow Will.

Will was usually last out. I looked at my watch. It was six thirty and I had some shopping to do. A message from Anna.

Hi James, are you home? Can I call?

No, shopping at Carrefour. Should be home in thirty minutes. I am now queuing up to pay.

Anna called anyway!

"Which Carrefour", she asked. *Oh Antibes. I was just passing there! Call me when you're home.*

Anna called me. Only to be expected. The days earlier catastrophe turned out to be a main fuse, allowed a regroup of the girls for a later lunch. The last guest had recently left, leaving Anna in a jovial mood that needed my attention,

So lunch with the girls was a success?

Oh yes and with the usual compliments. Don't know what I would do without Marta and I've managed to secure two practice matches tomorrow.

Marta. Can't let it pass a second time.

Who is Marta?
She is my house keeper who happens to be a splendid cook. Sorry, should have explained.
All became clear. Anna had a housekeeper. Of course she had a housekeeper. Why didn't I realise that? Perhaps because apart from the couples I knew who both worked and had that person who "does for them" once or twice a week, I was in ignorance of such "goings-on". A nod in acknowledgement, when discussed, of their seemingly endless task in finding the right one, would be my only input. That was my reality. A housekeeper? I'd seen enough Hollywood movies to be acquainted with the terminology but I must admit, I wouldn't know one if I saw one. Massive learning curve there James!
Then I hope you treasure her as the good housekeeper she seems to be, let alone good cook as the combination must be hard to find.
The perfect reply as Anna lyrics between the history of Marta as part of the growing family and her ability to be seen and yet not seen as circumstance dictates. Needless to say, my contribution to the said, day to day politics of having a housekeeper was somewhat limited as one did ones best to avoid any unacknowledged embarrassment by making no reference to the subject.
Two practice matches in one day? Isn't that a little excessive Anna? You don't want to be physically drained for the match on Saturday. Not even considering the mental approach if you lose both matches tomorrow. Do you have a coach? Don't answer that, as it's obvious to me, you don't! I think you should consider the option of understanding your weaknesses on court and practice accordingly. It is not about winning or losing tomorrow, it's more about honing your mental approach to areas that are disruptive to your game.
Did I just say that? And if I did, what did I say?
Dear James is concerned. How sweet! Actually, you make a valid point. As you know, I'm not good at losing, so integrating my weaknesses in the games tomorrow sounds like a good idea. As my, "unpaid" coach, how do you envisage I fulfil that requirement?
What? She was messing with my head. Of course she was. Anna aware I was giving her advice with no knowledge of the subject. I saw it as a continuation of that obviously absurd dialogue or coming clean and admitting I had no idea of what to suggest. You do that James, you admit to ignorance and this absurd dialogue comes crashing down.
That's easy Anna, unfortunately for you maybe not so. I'm assuming you know who you will be playing tomorrow and on that assumption you explain to said person your need to improve on your weaknesses. That's the difficult bit Anna. Accepting your weaknesses. Didn't someone once say, "It takes a strong person to accept their weaknesses?" Easy for Samson to say ... Until he met Delilah.
I had more to say but uncontrollable laughter from Anna interrupted my flow as she tried desperately to formulate a response.

James, you're unbelievable!
I am? You bet you are! Don't let the euphoria of the moment allow for some benignly weak follow up. No need to worry on that point as Anna had controlled her laughter.

For one second I thought, I need James as my Life Coach. You have a knack of turning the subject into something so far removed as to make it of secondary importance to the matter at hand. My example being. What has Samson's hair got to do with explaining to my competitor tomorrow, that I would really appreciate her exploitation of my weaknesses? Maybe it would be far from ideal to consider an explanation of said question to be beneficial to me, unless my Life Coach (pending) has conceived a cunning plan that envisages a change in my competitive nature to that with acceptable submissive tendencies?

Now it was my turn to laugh! Not so much because I found it amusing, which I did, but more to hide my momentary inability of having anything to say. I was locked into, "submissive tendencies" and that could be for a number of reasons. They were the last words used and therefore memorable within a jumble of others that my brain was finding difficult to compile into anything resembling an intelligent response. Or maybe I was asking myself the question, "Did Anna leave her reply open ended on purpose?" She could have concluded with, submissive tendencies on court, but no, she left it open. Did she leave that door open on purpose? I didn't think it mattered the reason, I was at a loss as to the formation of anything close to an intelligent reply. Submissive tendencies it was then.

Anna my dear, as your unpaid pending coach, it might be ethically immoral of me to comment further on my techniques as a coach, be it on or off the court. Or, to put that another way. If you think I'm giving away my secrets of guaranteed success for free, you're wrong. Oh and another thing, maybe until the time we know each other better, I suggest we don't discuss your submissive tendencies but rather discuss tomorrow evening.

Change of subject would help me right now.

I was thinking about tomorrow evening. If it's an early evening finish, how about seven to start? With my guarantee of you being home, dreaming sweet dreams sans hangover for the morning tennis match. So Anna, having given such an assurance, I do believe you have little choice but to consider this as a viable option. Don't you agree?

I agree James! I just wish I knew what I was agreeing to? Am I agreeing to considering your proposal or having little choice but to agree?

Yes Anna. You have a good laugh as to how clever you have been. It was clever and quick and yes, funny. I was sure she didn't expect a reply, wrapped up in that smug feeling of a well engineered example of oneupmanship. Did I allow it to pass and graciously Accept the loss of that battle? It was a tough decision as my immediate thought would be one of retaliation. Can't let her get away with that! Fortunately intuition kicked in as I formulated a response with the accompaniment of a wry smile.

Well done Anna on your decision to agree. So, seven it is then?

Seven it is James.

Before you go Anna, I have an observation I would like to share with you.

Oh yes?

Yes. Do you realise that almost every time the conversation is winding down to the goodbyes, you put the phone down prior to the good bye.

I do?

Yes, just as I'm about to say ....?

She'd put the phone down! Now that had me laughing. This girl was good, no doubt about it. I opened myself up to that one and fell right in. The opportunity could have been missed by another but not Anna. Straight for the jugular. I was left to clear up prior to bed. A few moments passed when I received a message.

You must have seen that coming James because I think you walked straight into it! See you at seven in Latino's. Cocktails on me. Winner pays, that's my motto. Now I must stop as I'm laughing too much thinking of your reaction to this message.

I decided not to involve myself in further banter.

As I lay in bed, unable to sleep with a constant cascade of thoughts that were channelled and then dispersed, I awaited the still waters.

At six fifty I woke to the sound of, "Castles In The Sand" and fell into my morning routine. Who was I kidding. By the time I was half way to the kettle my thoughts were of Anna, although surprisingly the thoughts made sense. The nights sleep had brought clarity. Emails. Phone calls. One date. Enjoy the ride James and with that thought, I headed for the shower.

The workshop was already alive with the sound of machinery that was competing with the radio when I arrived. I left yesterday evening as an area was being cleared for the initial build of a new stand which was now taking shape. It had reached that time in the season when private life took a back seat as there wouldn't be many with less than three hundred hours worked over the next month. The permanent team of four carpenters had blossomed into seventeen and the place was organised chaos. Anticipating the time when space would have to be allocated for the painters who would arrive shortly, I'd booked the first truck the week before. The following day the truck arrived, dropping off a seventy cubic metre trailer. More would follow as prepared stands were loaded into the first of many to arrive over the coming weeks. Deliveries of materials became a daily routine that fed the machine turning raw plywood into things of beauty. Accepting the premise, Beauty is in the Eye of the Beholder, I continued to keep a watchful eye on progress. It was just a matter of keeping the chaos organised. Thoughts of the evening were of a somewhat abstract nature, if I didn't get away by five. That having been said, why was I already trying to decide what to wear?

Sorry, what did you say? "Ah yes, I agree, put Fa on panel construction which should free up Philo to concentrate his skills on this hellishly complicated reception desk". The day forged ahead and was surprisingly shaping up to be a good one. No foreseeable problems standing in the way of a five o'clock exit.

Chapter Three

Anna had just text me saying she was entering the car park and would be in Latino's in five minutes and it was only ten past seven. Unfortunately, lateness was a familiar commodity in this part of the world and accepted. Fifteen minutes was most certainly considered, on time. I had been standing on that corner for twenty five minutes, keeping an eye on the bar in case there was the slightest chance Anna might be the punctual type. I headed for the bar in a direct line for the still empty table I had picked twenty minutes previously. I was given a cocktail menu explaining, "J'attends quelqu'un." "D'accord monsieur." There would be no mistake this time as there was only one approach from the car park and that gave me an uninterrupted view along the fifty metre walkway. No sooner thought when Anna came into view. For a tall woman Anna had a graceful manner. Honed to perfection, like her English accent. Dressed in light brown trousers set off with a multi coloured blouse and what looked like a jumper draped over her shoulders. I watched her approach while checking the menu.

Hello James. What colour shoes am I wearing?

I couldn't see her shoes. She was standing too close but I knew they were a pale yellow. It was obvious Anna had seen me watching or at least was fairly confident I did so and was alerting me to the fact. Put in that position, I felt honesty, was the best possibility.

Yes Anna, I was watching you approach and they are yellow.

"And?" *Said Anna.*

Here for barely thirty seconds and already demanding my opinion on her initial approach. I knew she was playing with me. I think the upturned smile and quizzical look helped to allay any fears I might have had. This was a game I could play.

If you hadn't been so intent on discovering that you were right rather than allowing me the good grace to compliment you on how absolutely .... You would have heard the remainder of that compliment in it's entirety! Looks like you blew it Anna. There's an English proverb that says, "Anything worth having, is worth waiting for." In this case, about twenty seconds would have done it."

As that initial flurry of exchanges passed I realised I was sitting. Albeit on a bar stool that gave us eye level contact. I slip off the stool and reach forward to give Anna the friendly greeting of kisses.

Oh James, would you deprive me of your compliments. You must have considered them on my approach? And for them to now be scattered to the winds. What a shame that would be and besides, I like compliments.

You are right again Anna, I did consider and now I struggle to remember those words, carefully crafted to be a more than, You look nice!

Anna waited. You are going to have to think of something James. No way was I going to get away with, "You look nice".

With every step you took you illuminated the walkway until the moment you were next to me and my world became immersed in a radiance so profound all around became of no consequence.

"Excusez-moi monsieur, êtes vous prêt à commander?"

The timing could not have been better. Anna and I laughed. We managed to order our drinks amid much smirking and maybe to the slight annoyance of the waiter.

We left the bar in jubilant mood. Anna insisting on paying but was considerate enough not to mention her reason for doing so. There was no need and she saw it. Unsaid things. Doesn't that development necessitate a period of time having to pass? Or perhaps the fact that Anna had promised this first drink and read in my expression the complicity of acceptance. Nothing more.

We walked side by side through the covered market talking about nothing in particular with Anna now telling me about her forthcoming visit to Geneva. I remembered her daughter lived there. "Visiting you're daughter?" Before she could answer we arrived at the restaurant. I had to smile as her pronunciation, at that moment, was perfection itself. "Is this the restaurant"? with every vowel gaining equal merit.

Is it just me or do we all have that initial moment when seated, of coming to terms with our surroundings? Glancing around wondering if a better table was available? Anna was already checking out the menu, maybe it was just me?

"Bruschetta definitely but which. Mmmmm."

I watched Anna as she ran through the options. She seemed oblivious to her surroundings taking great delight in, at one moment murmuring her decision, only to reject it the next. She looked up.

"What"?

I looked at her and smiled, saying nothing. It was her word, used when she caught me watching her. My response was always the same. A smile. I liked what I was seeing. She took it as intended and I knew she enjoyed the unspoken compliment.

The young woman who had seated us came over to ask if we would like an aperitif. Having already established Anna as a red wine drinker I quickly checked the list. My general rule of thumb? Out of the window. I went for the fifth, again. If you asked me why I changed the habit of a lifetime, maybe it was the wardrobe of designer labels sat opposite me? I didn't feel particularly intimidated by Anna's labels. Then why the fifth? We were enjoying each others company and more to the point I do believe my modest charm was something she was unused to. Yes, I do have modest charm and stating the fact doesn't compromise my modesty. A fact is a fact!

Gambetto Fettuccine Alfredo was Anna's choice. Swordfish with a tomato sauce for me.

So James, what are your intentions?

Here we go. Anna was in playful mood.

To finish this meal Anna?

Ok James, perhaps that was too easy to redirect but there are subtle connotations. I am very good with the daily chit chat, whether it be with my daughter in the car or a formal gathering of distinguished persons. Sometimes life changing decisions have to be taken. I'm not saying you are a life changing decision but I won't know without ...... compiling information about you, now will I?"

I couldn't fault her logic, or complain, when one was faced with Anna's doleful expression aimed at giving sympathy to her cause.

Ok Anna. My intentions. Accepting what I have to say is based on this second date and four thousand emails. This being the "second" date, I can but conclude, I must like you.

She laughed giving me respite. I was not sure where that was leading but seeing Anna wanted to jump in, I stubbornly continue, knowing I had to add substance to my previous remark.

Please Anna, give me this moment. You asked my intentions and without the time to think of a reply, please accept my digressions as a part of my answer.

That had Anna's attention.

God bless the untimely interruption of the waitress! "Voulez vous le dessert?" as she cleared away the plates. We decided a coffee would suffice.

I promise not to interrupt James as I can see you are intent on a reply. I just wanted to say, as I think you already know, I need, yes, I think need is the right word, I need to hear from you ....

Anna!" That had her attention.

Don't interrupt!" That smile told her all was well.

I like you. I could simplify that by giving you a score out of ten but how infantile would that be? No Anna, you most certainly deserve better. I am therefore going to open myself up to allow you to draw your own conclusions.
Now I'm in trouble! Why the hell did I say that? Time for digression. I was reaching out to this woman who unfortunately had the patience for my diversities.
Why do I get the feeling I'm closing a net around myself?
We laughed at that.
Ok. As you know, I've been married twice. The second time was love. Don't ask me why and certainly not when I tell you I knew within thirty seconds of meeting her.
Anna wanted to say something but was tactfully able to control but not conceal that urge. And I was left wondering, where was I going with this, not sure if I might be going in too deep. As long as it makes sense James, then it is up to Anna to draw her own conclusions.
You might wonder about my first marriage? That was friendship, as it turned out. Don't get me wrong. We have two wonderful children and spent the best part of twelve years enjoying each others company. You might now be wondering, where is James going with this? Well Anna, I will tell you. Two marriages and an …. acceptable amount of affairs later, I am able to categorise my emotional feelings for another woman rather rapidly. It's …..
I'm sorry James, I have to interrupt but I hope you remember where you left off because I'm so enjoying it! I think I told you before how I like to listen to your voice but as mesmerising as it it, I can't let that statement pass. Categorise your feelings! What software are you running? I took you as the more sensitive type?
I was glad Anna said, "Categorise your feelings" because I had totally lost the thread as soon as she spoke. Now I had material to continue. Sensitive type. Software. Bring it back to the original point in the conversation. Particularly as that often had the effect of impressing those one talked to. I remembered where I was. Quickly coming to the conclusion of my intentions. *On a score of one to ten. You get an eight!*
Where did that come from? Infantile behaviour perhaps? I had it in mind, to mention my sensitive soul. Or something similar. It didn't matter. It worked.
I loved the way she laughed. Initially it was tempered restraint, replaced with, what I can only describe as an emotionally charged laugh. She was opening up. This is who I am James. This is me underneath the facade. Would it be conceited of me to assume I had seen a side of Anna that was rarely shown? As I pondered that thought Anna regained her composure. Time would tell if I was correct in my assumption.
I have to say James, I do feel relaxed in your company. Even when we are playing our games, I can rely on you to give me a, "get out clause", thus saving me the embarrassment of losing. Or perhaps that should read annoyance?

She was smiling again.

But seriously. I spend too much time taking too many things, too seriously. So in my category of, Someones company I feel relaxed in. You get an eight and half out of ten!

There was that smile again. A good moment I thought to discuss the next rendezvous. Mmmm, I wondered how I'd do in the, "Assertive man telling his woman what to do", category?

You mentioned it unlikely you will have time this weekend for more idle chit chat Anna. So I suggest we get together early next week. Let's say Tuesday evening.

Was that assertive enough? Anna was looking at me with that hang dog look. It was not good news.

Oh James, I'm sorry. I'm going to Geneva on Wednesday. And so much to do. To make it up to you, I promise I'll buy some Swiss chocolate to give you on my return.

Anna was looking at me. Why did I get the feeling it was a look that had been used many times before? A look that begged forgiveness? If not, then something very similar. Was I reading her that well or was this a look that Anna knew worked? Was I being obviously manipulated? I think it more likely this was Anna's, get out clause. A look of, Please understand. If I could. I would. But on the positive side. I'd been promised some chocolate?

Not to worry Anna. It will give you time to compile more categories. I wouldn't mind applying for the, Man who you think about the most, category. I think I'm onto a winner there. Whenever you think about that category, you will think of me. Certainly as I've now implanted the thought in your head! Shall we go?

Out on the street it was not busy. Too early in the season and no school holidays to contend with. It was a narrow pavement but Anna managed to hook her arm into mine. Oblivious of the few people around having to take drastic action to avoid a collision. Fortunately, jaywalking is not illegal in France. Anna was telling me about her visit to her daughter living in Geneva.

She is more of a friend than a daughter. Did I tell you? I left her father when we lived in Holland with just the clothes on my back. Admittedly, I had a good job and was not exactly destitute but life had to start again. Tanya was eighteen months old at the time. Maybe I shouldn't admit this but I am looking forward to seeing my grand daughter. Yes. I'm a grand mother!

It is my turn to stop you, Anna. It is a real shame. I was enjoying your company so much! But I'm afraid I can't be seen with a grand mother! Could you perhaps walk a few paces behind?

There she goes. Giggling like a school girl. The jaywalking continued around us. We reached the underground parking as Anna rummaged through her bag to find her ticket.

I did promise to have you on your way early and sober Anna but I have to admit, I am now regretting that promise.

Anna found her ticket, giving me a look as if to say, Look at me. I'm in charge of my life. In an instant, she had changed. I don't think it was anything I said. I don't think she was really listening.

Anna, it would be wrong of me to say it was an enjoyable evening. So I won't! Instead, I will leave you with a thought . It might help to answer that earlier question regarding my intentions. Your presence ...... made the evening perfect.

Anna looked at me. That moment of insecurity loomed within me. Did I just get that wrong? Too much said? Great evening Anna. See you when you get back. Don't forget the chocolates. Perhaps that was all that was needed!

That gives me something to think about while I'm away James. I might have to discuss it with Tanya. She is very good with these sort of things.

Anna was laughing again. Giving me no time to ask her what she meant by, "These sort of things". Kisses on the cheeks and she was gone. As I walked in search of my car I pondered the evening. Actually, I pondered Anna. What you saw was what you got. Not in Anna's case. She was a complex creature. I wondered what drove her? She had a competitive nature and a commanding presence. One which was used to being heard. That much was obvious. I could see her, strolling through the crowd at a party. Picking and choosing conversations as she went. Perfectly adapted to her surroundings. But tonight there was another Anna included. It would be vain of me to believe I had a part to play. But I felt I did! I was going to go out on a limb and say, she liked me. Didn't understand me but perhaps that was what she found intriguing? Assuming she was finding anything at all. Having found the car, I sat for a moment. She liked me. I liked her. That was enough James. Lets go home.

Chapter Four

Saturday and you couldn't have asked for a better day to play tennis. Blue skies. No wind and seventeen degrees promised. Perhaps spring had arrived thought I, as I wondered through Antibes. Arrived at le tabac, The Times now in hand and but a few steps away from a coffee. Placed at a convergence of roads only wide enough to accommodate one way traffic. There was a small fountain and with the surrounding cafes using every available space to place chairs and tables, it was a good location and one of my favourite for a morning coffee. Café allongé, s'il vous plait monsieur. I made no attempt to read the paper, I was content watching the world go by. I looked at the time which was fast approaching the moment I calculated as being ideal to message Anna. Not too soon but not too late as to conflict with her thoughts of the up and coming match. *I know you said not to be there and far be it for me to go against your wishes Anna. I have therefore come up with a usable alternative. Please imagine me on the sidelines, cheering on your every move. Oh and I'd love to have a picture of the winner in her tennis outfit. Your choice on which outfit you wear. Good Luck Anna. James x*

I thought that was lightly put. Lightly put? Fortunately at that moment, I was distracted. A woman had seemingly "brushed" another with her pushchair. An argument ensued. These situations can often be amusing if not taken too seriously. Let off a bit of steam that could have been brought on by her husband breathing too loudly. You never knew. I just accepted it as the Mediterranean temperament.

Time to move along. I needed to go to Monoprix for bread. Wondering around Monopix I realised I hadn't planned the day. My thoughts were on Anna last night. I went to sleep with no weekend plans. I had to smile at that revelation. No plans and I didn't care.

The sun was shining on the terrace when I arrived home so after dusting off a teak chair from the cellar I opened the patio doors, coffee and paper in hand, ready to settle down for an hour or so. Paul called over, asking if I wanted to join them for croissants. The paper could wait. "Sure but I've got my own coffee". "I don't think I mentioned coffee", said Paul, as he disappeared behind the planted barrier that was all that separated us. Oh dear, am I up to Paul and his buoyant mood? Hell yes! Not only croissants but almond biscuits brought back by Paul from his recent trip to Genoa. There was a conversation about his racing schedule when a message arrived. Anna. With photo! For the next few minutes ….. I nodded to anything Paul had to say.

Have you ever considered becoming a diplomat James? My choice of outfit I'm wearing, as the assumed winner. So sweet. Win or lose this is what I will be wearing. Your support is much appreciated. Oh and Happy Women's Day.

A photo of Anna in her tennis outfit. Taken looking at the mirror. White T shirt with a pale blue jumper over her shoulders. White tennis skirt with white knee length leggings. Shoes to match the blue of her jumper. Topped off with a red Baseball hat allowing her ponytail access through the band. And such a ….. warm smile.

What is it? asks Chiara.

It's Anna. She's just sent me a pic in her tennis outfit.

I explained she had a tennis match.

Let me see!

I stopped explaining and handed Chiara the phone.

She looks lovely and have you seen the mirror? Very glitzy and possibly typical Russian in the choice?

I admitted to not having noticed the mirror. I looked at Chiara. She laughed.

Just joking James but you have to agree, it is a bit glitzy? Can you zoom in on the basin. Maybe we can see the make?

Chiara we aren't talking bathrooms. This is about how lovely Anna looks and all else is superfluous.

"She looks lovely James", said Paul.

Thanks Paul. Now about that race of yours. Where was it again?

Time passed until the plates were emptied. A good moment to make my departure, I wished the pair a pleasant day. Walked the fifty metres to my front door. My phone pinged.

I won! I can't believe it. I'm sure it was thanks to you being on the sidelines. Just enough time to enjoy buying the loser a drink before picking up Elena. Yes, I'm a chauffeur at the weekends too! I won and you are the first to know. Mmmm, I will have to think about that? Later James.

You'll have to think about that! I wasn't going to be able to concentrate on the paper for sometime to come. First to know? Was Anna just messing with my head or did she truly want, albeit subconsciously, to tell me first? Don't go there James. A good time for some lunch.

The day was staying clear and unusually warm for late March and it seemed a shame to stay around the house. A ten minute walk to the sea and veering right, taking in Antibes centre, would be about ninety minutes. Nothing better for thinking than walking. I had that vague idea I should have been keeping this in perspective. Do I take Anna's comments as more than a throw-away remark. She put thoughts in my head that had no validity in the meaning. She realised, after saying "I was first", that maybe, just maybe, she'd said too much, adding, "I will have to think about that". Thinking about why she would do that added to her mystic? Yes, maybe that was the way she saw it. I saw it as she wanting me to like her. Which wasn't a bad thing. She obviously liked me, otherwise what would be the point. Why would she care what I thought.

It was all making perfect sense. Or was that perfect nonsense? Either way I decided to reward myself with an ice cream. No ice cream parlours were open at this time of the season I was thinking, as I walked out of the Esso station, Magnum in hand. A couple of girls passed me by, speaking Italian and my thoughts drifted. Why? Why, for the remainder of my walk home did I think of Emanuela. My, Oh so sweet Italian. "I have been waiting all my life for you", I remembered her saying. The times we spent together. There was an openness about Emanuela combined with an innocence. Until one reached the bedroom that was. What times we had. Every second was a joy to behold. I had found my soulmate. Then she slowly disappeared. No more visits. The messages dried up. I finally texted her saying I was going to visit her the coming weekend. I had an almost immediate answer which had not happened in some time.

Please James don't come. Anyway I will not be here this weekend as I'm going to the countryside with my daughter.

I left it two or maybe three weeks and set off one Saturday morning at five to be in Torino by eight. I took a flask of coffee and cigarettes as I had decided to wait outside in the hope Emanuela would make an appearance from her apartment. Some might call this stalking. So be it. I must have been distracted, as the next moment, she drove past. Damn! I decided to wait for her to return. Saturday morning shopping was my guess. One hour and seven minutes later, she returned. I got out of the car and strolled towards her. She was facing the boot of the car as I arrived. I asked if she would like some help as she struggled to get her shopping from the car. She spun around and looked at me. *"Hello James",* she said as she reached forward to give me a gentle kiss.

I'm sorry Emanuela if I've startled you but if I didn't just turn up I had the feeling I might never see you again. Do you have time for a coffee?

She looked at me, eyes wide open with a quizzical expression on her face.

I'm going to have a late breakfast with my daughter and then she is off with a friend. Can we meet in an hour, in the park? There is a small kiosk under the trees. Just go to the end of the road and turn left. The park will come in view on your right. See you there in an hour?

Another kiss and a big smile from Emanuela before she turned, carrying her shopping to the main entrance of her block. Quietly elated, I headed for the park. An hour to kill so having spotted the kiosk I walked in the opposite direction. No need to rush. A stroll through the park on an early spring day. I had no problem with that! There was a lot of ..... "goings on" in this park. Joggers. Cyclists. Lovers. Dog walkers. I wasn't sure if I would have been surprised to see a brass band marching right on through this theatre of activity. For that was the way it seemed to be. A spirited hustle and bustle of people enjoying themselves. Was that the way we interpreted moments in our lives? Ones mood sets the tone. The world was a happy place. I was reminded of John Lennon. "All we need is Love." I could see where he was going with that. The kiosk was in sight so I sat to enjoy a real coffee. Italian style! Still another twenty minutes before beer time. Not really but I was getting nervous and a beer and cigarette would help. Not really but I had one anyway. I'd forgotten an important detail about Emanuela. She was never late but invariably early. Such was the case on this occasion. I watched her, half running, half walking. Remembering the second time we met. Emanuela spotting me across the beach and literally running into my arms from fifty metres away. I have to say that was one hell of a feeling. Very likely, similar to the feeling millions of men shared when watching Bo Derek in "10". She sat opposite me and grabbed the beer.

Lets finish this James. I know a place on the river where we can have lunch. The owner is a friend of mine. So if thats ok, I can book.

I'd like that. It sounds perfect.

The trip there, on the other hand, was not. In the passenger seat and unaware of Emanuela's abilities at the wheel. Was it a fact that the closer one got to the equator the less concern one had for other motorists? I knew Torino was on the forty fifth parallel but no one had told the Italians that! Emanuela joined the affray, throwing the large People Carrier around as though on a fairground ride. Three lanes in both directions with nothing separating them other than irate pedestrians stuck in the middle. I saw the river. Hopefully it couldn't be far. Impressed with Emanuela's parking, we strolled across the freshly cut lawns.

It's about a ten minute walk from here James but I thought you'd enjoy the scenery.

I'm enjoying the scenery just fine Emanuela.

She smiled, knowing exactly my meaning.

Lunch was pleasant but I felt Emanuela a little reserved. Not her usual bubbly self. Only to be expected? Not how she saw her Saturday panning out. We sat on the grass watching the rivers slow meanderings. Small talk prevailed until Emanuela asked the question foremost in her mind. One I feel had been sitting there waiting to be answered for some time.

James, if you moved to Torino, what would you do?
There we had it. Emanuela and her slow disappearance. It all made sense. The honeymoon period over, Emanuela looked to how it would work and came to the conclusion, it wouldn't. I never took her to be the pragmatic type. My mistake. If I'd known, could I have changed the outcome?
I was now surprised to find myself on the last leg of my walk. Twenty minutes had disappeared with thoughts of Emanuela? Turn left at the corner shop and but a few hundred metres from home. My last thought of Emanuela before entering the house had me convinced, I couldn't deny the feelings that still lingered. Perhaps Anna was my diversion? Was I creating an Anna in my life that didn't exist but was a useful distraction? Perhaps, but what a distraction! Perhaps that was the purpose I served for Anna? Her husband having died the previous year. A tentative first step to see who's out there. There could be more than just me! How do you feel about that, James? It's not unlikely. She was certainly a catch. (I think that was something my mother once told me.) I wouldn't say Anna was beautiful in the "Tabloid" sense of the word but it didn't take long, once having met her, to realise Anna's beauty lay deep. It conspired to overcome, utilising all the exuberance Anna had to offer. Her charm. Her confidence. Her intellect. Her ..... Anna. Well done James, you've just managed to convince yourself you're possibly not the only one! Why not go the whole nine yards and assume Anna was not going to Geneva to visit her daughter but instead was having a romantic few days away with someone else. I suppose it would have to be Switzerland, or no chocolate. Great consolation prize James. How the world turned. Was it only that morning I was staring at Anna in her Tennis outfit. She was getting to you James. Got to reign that in. But how?
It had started to cloud over drawing the day to a close that much earlier. I settled back with The Times to catch up on the days news trying to keep up with topical events that occasionally gave one that, "I know something about that subject", when being discussed in company. Not that any of this acquired knowledge helped come Monday morning. Monday mornings at work and there was only one topic to be discussed. Football. That encompassed not only the English league but the French also. I did try, many years ago, to take a more active role in knowing what happened at the weekend. I did believe there was a time, my input was occasionally rewarded with an intelligent knowing nod. The glory days of football adoration. It didn't last. My knowledge was inevitably found to be superficial and I was soon relegated.

Chapter Five

Chicken Curry for dinner and a new recipe. Actually not a new recipe just a different "all-in-one" sauce. Trying out a plastic sachet combining all the essential ingredients. Should be interesting. More so because of the price. The cost of that plastic sachet was well in excess of the price of the chicken. The point of the exercise was all about turning out a good curry. If successful, Paul and Chiara would be the first inline for a curry evening. Maybe I could invite Anna? Preparation almost completed. Chicken prepared. Paprika chopped. Just the onions to rough cut. I heard the message tone. No time for that and anyway I wouldn't want the excess chicken on my hands, smearing itself over my phone. Ok, I'd read the instructions just one more time to be absolutely certain the three easy steps had been assimilated. Twenty minutes later all was simmering gently in the pan and more importantly, smelling good.

I read the message for a third time.

Hi James, I realised it would be nice to catch up before I go to Geneva. There is a chance I can be in Antibes tomorrow afternoon about three. Could we have a coffee. Ideally somewhere near the carpark because I think my time will be limited. Hope so. Anna.

Sunday afternoon. Check the diary? No need.

Hello Anna. Three o'clock sounds fine. Give me a call tomorrow when you know for sure. There are two coffee stops directly in front of you as you walk through the archway. (Close to Latino's) Less than two minutes away. We can meet there. I look forward to the chance of seeing you. Take care, James.

Happy with that, I pressed send. Time for the rice. I'd made my decision for the evening. I'd watch movies. With a catalogue of over seven hundred movies on the computer, that wouldn't be a problem. An evening of thought was not what I needed. My lost Italian love versus the enigmatic Anna. Definitely to be avoided.

One thought did cross my mind as I piled the curry onto the plate. It was a fact I needed a distraction from Emanuela and I couldn't image one better, than Anna. I sat back to watch a movie. Any movie. Three movies would see the evening through. I fell asleep somewhere during the third. I was brought out of my slumber hearing Brown Eyed Girl playing on my phone. Anna!

Hello James, I hope I'm not disturbing you?

Of course not.

I think I had but a few seconds to wake up. Was it idle chatter or did Anna have something to say?

I'm in my office going through some papers and I stopped! I admit it. I was thinking of you. Why don't we make tomorrow definite. I will be there at three.

Is that three or the three, Anna time?

She could do no other than to laugh.

I have thought about that. If I call you half an hour before I leave the house, can you get there?

I would be there around two, I was thinking.

I'll have the helicopter on standby. Forget the helicopter, I'll be there at two. For the chance of seeing you, time is of little importance and there is always the possibility you might arrive early.

James, do I detect a slight touch of sarcasm in your voice?

Surely not Anna. As I think I've said before, I don't give out compliments easily, so why would I risk this opportunity of meeting you with compliments laced in sarcasm?

Possibly untrue as I found it even more difficult to throw out compliments unless there was a touch of sarcasm. A note for you there James. No sarcasm when complimenting Anna and at the same time thinking, that wouldn't be as difficult as it seemed. It was as though Anna offered herself up to compliments. I remembered when I said I was happy just watching her talk. She seemed to light up, radiating an inner glow. Complimenting Anna had it's own rewards.

Mmmm, I'm not sure I believe you but on this occasion as I most probably caught you asleep in front of the TV, I forgive you.

How did she know I was asleep in front of the TV?

"Only kidding", says Anna. *What are you doing anyway, if I may ask?*

Apart from trying to wake up in front of the TV, not much. But don't worry, I'll be fast asleep five minutes after you prematurely put the phone down. Don't you dare!

I won't James. I've been thinking. Can I ask you something?

Now was this the reason Anna called? I think I recognised that sweet non confrontational voice, it was the one my daughter used when she wanted something. "Daddy can I have. Daddy is it all right if I." My automatic inbuilt defence mechanism was wondering what was wanted.

You know we talked about intentions last night and I know this might sound a little old fashioned but are your intentions honourable? You never really gave me a straight answer on that. Or if you did, I missed it but I don't think I would have. What I mean, Oh this is not how I wanted to ask you. I can see me making a fool of myself if I continue. Do you understand what I'm trying to say James?

I had to answer that with a certain sensitivity. Anna felt she'd put herself on the spot. Possibly opened herself up to ridicule. This could be one of those defining moments when looking back realising where the mistake was made.

Anna, my intentions are honourable and if it helps I will admit to developing a fondness for you that would make it impossible to consider any other avenue of thought. I am who you see. Who I think you like. I would like to think there are characteristics you have yet to discover and will enjoy the journey of togetherness as we drive off into that sunset. Or do you think that was a bit of an over reaction to your question and a simple yes would have sufficed?"

She heard the humour in my voice and replied accordingly.

Thank you James for digging me out of that tight spot. Perhaps I think too much. I'm usually good at reading people but I have to admit, you have me baffled.

Anna paused. I wasn't sure if she expected a reply but as nothing came to mind, I decided to remain silent. It just so happened, it was the perfect "non" response.

You see? Most men I know would have something to say about that. Usually something challenging. Something defensive. Not you. You wait. How could you possibly have anything to say until I explain my reasons. You are a gentleman James and yet ……. you have no idea how to dress!

I was pleased to hear Anna giggling but surely I'd have to rise to the bait of dress? But then I would fall into that category of, "Most guys", that I am evidently not.

I have to say something. Anna expects it.

Fifty percent perfect? I can live with that.

No James, that won't do!

I'm not going there Anna. I'm not going to defend my taste in clothes. You have me in a corner. If I defend my clothes sense, I lose my gentlemanly status. Instead I will agree with you and hope you can educate me in this obvious faux pas on my part.

Oh James, I'm disappointed. I was expecting you to fall into the trap. But no, instead you agree. You see why you baffle me? I expect you to do or say something and you do the opposite! Don't change James. It's the bafflement that intrigues.

What was I supposed to say to that?

I don't intend doing so Anna. Not sure I could if I wanted to.

She knew I had a smirk on my face and this time, Anna waited.

If I'm not careful Anna, you will have me saying, What.

I could see that noncommittal smile on her face. From the other end of the phone, I could see it.

Oh come on Anna, give me a break. How am I supposed to answer that? It's not my intention to baffle you. I've always thought of myself as fairly straightforward albeit with a quirky sense of humour so perhaps the dilemma lies not in me but in your accepted idea of what men are supposed to be. And you've found an exception!

Now it was my turn to smile. And to stay silent. I thought I'd actually managed to turn that around. Putting into Anna's head the idea I might be an exception. Not that I thought she'd be fooled for a moment but I still liked the idea. While I revealed in contented smugness about the idea of being an exception, Anna spoke.

I hate to burst your bubble James but that answer implies you think of yourself as someone special. I didn't see you as the conceited type, perhaps more than you would admit or know, you fit into my, accepted idea of what men are supposed to be category, after all!

Two-one Anna. Or maybe forty-thirty? I was going to let that one slide. It seemed to work the last time? Better still, turn it into a joke thus avoiding Anna's latest attempt at scoring the winner.

You are right Anna, I'm not the conceited type but enough about me. What do you think of me?

"Ok James, I give up", said Anna. Barely able to contain her laughter. *I'll stop trying to draw you out so please accept my hypothetical olive branch and Coffee and Cakes are on me tomorrow. I'll call you tomorrow, sometime after two I would think......*

Anna?

Yes James?

I'm picking up on that, I'm about to put the phone down moment, so before you do. Good Night Anna. Pleasant Dreams and see you tomorrow. You were saying?

Good Night James

Giggling was heard in the background as Anna ended the call.

"Coffee and Cakes" at three, thought I as I headed for bed. Lying there, waiting for sleep to silence my thoughts, I knew the next day was to be all about three o'clock. From the moment I opened my eyes, which would be earlier than planned, it would be a count back from three. My day would be full. Pre three time. Deciding what to wear I knew would be a high priority. Arriving early to find a parking space. Perhaps I could lunch there? It would certainly secure a table. I'd think about that tomorrow. Then there was the post three time. Coming away wondering. Analysing. Reliving every minute. Did I manage to leave Anna with the impression, I might be worth pursuing? Thankfully sleep closed off any other avenues of thought.

Why was I nervous at eight fifteen? The realisation that no proactive pre Anna time was necessary until at least eleven, I settled back to wait for the kettle to boil. Keeping myself busy was the plan, so shortly after breakfast I decided to wash the cars. I always preferred to do it myself or perhaps it was something to do with never having worked out how to use those infernal machines on garage forecourts. Either way, I started with the Scenic always cursing the almost impossible task of washing the roof. Having to lean in so close invariably ends up with the "wet T shirt" look. My mind wandered off to Wet T shirts. Or more precisely, who was wearing them. Having finished the Scenic I switched to the Figaro. My little weekend car. Or Barbie car, was the name given by my colleagues at work. It was not so much that I was into cars but the pleasure of driving around the French countryside, roof down, was a joy. Invariably a stop for coffee or a beer at a passing bar brought quizzical looks. The Figaro became a point of conversation. Over the years of owning the car, I had the answers down pat. No, it's not English, it's Japanese. No it's not that old, it's nineteen nighty one and only twenty thousand were produced. Yes, only automatic. And so it continued. I made momentary friends of those around. Some say I bought it for the sole reason of making myself more attractive to women. All I can say is, if the Figaro was capable of such a feat, it had, in my many years of ownership, eluded me.

I thought of preparing a chilli for the evening. It always tasted better if preprepared beforehand. Then realised the smells would permeate the house and me with it. What if Anna came back after coffee? Hi Anna. Sorry about the overwhelming smell of chilli but hey! That would certainly endear. Chilli would have to wait. Those unfinished pages of The Times, now there was a time filler. The decision not to have lunch found me in Antibes just after two. The bar was not overly busy I noticed as I walked by. Plenty of empty tables to chose from but as I hadn't heard from Anna, too soon to sit. I could be there for an hour and half before Anna arrived and even by French acceptance of, you buy a coffee, you leave when you want policy, an hour and half over a coffee might be stretching their patience. I walked on by deciding to head for the open market, closed on a Sunday afternoon but as a place to head for, it was ideal. Turn right heading back into the town giving more options or left past the Picasso museum and around the ramparts. I decided to go straight on. A longer walk and if Anna rang I could take a short cut back. I was feeling bold and full of bravado, bolstered by my uncompromising feelings as though just becoming aware Anna was the reason for my being here today.

Brown Eyed Girl was calling.

Tell me you are not already here James as I am only five minutes away and you will get my most profound apologies. I am working on the hypothesis you have been here for at least thirty minutes and are already sat at a table.

As though stage acted, Anna's appearance through the archway with a big smile on her face was timed to perfection. And yes, I was sat waiting. On arrival Anna was apologising for the slightly overdressed look. My thought? She looked ….. sensational. Straight off the front cover introducing the Vogue Spring Collection. Not that I was much of a fashion guru, as Anna had already pointed out but I do go to the doctors and occasionally the dentists where there are magazines in abundance depicting women such as she.

She was wearing a dark blue knee length dress with matching large buttons down the front. Large pearl necklace and earrings and what were obviously, well crafted slip-on shoes. As she unraveled herself from her scarf I was wondering if the slip-ons were for my benefit.

I've just left my daughters school discussing her options for ballet. This is her last year and those that know best felt it would be more beneficial for her to quit ballet and concentrate on the academics. It turns out there is someone waiting in the wings to replace her. The reason given? This other person can carry the ballet agenda forward into the following year. I was fuming. I even noticed at one point I was wagging my finger at the dumbfounded administrator. When I had finally convinced this, this person, the direction she wished to pursue was not going to happen and she should be more concerned about the individuals needs and in this case desire to continue, rather than her own selfish motives, ……. she went quiet.

This was definitely one of those moments when staying silent was the best option. Anna reached for her preordered coffee but changed her mind. Seeing my hand on the table, her hand moved to rest on mine.

You know, this is the first time in a long time I have been able to vent my frustrations with someone who takes an interest. You're such a darling James. Let's order some cakes!

She tried to attract the waiters attention. Her persistence paid off and cakes were ordered.

Having dumped my frustrations on you I'm feeling so much better. Sorry for that James but it's true, I feel a sense of relief having done so. So what time DID you get here?

Anna's back! Impressed with the way she did that. Arriving in an obvious state of tension and yet managing to shrug it off minutes later. Thinking about that, watching Anna stir her coffee while deciding on her cake of choice, did her temperament change so dramatically because she realised she came away the winner? I digressed with my thoughts and wondered if Elena wanted to stay with the ballet. There was no provocation for such thoughts, at least not until I knew Anna a lot better so I returned to the reality.

Uhmm, I arrived ……. about two hours ago. This is my fifth coffee. Said in a way not to be believed.

Almost but not quite losing control of her cup, Anna managed to replace it before giving me the perfect smile. Generated from her eyes before encapsulating her entire face. And changed the subject.

Which one would you like James?

Not the one you've had your eyes on from the moment they arrived Anna, instead I'll have this one. I'm always intrigued by the percentage of difficulty the baker manages to achieve when it comes to what should be, the simple task of eating.

This was coffee and cakes. How one imagined the time being spent. Sat across from the most delightful company. Idle chit chat on a warm sunny day while taking in the ambience of our surroundings. An ambience that persisted. A French thing. An attitude. A place to talk. To meet friends. To meet lovers. A place for relaxation. There was no real content to our conversation just a lot of laughter. Helped by the obvious outcome of James versus cake.

So Wednesday, Switzerland Anna?

Yes, well no. I have to go via Milan. Meeting with a lawyer. Legal matters I have to sort out. So I'll be leaving on Tuesday. Bright and early as I need to be in Milan by ten thirty. In fact I shouldn't really be here now. There is so much paperwork to compile and I have today and Monday afternoon to find everything I need. After I get back from practice in the morning. Tennis, that is.

I now feel truly honoured that you've managed to squeeze me into your hectic schedule Anna. ..... Just one thought. You could be sorting out your paperwork now. Having cancelled the practice on Monday and we could've had a whole morning together. I must therefore conclude. As honoured as I feel, I do believe I am taking second place to tennis.

A brave move I felt but worth taking the risk, particularly as said with my usual off beat casual manner. Anna wanted me to feel thankful that she found the time for me. Which, admittedly she did but not placed so high as to interfere with tennis. The fact that I noticed was what I hoped Anna understood and in doing so ..... I awaited her reply. She was in thought mode. It was an expression I'd rarely seen. Rarely. We'd only met twice before but I think it still counted. The times together, although in time not amounting to more than but a few hours, I'd come to realise Anna didn't need time to think. Sometimes I felt she was a few questions ahead of me. Now she was thinking and as she looked directly at me, I was thinking, cowardice could have been preferable over a not so brave move

Sorry James, you're waiting for a reply. I've been trying to decide if I should hand over my social calendar to you as your skills in seemingly knowing what is best for me is beyond reproach, or get up and leave.

Oh shit! I think she might actually get up?

I think your best option Anna, would be to email your calendar to my secretary and I'll see what I can do.

That having been said with a, dead pan face, I could now only wait.

Damn you James, I can't even threaten you with leaving.
Anna was laughing! Yes, it had worked. But I needed to backtrack.
I'm sorry Anna. I realised, no sooner than it was out of my mouth, I had overstepped the boundaries of acceptable behaviour. I have no right to suggest how you spend your day and to continue in said vain I'll add, I took your threat very seriously, hence the apology.
I raised my coffee cup. Anna raised hers. We chinked cups which admittedly, didn't quite chink but who cared?
"To an enjoyable time in Switzerland", I said.
Thank you James. I'm looking forward to seeing the family, particularly my granddaughter. It's her birthday while I'm there and we have eighteen under fives to keep entertained for the afternoon.
It won't be a problem. There is a really nice restaurant just outside Geneva that specialises in lunches for children. So I've booked for twenty. Tanya and I can relax. Have our lunch by the pool while the staff take care of the dear little ones.
Sounds like a very good plan Anna. I can remember when my daughters sixth birthday came around, my ex wife had conveniently organised three weeks in Australia. Don't worry she said. Everything's been organised. There are seven or eight for a party in the garden. I've organised a bouncy castle that's arriving in the morning, so if you can be here when they arrive. Oh and buy a few things for them to eat, ok?
"Right", said I, not really sure what I was agreeing to but Kat's birthday wasn't for another ten days or so. Plenty of time to discuss with my future ex wife Susan.
So when are you leaving, exactly?
Tomorrow, just after lunch which is why I'm calling. Can you pop around this afternoon and pick up the house keys? Momentarily my mind went to overload Anna. Six year olds, I'm thinking. Birthday party. How does that work? It' not a laughing matter Anna. This was in the category of, seriously out of my depth. The last time I had that feeling I was about four years old and my father decided it was time I learnt to swim. Off we went to the local swimming pool. My father was a very proficient swimmer. I'm in good hands. Or so I thought. As we walked around the pool, my father pushed me in, saying something about, this was the way he was taught. I was four bloody years old for christ sake! Somewhere around my third attempt of enacting the role of a lump of concrete, my father fished me out. I lived by the sea for the first thirty years of my life. I wonder why I never really got the hang of swimming? So Anna, when I say out of my depth, we are talking life and death here. But I think I digress?
Oh James, surely you are being a little over dramatic?
I recognised that tone. Anna was doing her best to contain her obvious delight at my predicament.
I've lost count as to how many birthdays I've organised for the girls.
I jumped in.

Exactly Anna! You've organised thousands. I've organised zero!
Should I continue or do you feel I've suffered enough, envisioning that memory?
I'm all ears James, I haven't enjoyed such as this since I visited India and saw a holy man lie on a bed of nails!
I decided to ignore the comment but was secure, in knowing Anna, was enjoying the telling.
It can take anything between thirty minutes and an hour and half to get to Susan's place, depending on the traffic. I get through Ealing and arrive in twenty five minutes.
Before I continue Anna, I should remind you that Susan and I had been separated for less than six months. Still a lot of raw nerves out there.
On the drive there the questions began to pile up. Exactly how many? Do you have a list of names? All girls? How to keep a group of six year olds happy for however many hours? And then there is the food? What about Matt? My son. Is he going to be included? So many questions and all to be asked in a non provoking manner. There was no possibility, if I wanted to keep this conversation amicable, to suggest it would have been nice if we could have planned this event some time ago. Do I talk about her up and coming holiday or would that be misconstrued as invasive?
Susan very quickly assumed the frosty posture and couldn't understand why I needed so much detail. "It's a six year olds birthday! How difficult do you think it could be?" Then came the bit about, "I have to look after them twenty four hours a day. It's not asking a lot that you look after them for three weeks". Before Susan could say another word, I really did feel I'd missed something. If the time it took for the penny to drop, could be measured, it would be so infinitesimal as to become meaningless. I'm staying here for three weeks! Not just the party in ten days but for a whole three weeks! There was a phone conversation, three or four weeks previously about, Will it be ok if I look after the kids while I'm on holiday, kind of conversation. So it starts tomorrow. Was I suppose to know that?
Anna was watching me. Amusement written all over her face. I wondered if she realised how I digressed from the original point. We shall see. The art of digression? Always return to the original point!
This is now a whole new ball game. The birthday party becomes almost manageable when stacked up against three weeks that I'm totally unprepared for. I'm now wondering whether I should mention that small detail of, Wouldn't it have been a good idea to have given me some notice or ideally a meeting beforehand to discuss their needs over the coming weeks? No sooner had the thought appeared I concluded it was potential provocation. Instead I suggest we run through their daily routine. Susan led me to the Breakfast Bar and proudly points to a notice on the fridge door. I started to read about the dates and times Matt attended Judo lessons after school. Thursday Kat would need picking up from her friends house. Address in brackets. It's a long list. Susan is keen to

move on. "Matt usually has cereal in the mornings. Kat just does her own thing",
she said.
Does her own thing? What does that mean? I have an image of Kat. An
extremely sharp knife in hand, slicing carrots at a hundred miles an hour,
casually tossing them in the direction of the juicer. I let it pass. We go to Matt's
room. Susan mentioning something about him watching too much television. He
has a TV in his room, could that be a contributing factor? Once again, I let it
pass.
He has enough school clothes in there for the next week. I usually wash them
all at the weekend, rather than half during the week. And so it continued. We
moved from room to room. A brief description of the function attributed to each.
Oh, and don't forget to tell Matt to sit down when he goes to the toilet. Or at least
lift the seat up first.
It might just as well have been a lecture on the inherent future of the 3D printer
and its role in the field of molecular science, thought I.
I left Susan's house dazed and confused heading straight for The Kent. A
Fuller's pub that had a large garden. Shouldn't be many customers there at that
time of day. Even for a Friday, three thirty would be regarded as too early. A pint
of Pride in hand, I headed for the garden with enough forethought to come
prepared with pen and paper. Nowadays, one's phone would be enough. We
are talking mid eighties. The era when music took a nose dive.
I do believe I was enjoying myself. I took a sip of cold coffee giving Anna that
brief moment I felt she was waiting for.
I don't mean to interrupt James but you know I will anyway. How about a glass
of wine? Monsieur, deux verres d'un vin rouge, s'il vous plaît.
Cold coffee had now become red wine? Someone used to making decisions
and acting on them. Although maybe more consultation time might have been
appreciated? That was Anna. I laughed. Collected my thoughts and continued.
Half way through the third pint, notes completed and although not completely
at ease, confidence was returning. I looked around and to my surprise I found
the garden alive with activity. Most bench seats were occupied, mine included.
It's a typical pub garden set up. Two bench seats fixed to a table between with
the possibility of seating six. I was collecting my notes together that had
amounted to a tidy bundle of A4 when I caught the eye of a lady sat diagonally
opposite. There were just the two of us at the table and we acknowledged each
other's presence with a smile. Now this is where it got interesting. It turned out,
she had two sisters and they organised kids birthdays. Prepare ready made
meals and provide babysitting. She and I became instantly good friends. I have
to say at this point Anna, you are most likely thinking, how callous. But it wasn't
like that. Our initial connection revolved around my dilemma of the next three
weeks and how she could help. There was never any thought of, anything else.
As it turned out, I got it at cost price. As a thank-you I paid for a weekend in New

York, for her and her sisters. Petra and I still keep in touch. She moved back to Prague about twenty years ago and has two grown up girls.
  Susan returned three weeks later. I helped her in with her bags while Matt and Kat ran rings around us. A while passed before normality returned and Susan sat with tea in hand telling me about her time in Australia. Time to make an exit. A gradual exit. Well Susan, I'm sure you don't want me hanging around, so just to bring you up to speed. Weekend meals in the freezer. Clothes all washed for school on Monday. There have been changes to Kat's ballet lessons. It's all on the fridge door. You know, I've really enjoyed the time here. Oh and I took lots of photos at Kat's birthday so I'll give you a copy when I get them developed. I said goodbye to the kids and was out on the street, heading towards ..... The Kent and a late afternoon drink .... with Petra. I will therefore admit to fortuitous circumstances developing into the contributing factor that turned a potentially disastrous three weeks into a pleasure, including a well organised Birthday. So you see Anna, to this day I've never organised a children's birthday party, let alone for eighteen! To three ladies from Prague, I say, as I raise my glass.
  Did you just make that up?
  I'm sure Anna was not wholly convinced about the authenticity of my story. Rightly so, as most was fabricated. There was a core element of truth, just maybe not so obvious.
  Yes. Well not entirely. My ex wife's name is Susan. Then there is Matt and Kat. For the rest, lets say, poetic license.
  You just made that up! Didn't you?
  I just filled in the gaps. Ok, they were rather large gaps.
  Anna raised her glass.
  To an entertaining story James, loosely based on fact. Very loosely.
  I was watching her again.
  What?
  That was the catalyst. Laughter ensued. Anna reached into her bag as her phone rang. What seemed to start as a jovial conversation soon turned into one of noticeable concern. I said seemed as the conversation was in Russian. Anna put the phone away and said she had to go.
  I've lost all sense of time. My daughter is waiting to be collected. Monsieur?
  Don't worry Anna. I'll get this. You go.
  Are you sure. I did promise?
  Enjoy your time in Switzerland and we'll get together on your return. Now go.
  Thank you for a wonderful afternoon James. And yes, see you on my return.
  She placed her bag over her arm and stepped around the table. A most elegant exchange of kisses on cheeks. A big smile and Anna was on her way. I watched her go wondering if a last wave would be forthcoming. She approached the

archway, the last chance to turn. But no, she was gone. I sat back down not unduly concerned that Anna hadn't turned, as I ordered another glass of wine. A wonderful afternoon? Yes it had been. Two hours had passed unnoticed by both. Anna, at her most vibrant. Full of information and questions. And yet she could sit and listen with equal enthusiasm. She was a joy to be with. A lady with a natural positive nature. Open to new challenges. New, as in me. Glass always half full. I wondered if she saw me as a challenge and if she did, how long before the challenge would run its natural course? Let's not entertain that idea James, instead, glass half full. As the sun disappeared there was an almost instant chill. I finished my glass, paid and left. A feeling pervaded me as I walked away. A feeling not dissimilar to that of concluding the world could be a beautiful place sometimes. Once home I put off the dinner preparations and sat down. Sat thinking of Anna. Reality disappeared as fantasy took over. An hour had passed before I'd managed to shake loose of that one. Get some dinner sorted. It was a Sunday evening so there were always a couple of "version originale" films to choose from on French tv. All of which kept my brain occupied on something other than Anna. Bedtime wasn't so easy. No distractions. I was tired in the morning when I sent Anna a message.

Knowing this will be read at the lights, I'm keeping it short. Good Morning Anna. What a beautiful day!

An almost immediate response.

Oh Good Morning James, how are you today?

How am I today? Too generalised a question. How am I relative to the time I broke my shin bone. Or to the time I found fifty Euros in a jacket I hadn't worn for awhile. That I could answer.

You broke your shin bone? When?

Fear not Anna, I didn't break my shin bone, although I must say, it is comforting to think you are concerned about my well being.

This could be interesting if Anna wanted to pick up on that remark. I think admitting to being concerned was not something Anna would be willing to acknowledge, well, not yet. If face to face we would be laughing at the possibility of Anna's concern. Text was different. It cannot pick up on the nuances associated with conversation.

How are you relative to yesterday afternoon James?

So much for the possibility of Anna picking up on that then! A straight question. Was Anna smiling when she wrote that or annoyed by my petulance? Or possibly just fishing for compliments? Time to reassert her position, on that pedestal.

I think you can envisage my response Anna but I will try to enlighten you. Compared to yesterday, my day feels empty of purpose. I drift between moments in my day with no rhyme nor reason. A shade, drawn over my eyes that keeps locked within me those precious few hours. Not wishing to embrace

the day for fear of losing the smallest detail of the memory I have of yesterday afternoon.
You're being sweet again, aren't you James? You seem to have a knack of knowing when to deliver. I considered what you might reply but in future I will cease with these considerations as I'm sure to be as way off the mark, as now. "Yesterday afternoon? Nothing is relative to yesterday afternoon!" *Might have been more what I was expecting but as it turns out, this is not what I should expect from James. Maybe I should be concerned about your wellbeing? Something more to discuss with Tanya. Oh aren't we girls going to have fun. Now off to have my nails done. I think a pastel shade this time. Perhaps a light pink?*

The temptation to discuss pink was there. I decided to leave Anna to her nails. Giving me time enough to finish a few outstanding emails before lunchtime. April approached so the work load increased as we prepared for Miptv, our second largest show of the year at the Palais de Festival, in Cannes. Being a small subsidiary of our parent company in New York, necessitated the need to call in extra labour. Most will be local but that left thirty or so from countries throughout Europe and Canada. My initial contact would be a phone call, followed up with a conformation email giving start dates etc. The phone call? Just to create a "rod for my own back"! It didn't start out that way. Many years ago, when I took on the role of labour organiser, few people had fax machines! Computers? I think most could spell the word but few had ever seen one. As the years progressed the habit remained. Now, everyone I called who I would have seen five months previously, wanted to chat. Multiply that by the thirty or so and it was somewhat time consuming.

No more news from Anna during the day, I therefore decided it would be best to reciprocate. It must have been late when I left for home that evening as there was very little traffic. The evening was to be an evening of relaxation. Heating on full. Sit back with a coffee and cigarette while thinking of Anna. Not really taking into account the problems of the day and the infuriating way the mind had of disregarding my intentions. Evidently I had a sudden inspiration. A nagging problem of the day seemed on the breakthrough of a solution. I reached for the iPad and started taking notes. Feeling confident that when proposing my idea the following morning, it would be met with enthusiast approval, I was in the, resolve all today's problems in the belief I can, mood. Three coffees and an equal amount of cigarettes later, I might not have solved all the days problems but well on the way to minimising the impact of quite a few. Too late now for anything other than bed. Anna's time would be had prior to sleep.

The alarm, set for six forty, was the first realisation of a new day. Somewhere between stirring the porridge and being attacked by a hot teabag, my thoughts were of Anna, or more to the point, the thoughts I didn't have of Anna the previous night as sleep overcame me before I had the chance. Too late now.

The morning routine took over. As the first to arrive I had time alone to write a message. I was looking for something casual and amusing but my brain refused to focus.

Good Morning Anna. I would like to say my every thought over the previous day was of you but that would be lying. Suffice it to say, I am thinking of you now. I did intend giving you my most precious slot. That being the time alone in bed when my thoughts have most clarity, unfortunately, and this is most unusual, which I can only put down to the pressures of the day. I fell fast asleep in conjunction with my head hitting the pillow. I feel sure you will be busy with last minute preparations for your forthcoming trip. Passport and credit card. Anything else you remember is a bonus. I find knowing that allows a more relaxed approach to packing.

The guys started to arrive so I put the phone away, satisfied that enough was said to give Anna potential, "fuel for the fire". As expected the conversation soon revolved around the previous evenings match. Marseille vs Nice. Always a match that brought controversy amongst the crew. With two hardened opposing sides in the camp and enough interest by others ready to poke fun at any given opportunity, one could rely on a heated debate. An undeserved last minute goal seemed to be the main topic. My attention was drawn towards Shep whose interest in football was equal to mine. Shep, a hive of information. He was knowledgable in a number of diverse fields. From ladies fashion to history of the Middle Ages. I asked him if he had heard of Ferragamo shoes. Oh yes, he said. Not cheap. Was his opening line. Followed by a brief foray into the life and times of Ferragamo shoes and the price demanded for such quality and individualism. It became obvious, Anna liked her shoes. I heard from behind me a familiar voice. I turned.

Hi Ricky, I'd forgotten you arrived today. It's always a mixed blessing seeing you. Great to see you again but it means the crazy time approaches once more.

He laughed, knowing what I meant. Ricky had arrived in town from Austria to run the on-site show. Three weeks before the install and with seventeen stands to construct in less than a week a lot of planning was necessary. This occasion was no different from most pre show times. A new stand now approaching its last details of construction would be taken apart tomorrow to be painted and laminated. Crews needed to be standing by once it was down. With another stand under construction and ready for the initial pre build, and only the space for one construction at a time, the timing could not have been better planned. It was going to be one of those days. I thought of Anna and in some way was thankful she was going away. There would be some long days ahead. Long tiring days and the thought of entertaining Anna after such a day would push my capacity for interesting conversation to the limit. I heard the phone acknowledging a message. No time to read just now but yes, I saw it was Anna. Two hours had passed and having been pulled in all directions for advice and information, I managed to find a quiet corner in the electric room while the guys were having a coffee break.

No reading at the lights this morning, it's half term. Thank you for those thoughts James, particularly the passport, credit card detail. I will invariably spend a couple of days shopping with Tanya when in Geneva so this tactic will alleviate the need to take a full suitcase. Better to arrive empty and return full. What a wonderful excuse for more shopping. Well done James! What I don't understand is how you could possibly fall to sleep when you have me to think of. Disappointed, James. The Swiss chocolate is looking decidedly uncertain. Got to dash.

Taking my advice and reprimanding me at the next turn but she did it so well. I thought of the conversations we'd had and in the main they followed a similar vain to the text message. A competition of words. There was an edge. An underlining oneupmanship. It seemed we had set the ground rules. It was yet to be seen if the ground represented a solid foundation. There were times the subject was serious. Conversations about her early life in Russia. Even about the sad demise of her late husband was something Anna was willing to share although not too deeply which was perfectly understandable. Anna had already asked about my intentions which led me to believe she was either a naturally cautious lady or had been hurt by someone. I couldn't imagine it to be the latter as it was only five months since the death of her late husband. Caution it had to be and yet Anna didn't strike me as the cautious type? There were contradictions that I found confusing. She was outgoing and yet reserved. It would be interesting seeing Anna in a group that consists of more than just the two of us. Hopefully, one day, I would get the chance. I was imagining the introduction of Paul and Chiara. Two formable women. I think Paul and I might enjoy that encounter. Something to think of, but too soon to contemplate. It was too soon to think Anna perceived me as anything other than a distraction. Or perhaps too soon to be making any evaluations at all? Let it go James, there was at least another week before a chance of another meeting. I smiled at the thought as I looked around at the organised chaos that surrounded me. My work was an unforgiving distraction. No doubt about that, compounded by the reality of taking ten minutes to get to the office while being bombarded with questions needing quick answers. I had to laugh at the quandary. In order to answer the questions, I needed to get to the office but that seemed unlikely as the questions kept coming. Having reached the cocoon of the office, the quiet engulfed me. The only addition to the office staff was Ricky who was checking his notes from the last show. Never a good sign I thought.

James?

Yes Ricky?

Were the changes on Fox completed?

Yes Ricky, in combination with the inventory. If you check the Punch List you'll see what's pending and what's completed.

My way of saying, Check the information at hand before bothering me. Ricky smiled. He got it.

I was surprised to find it was now approaching seven. Surely not? I've only just finished lunch? Time to get out of here. I saw Ricky had already left. He couldn't afford to miss that ten to seven bus back into Cannes. Looking through the open plan office at John hunched over his computer in the semi private area befitting our General Manager. Will, was still here, sat opposite me but that was no surprise. "Good Night All", I said, as I grabbed my coat.

Once home, the first on the agenda was rolling that cigarette. First of the day. Pleased with myself that the, not smoking during the day commitment, was working, particularly as it allowed for a more pleasurable moment. Rather than one of many smoked during the day, it was the first! Beer and cigarette in hand, and already compiling in my head, the thoughts for a message. I'd barely sat down, ready to put "pen to paper but the problems of the day were still fresh in my mind. I managed to put those thoughts aside and instead compiled a message to Anna. Ok, admittedly there were some interesting possibilities for a message. I reached for my phone. Opened Notes and put down a couple of headings. Satisfied they will jog my memory later, I relaxed. It was interesting how the mind worked. I imagined a fisherman standing in his boat, the net on a pole, in hand. A shoal of fish leapt from the water. He reached out and a fish fell, totally randomly, into the net. It was how my mind worked when I had the time to give it the luxury. Thoughts tumbling around until that one was netted. Initially it had the feel of a random catch but having been given this particular problem, more often than not, it led to, if not to an answer then to a promising avenue of constructive possibilities. I had to stop, or the self indulgence if left unchecked, would consume my entire evening. Not that there was much evening left. Getting home at seven thirty would do that.

Showered. Plants watered. Last coffee of the day drunk. I realised I hadn't sent that last message of the evening and it was not the time for inspiration. It might take awhile I thought, staring at the blank screen.

As it's so late I have three hopes. Firstly you are fast asleep Anna, as you have an early start tomorrow. Secondly .... the ping of my message doesn't wake you and thirdly you are reading this in the morning. Have a safe journey. Enjoy your time with your granddaughter and may I suggest when talking to Tanya just a short summation? Something like, James? He's Fantastic! It could save hours of frustratingly watching your daughter fall slowly to sleep. Shop till you drop. Oh, and if the "decidedly uncertain" magically mutates into decidedly certain, I prefer dark chocolate.

Feeling confident Anna would find it amusing, I headed for bed and once again found myself thinking of Emanuela. Where did that come from?

The alarm woke me at six thirty. Didn't I just fall asleep? Was it Thursday or Friday? Not really of any consequence when working a seven day week. It was Friday. Friday the twentieth of March. Mike was due to fly in from Austria and the plane landed in two hours, according to my phone. No problem as the morning rush hour would have past. I reached Nice airport, unwisely not having confirmed Mike's arrival time before departing. Typical, a twenty minute delay. I got back in the car and drove five minutes out of the airport to sit it out. I thought back to those earlier years when all this started. A friend of many years, Mike and I received an offer we couldn't refuse. It would be twenty five years ago since Ricky invited us to join him here in Cannes. "How would you guys like to come to the S. of France and build a stand for Warner Brothers?" He said. It was September in Kitzbuhel, undecidedly wet and chilly. It didn't take long to make that decision. Time had moved on. Ricky runs the on site campaign while Mike had been organising the Fox builds for twenty years. And me? After commuting twice a year, first from Austria and later from Holland where Josey and I decided to settle in her home town of Dordrecht, it was seven years later we found ourselves living in Fayence, the South of France. Full time employee and gradually accepting an ever increasing amount of responsibility. Certainly those earlier days were more carefree. I checked the time of arrival. Mike was on the ground. Time to make a move. Timed to perfection as I saw Mike ambling out of Arrivals. By the time we reached the motorway the conversation had taken the inevitable step of being work orientated. Who's coming to this show? Who's not? Office politics and the latest rumours of that possible new client. By the time we left the motorway, Mike was up to speed.

From the very beginning, Mike and I had shared an apartment, supplied by the company and as it was conveniently situated close to the office, I'd seen no reason to stop that tradition. I dropped him off and continue on to work. As per tradition, I'd join him the next evening. Giving him time to settle in. I got a text from Mike. What time for the supermarket? Another tradition. One which I would have preferred to have avoided. Mike won't pick up the hire car for another week so it fell to me to be available for that first big shop and I'd already lost a couple of hours of the day due to the airport run. Simultaneously as I enter the office my phone pinged. It was Anna. There was no time to consider the possibility of reading the message let alone reply as I saw Ricky giving a bad example of a man patiently waiting.

Um, James, when you've got a moment?

And so the morning unfolded. Thankful for the sanctuary the Electric Room provided I managed to read Anna's message, two hours later.

Hi James. Stopped for a coffee mid journey. Your hopes were vindicated. I saw your message this morning. No time to answer as I spent that valuable answering time having discussions with the builders. More of that some other time. If dark chocolate exists in Geneva, you will get some. Your message put me in such a good mood, I sailed through the problems with the builders and I swear the Mistral wind had reversed it's usual direction and was aiding my journey.

I've been thinking about the "sleeping daughter scenario". Taking it to it's conclusion, I have to ask myself, Why would she be sleeping? She is bored. Obviously that is what you meant. So to alleviate that pain, I've decided to say nothing. Don't you think that is a brilliant idea. The alternative would be to, lets say, to distort the truth. (To save your feelings.) Unfortunately as good an actress as I can be, I find it impossible to lie with conviction. I think the best I could do would be, James, Yes, he's ok. Therefore I'm certain you will agree my dear that my daughters ignorance, might serve you best at this time. I'm now heading off to get more of that assisted Mistral in a joyous mood. Maybe you do have your uses? Maybe not Mr Fantastic more, Mr Useful. Oh Joy, Oh Joy!

Very good Anna. Very good. Touché. But before I could totally absorb Anna's message, duty called. It was lunchtime. My turn to drive. Just the four of us. Will, Fa, Philo and myself. Having arrived at the restaurant, I was surrounded by football managers in the making. It was Friday so there was the prematch conversations. Who's playing. Who shouldn't be playing and why they continually get picked. It continued, partially in English but mostly French. I switched off or maybe it would be truer to admit, I'd been switched off. The general consensus would be, James hadn't anything of interest to offer on this subject. I tried to recall Anna's message but could only remember the general gist, although, the general thrust would be a more appropriate thought. Anna had certainly thrust her salient points upon me. This needed thought and I was wondering if ignoring the message might be in my best interest. A short, Well done Anna message and switch topics. Either way, as I was unable to devote any serious thinking time to the subject until the evening, I put my thoughts aside. The evening? When Anna would be with family? It was all about timing and if I could co-ordinate the arrival of the message with that after dinner chat mother and daughter would invariably have …… it could work to my advantage. All I needed was the content but I thought I might have stumbled onto the possibility of a vague outline. Imagining the two together where the conversation, no matter what Anna had said, will eventually land squarely on me. What I wouldn't give to be that fly on the wall. How perfectly I could time the moment to press send. With a message so relevant to their present conversation, certain there would be a turning of head by Anna, just to check I wasn't there. Now that would be, Oh Joy! We paid for lunch and in the process of leaving I decided ten thirty would be the ideal time to send a message. At the same time wondering if I would keep to that. Shame about the fly.

Later that afternoon, "Don't look behind you", was added to my Notes. Pleased I'd managed one offering for the evening. More would have been better but realistically unlikely. There were no longer those moments in my day, admittedly all of my own making. Accepting just that little more responsibility every now and again, I found myself spread so thin it would necessitate the use of an electron microscope to realise there were parts of the whole, still connected. But it sure made the day go by.

Driving home thinking about the message, I saw it broke down into four categories. Generous Anna. Happy Anna. I think I am so clever Anna and Check out that comeback on Fantastic Anna. Still not convinced a direct attack would be the most convincing approach was not a reason not to include the possibility and anyway, the distraction was an added bonus when playing with the evenings traffic. Oh my goodness, I didn't believe it, someone was actually indicating. Ok, he had already changed lanes but at least he thought about it. Happy Anna shouldn't be too difficult. It was a true emotion revealed as a compliment therefore, a thank you of sort, would fulfil that requirement. A thank you of sort? Was I now opening myself up to complications? Glad I made your journey more agreeable, just wasn't going to work anymore. The thoughts occupied my mind as I buzzed the gate open only to see the neighbours cat looking rather disgruntled at having to move out of her sunny spot. I apologised to the cat and hurriedly closed the gate. Sat in front of the computer. Cigarette in hand. Beer on the desk. I opened Notes. My iTunes library is quietly playing Sam Cooke's Frankie and Johnny. I turned it up. Not a song I was familiar with. One out of twenty thousand makes it hard to keep track. I think that can go down as a double entendre? Either way, Sam was certainly setting the mood.

Hi Anna. May I start by thanking you for considering such an undertaking. The only bar of dark chocolate in Geneva! If it helps I've Googled the possibilities and it seems there is a chocolate shop selling dark chocolate on virtually every street corner. So you cannot imagine how relieved I was to discover this as my original thought was of poor you stumbling through the cobbled street of Geneva in your Ferragamo shoes. Also, glad to hear my poorly deserved attempt at witty repartee aided your journey. I do believe you could be right, not discussing me with Tanya. It is such a shame your enthusiasm will get the better of you. I can imagine the conversation between mother and daughter once the little one has been soundly tucked up in bed. Quite possibly the conversation that is being enacted as I write this very message. "So mother, what's happening at home? I've noticed you are in a rather effervescent mood of late". And you are seriously telling me you will resist the temptation of spending the rest of the evening not expounding my virtues? Mr Useful will fly straight out of the window to be replaced by, maybe not Mr Fantastic but something close. You might try, Oh he's ok knowing full well Tanya will not accept that abridged version. Tanya will become sceptical of this adoration you seem to be extruding from every pore, playing devils advocate to your enthusiasm. What I cannot know is who will emerge triumphant from this debacle. I'm sure there will be words of caution which you will pooh pooh as being irrelevant, adding something about how you can take care of yourself. (Am I close so far, leaving you wondering, How does he know that? I suggest you don't look behind you.) You are now a few glasses of red wine later. Quite possibly late in the evening, if not, early morning. But what do you really know about him, asks Tanya? Ah, she's got you there! (Text me at this point and I'll gladly help where I can.) It's three o'clock and both decide to adjourn til light of day. For some reason a John Sarstedt number comes to mind? Where Do You Go To My Lovely. And that, my dear, is where you are now. With your thoughts of the evenings conversation spreading like oil on water. I wish you well as you grasp for those straws but I leave you with some hope. My mother used to tell me, Everything will be alright in the morning. It never actually was but as a glass half full girl, who knows, it just might. Right now? I'd advise counting sheep. It will all be fine tomorrow. Good Night Anna

The question was, did I send this message pre conversations of the evening, which could be of advantage as I was sure the girls would find the possibilities of my inferred conversation amusing. Try to time it mid conversation or leave it until later when there was the possibility of it being too late. Anna already tucked up in bed. The choice was simple. Earlier rather than later believing Tanya will respond in a more favourable manner knowing I at least had a sense of humour. Nine twenty. I decided to send at ten. It had taken me the best part of a half an hour to write that message. Not sure who's fault that might have been but I had good idea it was I who instigated the amusing battle of wits in the very early stages of our verbal relationship and having since met Anna I felt fairly confident it was the only way forward. If it had been, during those first fragile messages, Hi, my name is James and I think your photo is great, it would have fallen like the proverbial lead balloon. No, it was the right choice. Trying to stand out before a number of unknown adversaries. Given time it would hopefully disappear as the verbal becomes superseded by a more personable, one on one. I didn't know if I was winning that battle of wits but I felt I was still in contention. May the best man win and in this situation, I can only hope Anna gives me the opportunity of becoming said man.

An hour since I sent the message and no response from Anna. I went to bed, a little disappointed but not downhearted. After all, it was I who imagined the scenario and if I was even close, they would be too preoccupied for Anna to consider replying. Tomorrow was another day. Another working day as I said good night to Friday.

Nothing waiting for me that next day. No problem, I told myself. She was a busy lady. She was with her daughter and grand daughter. Admit it James, you were disappointed. Sunday morning and still nothing waiting for me? Not to be discouraged with the thought of, Everything comes to he who waits, in my head, my morning rolled by. It was late morning when a message arrived.

Hello James. It was two thirty and three glasses, other than that I would have to say, your perception of events were played out almost verbatim and I did look but you were not behind me? So how did you do that? As you might imagine, it is a late start for me. Well, it is Sunday! Not so for Tanya who had my sweet, ever so hyperactive granddaughter to contend with. We have planned a stroll across the park followed by brunch in one of our favourite restaurants, Le Café du Centre which as the name suggests is in the heart of the city. A brunch that will necessitate a minimum three hard matches to expunge the over indulgence of such a tempting menu. Which unfortunately means I have to leave you now because as per usual, I am running a little late. But before I go I will return to the, How did you do that? This leads me to believe you will anticipate my following request. Please provide me with ten known facts that will help to sway my ever so sceptical daughters opinion in your favour. And perhaps for the future you have learnt, it is not always wise to be such a smart ass! Be grateful I have given you something to do on a rainy day in Antibes. All for now from a very sunny Geneva and a big sunny smile from Anna.

Sunday. Almost eleven when I received that message but I knew there was no way I would be supplying ten known facts even if I could think of ten but there would have to be an acknowledgement of kind. Maybe something about, there was only one way you'd get to know those, and that was first hand?

It was now approaching midday and there was a glimmer of hope I could finish up by lunchtime. Even Ricky was wondering about his presence and what more he could achieve if he stayed. I suggested we try to get it wrapped up. Have lunch and call it a day. My shout. Ricky, never one to miss out on a free lunch, smiled in acknowledgement. Mike, who came into the office and caught the tail end of the conversation characteristically, invited himself along.

The Three Brown Shirts having lunch. The three of us living in Austria during those early days with the company, it didn't take long before the rest of the team came up with that nickname which stuck for many years.

We left the office a little later than intended but managed to be seated by two deciding on the Plat de Jour and a carafe of rosé. Before one had those few seconds to sit back. Work out the geography of ones surroundings, Ricky was talking. Mike and I had been there before. It was difficult sometimes for Ricky to turn off work mode. Mike was formulating a plan. I'd seen that look before. "Actually Ricky I don't mean to interrupt", Mike was saying, "But right now I'd rather hear more about James's Russian girlfriend. Didn't you say her name was Anna, James"? I had told Mike the day before about Anna. He'd asked at the time if it was private knowledge. Not really, I answered but not necessarily for general distribution either. Mike knew this to be acceptable collateral damage particularly when the alternative would be a work orientated conversation.

Ricky took the bait.

A new girlfriend James? What happened to the Italian? Wasn't she, the one? So who is Anna, hopefully not Russian Mafia. Does she speak English?

English Ricky, that's a good one coming from someone born and bred in Leicester. If you must know her English is what you country folk call Queens English although her deceased husband was Italian so perhaps there is a Mafia connection.

"Who is she?" Questioned Ricky

She is an educated, intelligent, light hearted, charismatic, one would say beautiful individual who is a one-off. She certainly has taste, ... but before I could continue Ricky leaped in with the obvious line.

She can't have that good a taste if she likes you!

Thank you for that Ricky. I almost didn't expect that considering it's a line so well used it has a breaking strain that wouldn't support the worm attached. No pun intended.

Fair enough James. So she has taste?

Yes she does. Her decorum is that of a lady accustomed to the finer things in life.

So, she's a rich bitch?

Thanks for that Ricky. I tell you what, why don't we just talk about work. You're on safer ground there.

Mike interjects.

Anybody saying no to another carafe? Monsieur. Un autre pichet de rosé, s'il vous plait.

Ricky and I laughed.

"Well", said Ricky, A toast. "To James, Long may Anna's tastes remain obscure".

And so the afternoon continued, ending just short of ordering that third carafe.

Home at the unusual hour of four o'clock. I say home because knowing Mike was going out that evening, I decided to head for home. A chance to water the plants and relax in comfort. It was a Sunday but just another day and will be so for the next three weeks. I decided to make use of the larger screen of the iMac for some preliminary note taking on this raining afternoon as predicted by Anna. Now I'm wondering if she is behind ME.

She and Tanya talked about me as Anna's message implied. She also implied it didn't go so well with Tanya as she needed ammunition to defend her position. "What do you really know about him". Did she say that? Or was Anna playing with me? For all I know, Tanya was perfectly happy with her mothers upbeat mood and wished her all the best. If I was to take this request seriously, it could take hours to work out a reply. Acknowledgement of kind, Still believing it was the way to go. So I was accused of being a smart ass. Mmmm

Hi Anna, so pleased to hear from you this morning and you with a fuzzy head. How endearing. Although I have to say, it was somewhat harsh in places. I do understand. You were put under pressure from Tanya and on one of the few times in your life, at a loss for words. Very frustrating for you. And as that previously stated, understanding fellow, I really don't mind you venting this frustration out on me. I can be a pillar of strength. I have therefore, as that understanding fellow, thought long and hard about the necessary facts that would benefit your position. It is simple. In fact so simple I'm surprised you hadn't thought of it. Let me walk you through the obvious. Girl meets boy. They like each other. They meet again. They phone. They message. All the time learning a little more about each other. I therefore conclude. Time will answer these questions. What do you really know about me? Time is the only true answer to that question. So I suggest you say to Tanya, I like him and that is a good start. The rest will be decided with time. I might even suggest you told Tanya this answer was my idea. You could also tell her, as I've told you, my intentions are honourable. At the moment it is a simple formula based on trust and understanding and in the process, enjoying each others company. Come on Anna, admit it, that is not bad. How could Tanya not endear herself, if not to the person, surely to my obvious depth of character. Not only am I a thoughtful, understanding fellow but I am also a concerned one. Yes concerned for you. Off you go tomorrow, looking for those well fitting clothes and what do you find? Your stomach seems to have taken on a life of its own. Where did that come from, you are wondering? If you haven't already worked that out. That's right! Brunch! You see how concerned I am. Any other day it wouldn't matter, as you said, you can work it off but tomorrow is Shopping Day! No chance to work it off. I will not be able to relax knowing the day could be ruined because of a slight overindulgence.Please note the lack of Smart Ass repartee which should affirm my position as not only a good listener but also one who has a positive outlook regarding such constructive criticism. I've counted many facts entwined within the above that doesn't include, creative, interesting, amusing, nor even handsome (yes, it has been said.) Perhaps you girls are smart enough to discover them. I can now press send and sit back knowing that I have given an honest and in my humble opinion, accurate description of my psyche. (Honest nor humble are facts not listed above.) I've just realised. I'm about perfect if one doesn't include a slight egotistical streak. Enjoy your evening Anna while I watch the rain falling and wonder why I brought my motorbike out of winter storage.

I'd reread untold times. Changed words. Changed sentences. Deleted. And spent two hours doing so. Albeit staring at a blank screen for the best part of that time, having no idea where it was taking me and having concluded with an Off The Wall remark. I would say, I was satisfied with the outcome and was now wondering if the message for Anna would appease Tanya. I pressed send and almost simultaneously I was aware, it was not for me to be satisfied. Time would tell if I'd hit the right note as I looked around only to find, I was sat in darkness. Where did those last moments of daylight disappear? Sitting in the dark listening to the rain soothed the soul allowing my thoughts to drift away. Anna didn't work. She played tennis. Drove a Mercedes and attended functions. She undoubtably had charisma and her, oh so perfect English, certainly got her noticed. So what did she see in me? The sixty four dollar question, was what that was. What was it that interested a well educated woman? Well James, I said to myself, whatever it is you're doing, I hope you can keep doing it because interested she was. I dwelt on that thought for awhile and conclude the best option was to be myself. It had worked up until now. Why fix it when it wasn't broken.

Maybe there was a good movie on the television that evening I thought, as I reached for the light switch. Time enough to grill the fish. With a few herbs, olive oil and a touch of ginger certainly very palatable. In fact, time to relax, as it had only just turned eight. And then Mike called.

Hey James can I come around. the wifi is not working at the apartment.

But I thought you were going out Mike?

Yes, I was but I've got a problem in Italy. Their server seems to have gone down and ......

Ok Mike. What time were you thinking of arriving?

In about an hour, if that's ok?

Yes, that's fine. See you then.

I was pleased to have gotten away so lightly. Once Mike started talking about his real job, as a computer programmer running his own system in various countries, one lost the will to live. Normally he could be side tracked but when he had a problem or in this case maybe a small catastrophe, Mike became focused on that and that alone. The best one could hope to achieve was to stay out of the way. That settled it. No beer but straight into dinner. There was only enough fish for one and if he arrived hungry, there was always the frozen pizza. With dinner out of the way and the thought of a little more ginger the next time, I saw it was fifteen minutes before that agreed time of Mikes' arrival. Always best to think about the agreed time and then discard it. Timing not being one of Mike's strong points. Sherlock Holmes was on TF1 in ten minutes and I didn't think I'd seen it. I would follow the usual upbeat mental process, giving the possibility of having the original soundtrack as somewhere between no and no chance. Glass half empty it might have been but less chance for disappointment. It just so happened this time VO meant VO so I sat back knowing the agreed time had lapsed and not surprisingly, Mike was nowhere to be seen. It was an hour later before Mike made an appearance and with a quick Hi, dashed upstairs and reappeared just as Sherlock finished. Which happened to be the exact moment my phone informed me I had a message. It was not my form to interrupt someone talking by reading phone messages. Rather bad manners I felt. So I resisted the temptation to see if it was Anna as Mike explained why the wifi was failing at the apartment and if he could only get a booster preferably in the range of ...... and so it continued. Mike stopped for thought. My chance.

Did you manage to get the server back on line? How about a coffee?

Uh, yes I did and I will. Have that coffee that is.

I got up to make the coffee as I did so, I tapped the screen. Yes it was Anna. There won't be a time to read that until Mike leaves and that didn't seem likely anytime soon. I hadn't really concerned myself about Anna's reply until that moment and now I visualised Anna and Tanya deliberating over the reply. Concern had just upgraded itself to trepidation. Nothing I could do would change anything the message had to hold so I reluctantly slipped back into attentive host mode as Mike concluded his dialogue on Protocols within the wifi system. "I know mine is slow", was the only reply I felt might, in some small way, adequately encompass the problem. Offering some compassionate understanding of the dilemma Mike faced. It seemed to work? Over coffee the conversation inevitable turned to work or more precisely, to Fox. The largest and most prestigious stand the company installed and Mike took a personal and passionate view in anything relating to his stand. Arriving four or five days before any other stand leaders making sure all had been prepared correctly.

It was half eleven before I managed to gently usher him out the door. Whatever Anna had to say, a reply would be out of the question that evening as I needed to be up at six. Deciding on a final decaf and cigarette to accompany the reading, I recharged the Nespresso and rolled while waiting for that last gurgle of machine telling me my coffee was ready.

Hello James, That's all I can manage. It is not true of course but I have no idea where to start. How about from the beginning? I read your message not once, oh no, but more times than I needed to. Tanya and I were about to have dinner. (A salad was the choice made by both. After the Brunch, that decision was inevitable.) The following hours of conversation washed over me. Finally I gave up. I decided to share your message. You did say I should tell Tanya? I eliminated the intermediary and passed my phone over. Tanya read and like myself, not once but twice. (Actually I read it four times.) Having skated over the message once more but this time together, I felt duty bound to initiate the conversation in a manner befitting two girls at a loss for words, Well Tanya, don't you feel James has a point? I mean about time being the decider. I don't know? She said, Ok, I'll admit he has an open book delivery and that in itself is ……. unusual. I'm just saying, be careful.

Do I need to be careful James? Are you that open book? Don't worry too much about those questions, it's just the cautious me. Accept them as thoughts, meant to be heard but not acted on. Enough thoughts. You can be very profound James. Time being the decider. I have to say, it threw Tanya for a moment. Her, "What do you know about him", lost instant credibility. What does anybody know when meeting someone for the first time? We had over a hundred mails prior to our first meeting. I stopped at this point, thinking of what next to write and a thought occurred. I thought we would have had an advantage. We knew each other via the mails but I've realised since, that it's not true. We've met three times? You are not the person I expected. Receiving those mails were a key point of my day. I knew who this person was, or so I thought. That vision practically disappeared within thirty minutes of that first meeting. You were far more than I expected. Your capacity as a good listener is correct and I know what you are thinking. "One has no other choice with Anna". Ha, you see, I was right, you are thinking that! Shame on you.

A very interesting game you set, and with pen and paper in hand, Tanya and I set about listing your somewhat disguised qualities. Not really understanding your sense of humour, Tanya took some time to warm to the challenge. Half an hour later amongst gallons of giggles we came to the conclusion you are right. You're egotistical but in such a way as to not take too seriously. To put that another way it was a unanimous decision when declaring you harmless. (I didn't see that listed in your correspondence?) I didn't say anything to Tanya but I think of you as far from harmless and I'm not sure you even realise that. Perhaps one day I'll explain but for now suffice it to say, looking forward to seeing you again. Which, by the way, might be awhile. Just heard, Elena has been accepted at Uni and so we are off to deepest, darkest, North of England at the end of the week and I have to go on to Germany for a few days after so it will, as mentioned, be awhile before I'm back to Biot. Around mid April which might happily coincide with the end of your busy period? Now off to bed early, as tomorrow is, Shopping Day! And talking of shopping, you're chocolate is still in the shop but not for long! I'll finish with a, Thank You for your concern but looking at my flat stomach, I do believe it was misplaced. Lucky me.

Good Night James and don't work too hard. x

ps: You can ride your bike tomorrow. The sun will be shining. How do I know that? The sun shines on the righteous.

A smiley face at the end of the ps. Was I confused with that reply? Most definitely! She read it four times. Was that because she didn't understand or was it to absorb the content? Not what she expected and yet harmless. Ok admittedly, retracted later but definitely egotistic. Oh my! I put the phone on charge and went to bed. Three weeks before the next possibility of meeting! Sleep did not come soon enough that night.

Chapter Six

Barely out of the shower and the phone rang. My heart leapt, or so the expression goes. But no, it was Ricky, wondering what time the office would be open.

I'll be the first there about seven thirty Ricky.

Ok, see you then, bye.

Yes, I'm fine Ricky, How are you? Did you sleep well? Have fun last night? Oh no, not Ricky, not when he was in work mode! He's an Englishman living in Austria. I sometimes wondered if he wasn't Austrian, and should have been living in England. He had mastered the language along with his decorum, that had also become Germanic. Although, knowing a number of Germans and having been a regular visitor to numerous locations in Germany perhaps it would be better to say this was Ricky's perception of Germanic. In fact Susan, his wife, was more English and she is Austrian! All the same, I wouldn't want to change him. Those thoughts had lost me ten minutes of, Get Myself Together In The Morning Time, as I would normally arrive about twenty two eight but knowing Ricky as I did, he always wants earlier so I gave him my earliest.

I preferred to arrive early for two reasons. Less traffic being the decisive factor but those twenty minutes or so before anybody arrived were the peaceful, reflective moments I enjoyed. Ricky, unsurprisingly, was pacing the yard as I pulled into the car park.

Morning Ricky.

I've already been here for ten minutes hoping you might arrive earlier.

"And a Good Morning to you James", I said.

Yes, sorry James, my head is elsewhere. Have you read those emails that came in last night?

I glanced at them.

Did you see the changes we've now got to make to the reception? In fact it looks more like a rebuild of the entire area.
Well I'm sure the changes will still be there in twenty minutes Ricky. Time enough for a coffee in the sunshine.
I opened up and headed for the kitchen. Made a coffee and sat, basking in the warming glow of the early morning sun, just rising above the skyline. This was My Time. The first chance to re-read Anna's message. No chance to formulate a response but a chance to become familiar with the content. Ricky appeared.
James, can you help me for a moment? I don't seem to be able to connect to the File Server.
Sure Ricky.
My Time, just disappeared as I followed Ricky to the office.
It was ten thirty and a break for coffee before the first chance materialised. Uncharacteristically I sat apart from others, wanting the solitude needed to reread the message. Mistake.
Hey James, what are you doing? Writing secret love messages. This produced the obvious laughing response from all. Needless to say the content of Anna's message remained a mystery until later that day. An hour or so before lunch John asked to see me.
Can you go to the Palais this afternoon James. Evidently there seems to be a few measurements in dispute amongst the design team. I've marked the areas that need checking and Lily has made an appointment for three at the Palais.
Sure. No problem.
Before lunch I'd need to see Alex and make sure he knew what was happening. Getting him up to speed on all the many aspects of construction underway, would take some time. Alex pointed out I'd only be gone a couple of hours and it was unlikely the place would come to a grinding halt. Laughing, he continued by saying, "I'll make sure the machine gets fed". He was right of course. I should have spotted that. "A slight over reaction on my part"? said I, now joining Alex in laughter. A good moment to make my exit.
I think I'll get out of your way for awhile Alex, let you get on. Oh, one thing. We are expecting a laminate delivery this afternoon and Fa will be needing it. A Gossamer 9001A-43 laminate. Seven sheets.
Ok James. See you later and don't worry, it will still be here when you get back.
Rounding the corner and making my way to the office stairs, I could still hear Alex laughing. I had to smile but wondering if my concentration on the work at hand had slipped. Replaying in my head a part of Anna's message. One minute I was harmless. The next, not so? Time for that later, right now there was work to be done.
Having arrived early at the Palais I set about defining angles and lengths, which was completed in record time with the help of a bored Palais guard. I decided to reward myself with a coffee. Crossing the road and heading for the Cafe Roma

I was aware that this was not a reward. I was kidding myself. It was not what I'd normally do. Job finished so back to the office but the coffee would give me time to acquaint myself with Anna's message.

Cafe, s'il vous plaît, as I took out my phone.

I read and reread the first paragraph which itself, was split in two. Happy go lucky first half and then passing the phone to Tanya I felt the mood had changed. Understandable. Daughter looking after mothers welfare although I was seeing more. Anna needed approval from Tanya? Even if I was partially right, how important was that approval to Anna? I glanced up as my coffee arrived and for the first time noticing the people around me. The people on the street. I sometimes try to guess their profession. I thought about that and slip back a few years. Laying on the beach at lunchtime with colleagues, in early October during a build at the Palais. All tourists long departed and there not five metres away were three girls. Sunbathing topless in their knickers. At that moment one of the girls turned our way. I'd seen her before. Recently. Hoping it would come to me, I turned to get a better view of the almost naked girls. As I turned back the realisation hit me. They worked at a bank. In fact they work at the Credit Agricole off the Rue de Antibes. I was there yesterday. A cunning plan was materialising.

I looked at Alex saying,

Some time ago I spent time on an in-depth research regarding underwear verses occupation. It was part of a thesis I was putting together.

No way! Interrupted Alex. *So what's their occupation James?*

I paused for effect.

Difficult one Alex. Not much to go on and that's an understatement.

The others laughed.

"Ok? Yeah sure", said Alex.

A few of the other guys, I noticed, were regarding the whole episode as "interesting". They didn't know where it was going but I saw by the looks on their faces, they thought something was going somewhere.

Look Alex, do you want to know or not?

Five to one says you're wrong.

That will be your five pints to my one. Is that right Alex?

Just get on with it, he replied.

Well, they are not shop assistants. They tend to go for the more, "flowery" underwear. These girls are serious girls. Solid lines with no frills. Have to be office girls? No, not that. You see the girl on the left Alex? She's eating an apple. Before that a salad. Tuna I think. Not the meal for office girls.

Alex now had that, You can't be serious, look on his face.

You don't get it Alex. There is a lot more than clothing that distinguishes someones occupation. As you're putting me on the spot I'll give you my answer but please accept it's based on incomplete data. They work in a bank and if my

memory serves me correctly, there is only one bank that has a split lunchtime shift. Therefore I conclude they not only work in a bank but the Credit Agricole.
"I'll take that bet", said Fa.
"Me too", I heard from Gary.
First off, there is no way he can know they work in a bank, let alone a specific bank and secondly this is a bet between James and me! Not for the rest of you!
"So how are you going to find out Alex", asked Gary.
Well, James can ask them.
"No way", said I. "I've done my bit. It's now up to you to disprove it".
A general chorus of, "Yeh Alex", met him from the other guys who were by now keen to see this through to it's inevitable conclusion. Meanwhile the girls were getting dressed.
"I'll give them a minute to finish and go and ask", said Alex.
Even before he'd finished the sentence Alex became aware, these girls were wearing uniforms. Not exactly the same but similar as to make no difference. He took one look my way and headed off across the sand. But he didn't stop, just carried on past? Taking a wide circle, watched by all present, he returned.
How the hell did you know that? Alex went on to explain he had no need to ask. On the label pinned to their jackets was, in big bold letter, Credît Agricole. That kept the boys in a fun mood for the rest of the day. That was all except Alex, who was obliged to keep me in beer for the rest of the evening. I never did tell him. Perhaps I would. One day.
That walk down memory lane has cost me time. I had to accept not only did I seem to have more questions than answers from that first paragraph but it was also time I returned to the office. Resigned to accept the inevitable, I put the phone away, knowing it was going to be sometime before I had another chance of returning to that message. As I drove along the bord de mer another realisation hit me. I was staying with Mike that evening. There would be no chance to even glance at the message. Once there the beers would be brought out to the terrace and before long one or two others would arrive. It was what we joked as being, part of the tradition, repeated twice yearly. Someone invariably started rolling that first one and the evening would bounce from unrelated subject to unrelated subject. Through experience I'd found it best not to follow the conversation but be ready to interject with an "Off the Wall" remark. Thus sending the conversation in another direction. The table would slowly fill with empty bottles and cigarette ash. The ash, in the main, supplied by Robert. He never had accomplished that knack of flicking ash into an ashtray. Or as Mike liked to call it, A Tray of Ash. Either way, Robert couldn't do it. I thought about that as I drove. It didn't look good. I needed to formulate a plan. I'd try to get away from work early. Mike had a tendency to stay later so I could have a couple of hours before he arrived. That would work. I was satisfied with that plan

as I drove into the carpark. As I got out of the car, John appeared from the direction of the office.

Hi James. I'm off home. Everything seems under control. The painters and laminators are leaving at six this evening. I'd suggest you give those dimensions and angles to Cochrane and get out of here.

Nice idea John and thanks for the thought. I have a couple of emails I need to write and I would like to have a quick run through with Alex about the progress in my absence.

John is giving me that, "I told you to get out of here look". I checked my watch. *I'll be out of here by six.*

"Make sure you do", said John, with a smile on his face. "See you tomorrow".

Finally the time arrived. I was sat on the terrace, beer in hand and reading that message. Inspiration! I opened "Notes" and started to write. Later when satisfied, I would copy/paste and send.

Do you need to be careful? Am I that open book? As you said Anna. Just thoughts. Not something to be acted on. I will therefore take your thoughts on-board in a way I can only describe as, passively.

I thought I'd managed to avoid any further discussion on the first paragraph. Harmless. I need to say something but what? It had been decided I was harmless and yet Anna later declared me to be far from harmless.

There is no fooling you Anna. You have seen right through my pitiful attempted charade of enacting harmless. To be discussed.

Have fun in deepest darkest but remember, if you are asking directions or in some other way needing to interact with the local people, don't expect to understand the reply. Another thought has just occurred. Elena might adopt the local dialect while at Uni. This might sway the opinion on whether this is the ideal Uni for a daughter who might abandon her Queens English for something more conducive to the area. Just a thought but not meant to be acted on. As a concerned person I am delighted your shopping day will not be ruined. Admittedly intrigued by the remark regarding your flat stomach but then I would be, wouldn't I Anna. After all, it was the reason for including that snippet of information. "Let's see what James has to say about that ". *Well Anna I'm not surprised you have a flat stomach. From what I know about you, you strike me as a Lady who will not be satisfied by an appearance that runs to second best. I am not sure if it's personal pride in all things you, or the possession of a shallow outlook on life where second best is frowned upon. To be discovered in the process of time unless it's the latter which, being too close for comfort, could deny me any future correspondence. I'm not worried about the possibility of abandonment Anna. I'm a harmless chap who shouldn't be taken too seriously. Isn't that so, Anna?*

I'm not going to deny I was overcome by emotion upon hearing you are embarking on this mini tour of Europe and will be, out of touch, for the next few weeks but your rational shone through, particularly when realising you are right. I will certainly not be at my best in the coming weeks and for us to meet would certainly condemn me to second place. I therefore concur that your timing, to be a blessing in disguise. I'm sure you will enjoy the North of England. You will find the people warm, open and friendly. (Don't let me down, N. of England.) Much like yourself, I hasten to add. I do believe this paragraph contains a little more, praise to Anna, than I intended. Which actually pleases me. The thing is Anna, I don't like to lie. I'm not saying I don't, just that I don't like to. Telling the truth or at the very best avoiding the truth by changing the expected answer just ever so slightly, invariably gets me into trouble. An easy example. Girl enters room and asks how she looks after spending time "getting ready", equivalent to time itself. My reply could be, Absolutely gorgeous. You look stunning! But what if she doesn't? The best I could do would be, You look nice. I'm now in trouble. So you see Anna, I am pleased that telling those truths will please you. Having pleased you I am hoping you will forget any "indiscretions" that might have been touched upon earlier. It doesn't seem particularly logical to inform someone about something one has hoped they'd already forgotten but it seems, I just did!

I was intending another three pages of idle chatter but you will be relieved to know, the guys have just walked in. It will take about two minutes to shuffle around in the limited space that is euphemistically called the kitchen before the essential ingredient, chilling in the fridge, is handed out to all concerned. I notice the shuffling is receding and beers in hand they are heading my way. So I hurriedly wish you a pleasant evening hoping you "Shopped till you Dropped" and now lie exhausted on the couch with a contented smile on your face while considering all those wonderful purchases you made.

Good Night Anna

With no chance to reread, amend nor change, I pressed send.

Hey James, what are you doing in the dark? More importantly why are you doing it without a drink?

Hi Robert. How's it going? I'm fine reference the beer, I'll have one in a minute. You're not fine. Mike, another beer out here.

One can always rely on Robert to make sure you're, "Fully stocked." I wasn't sure if it was a benevolent gesture on Robert's part or that he felt uncomfortable in the company of someone without a drink. Keep everybody topped up then never the accusation be made. Whatever the reason you wouldn't see anyone refusing Robert's good nature. And so the evening began, in that inevitable way "tradition" dictated. Beers on the table, although at times I did wonder just how long the beer remained on the table verses the time it took to be drunk. Robert, who had been in town for about thirty six hours had managed to score. He threw the weed in my direction. Tradition dictated. It was out of my hands. Metaphorically speaking. As ones hands are an integral part of the rolling procedure. The evening progressed and I played my part but there remained a part not connected to the whole. I shrugged it off, time and again. This was not the time for thoughts of Anna. I managed, with some effort to put those thoughts aside and concentrate on the company present. I could see Gary was well on his way. Not being a drinker, when he did, it tended to hit him hard. He was close but just before complete breakdown, he managed to give everyone a short rendition of his months in Bali. Gary knew what he wanted to say but couldn't quite get the words out, or when he did, not necessarily in the right order. I could see Robert was ready to pounce. Once he did, the conversation would degenerate into a free for all with the sole intention of prizing from Gary his closely guarded secrets. Usually those involving females. "None really", said Gary, "I was concentrating on the surfing and as long as I had a good book, the evenings tended to take care of themselves".

Robert wasn't going to let this pass. *Yes, ok Gary, but you were there for almost three months, there must have been someone?*

We were informed, Gary surfed with a girl. They had drinks occasionally. Robert wanted more information.

"And?" Said Robert, not to be put off by Gary's reluctance to share more. *You're hut or hers?*

"It wasn't really like that," said Gary. "It was more about having mutual interests".

"Ok", said Robert. "But in who's hut did these mutual interests take place"?

The mood jovial and Robert's prying for details focused the attention on Gary. I thought, time to get Gary out of the spotlight. Knowing full well, he was not going to tell.

Hey Robert, what was that I heard about a cabinet being built back to front?

Yeh well, that wasn't my fault. Cochrane's drawings were wrong.

So you're saying he gave you a drawing that was back to front? Did you try that old carpenter trick of using a mirror?

Gary glanced my way, realising my intentions and gave me a slight nod, with a growing smile. Robert's was now on the spot. And so it continued.

The following morning, once more tradition dictated. Arriving at work with, depending on who you talked to, a minor or massive hangover. There were four present who would rather not have been there. One asked oneself the obvious question. Asked approximately every six months. Why did I continue to do that? The answer was always the same. It was tradition. So, trying to remain alert to the possibility of any eventuality was not the way the day started. Maybe another day but not today. I looked around the workshop. Tomorrow this place would be empty. Everyone here with the exception of Alex, Stuart, Myself and Nico. Nico the general labourer had, over the years, become a valuable member of the small team remaining. A workforce of seventy descending on the Palais des Festival becoming a logistic nightmare for Ricky. No two shows were the same. Problems on stands that previously didn't exist could create hours of unforeseen labour and material costs. Thinking on ones feet. If you couldn't do that, it was not the game for you.

Last truck to load and Stuart had volunteered. The carpenters were starting to clear their benches while preparing their on-site tool boxes. It was eleven thirty and those guys would have already calculated the time until lunch and how best to fill that time. I was now feeling almost normal. Nothing from Anna but at least the day was on schedule. An invite for lunch.

Business lunch, said John. *We'll get together with Ricky and Will to run through the Punch List.*

To put that another way. Let's go have an hour or two, or maybe a bit longer, lunch. Mental note. Stick to beer and a lot of water. It didn't happen. Getting back, just before four and finding the place, almost as I'd hoped to find it, certainly gave my somewhat intoxicated brain a moment of relaxation. There were four guys sweeping the construction area. Stuart was putting the remaining two pallets on board and Nico was already clearing bays. I headed for the office in need of a strong coffee. Replies to a couple of emails sent. Time to hit the shop floor. Second coffee in hand I saw Alex approaching.

We've just packed away the last of the light boxes. Led's checked and I've included a couple of spare transformers. I think that's about it.

We'll have a look around. I'm sure you're right but hey!

We both laughed. I'm not sure if this was a technique, readily learnt in any, "How to be a Manager" book but for me it was obvious. On an inspection tour, which this was, start upbeat. Walk through and praise. It would never be perfect. That was expected. You're the boss. You get paid more because you see things others don't. I had to admit, it had become increasingly more difficult to notice any faults.

It's all good Alex.

I see you looking at the mezzanine James. Last job of the day will be bringing forward the remaining pallets for loading tomorrow.

I'm going home Alex. I'll be in at seven tomorrow but see you and Nico at eight, ok? Later!

Alex was saying something but then he always did have something to say. I gave a backward wave and walked to the car. The end of the day and it was only five! Five, and I was leaving on the day before the build-up. Never happened before. As I drove back to the apartment my phone beeped. Why did I immediately think it might be Anna? This was our busy period. It could be a message from any of sixty plus people. I parked in the underground carpark knowing I now had no signal. That's cool. I was a patient man. I could wait until I got to the apartment. It was thirty metres from the lift to the front door. I fumbled and dropped the keys thinking, those vital seconds of running along the corridor have now been lost, as I searched for my keys in the semi gloom.

How was your rainy weekend James? I'm enjoying beautiful sunny Zurich! Your chocolate is still in the shop. Not for much longer I hasten to add but you were right. We shopped and have now dropped. I quickly glanced through your last message and I do believe I noticed some flattery James? When I have sipped through a well earned glass of iced water. Taken a shower. Tried on my new attire. Had dinner and am sat relaxed, gazing on a view to die for, I will take the time to read again. Hope you are not working too late nor having too many drinks with the boys after. Bye for now, Anna x

Well Anna, it stopped raining yesterday and the sun was out, I said to no one in particular. There was an hour of setting sun on the terrace which we rarely got a chance to enjoy. I saw Gin and Tonic in the fridge, brought by Robert no doubt. Not an automatic choice of mine but I felt this particular evening called for such as this. Did we have ice? A slice of lemon might be too much to expect. Ok, maybe not the view Anna was enjoying but this one ticked most of the boxes. The start of the rush hour traffic, barely a hundred metres away not to mention the occasional goods train passing virtually under my terrace, wasn't perfect but the view with the setting sun lighting up the cloud formations ……. even the buildings which in some light resemble the picture of drabness, came to life. I had a view of the bay looking out towards Madelieu-La-Napoule. There was barely a ripple on the water as it lapped the beach. A melancholy mood overtook my thoughts. Emanuela. Emanuela again? Where are you now? Do you have a boyfriend? Are you happy? I thought about the times we spent together. No matter what the day nor the place they followed a similar pattern. A pattern full of happiness. Full of love. I wondered what happened Emanuela? What changed your mind? I'd been there too often so I was grateful hearing Mike arrive.

What is that you're drinking?

Oh, um, it doesn't matter, I've finished it. I'll have a beer if you're offering.

Mike returned dropping two beers on the table.

I've just been for a swim.

You're joking. Lucky if it's fifteen degrees. You're mad!

I admit it wasn't a very long one. About forty seconds would have been about it.

You're still mad. So what time has Ricky pencilled you in for tomorrow at the Palais Mike?

It's a six o'clock start for most but I'm holding out for seven.

I'll be going to the shop about that time, so alarm set for six fifteen. Mike and I had been doing this for over fifteen years, twice a year. We had a routine.

"Six fifteen works for me", said Mike.

"So", he said as he sat, "What's happening with Anna"?

Actually Mike, I haven't seen her in awhile. Constant communication but no date! She's traveling around at the moment and will be back about the time this

all wraps up. Demontage finishes Saturday so I'm hoping she'll be free on the Sunday.
"Did you hear the latest with Gary and Fa", asked Mike.
No. What have they been up to now?
Evidently Gary had thrown Fa's shoes on top of a truck at lunchtime. When Gary left, he couldn't find his pushbike until someone pointed to the roof of one of the trucks. There laid Gary's bike. Put there by Fa with the aid of the forklift.
"It's going to end in tears", said Mike with a smile on his face.
I think a quiet night after last night, what do you think James?
I'm with you there. Did you happen to bring any movies down from Austria?
I think I'll sit here a little longer if you want to be first in the shower Mike. Looking at the time we should manage to finish a movie before eleven.
"Could be an early night", said Mike laughing, as he headed for the shower.
Even if I wanted to I couldn't reply to Anna's short note and apart from talking about my weekend which I'm sure she wouldn't be interested in, there was no real reason to do so. I hoped I'd got that right? If I had I should expect a more in-depth reply in the next twelve or so hours. Emanuela returned to my thoughts as I sat alone. What are you doing now Emanuela? Right at this moment. Are you thinking of me as I am of you? Are you thinking of times we spent together? The time we looked for somewhere to eat on a rainy afternoon in Torino. In the end, the idea of an Italian lunch gave way to lunch in an Irish Bar, that was always open. Two burgers and chips later we were back on the streets not only having to contend with the rain as before but now the unwanted gusting winds. Fortunately there was a bus nearby that took us within a short walking distance of home. Forty five minutes later we found ourselves carefully peeling off multiple outer layers on the porch. Emanuela rushed off shouting, "First for the shower"! I remembered it was a little later when laying relaxed on the couch, Emanuela turned to me and said, "I think you are amazing. We seemed to spend hours battling the wind and rain but you never complained, in fact for most of the time quite the opposite." I remembered somewhere about then, I interrupted, more to save myself any more embarrassment. I don't handle flattery very well.
You know it's not bad weather that's the problem. It's bad clothes!
We both laughed.
I have to ask you James, that trick! When you stood against the corner of that shop window. Where do you know that from? It was very childish you know but very funny.
"Harry Worth", I said.
"Harry who"?
"Youtube it, you might find the clip. Try, Harry Worth Shop Window. That might do it". Having written that down Emanuela put her phone aside and turned to face me. I still remembered those feelings that flashed through, possibly my whole body. We had been together perhaps seven weekends in our two month

100

love affair. That first time meeting at that beach bar in Pietra Ligure with the obviously, full intention of moving onto the beach. Go for a swim. But no. We sat in that bar the whole day. Coffee. Beer. Food. More coffee. More beer. It was intense. Intense but not in a way where one felt uneasy. It was intense because when two people have an instant connection, nothing stopped the flow of that conversation. There were no barriers. We knew there were mutual unasked questions but no need to ask them. Certainly not now. The more we talked the more connected we became. It was a wonderful day that cumulated in a ten minute walk to our cars, that turned into forty. Kissing being obligatory ever twenty or so steps. Holding each other close before reluctantly prizing ourselves apart for our separate journeys home. The feeling that enveloped me, as we kissed. Was a feeling I would never forget.

I glanced at my empty beer and as on cue, Mike returned. "All yours", he said. I headed for the shower. Mike doesn't smoke and as it's a shared apartment, it was only right smoking was for the terrace. I was pondering this thought as I showered, knowing full well in about twenty minutes I'd smell like the preverbal ash tray, or was that, a tray of ash? Must give up one day. It had been awhile. Generally speaking I did manage to avoid smoking during the day but this could be a hard week. We sat on the terrace while going through the possibilities of Mike's collection of movies. As we both liked a good sci-fi, Mike had managed to include a few in that seasons, hot favourites but as any sci-fi aficionado will tell you. There are very few good, sci-fi movies. The decision was made. Inception it was. Which, as it turned out, was given an eight plus by this, the selective audience of two. Good movie. With the added bonus of bed looking possible before eleven thirty. No news from Anna as I headed for bed.

It was turning out to be a good day. The first day of the build and it was a good day. Busy but staying ahead with the truck reloads. It was all about servicing the machine. Eighteen fully loaded trucks were delivered in an established order. At the Palais it was seven forty five and forty guys would be standing about, loosely gathered in small groups, chatting with old friends not seen in five months. Plenty to catch up on while waiting for their valid entrance badges. I imagined Ricky rushing around not wanting to chat. He didn't do chatting when there was work to be done. Just get the passes out and get the guys to work. I smiled to myself as I headed for the office, pleased I wasn't at the Palais. The beauty of being busy was lunchtime approached at the speed of The Flying Scotsman. Alex decided to join Stuart and I at the African for lunch. It was actually not now called The African. Many years ago it was The African Queen but lost that name. Something about ownership. Two names later and it was still the African as far as we were concerned. For the last week there had been as many as twenty for lunch but most were now doing their own thing working down the road at the Palais des Festival. There were just the three of us, all knowing what had to be achieved before the end of the day and that day normally finished around seven. I didn't expect the day to deviate from the normal pattern of, first day montage. It was around six when I heard a ping on the phone. I looked. It was Anna. No chance to read as I was helping Alex reload a pallet of particularly skittish chairs that had decided being shrink wrapped to a pallet, wasn't going to stop them from abandoning said pallet. Alex was adding the final touches when Ricky called.

Hi James, we seem to be missing a particular crate for Dreamworks? Jan tells me it's crate nine. They need to get it in place before they can continue.

Ricky was in work mode and as such could be somewhat condescending at times. It was day one so I let it pass. Spending the years I had as logistics manager, I knew a stand by its components. I was also the unofficial photographer of the stands. Some pretty shots but mostly to establish the exact location of graphics, of spotlights, of where a wall ends in relation to the Palais wall, of the furniture layout, of the storeroom and its contents which will invariably include a fridge and coffee machine. So I thought it was fair to say I knew these stands, inside and out but I let it pass.

"Crate nine was on the truck that would have arrived around eleven", I told Ricky. "There were some E One, Content and three Dreamworks pallets plus that crate. It's either somewhere close or may I suggest you check the E One area".

Ok James, I'll get Jan's guys to check again, meanwhile I'll take a look across the way.

Oh, by the Way Ricky, but he was gone. …… *Just wanted to let you know, we will be finishing at seven.*

I checked the phone again but I had to resist the temptation of reading for another forty minutes or so.

Alex, are we getting the two empty trucks tonight?

I'll check and get back.

"Nico can you start bringing the furniture pallets forward. I'm sure those trucks will be here before lunchtime. Well at least one," I said, giving Nico an expression of hope.

"Sorry James", said Alex. "It's not going to happen this evening but he's promised one before lunch tomorrow".

I looked at Nico, he was now smiling at me.

Let's just make that enough pallets for the one truck, shall we Nico?

He nodded and moved on. A young man of very few words and I felt it was born from being a naturally reserved character. With his friends he might talk more but not much. He listened and by doing so, he learnt fast. Nico was not one you would class as a high achiever and yet excelled in what he did. I knew what I was doing. I was giving my thoughts to Nico's capabilities. Distraction, was what

I was doing. It wasn't working as I'd hoped but it was helping. Just enough, as I once again, thought of Anna. Lily walked past.

Oh James, I'll have the on-site reception desk and cabinets filled by about eleven tomorrow, so can you get them to the Palais in the afternoon?

No problem Lily. I'll make sure a couple of reception stools go in the same truck. It was our little private joke. Many shows ago the stools were forgotten. In fact for many shows after, they were forgotten. One day I received the familiar call from Lily asking for the stools. I called Jan. "Ok Jan, can you take the stools around …. now"? I'd earlier told Jan what I wanted to do and he was only too pleased to comply. The stools had been delivered to Jan's stand and were left, waiting. Thirty seconds from the moment Lily put the phone down, the stools were there. I called her back. "Sorry about the delay with the stools Lily". And bless her, she got the joke. Although I might add, that would have been, to a large extent, down to Jan's German crew. The stools arrived yes but dressed in pink ribbons. (I never did get a straight answer about that.) They had managed to, evidently as told by others, sew a backing to both chairs. Lily's Chair said one. Lily's Guest, said the other. Lily's chair had a soft cushion. Even arm rests had been added. Her stools had not been forgotten since that day but it was still fun to run over the old joke. I only got two chances a year. Use them or lose them. That was the workers company motto. Take that break or lose it. Take those days off or lose them.

"I'm sure you will James", said Lily. "But tell Jan there is no need for the ribbons", as she walked on by, laughing.

Lets start locking up Alex.

Nico can you get the glass A frames out and ready for loading first thing in the morning?

Nico pointed down the aisle. Glass frames ready and waiting. I gave Nico a sideways smile before heading to the office. No urgent mails. I saw Page flies in tomorrow. The first of six Project Managers based in New York who would be arriving. She would need picking up from the airport. It was a late afternoon arrival. That can be organised tomorrow. Time to leave.

Getting back to the apartment I knew I had at least an hour, possibly two, before Mike returned. He wouldn't be leaving before eight and being the first days build he might be tempted to a couple of beers after work. I was hoping for the latter. Kicking my shoes off I forego the early shower. Finding my tobacco I headed for the fridge. Once settled on the terrace, I opened Anna's message.

Hello James. I had the full intention of expanding on my earlier message yesterday evening but I'm sure you already knew I would be too exhausted to do so. Didn't you!? Coincidently another reason for delaying my message came to mind last evening. We will be visiting the university tomorrow and will spend some time touring the local area. If I cannot converse with indigenous population, we will be on the next plane home and possibly take advice from you on the preferable list of universities. Actually that is not true as I didn't believe a word of your cynical remarks. Ok, not true. I was completely unconvinced of my conviction, because I know you. That alone is surely enough? But no James, your ……. I'm not sure how I describe it? Your, simplistic approach. It begs to be believed. And I fall for it every time. I know you're lying but it is enough, minuscule as it is, it's enough to sow the seed of doubt.

I now leap forward twenty four hours, well prepared to respond to your message. We decided on an early breakfast and having plenty of time before Elena's interview at three thirty, decided to take in the sights. We left the hotel around eleven. It would have been earlier but the weather had changed so dramatically after breakfast we had to rethink our entire wardrobe. Once on the streets I thought of your message and immediately curse myself for doing so. With that seed firmly in place, we started to investigate the neighbourhood. You lied to me James! I knew it! Everyone we met were helpful and charming and I might just as well add, totally understandable. But you knew that James. I can only congratulate you on managing to sow that seed. When I later told Elena she wondered how I could be so gullible but thought it a highly amusing tale all the same. I would appreciate your thoughts regarding my gullibility. Not that I expect you to say anything more than, "Gullible. You Anna? Not the remotest possibility." Or something very similar James. I will email you a photo of our lunch later. I think you will be impressed. I do believe it is what's called a pub lunch, complete with pint, I might add. After lunch Elena was a little nervous regarding her forthcoming interview so I suggested another hours shopping wouldn't go amiss. Strangely enough when she later disappeared through the doors of the college, it was me who felt nervous. Success. Elena has been accepted. Some formal paperwork but she has been guaranteed a place in September under the assumption she obtains the necessary grades.

One small point I'd like to touch on before we head back to the hotel to prepare for our celebratory dinner. I see you are now enacting your state of harmlessness. I believe it is time to correct you on your assumptions regarding my definition of harmless. You will remember I declared you far from harmless. Simply put, you encapsulate all the qualities a woman requires (Well most) and yet you are unaware of this. Your enactment of innocence is part of your charming character James, but it's not an enactment. No one could keep up that act for as long as you have. Why do I feel I might regret saying that?

I leave for Germany on Thursday while Elena returns to Biot. Hopefully it won't be too drawn-out an affair. Just business my dear. Oh, some bad news. I have eaten your chocolate. Well strictly speaking it was Elena and I. Don't hate me? Looking forward but for now it's off to prepare. Anna x

A most agreeable message. Anna had taken the time to involve me in her day. Plus an email photo of their Fish and Chips lunch. Shame about the choice of beer. More importantly harmless had, for some unknown reason, been recognised as a positive trait. I do believe I'd told myself, "Whatever it is you're doing James, it seems to be working and continues to do so". Perhaps I should analyse this trait in myself? Time enough for that another day but worth adding to the, To Do list. I glanced at my watch. Mike could be back in less than an hour but I was counting on him being unable to resist that after work drink with the boys. Could I report on my day? Not really as it was fairly uneventful. I did hear a good joke today which could be worth passing on. It would be interesting to see what Anna made of it. Not sure if I should continue with the harmless topic to anyones advantage so perhaps I should ignore that part. Yes, of course you will James. Ignore the part of the message that intrigues the most. Finding the starting point for the message was the hard part. Ok, I'll start with a thank you. Well maybe not.

Hello Anna. I am wondering if our relationship is of any importance to you? You've eaten my chocolate! Why would you do that? I am devastated. You are obviously unaware what that small gift of chocolate would have meant to me. Hate you? I might never speak to you again. How did I do on the Simplistic Approach? Did it "Beggar belief?" Sorry Anna, I didn't mean a word of it although that is not to say you are completely off the hook unless that is, you did believe it. In which case you will have suffered enough and therefore I forgive you. How am I doing Anna? Let me hazard a guess. It's unlikely I'll be receiving any gifts in the foreseeable future, albeit I've forgiven you. Don't blame me, that's mans logic! The cold beer in the fridge, Man's logic.

Moving swiftly on. So grateful for the photo. Then again possibly not. I could almost smell that wonderful aroma. Some ask, "What do you miss the most from England?" You mean apart from my family and friends? Yes. That's taken for granted. I have to be honest. I enjoy certain drinks. Certain foods only available in England but do I miss them? Not really would be the answer. But seeing that Fish and Chips and knowing it was recently eaten, that got me. I should have been there. You could have eaten something of inferior quality and not realised it. I have to say, generally speaking, the best Fish and Chips will be found in a Fish and Chip shop, not a pub as they tend to be of the pre-made frozen variety and some of those can be rather dire.

Enough James, unless it was your intention of sending Anna off to sleep.

Where was I? Ah yes. You're potentially regrettable remark. You will not get any backlash from me Anna. I was somewhat overwhelmed but after consideration, I saw a flaw in your assessment. If half of what you say is true, I have two ex wives that spent a time in our relationship, in denial. They thought they hated me but in fact they were wrong. Maybe not so much encapsulate, more crushed like a nut, was the way I saw it. We all have our faults Anna and one day, I might just happen to find one in you.

I knew what I was doing. Saying nice things to Anna. The question was, Why? Was it the honest truth or something I knew she would like to hear. It didn't take long to realise Anna enjoyed, on some level, praise given but she was an intelligent woman. Flattery will wear thin. I'd understood that, "line of enquiry" approach for many years. Ask questions. Sound interested in what they are doing. Mr Super Charming. It couldn't be maintained. Unless those people really existed, and I had my doubts, why do it? There was only one conclusion I could draw from this. She seemed perfect. Actually there was another possibility. She was Mrs Super Charming.

Off to Germany tomorrow Anna, but hopefully not the north of Germany. It seems they are having some problems with snow. That aside, I think you've had a good time "Up North" and may I say, duly acceptant of your daughters choice? (Did I not mention you would find those northerns to be friendly and always willing to give help where help was needed? I'm sure I did?) It's now eight thirty and there is a possibility, how ever slight, that you might be out-on-the-town by now. If not, you are late! I was about to conclude this message in a timely manner but Mike has just walked in. I'm sure you will enjoy your last evening. It therefore leaves me but to wish you a restful nights sleep while crossing ones fingers you awake, sans hangover. Je te souhaite un bon vol demain. James x Hi James.

Hi Mike. How was the day at Fox?

Not the kind of question one should ask Mike. Too much scope for indulgence. It took some time to answer that question and even then if Mike's stomach wasn't calling, it would have been longer. Not that Mike's conversations were boring. Far from it but he did like to digress. I made a casual dash for the shower while Mike ate. We had a, "What James did today", half hour on my return. Mike was still eating. Captive audience. Time had finally beaten us. No movies tonight although I knew once in bed Mike would tune into something. Usually falling asleep as the tv counted down to the timers, already preset moment, of "off".

See you tomorrow Mike.

I got to my room. Just check my alarm was set for the right time. "You know it's right James". Oh look. Surprise. No messages. And guess what? The alarm is set for the correct time. I closed my eyes.

Sitting in the unusually quiet workshop the next morning, sipping the hot instant coffee gave me the twenty minutes needed to run through, what I knew of the day so far, while trying to allow for the inevitable disaster. Over the years I'd discovered that attitude of expecting the worst actually worked. If I thought our small team was reaching it's capacity, extra work could be deflected. Many years ago, when I first started, if you had a problem, it was an "on-site" problem. That had all changed. Capable carpenters were now encouraged to send items back to the workshop for repair/alteration. If I told Ricky we'd reached capacity, the carpenters on-site would be informed that for the time being, unless they could

wait, any further changes would be down to them. The group of Germans working at the Palais, I never heard from. They built four stands and in the ten years they'd been contracted to do so, never a word. The only time I saw them collectively was during the, "Job is over now lets hit the bar before departing" time. There were six of them. I would ask them, How was the show?
Eet vas ghood James. U vant a beer?
Great bunch of guys. German mentality. Work hard. Solve problems. Get the job done. Then party!
I was wool gathering. Perhaps ten minutes before the guys arrive. Still two furniture trucks to load. Stuart wasn't busy, he will enjoy that. The broken LED on the reception desk, that was something for Alex. Nothing outside of the usual. Three days before the show and everything on automatic.
The guys arrived. No one late. They knew me. It was my job to keep ahead of any potential disaster. That big picture. Over the last three weeks, I'd tried, occasionally unsuccessfully, to keep ahead of the machine but not fully in control of the big picture. But now. I had my big picture. It was my machine. It worked in one of two ways. Pro active. That came with experience. Knowing when deliveries of essential items should arrive. Not easy when a round trip in a twenty cube could be up to two hours. Two twenties at my disposal cut down that time. Ever evolving logistics. That was the experience. The other way? It had been called many things, some more grand than others but we called it, "Winging It"!
I was grateful I had Stuart on stand-by. "Stuart, a damaged laminated panel coming in. It will need a fast turnaround. How long"? He asked me the obvious that we both knew were associated with laminated panels. Satisfied he said, "Two hours. Three at the most if it's one of the old panels". I got a call from Ricky. A large glass panel had been dropped. Having given me the sizes, I checked the stock. Sorry Ricky, we don't have a spare. Taking a look at the drawing, (a good distraction when Ricky had one of his, "What the fuck we gonna do", moments.) I realised he was talking about a stand-alone piece of glass.
Ricky, if it's the one behind reception, we have something close. Stuart can make up a frame giving it the necessary bulk to support the header. What do you think?
Yes, that will work James. I'll send you the dimensions. Great idea, by the way.
During the course of ...... actually during the starter of three courses, of lunch outside the Palais, Ricky would be praised by the owners for his quick thinking after telling the story of how he saved the day. C'est la vie. Meanwhile, Stuart got to work on the panel.
Lunch came and went and by close of play that evening the warehouse had that, empty look. Everything left to go had been neatly stack, in order of clients and to some degree categorised by priority. The upper mezzanine, already hoovered, with some empty pallets that had recently returned from the Palais, placed according to stand. I thought, 'We are ahead of schedule". Tomorrow will

be the rush on empty pallets and crates returning. That was no problem. We had two forklifts at hand to ferry most items close to their destination. It was a strange affair. Eighteen trucks ferry the materials to the Palais. The empties are returned only to be put back onto trucks that then took them back to the Palais to return full. Put like that I was wondering why the days became so stressful? Perhaps I was missing something? After twenty five years in the business, I was still not getting it. That was one possibility or perhaps it was just not that simple. Either way, it was now time to leave. Tomorrow was another day.

Getting back to the apartment, I amazed myself when deciding to start with the shower. Sitting on the terrace, watching the sun going down across the Bay of Cannes while consuming an ever so slight morsel from Robert's bag, I realised, it could be worse. Not sure if it was the post shower me, or the ever so slightly stoned me, version. I didn't care. Life was good.

The sun had set when Mike walked in the door and I'd just finished my second beer. "While you're there Mike"! He'd put his bag down and was reaching for the fridge. In a mellow mood I decided to open myself up to the inevitable. "How was the day, Mike?" So Mike told me. It turned out it was a good day. Ahead of schedule but then there was Stephan. Stephan the guy who set the computer controlled lighting cables and had missed two. And the painter who painted the wrong shade of cream on fifty percent of the cabinets. The usual problems with the tent guys. A stolen screw gun. A couple of the team coming back late from lunch and if my memory served me well, the safety officer paid a visit and Mike had to spend two hours walking him around. "And you say it was a good day," I asked in a quizzical manner. I think that thought caught Mike out for a moment. "Yes", he finally said, while still thinking, the penny dropped.

It was Ricky! We didn't see him all day!

That brought Mike's story to an amusing end.

Chapter Seven

Nothing from Anna the previous evening but not really expected, she was enjoying the last evening with her daughter. I had my morning coffee sitting at the computer checking for any recent Wish Lists that might have been sent by Ricky but as the Project Managers had now descended upon us from New York, I expected more than I saw. Could be turning into a good day. Still only seven thirty, I had time to pen Anna a few words.

Good Morning Anna. I'm going to hazard a guess. You had a wonderful evening with Elena and due to your amazing self control, you gracefully refused an overindulgence of alcohol. Thus waking this morning with a clear head ready to face the day.
Did I get that right?
Remember. Passport. Credit Cards. Anything else, is a bonus!
Have a good flight and hoping all works out well.
James x
Short, with amusement and a constructive conclusion. I could but wait.
"James, are you up there"? A call from the workshop below. So started the day. I put aside thoughts of Anna as I left the office. Thursday and Friday passed without major upsets to a roughly planned routine. First thing Saturday morning the twenty cube left the warehouse full of client materials. The second truck being held back until late morning as it was a kleptomaniacs dream come true at the Palais. Carefully stacked in the original cardboard boxes. Big pictures of computers, laptops, iPads and plasmas on the sides. That Apple logo, was an obvious target. I looked towards the workshop. Stuart was sweeping up. A little presumptuous I felt but at the same time, I admired his optimism. It was client day. Anything could happen, particularly considering there were three new stands out there, of which, two were new clients. My solace lay in the belief

Julian, as the leading Project Manager, would not be easily appeased. Necessary changes impacting on the workshop at this late stage on the whim of a client, would not be tolerated by Julian and less so by John. Carry on sweeping Stuart, I thought, but I could not allow complacency. Not that I was worried. I rarely got worried. What was the point? Vigilant would be more appropriate. Were we in a position, excluding all that might be expected of us over the next thirty six hours, to allow for the possible inclusion of any major changes. As I climbed the stairs to the office I glanced in Stuart's direction who was still sweeping. Bring it on, I was thinking. Lunchtime approached when I received a message from Anna. There would be little or no chance of reading during lunch as there were four or five guys accompanying me. Why did they always seem to arrive at an inopportune moment?

"Come on James, let's get off to the African!" said Robert. I glanced at my watch which encouraged Robert to add, "It's only five minutes James, the boys are waiting". It was actually ten minutes but I shrugged my shoulders and led the way to the car. As designated driver, it seemed the sensible thing to do. The conversation at the restaurant resembling that of the cat playing with the preverbal mouse, again.! Robert and his technique. Have a little word with the guy next to him. Then he might mention it, as a partial address to those within ear shot. Until finally he would put it to the, now not unexpected, adversary.

So Steve, I hear you were late in this morning?

Yes. I think I forgot to set the alarm.

Nothing to do with the blonde that was seen leaving your place?

Robert knew he now had the backing of most. This would not be pretty. It might have been a rumour Robert had picked up on and in his, oh so sweet way, was giving his sparring partner a chance to redeem himself, or not. Invariably there would be some degree of humiliation but never rising above an acceptable level. Robert had Steve pinned to the ropes.

What blonde?

The same blonde that was with you when you left the bar last night?

Others joined in the taunt. Steve was showing signs of discomfort but believed if he continued refusing to admit to any indiscretion, he could fair the storm. Personally, as I watched the debacle unfold, I felt Steve would have had a better chance if he'd admitted all. Steve added a remark about Robert being jealous. Throwing Robert into defence mode. Wrong move! Steve suffered that lunchtime. Robert rarely tried that tactic with me nowadays. He knew only too well, my sarcastic repertoire was difficult to comprehend and would invariably lead to confusion. Not that sarcasm was the standard response but on those, now rare occasions he tried, it worked.

The afternoon followed without incident. The last day to get clients to accept any modifications. The Wish Lists started. Client changes. Stuart had a cabinet to construct and laminate so was fully occupied. The twenty cubes, returning on a regular basis to unload their empties. Nico, on the mezzanine, creating order with this ever continuing supply of empties. It was left to Alex and myself to concentrate on ploughing through the Wish Lists. Most were straight forward enough. Missing a door handle. Needing two more long arm spots. More Velcro. It was the cutting lists that were time consuming. Four lengths of eighteen millimetre ply, cut to such and such dimensions. An overlay missing. One metre by sixty eight millimetres and painted please. I hadn't had the chance to glance at Anna's message and it was going to be a long day. Ricky called just before seven.

Hi James, just thought I'd let you know the last twenty cube has just left.

That's good news and reference the Wish List items, all have been completed. Alex is putting a couple of undercoats on that overlay. Do you want it first thing and paint the top coat on site or get it later if Alex paints it?

First thing would be good. There is more painting on the stand so another overlay will make little difference.

Ok Ricky, in that case I'll send the guys home and wait for that last twenty. Talk to you tomorrow, no doubt.

Talk tomorrow James, later.

It was eight fifteen as I walked into the apartment and was tempted to throw myself on the ever so inviting bed. I resisted and decided a shower would be the better idea. Finally, the terrace. I reached for my phone.

Hello James, sorry I haven't replied. It's all been rather hectic. To be honest, I'm annoyed. Not with you! German bureaucracy! Accepted, it is far removed from the French system but infuriating nonetheless. It's Saturday, late morning and I'm trying to relax in the comfort of my room. Maybe I shouldn't admit to this but thinking through the process of this conversation, is helping. A lot.

Before I forget to mention, I forgive you for your "man's approach" regarding logic. As fascinating and amusing as it was, there seems to be one minor detail you obviously preferred to ignore. Using the word "man" in conjunction with "logic", defies logic! Your aptly phrased subject changer ..... Moving swiftly on, knowing as we now do that I forgive you, I'd like to apologise for the Fish & Chips photo. I had no idea you would feel so strongly. If only I'd known, I could have bought you some. Wrapped them in a plastic bag and presented them to you when you pick me up at the airport. So who said it's unlikely I would be presenting you with other gifts? (You know, I'm really starting to enjoy my day!) I thought I was going to regret my earlier remarks but no, James in true modesty, turned the whole thing around and deemed me perfect! (As you like to say James, poetic licence.) Moving swiftly on, (I'm getting to like that one. It seems to put closure to anything I've previously said. Most delightful!) I mentioned picking me up. That is part of the good news and the other part? I'm returning to France on Tuesday at 21:30. Therefore, how about Wednesday evening? You can tell me on Tuesday evening when you pick me up. I will keep

111

the evening free on the off chance you say yes. That could have been the last of the good news but no. I have one more to add. You will therefore have the pleasure of my company, two evenings in a row.
Planning your Tuesday and Wednesday evening? I hope you don't mind. You can't blame me. It is what I do. It's an acquired skill and I am good at planning. And then there is the other part of my beautifully composed message. I have to admit to a sense of satisfaction at beating you at your own game. I can now go about my day at peace with the world. Anna x

I had to agree on two counts. It was good news and yes Anna, you are good at planning. Certainly planning for me. I wasn't sure if I should sit back and enjoy being planned or launch forth with my own itinerary? I would sit back but I had to be careful, Anna would surely expect input sometime in the future. Why did I get the feeling I was the latest, pet project? Perhaps I should keep my reply short. Ok Anna, I'll see you at the airport and looking forward to Wednesday evening. That worked. But you're not going to do that, are you James? I would sit there with my Notes open and try to compile some drawn out but hopefully witty analogy based on Anna's previous message. Good Luck with that one James. At that moment I could barely remember where I might find the fridge as tired as I was, so how was I possibly going to construct said repartee?

It was of little consequence, as I heard from the terrace that Mike had arrived. Opening the fridge and pulling out two beers.

Hi Mike. So that's where the fridge lives.

"Well now you know, you can get the next two". Said Mike, taking a seat.

Tell me you had a good day Mike. The stand is finished and the client is elated!

Yeh, that's about it. Except for the list of, "Things to do tomorrow", which is quite long. How about you?

Mike wasn't going to list the items? Say nothing of his day? I was confused. Don't be confused James. Don't miss the opportunity to talk about my day. It was too long a pause as my thoughts recollected a question once asked. "What is the definition of a millisecond?" The time it takes a Frenchman to honk his horn when the lights turn green. That light was green and Mike took the opportunity to talk. But to my surprise Mike asked if I'd heard from Anna. I now had enough material to discuss my day and talk of Anna for the next thirty minutes. Maybe longer? Then it was film time. Oh what an exciting life us exhibition employees live. So Mike sat, listening attentively. Work? I gave that five minutes. Anna was given top billing. By the time Mike had showered it was once again, too late for any movie. A couple of episodes of South Park and I made my excuses.

"Castles Made Of Sand" was quietly building in the background allowing a few seconds for my brain to adjust to that first morning contact, followed by a body that was not happy. Don't think about it just get up. At least it was Sunday. Put the kettle on and disappear to the bathroom. I wondered who those people were that spent time in the shower and then reappear feeling refreshed and ready to face the day? Who ever they were the shower gel adverts seem to have the monopoly. I felt like shit. Having checked, my iPhone app, it proudly concluded I'd managed twenty three point four kilometres the day before. Considering our building was contained within fifteen hundred square metres, that was a lot of walking. Eddy Izzard is glorified, and rightly so, for achieving however many marathons in however many days. I had twenty five days of this. Does Eddy climb the stairs to the office as was beholden to me with such repetition that on occasion I wondered, was I going up or coming down?

Nine thirty and I needed to reply to Anna. It would have to be a short one as the day permitted no more. It was the last day of the montage and although busy I saw there just might be that window of opportunity that could manifest itself around late morning. I'd hold off on that reply for awhile.

Dear Anna, it would be churlish of me to do any other than compliment you on your self appraisal. If feeling that you have somehow beaten me at a game I didn't know I was playing, makes your day, then I am pleased. I only wish there were more like you who could be so easily satisfied with so little achieved. Am I getting too competitive Anna? Lets change the subject and talk about your anticipated delight at the prospect of seeing me two evenings in a row. Consider it a, must do. I'll be waiting at Arrivals. Twenty one thirty. Perhaps you could be kind enough to forward the flight details? FYI. The company has decided, which is normal for this time of year, that I am obliged to work twelve hour days, seven days a week until the nineteenth of April. (I just love this company.) Nine thirty will therefore suit me for Tuesday and Wednesday of course, is a yes. As you said, two evenings in a row, how could I possibly resist. No chance to add more as work calls. See you Tuesday.

That worked for me. Focus was back on work. See the Sunday out to it's conclusion which didn't seem as daunting as I thought it might be. The day cruised on by with barely a ripple. So unusual for a last day build. Maybe after twenty five years at the Palais the company had finally got it right? Twenty one hundred and it was over. Another montage completed and I was seeing Anna in two days.

Monday morning. It was six thirty. Many years ago I thought it might be a good idea to have photos of the stands we built. The "nuts and bolts" of the stands. Photos showing how certain aspects of a stand, fitted together. Plus the pretty pictures. Digital photography had only recently taken off and to be able to transfer directly to the computer was a revelation. Needless to say, all agreed it to be a good idea. Twenty years later and here I was, at six thirty entering the Palais to take photos. The unofficial photographer. I was wondering how many unofficial roles filled my day? The more I thought about it, the more I was convinced my working life was full of unofficial. Maybe that answered the question often asked of me, "What do you do?" I found that a difficult question to answer. Now I understood why. In future when asked this question, I could honestly reply, "Most of what I do is unofficial." If said with a suggested undercurrent of, "You know what I mean". I do believe it could stop any further enquires in that direction.

Tradition played it's part in that, the first day of the show. Meeting with Ricky at nine thirty. Obligatory. I crossed the road from the Palais at nine thirty and headed down a side street to meet Ricky for coffee. Alan and Ingrid were there, as normal but no sign of Ricky? Ricky was late! The show, that repeated itself on a twice yearly basis, was the only time in the last few years I got to see Ingrid, who now lived in her home town of Vienna. A wonderful lady. Always charming with a delightful ability of putting a positive spin on the day. Alan lived locally. An equally charming fellow but who had a known affliction. He was from Glasgow. It was lucky if anyone understood one in three words he said. We still loved him though. We managed a brief, "Whats happening in your life", moment when Ricky arrived. Thirty minutes later I decided to leave, with Ricky and I promising to discuss the demontage plan the following morning.

See you here at nine thirty James?

Is that my nine thirty Ricky, or yours?

Ricky was never late. Or so he liked to think. Alan and Ingrid laughed, understanding my dig at Rickys', never to be repeated, lateness. Ricky just smiled. I spent the rest of the day in the office. The guys had played this day out on so many occasions they didn't need my interference, I left them to it. Catching up on the paperwork presented itself with a feeling of deep satisfaction. Rarely was I this far ahead in the practicalities of the up and coming show in Monaco. It was six o'clock and I decided to leave.

I'm off Alex and I don't see any need for anyone to be here after seven. Just give Ricky a call about six thirty and tell him you're closing down for the evening. I should be here at about ten thirty tomorrow morning.

I was back at the apartment with a whole evening in front of me and little chance of Mike returning before ten. Start with a relaxing bath and follow through with the inevitable beer on the terrace, knowing there would be time to update the previous message to Anna. I wasn't ten minutes out of the bath when Robert called.

Hey James you couldn't do me a favour, could you? I've got a blocked ear and need something to shift it. Can you pop across to the Pharmacy before they close? I'm not finishing before eight thirty and it will be closed when I get back.

Yes sure Robert, I'll go over now.

Fifteen minutes later and I was back, beer once again in hand staring at my phone and waiting for inspiration.

Hi Anna. I thought I should follow up on that rather uncharacteristically sarcastic previous message by invoking the more sensibly amusing me. I know you enjoy playing these one-upmanship games and if you've already read my previous message I'm sure you're compiling an apt response. Alternatively you're out on your last evening enjoying yourself and giving little regard to my message. If that be the case then enjoy! Personally I'd like to believe the former but then I would say that, wouldn't I. I digress, again. The sensible me would say, God knows what you see in me! But that would be self defeating so please ignore that remark, instead concentrate on my good points. What are those? I have no idea. Can't help you there but I must have some otherwise why would you want to incorporate two evenings in a row with someone lacking that, Je ne sais quoi. On the subject of, Je ne sais quoi. You have it in abundance Anna. A fascinating woman that I hope will be my pleasure to get to know better. Get to know what makes you tick. What life was like in Russia in the seventies and eighties before you left. Your politics. (Maybe we can save that one for sometime in the future. Always an emotive topic.) I should stop now. Lets not feed the Lady too much. Save some by reserving the best until later. What is the best? All will be revealed with the passage of time. Putting that another way, The best is yet to come. Don't let me down Anna, I'm looking forward to making those discoveries. Well, a sensible and complimentary message. What is my world coming to? Enjoy your evening Anna and see you tomorrow.

The "Sandcastles Made Of Sand" were calling once again. I arrived at the Palais at six thirty wearing my unofficial photographers hat having checked my messages for the umpteenth time. No reply from Anna. Not surprising having reread the message I sent. Coffee with Ricky and trying to extract just one small piece of information.

Three trucks ready to be loaded with empties. What do you want in each truck Ricky and in what order do you want them delivered. Or, to put that in a way you might find easier. Same as last show?

It must have taken thirty minutes for Ricky, having explained the complications involved in the truck rotation, something which I was well aware of, to say, "Yes James, the same as last show". I could now go back to the workshop to give the ten or so guys direction. Who by now would have filled the carpark with crates, pallets and pump trucks just waiting for said information. Driving back and arriving in time for tea break was no accident. Everybody was in the same place. I only had to say it once. No need to catch up with individuals to explain. It was another occasion for Fa to shine. He really didn't like the responsibility but he did it so well. He would run around on the forklift giving direction of what he wanted next as he loaded to perfection. It took the best part of three days to load the trucks. A tight schedule so who better to put in charge than Fa. Meanwhile I was able to concentrate on the details surrounding the up and coming demontage.

I took a walk around the yard trying not to interfere with the organised chaos that was taking place. Lunchtime approached and I received the message I'd been waiting for. Could I find a moment to read? Of course not! John decided to join us for lunch which was going to be a company credit card lunch with the usual bonus of lunch being extended beyond the normal hour. It was quarter to lunchtime hour but John was ready to leave.

I'll join you in a couple of minutes John, I've got to get this email off in the hope I get a quick response.

Ok. See you downstairs James.

I'd just received a short but positive message from Anna that I was able to digest in the milliseconds I had before John became impatient. I put my phone away ready to indulge in a lunch with a warm feeling of contentment.

Hi James. You never cease to amuse me. I have had an unscheduled meeting this morning and am therefore running behind my own schedule for departure. I look forward to catching up this evening. ...... when you join me for a drink à chez moi. It will give me a chance to better respond to your latest, mildly antagonistic, message. See you this evening. Anna x

My day was now arranged to correspond with the, arriving at the airport on time. As I sat listening to John during lunch, centre stage with the captive audience of six, the seventh, although giving the correct facial expressions had his mind elsewhere. I was busy working my schedule back. I leave at seven. Home by half past five giving me an hour and a half to prepare myself. Now there was that thought again that I rarely had. Prepare myself? Have a shower, grab something from the wardrobe and go. That would be my preparation. It wasn't something I thought about and yet there I was, running through the inventory of clothes in my cupboard. Again! Can I wear this? Should I wear that? Interesting.

James, are you receiving?

I momentarily looked up to see John regarding me with interest.

Unless it was something to do with my evening ahead then no. No, I wasn't listening. If it was something to do with work ...... I'm having lunch.

There was a chance it could have backfired but, it didn't.

You carry on James, I'll let you know when we're leaving.

That was met with resounding laughter. Much to the appreciation of John. I was left alone with my thoughts for the remainder of that lunchtime.

I left at five thus giving myself some unwind time before having to negotiate my way around that, flight arrival, preparation.

As I strolled from the airport carpark, Flight Tracker told me the plane had landed. Perfect timing I thought as I managed to find a seat with a good view of the arrivals. There she was looking immaculate in her light grey dress that moved around her. I couldn't imagine I would ever again have the privilege, yes privilege of a more captivating sight than Anna who was attracting subtle attention as she walked towards the exit. Privileged because very shortly I would intercept her and the spotlight would fall, ever so briefly, on me. It was only a short flight but she seemed to stand head and shoulders above the others, who looked in comparison to have just completed a non stop trip from Australia, in cattle class. I had to smile as I watched Anna seemingly oblivious to those around her, strolling towards the exit pulling her luggage. I managed to intercept her at the door with a, *"I'll take that Anna"*. She turned and smiled, allowing me to relieve her of the luggage. *"Hello James"*, she said, as we politely kiss on both cheeks. Being a little more observant I realised we were blocking the exit. "We are over there", I said, guiding her towards the carpark thus avoiding any confrontation that could often transpire with the local attitude of, "Get out of my way"! Which would be unacceptable in English but in local French dialect, it was far more intrusive. It took thirty five minutes before we arrived at Anna's house, allowing us the time needed to feel relaxed in each others company. After so many weeks apart, it was time well spent. I distinctively remember Anna touching my leg, albeit for the briefest of moments, on more than one occasion as she alluded on her time in Leeds and Germany. My composure became less than composed as we waited for the gates to open and even less so as I turned into the driveway trying to avoid that dumbfounded look as I took in my surroundings. The covered porch was larger than my living room. Anna was out of the car and waiting at the door but I felt I should avoid being rushed. Be casual James, I was thinking, as I unloaded the suitcase from the boot. Whatever happened I was going to take it in my stride. Anna opened the door and was now waiting in the hallway. The hallway that extended into the open plan living area. I rolled the suitcase to a stop knowing Anna was watching. We faced each other across the hallway. Anna was smiling again.

Yes James, I'm rich.

What could I say to such an obvious reality? I said nothing. I just smiled in return.

"Come on, lets have that drink I promised you. Is red ok"? She said, reaching for a bottle in the rack. Actually I'd prefer a chilled white, I was thinking but who was I to complain over such trivialities. We sat on bar stools around a central island called the Breakfast Bar.

A toast James.

Normally speaking that would entail the lifting of my glass while saying, Cheers. I think Anna was looking for a little more.

I remembered a time when I was about seventeen thinking this was not for me. Here I was, two years into a five year apprenticeship as a future electrician. It worked for now but not something long term. A conversation I remembered having at that time, revolved around Lyndon's latest girlfriend. Lyndon who I'd know since I was seven. "Yeh", he was saying, "and er Dad's rich. Ee's got a Mercedes and ee lives in one of those big ouses up at Derriford". (Love that Plymouth accent.) I had drifted off for a moment but it was helpful. Avoid that trap James.

"So Anna", I raised my glass and said, "To Unfulfilled Dreams".

To Unfulfilled Dreams James and who knows?

I looked at Anna.

What?

Ok if you must know, I was wondering if that was a throw away, "who knows", or an evoking remark based on the few times we've spent together. There is no need to answer, after all, it was just a thought.

Anna turned to look at me.

Are you hungry James because I am and I know Marta has left some meatballs in the fridge. I'll warm some up. Did you know Marta's meatballs have to be included in all my recent functions? There were about ten on the first occasion and the word soon got around. It has therefore been included as a part of any lunch or dinner I've had since, so feel honoured and while they are warming, let me show you around the garden.

Pressing a button, ten metres of patio doors slid silently open. I say patio doors, more, a wall of glass that just disappears. The terrace must have been twenty metres deep at least and expanding to the far corner where the Pagoda sat as a cover for what looked like a perfectly matched set of table and chairs.

Come on James, I want to show you the start of my jacuzzi. The pool house has never really been a functioning part of the pool area so I decided on a conversion.

We walked down the wide and subtly lit steps towards the pool, placed front and centre. Including the lounge area and grass surround I felt, with some poetic licence, a football pitch would struggle to encompass all before me. Anna was strolling ahead so I concentrated on my immediate surroundings. Catching up as Anna swung the door open to reveal a building site. I could see through this, having spent many a year on my own building projects.

So James, this is the sauna area and over here will be the showers and a toilet. They managed to lay the floor and build up the steps to the jacuzzi while I was away. It has underfloor heating which I'm told will be sufficient for my needs but I insisted on a few radiators. What do you think?

I think it's going to be very impressive when completed.

"Do you enjoy a jacuzzi Anna"? I asked.

Not particularly. It's all about the bling James.

I couldn't help myself. I laughed while thinking, this was another world. A world that I had to admit, was almost beyond my comprehension. Anna, I believed, was assuming my laughter was a response to her casual remark about bling. Better I allowed her to believe so, I was thinking, as we headed back to the house. A pleasant aroma of meatballs greeted us as we entered.

This will only take a few minutes. Could you get the cutlery in that drawer and the plates that are warming in the oven.

Duly noted, I complied with the request. Five minutes passed and we were tucking into possibly the tastiest meatballs this side of Moscow.

"How long have you lived here Anna"? I asked, believing it to be a question that would allow Anna free reign with her reply. I was not disappointed.

We bought the place five years ago and began a complete transformation. Walls and windows removed with a state of the art heating system installed. We travelled to a quarry in Italy to find the exact marble flooring we desired which was delivered and installed by the same company. Actually, once finished we discovered a small area where the grain, or lack of grain, didn't match the rest. No problem said the company, who returned two weeks later to dig up the offending patch. Replaced with something more to our liking. Spent another day polishing it in after the replacement. There was a lot of project management required just to keep up with the progress of the work. There are six on-suite bedrooms plus two separate toilets. Choosing basins, baths, showers and tiles seemed to take forever while constantly under pressure from the various trades to make decisions. There was a lot of stress trying to comply to their wishes but also a lot of fun. Spending money on the refinements of a house is always fun.

Watching Anna more than listening, as I found an exuberance that readily flowed through to a distinctive body language that was captivating. Wondering if I would ever have the long lasting opportunity to become bored with such as she, I continued to watch.

"If you've finished", said Anna, looking at my empty plate. I'll show you a feature that was worth its cost and before you ask, yes James it's bling at its best".

Yes Anna, finished and that was delicious. You must pass on my compliments of such a fine cuisine to Marta. I'm sure if she was to flatten them, place them in a bun and set up shop, she might end up wealthier than you!

I don't think I'll be passing on that suggestion James, if you don't mind. Come on, follow me.

We walked to the other end of her expansive lounge where Anna indicated I should sit. She sat opposite as she reached for a remote. While pressing a button Anna explained.

As you can see, it's a rather long way to gather refreshments from the kitchen so I came up with this idea.

While Anna was explaining, the floor between us started to silently rise. All six square metres of it, to reveal a double sided fridge, hot plate and various drawers and cupboards. It came to a halt about a metre and a half above the floor.

There is chilled wine and champagne in the fridge. The red wine is on your left in the large vertical drawer.

This was my cue, or so I perceived, to open said drawer. Not possible until I had closed my mouth in amazement. Sure enough, red wine in abundance.

Of course, there is only the wine here at the moment but when I have guests, this will be stocked with all the necessities needed to enjoy lunch without having to leave your seat. Let's assume for a moment you've decided on your entree

119

and have regained your seat. You'll be wondering if this is a, "Plate on your lap", scenario. Oh, I'm sorry, I will casually say. Just press the green button on the left hand side. Guess what happens next James?
I pressed the button and a small table slowly raised itself. I now had a marble topped table, stopping at just the right height.
"Don't you just love that", said Anna.
Very impressive Anna. Do you use it often?
Not really, it's just for the ....
For the bling Anna?
You're catching on James.
Ok, I was sitting across from this woman who self admitted to being rich and although having spent most of her adult life living outside of Russia seemed to have maintained her Russian heritage. A fascination for all things expensive with a taste that one can only describe as, ostentatious. I could see Anna enjoyed this showmanship so who was I to disappoint.
I am suitably impressed Anna and concede in accepting your reign as queen of bling! I would like to add, if you have any more surprises, could we please leave them for another occasion. I'm not sure I could deal with anymore. Perhaps I'm having a bling overload moment?
Anna laughed. It was one of many redeeming features Anna possessed which, for some unknown reason, would set me at ease. Having thought that, I wondered if it was usual for me to need that .... that blessing of Anna's laughter. I admitted to myself, it was not. Why did I deliberate on that matter? The answer to that was simple. I'd never met anyone like Anna. It was not because of her obvious wealth. That was a recent discovery. It was the complete persona. How real was this woman? Her confidence obvious but what lay beneath? An accomplished and capable woman who'd had practice in hiding her true feelings. Ok, then I would accept that thought, believing that time would reveal all and for the present time, I would carry on as normal. Normal? No chance, as I took in my surroundings.
I'm not sure what to make of you James.
So much for feeing normal.
Don't look so defensive James, it's an observation, nothing critical.
And there was me believing I had that remark covered. Needed to work on that body language as I now realised I was far more transparent than I'd hoped.
*Let me put it another way. You say the right things at the right time. You are attentive. Very amusing. Intelligent conversation, well sometimes. (*Said accompanied by laughter.) *I feel totally at ease in your company and yet I cannot for the life of me, figure you out. I'm usually very good when character assessment is called for.*
"Maybe you're not asking the right questions", I suggested.

If only it was that simple James? Character assessment, apart from the obvious body language, is not necessarily about asking the right questions but more about understanding the answers.

I think I must have had the, I've got no idea what you are talking about look on my face and Anna had spotted it. Not because she was so adept at recognising the signs. People have been recognising those signs in me all my life. Without barely a pause Anna continued.

For instance. A few weeks ago I played a league game with a woman I'd never met before. We spent half an hour in the changing rooms, pre match and I found her to be very casual and likeable. The conversation revolved around tennis and at one point I said, "Gosh, I hate losing. I get so mad with myself. My friend said it was because I was insecure. Maybe that is so, I told my friend but it is so difficult sometimes. The children. Money problems. It's not easy since my husband ran off with a younger woman". You know, she might have been able to play tennis but the psychological advantage laid with me. Poor me. As it turned out, she was the better player but I won.

If I understand you correctly Anna, you built up a false persona hoping it might some how affect her play.

That's ...... close I suppose but the point is, I won. Please don't hate me James".

The ideal moment had arrived. Not that I was particularly looking for it but there it was. Anna was feeling vulnerable. She was waiting for my acceptance of her previous comment.

Would you mind if I kiss you?

Before she could answer, I leant forward. Placed my open hand on her cheek and kissed her. It was intended as a, "There is nothing to forgive Anna, I like you", sort of kiss but Anna responded. Sitting on bar stools while facing each other was not the most ideal scenario when it was obvious that it was restrictive and awkward. Without wanting to disturb this free flow of kissing, I slid off my stool and as I did so, Anna opened her legs. My mind was in turmoil! We were close contact kissing, I thought, as I moved my hands around her face and head. Minutes passed and I wasn't sure what to do next. Your bedroom is where? Came to mind but I momentarily pulled away. Not so far as to make any difference but far enough. Our eyes met. If only I could have read the message they willingly portrayed. No such luck! I felt I had to diffuse this situation. Not because I wouldn't love for it to carry on to an inevitable conclusion, it was just that I couldn't be sure that it was the way it would go. I had an image of Anna looking startled and asking me to leave. So I played it safe. I moved away and in a continuously fluid motion, reach for our glasses. Handing one to Anna I said, "To winners. May they always utilise their advantages to the glory of the one". Anna understood immediately (or so she seemed to think.) and said, "Thank You James, perhaps I'm now getting to understand you a little better". I have no idea what she meant by that. What did I just say? Something about the glory of one. Why was it all the seemingly important things I said, I couldn't recall? Perhaps I would remember later when I had a moment void of this wonderful distraction. Or perhaps it was the kisses she was referring to?

I think we might both later come to realise this to be the ideal moment for me to say, Thank you so much for such a, most memorable evening Anna but it's getting late and I should leave you to ...... to have a clear conscience when you wake in the morning.

Have I overstepped the mark? I was smiling as I said it.

"Amusing, understanding, and so sweet", said Anna, as she leant forward to momentarily, devour my lips in hers. She pulled back slowly saying, "Let me walk you to your car".

There was no sign of disappointment but neither one of relief. Anna hid her feelings well or she was signalling her intent and I completely missed it. It wouldn't be the first time.

Almost forgot Anna. I've booked a restaurant for eight thirty tomorrow evening in Antibes. Would you like me to pick you up?

Why don't I pick you up. You live near the hospital in La Fontonne, don't you? It's on the way. I'll arrive early, that way we can have a glass of wine before driving into Antibes. Message me your address and I can be there for eight.

Two thoughts sprang to mind. Anna was taking charge but more importantly, I had about an hour and a half to tidy up after work before Anna arrived at eight. I'd leave work early. As I headed down the drive, I saw Anna from the rear view mirror wondering if she would wave. She didn't but I did, just before I disappeared out of sight. There were moments during that fifteen minute drive home that I tried, without much success, to understand what had happened in the last few hours. Certain details flashed through my head with absolute clarity. Anna was rich and surrounded by that richness one could almost assume she was born to into. It was the same Anna I met that first time in the pizza restaurant. Was it the surroundings that confused me? Why would that confuse me. After all, spending time with a beautiful, intelligent Russian millionaire shouldn't be confusing. You want to bet! Just concentrate on the drive James. Just concentrate on that. And so I did. Once home, a decaf Nespresso and cigarette in easy reach, I unravelled my thoughts. Not in the same league, was the prominent thought. Consoled knowing Anna was aware of this, separation. I couldn't avoid the question. "What does she see in me?" I decided not to dwell on that aspect of the equation and so I turned the whole thing around. Did I feel comfortable in Anna's company? Yes I did, was the answer. Therefore it was simple. Go with the flow and see where it took me. It was after midnight when I headed for the bedroom, satisfied I was in control of my life. Bring it on! (Oh what bravado.)

The following day was a sunshine day. A cloudless sky with a warmth in the air, which suited my mood to perfection. As I locked the door prior to leaving for work, I changed my mind. I unlocked the door and grabbed the keys to the Figaro. A day for the open top. There was the added bonus when taking the Figaro, people smiled and even waved in appreciation of that unusual car which enabled me to maintain that upbeat mood. Arriving early, as always. A chance to send Anna a quick message.

Good morning Anna. How is the conscience this morning. Intact, I think. May I suggest, now knowing where you live, we meet in Biot. I know most of Biot is closed at this time of year but there is the Café Brun. Ideal for a late evening drink. I'm sure you're off to play tennis so get back when you can. ps: A very most enjoyable evening and I'm sure you will pick me up on my usage of the bad English language. In fact it was a, very very most enjoyable evening. Later Anna x

A cunning plan that availed me the need to "clean my place up". Not that I minded the idea of Anna coming around but I would need more than a few hours to bring the place up to scratch. It was early that afternoon when I received a reply.

Hi James. Yes you were right, tennis was on the agenda, in fact I have just finished a good match with my friend Bev and am now sipping an ice chilled orange juice.

The obvious answer to that Anna would be, Lucky Bev!

Yes. That's what she said when her husband went to work in Africa for six months! Did I detect some jealousy in your previous remark James?

To answer that question Anna I would say, once women get to know me they find it difficult to live without me. So jealousy has never had the need to figure in my life. Did I mention I have an ego problem?.

Will Anna understand the humour?

Is that a veiled attempt at an invitation to get to know you better or just a boastful remark James?

Well read Anna. It was a boastful attempt at getting an invitation. I have to admit, getting to know you better would be a joy. Which conveniently brings us to the subject of this evening. I should be able to make Biot sometime after eight thirty.

Lets make it nine James which would suit me better as I have a late school run. I am picking up Tanya after her ballet lesson. We can meet on the corner at the entrance to the village. A busy day ahead. Tennis. Lunch. Nails. (I'm thinking of a Pale Rose.) School run and You. Lunch has arrived so we can talk later. In fact, why don't you call me this evening. Anytime after eight would be nice. Have a pleasant afternoon James. x

"Hey James, are you going to stare into space much longer or are you coming?" asked Stuart. It was lunchtime. Which meant the guys were waiting for their taxi. Two cars needed today as there were nine for lunch and I just knew without having to think about it, there would be little chance of getting back on time. Why was it only I who had concerns over a late return? Needless to say, on our return, we all booked the extra half an hour.

Working back from the meeting at nine. The phone call around eight. I deduced, six would be the ideal time to leave the office which nicely coincided with my thoughts of all being achieved for the day by that time. The final hours rolled slowly by. I found myself on my sofa, ready and available a good half an hour before the phone call. The thought crossed my mind that maybe I should be compiling a list of topics to discuss when talking with Anna. It was a process I'd often debated but in the end I inevitably believed, winging it, was the preferred method. I was not a list person. I should be, as my memory was never one of my strong points. What were my strong points? A conversation for another time, I was thinking. Now where was I?

Hi Anna. I have to admit I'm unsure as to the reason for this call as we will be meeting in an hour or so but your, undeniable not presumptuous wish, is my command and before you chastise me for that presumptuous remark I have to add, I'm winging it. The problem with this approach is the inevitability of getting it wrong on occasion ......

Before you say more James, I think you should know, I've just picked up Elena and you're on speaker phone. Perhaps you can talk with her as I drive? Just joking, particularly as Elena has a most horrific look on her face and I can imagine yours as not being, shall I say, overjoyed with the possibility. I'm sorry James, I was enjoying the thought of testing your "winging it" theory to the limit. But you must admit ....

Hi Elena! Your mother finds it amusing to think there would be no chance of me pushing my limits. I'm not sure how you feel about the possibility but for me, how could I be pushing those limits when I have the chance of talking with, as your mother describes you, an absolute jewel. How are you Elena ?

I'm very well, thank you James. Actually my mother described you in a not dissimilar way, in fact ....

Ok you two, stop it! The two of you ganging up on dear sweet moi. What have I done to deserve such as this? And Elena stop looking at me with that oh so innocent look. Fortunately we have reached the gate so just a chance to say, see you at nine James .... maybe!

I didn't bother answering. It was surprising how quickly one got used to Anna ending her conversations on the phone with no thought of waiting for a reply. I didn't see this as a character flaw, in fact I found it somewhat refreshing. When on FaceTime with Tony, one of my closest friends, there was that point when one of us would say, "I think we're waffling now?" To which the other would agree. We ended the conversation with a, Catch up soon, and were gone. So many conversations revolved around trivia in the latter part of said conversations. A ten minute conversation could quite easily be reduced to five.

Anna's delivery was therefore refreshing. That was how I saw it. With the plus, on that occasion, of hearing Anna barely being able to contain her laughter throughout. Note James. She has a wicked sense of humour. Had I noted that before? That memory of mine!

Time had passed but still time enough for a cigarette and beer before the shower when a thought struck me. I'd created a ritual. My shower time had to fall after the last cigarette and before Anna. Shower. Clean clothes. Teeth cleaned and just as I leave, the sucking of a few Tic Tacs. Was it worth it? It was not being me. If there was one thing I'd learnt about women, it was the no bullshit approach worked. If for no other reason that it threw out confusion but with a certain amount of respect. Honesty was an approach that just seemed to work. And here I was, entering into subterfuge. Ah well. Rituals were ok. ...... In the right circumstances. And I did believe, that could have been one of those circumstances.

Nine o'clock and I was dutifully waiting on the corner. Twenty minutes later, Anna's Mercedes came into view. I walked to the car park to meet her.

Hello James. have you been waiting long?

I could have lied and said, "No, I was running late and arrived just before you".

How is you're simple arithmetic Anna?

She was looking at me with a questioning look.

If you were to work on the time we were to meet and allow ten minutes as the minimum time I would arrive beforehand so as to be certain not to keep someone waiting, that would come close to the time I've been waiting.

She laughed as she strolled over to give me a kiss on each cheek.

You've just told me off, haven't you James?

I was about to reply but I could see Anna had already moved on and was no longer interested in a reply and as we walked up the hill from the car park, Anna put her arm under mine. I was wrong. Anna wanted a moment or two to get her thoughts together.

I can see you are not annoyed. You compiled an, oh so delicate way, of reprimanding me for my lateness in a way that I'm not familiar with. What does get you annoyed James?

"Middle lane drivers?" I said.

I was sure that wasn't the answer Anna was expecting but I wasn't sure I wanted to involve myself in such a philosophical discussion on relationships while out of breath climbing that hill from the car park.

No, I mean what gets you annoyed in relationships.

Only another twenty metres and then it flattens out. Take a deep breath James.

Why don't we discuss this in the warmth of the bar once drinks are served?

"Alright James", said Anna as she drew herself towards me.

It had been a number of years since I'd frequented that bar and those times were summer times. Sat outside in the early evening enjoying that shady cul-de-sac with a circle of friends. Rarely visited in those, post winter, early spring months. The bar was all but empty. Three guys at the bar and a couple in the far corner. Not quite the ambience I expected. But hey! The log fire was burning which immediately drew Anna's attention.

"Can you get me a red wine?" asked Anna.

I walked to the bar and recognised the barman. Some things never change. We exchanged greetings with neither knowing the others name but recognising familiar territory. "Goede avond", I said. (At least I remembered he was Dutch.) "Hi", he replied. So much for the sincere greeting.

Could I have a glass of wine and a small Kilkenny, if you still have it on draft.

"A small Kilkenny"? he asked. I was caught out. Subterfuge reared its ugly head. Where was the honesty in ordering a small beer? I was assuming Anna would rather see me drinking a small beer. Actually, I thought, she would prefer if I joined her in a glass of wine.

"You're right", I said. "Make that a pint". Anna having made the decision on appropriate seating as we walked in, I headed towards the table chosen, close to the fire. The, "What annoyed me", conversation in my head as I approached. Having no idea how I would reply to such a question there was a part of me hoping it would not be the key conversation of the evening.

I must apologise for keeping you waiting James but you will have to realise, time keeping is really not my strong point. Actually that is not true. I'm always on time for tennis. For picking up and dropping off Elena. Appointments with lawyers and the like, it is the social engagements that let me down.

That was going in the right direction. A direction that was not about me but Anna's time keeping. I noticed her nails. A pale rose.

It's not a problem Anna I will make sure I have a book to read for any subsequent meetings and anyway, how could I not forgive a lady with such beautifully prepared nails.

Well thank you, kind sir. I took the appointment today especially for my nail addict. I might not be good where time keeping is concerned but you see, I can be thoughtful in other ways.

I already think you're thoughtful Anna. I am trying to play down my nail fetish, which has only become apparent in recent months, thanks mainly to you. I have therefore decided to encompass all possible future fetishes within the boundaries of acceptability. I do feel obliged to mention, your continual reminder of my one and only, recently acknowledged fetish, isn't helping me! On the plus side. I appreciate the effort of having nails immaculately presented.

We were getting along just fine. Compliments had been paid and duly accepted. All with an air of casual humour. A group of four arrived. The two girls sat a few tables down while the guys headed for the bar. It was an instantaneous distraction that lasted no longer than a few seconds but enough time for Anna to change the subject.

126

So what annoys you James?
She was, at the very least, expecting a short list of annoyances. Do I make them up? Or was this a moment that needed thought before answering. After all I'd been involved in enough relationships. I must be able to resurrect something.
Let me get you another drink Anna.
Why? Do you think I'll need one after listening to your catalogue of annoyances?
I smiled and turned, noticing the guys had just left the bar. Talking of timing, I was thinking. *"Same again, please."* I now had maybe two minutes to compile that list before the drinks were served. What annoyed me in relationships? Come on James. It couldn't be that difficult. Placing Anna's wine and my beer on the table I sat. Anna was saying nothing, just looking at me with the expression of someone expecting answers.
Ok Anna! If you could please turn off that, Spanish Inquisition look and turn on that, Oh what is my beloved James going to tell me look, I might be able to answer your question.
She laughed.
That look has always worked James. Nobody has thought of asking me to assume another. Perhaps I'd be more interested in knowing how you saw through my facade of Spanish Inquisition. You are looking at me James with a smug regard that tells me I could have difficulty in extracting that information. Let me tell you something about me which might help you understand why I am the way I am.
That was fine with me. Anything to change the subject.
For many years now I have lived in an environment that precipitates a possible disaster. When I say disaster, I mean it in the loosest possible sense of the word. My disasters are of the social kind. When one invites fifty or so people around for a Tea Party, some are friends. Some are acquaintances. Others are people invited for business reasons. As I believe I've already mentioned, I do have a skill in this department but so much of those learnt skills, are of a false persona. Sometimes I have wondered who is the real me? But I digress. The point is, I thought I was accomplished in the art of deception. I am not saying I'm devious, it is after all, just a facade but it's a facade that I find necessary.
Anna was looking straight into my eyes, as she had been doing while giving me the low down on something I vaguely understood. I was not saying I didn't understand the concept. Most of us are guilty of some kind of "cover up" which was dependent on who we were with at the time but Anna when she was talking about Tea parties, …. it was but with a vague concept of such a life. I'd seen it in the movies and as I tried to place Anna in a similar scenario, she continued. Actually, she didn't? She was just watching me. I got the feeling she was waiting for something. Had she figured out that for the last brief seconds I was wool gathering? I gave her my full attention.

I see you're back now James.

She did realise I was wool gathering! Shit. She was good.

I've been wondering how to phrase the next part. You've managed to provoke an inner me that I usually reserve for myself and to a certain extent, for my girls and housekeeper. Don't look so worried James, I think this is a good thing.

This isn't a worried look Anna. This is a look of bewilderment.

Oh James how you manage to turn my serious moment into trivia and I don't mind in the least. But I will not deviate from my original thought. So you will just have to sit there and be bewildered. I'm trying to tell you. Gosh! What am I trying to tell you? This is unlike me to divulge such personal parts of my character so I will just say, I feel at ease with you James and strangely for me, I feel I can trust you. I do hope that is not a misguided thought?

Once again, Anna had my mind reeling. How was I supposed to answer that. As answer it, I must. I reached out and placed my hand on hers. (Was that Harry met Sally?)

I am going to answer that with the most serious intent I can muster Anna. As the Bishop Paul Morton once said, "I am what you see." If you see a trustworthy man, then that's who you see. I'm not hiding who I am from you Anna. So believe what you see. I'm sure, as time goes by, my idiosyncrasies will begin to shine through.

Anna smiled.

But to continue in a serious vain. I enjoy being in the company of intelligent women and you are certainly that. I don't think you are deceptive Anna. You are the many faces of a person trying to come to terms with who you are. You are alone for the first time in a long time and are placing that toe in the water with every reason to be concerned about what might bite.

Absolutely no idea where that came from but I seemed to have Anna's attention, perhaps I should change the subject. Back to the original question? Go for it James!

You asked me earlier what annoyed me in a relationship, well I can say with much certainty, you don't. You do like to talk and in the past I have, on occasion, found that annoying but in your case, I like to hear you talk. Even when you seem at times, to be talking for talking sake.

Do you really think so James. Do you really think I sometimes talk for talking sake? I prefer to call it effervescent!

Anna reached across and placed her hand on mine.

You still haven't told me what annoys you, apart from possibly talking too much.

Ok Anna, let me think. Jealousy, as it creates restrictions and therefore constrictions in a relationship. It's all about trust. It's not something one has to earn, it's something to be given. If one trusts ones partner completely I feel everything else will follow. Love and trust.

I placed my free hand over hers and with as much sincerity I could muster, I said,
Can I trust you Anna?
Inevitably, the smile from the corner of my mouth, gave me away.
You can get me another drink James and maybe I'll tell you.
Saying so with the start of laughter in her voice as she pulled her hands free from mine but squeezing gentle as she did so. The barman, seeing me approaching reached for a fresh glass and started to pour a pint. The four at the table were watching me with a quizzical look. I'd seen that look before.
Excusez-moi mais savez-vous à qui vous ressemblez?
"Gordon Ramsey?" I replied.
Oui, C'est ca.
I replied, with a smile, in English. "I might be English but no, I am not Gordon Ramsey". "Eleven euros fifty", said the barman. I saw a possibility and was wondering if Anna would be up to it.
"Would you like a photo of the five of us?" I asked the group. I could see by their reaction it was the right question to ask.
Anna can you take a photo of the five of us?
Not only did Anna leap up at my request but strode across the floor to organise the group while suggesting she took photos from everyones phone. We left the group full of smiles and bonne amis. That brief interlude had changed the dynamics of our conversation. It became lighter and more carefree. Anna was telling me about her up and coming visit to Geneva.
It's so convenient from Nice. Forty five minutes by Easyjet and Tanya picks me up at the airport. We head straight to the Birdie cafe. They do an amazing brunch and the coffee is second to none and of course, there is always time for shopping before heading back to Tanya's.
So when do you leave?
Sunday morning, getting into Geneva at ten twenty and before you ask, I'll be there for about ten days.
I wasn't thinking of asking that. I was more thinking about the possibility of getting some chocolate, this time around.
Anna laughed.
Actually Anna I was more interested in your departure time as I'd like to take you to the airport.
Oh James! How sweet of you but I've already arranged for Bev to take me and it just so happens, it conveniently falls at a time when she has to be in Nice.
Although I fully intended on taking Anna to the airport I was, to some relief, grateful of the outcome. Sunday morning would be the time the last trucks were unloaded. I wouldn't necessarily have to be there but it wouldn't be right if I wasn't.

The offer stays open Anna. You never know, Bev might have a chance of playing tennis with "That" guy on Sunday morning.
Anna was looking at me slightly confused. Why did I say that? I had to talk my way out of this one.
Oh come on Anna. Are you telling me there isn't a particular available and desirable male at the club who has not come to the attention of you single women? And if what you have said of Bev, possibly a few married women as well. All I am saying is, if I was you, I would call her Saturday evening to check on that possibility, or the next thing you might hear are the stories circulating around the club of Bev's sudden disappearance with ...... André, the tennis coach. So ..... take solace in the thought you would have me as back up driver.
Anna was reaching uncontrollable laughter as I gave her my best look of, "Innocent of any reason for her laughter", as she approached her, "Giggling like a school girl" moment. There was something I'd often wondered about and now might be a good time to ask. It could help Anna control her laughter.
How did you manage to achieve this air of Englishness? Apart from when in uncontrollable moments of laughter. I mean, for christ sake! You're Russian and yet your pronunciation and eloquence would put many a BBC newsreader to shame.
Anna managed to control her laughter.
Well James, I think that's a conversation for the next time. It's getting late and we should be making a move.
I checked my watch. It was eleven thirty. Early start and a long day tomorrow. As much as I'd like to spend more time in Anna's company, I had to admit, she was right. With a show of reluctance, I agreed with Anna and started to rise.
For the next time Anna. I look forward to that tale of discovery. "Let me help you with that", I said, as I reached for her coat.
And so gallant James.
As we headed for the cars Anna once again put her arm in mine. Only this time I was sure she was doing so with more affection. Maybe just my imagination? We walked in silence for awhile which was unusual, certainly for Anna.
I was just thinking James and while doing so I realised we are walking in silence.
Was this woman reading my mind?
..... and do you know James, I feel comfortable with that. I think that is a definite plus. To be able to feel at ease during the silent moments.
I was thinking of saying, "Not too many of those while you're around Anna", but thought better of it. Instead, I smiled. Small talk entered the equation until we reached Anna's car.
Thank you for the evening James. Most enjoyable.
A kiss on each cheek followed by a slightly uncomfortable hug and she was in the car. Seat belt on and gone. It was not just a phone thing, I realised. Anna made a quick exit and possibly one could say, abrupt, in any and all

130

circumstances. It was her way. No dilly dallying. Everything had been concluded so why hang around? I was left wondering as I drove home, if it wasn't a Russian trait. Must Google that.

Hello Anna,I started to write you an email. Unfortunately by line four, I realised it barely made sense. Therefore, I will revert to simplicity.
Delightful perfume.
Delightful company.
Leaving one wanting more.
Sweet Dreams Anna. x
Timely wish of sweet dreams James, as I am already in bed.
Had a great time, although we both were tired. Thank you for the evening. And sleep well.

Not quite the response I was hoping for but then again, nothing negative. Time I went to bed.

I received a message the next day around eleven.

My last morning of tennis before departure and I've put my shoulder out! Fortunately I have an osteopath who will always find time for me. I'm seeing him at four. God it hurts.

Once again, I had no idea how to respond to that. No, Hi James. How was your day? Hope not too chaotic? Oh and btw, I've hurt my shoulder playing tennis but it's ok as I have an appointment with an osteopath this afternoon. How much of a sympathy vote does Anna need?

That's awful Anna. You have my most profound sympathy regarding the pain you must be enduring. (Do you think that was a bit of an overkill?) I'll get in touch later to see how you are doing. I'm sure your osteopath will have you "right as rain" in no time. In the meanwhile I will send an aura of positive thought your way. I'm sure it will help.

No response from Anna. Then why would she? Everything had been said and we await the conclusion. Post osteopath.

Managed to have everything wrapped up by seven so I was back in the apartment by seven fifteen. Beer from the fridge and as I sat on the terrace I noticed something on the floor. It was Robert's grass. To hell with it. Half an hour later and I was writing Anna a message.

Have been thinking about poor you. Hope all went well with the osteopath. If in need of TLC, I know somebody available after 21:30 most evenings. Wishing you a restful sleep. J x

An immediate response?

Oh thank you James, you're so sweet. I am indeed feeling miserable today, but my shoulder is much recovered. TLS (whatever it may stand for, but I guess, something to do with saving lives) is not to be shunned. "Tender loving care" or "Tremendous lullaby song" could be both appropriate. Btw, could you give me the number of that somebody? Just in case…

131

Tender Loving Care is what it is Anna, and reference that number, I do believe you have it. (Look under James in your contacts.) I could try reading by your bedside. Guaranteed you'll be fast asleep in ten minutes.
I received an immediate reply.
Zzzzzzzz Good Night, James.

Chapter Eight

And that was where I thought it ended. I left messages over the next few weeks which finally cumulated in a drawn out email with no particular content as I had, by this time, accepted Anna's disappearance to be permanent.

Six weeks since my "Good Night James" message I found myself in Paris. An annual event for the company which Will and I had managed to keep to ourselves for five years. Six days at Roland Garros. A days work leaving five to enjoy the tennis and be paid for doing so. It had become the bane of our colleagues lives. No sooner was April over than Roland Garros reared it's ugly head. The time when Will and James went to Paris to watch tennis. I would spend two or three days preparing the set for ease of installation. It wouldn't do to miss out on more tennis than we had to. Not including the added bonus of five nights in Paris. Will and I would pass comments between ourselves on the good times ahead while the guys pretend not to notice. Either that or cries of, "Enough of Roland Bloody Garros"!

So we found ourselves in Paris. The set built and the next morning we decided to check out the Suzanne LenWill Court prior to opening time. Once in we climbed to the uppermost seats and sat to watch a couple of guys practicing, soon to realise, one was Andy Murray. I took some photos with the virtually empty stadium as a background. After awhile Will and I moved on. Time for coffee. Working in Paris for an American TV company meant they were set up. (Is that a pun, I wonder?) They had a Tuck Shop. Coffee. Tea. Toast. Chocolate. Biscuits and an abundance of fruit. It was half an hour before the gates opened and as it was a pleasant morning we decided on coffee on the terrace, on the top floor overlooking three outdoor courts. If needed we were a phone call away and two minutes from the set. Past experience had proven we would not be needed until the Director was satisfied with the layout which wouldn't be until tomorrow, about midday. Will decided to go for a short walkabout while I stayed on the terrace happy to have another coffee. Checking out the photos I'd just taken, I had an idea. Send one to Anna with an amusing anecdote attached. Deciding on one of many photos was not an easy task but a decision was finally made. A photo of an almost empty stadium with, off in the distance, four players on court. "Hey Anna can you see me. I'm the one just behind Andy Murray. Third row up on the left."

I knew I could have done better but I'd pressed send and to my dumbfounded surprise, I got a reply a few minutes later.

Yes, I think I see you. The blue shorts and knobbly knees.

I hadn't expected a response. Having received one I didn't know what to do about it. First reaction was the realisation that Anna had come back, and with humour. That was a good sign, wasn't it? Now what do I say? Do I leave it until my pulse rate reduces and am then able to collect my thoughts? The decision was taken from my hands as Will returned. "Did you get the message from Bill"? asked Will. Obvious from my non plus glance Will realised I hadn't. He continued. "We are needed on the set. Something about wanting a backdrop". Once on the set, Bill explained. "We need a plant against that post about six feet tall (and about three wide to hide the background". "Sure Bill", I said. You don't say no to the Director. Not possible. Will, already on the phone. No doubt scouring addresses of the local florists. We had just passed security and were heading into the TV compound. I stopped Will and suggested he looked sideways. To hide the "ugly" opening of the compound, potted plants had been arranged on both sides of the entrance. Will, being a Liverpool Lad of old, understood immediately. "You're suggesting we steal one of these"? said Will. I gave him my innocent look. "I was thinking of borrowing one", said I. "And how do you see us carrying that past security"? "I was thinking of getting a small trolley and wheeling it past", said I. And that's what we did. Bill was very happy and as we wondered off set, the Floor Manager asked how the hell we managed to come up with a small tree so promptly. Will answered. "It's what we do"!

An hour has passed but still no chance of seclusion.

"Let's go for lunch before the masses arrive", said Will.

It was the middle of the afternoon before I had a chance to think of my reply.

No Anna, that's Andy Murray. I'm the fit looking one giving Rafael Nadal a run for his money. Andy is watching. If you zoom in you might just see he is sat there, open mouthed with a look of amazement on his face.

There were a thousand possible replies spinning around my head. For no particular reason, I chose that one. I wondered if I should add more but decided ridiculous and simple humour to be the way to go. Maybe I was wrong. No reply all afternoon. As Will and I walked back to the hotel that evening, I kicked myself for thinking the reply would contain any substance that might intrigue Anna. We stopped at our usual bar on the way to the hotel in order to down a beer, or two.

Two is the limit as at ten Euros a pint, half our daily allowance disappeared. It was eight when we reached the hotel and as Will had the smoking terrace we agreed to meet in his room about nine, having already decided, not to venture out that evening. Eight thirty and I was ready to leave my room when I got a message.

It's been awhile James. All I can say is it is me, not you, so don't worry. I'll get back to that one day but for the moment I have to admit to forgetting your ways. Perhaps I should have reread earlier emails before I responded? Then I would have realised it wouldn't have been an obvious response. I congratulate you. Before I write more, I have a simple question that has no need for your funny repartee. When do you return from Paris?

"Wednesday evening about six", I replied

She asked a question. I'd answered. Was she expecting more? Where was Anna going with this? Whatever she was thinking I was feeling optimistic. Nine o'clock approached so I gathered together, a six pack and headed, once more, for the door. I got a reply from Anna. I put down the six pack and read.

Six. That gives you time enough to tidy up and arrive á chez moi for nine. I'd like to explain.

I was glad I'd put that six pack down. I would have dropped it! Six weeks had passed and Anna would like to explain? What was I supposed to make of that? She would like to explain and I needed to respond. Will called. "Are you coming up or am I drinking alone"? My head was spinning. A drink at her place. You don't do that if you intend a goodbye? "On my way Will", was my reply. I tried to empty my head of the bewilderment.

I've thought long and hard over my response Anna. As becomes obvious when one considers the amount of time that's passed between us. I count fifty four seconds since your last message but you know I am referring to our last meeting. I'll be there! Now off to get very drunk and when I awake tomorrow, my hangover will be consoled when I can focus long enough to reread your invitation. I wrote but didn't send, in the hope when I reread the whole, it made some kind of sense. I faltered but still didn't press. I picked up the beer and headed out.

Stood outside of Will's door, after the thirty seconds it had taken me to get there, I had second thoughts about pressing send. Should I really send this? Couldn't I just leave it at, "I'll be there"? No I couldn't! Anna was expecting more. I pressed send. I was giving her more I decided and now it was up to her to decide if I was actually going to get very drunk. I didn't get very drunk but being in a very jubilant mood, let's just say, the corridor seemed a lot narrower on the way back to my room. My phone! It was on silent! Anna had replied.

I know you're not going to get drunk James because if you were you wouldn't have told me. (I must say I am quietly pleased with myself for what I am sure is a correct analogy between what you say and what you do.) I realise I am asking for trouble when divulging my thoughts but maybe I only did so to get a reaction. You are now aware James, I can be as perspicacious as you.

Ok. Two thoughts. What does perspicacious mean and when did she send that? Forty minutes ago. Almost two hours since I'd sent my message. In the right time frame for a reply but I hesitated. Then I hit on a response.

Sorry Anna but too drunk to read your message. I'll try in the morning if my hangover permits.

Feeling good about my reply. I checked for spelling mistakes as my keyboard could often be in French. Then read it a few times. Send! It was late so unlikely to get a response tonight, I thought, slipping under the covers. Life was good. No sooner my head hit the pillow Anna replied.

I KNOW YOU'RE NOT GOING TO GET DRUNK JAMES BECAUSE IF YOU WERE YOU WOULDN'T HAVE TOLD ME. (I MUST SAY I AM QUIETLY PLEASED WITH MYSELF FOR WHAT I AM SURE IS A CORRECT ANALOGY BETWEEN WHAT YOU SAY AND WHAT YOU DO.) I REALISE I AM ASKING FOR TROUBLE WHEN DIVULGING MY THOUGHTS BUT MAYBE I ONLY DID SO TO GET A REACTION. YOU ARE NOW AWARE JAMES, I CAN BE AS PERSPICACIOUS AS YOU.

Thinking of you struggling to read the message in the morning I thought I should repeat in capitals. Good night James. x

I didn't reply. There was no need. Anna had given her parting words. Good night James. Good night Anna I was thinking, while drifting off to sleep wishing tomorrow was Wednesday.

Will and I were first on the set the next morning and fell into the unasked for routine of taking the protective bashes off the cameras. We were used to an early start but it was evident the camera crew didn't see the necessity to be quite so punctual. Invariably arriving with a pronounced hangover. There but for the Grace of, thought I. It was eleven something before I had a moment alone. I found a relatively quiet spot inside the compound and tried to analyse Anna's last two but the same, messages. The same but with a little extra. The thought of a response wavered between continuing along the same vein of accepted hangover morning and what that entailed or changing the subject. "Just woke up Anna. Could you please send the message again but in even larger capitals, if possible". Implying I was drunk or, I'm still playing the game. Would that frustrate Anna? Still not knowing but maybe at the same time realising she wouldn't mind either way. That was the risk.

Hi Anna. For the record, Will and I sat on his terrace and consumed no more than two bottles of red. To which I attribute less than half a bottle to myself. Now back to the tennis and the glorious sunshine. (Actually its cloudy but I don't seem to notice. I wonder why?) I look forward to the trouble you will cause while divulging your thoughts. Enjoy your day Anna.

Time to catch up with Will as it was approaching lunchtime. I called and we arranged to meet at the cafeteria. On the way I thought of Anna. Oh what a surprise. Acknowledging the obvious with an inner smile but unable to work out why Anna reestablished contact. Did it matter why? She had, that was surely enough. Try to go with the flow, I told myself. I received a nudge in the back. "Hi Will", I said without turning, realising I'd stopped moving and the queue was building up behind. Chicken a la orange with stir fried vegetables. While eating we checked the afternoons tennis schedules. No Brits playing but there was the possibility of a cute Serbian on court nine around three. Worth a look we decided. I put thoughts of Anna aside as we headed out to court nine. Always remembering to put phones on silent, we sat. Not too many people as neither were seeded. By the finish, the place was full for what turned out to be an excellent match. And she was definitely cute. Unfortunately, she lost but not for the want of encouragement as she seemed to be the favourite among the majority of the crowd who, as it turned out, were mostly male. We remained seated waiting for the crowds to disperse.

You seem to be in an "enlightened" mood James. Or to put that another way, Who is she?

"Anna", I replied.

The Russian?

Yes, the Russian.

Now expecting a throw away remark from Will, I was surprised to find him interested. So I told him about the, turn of events. Wills reply brought a smile to my face. "Go with the flow", he said. "Good advice. I'll try and do that". Was my reply.

The days, so slowly drifted by. I could have and was very tempted to inundate Anna with message after message but sensibly considered that not to be the way to go. So I kept it to a minimum. I sent a few photos with short messages. One I didn't send was a picture of me wearing a T shirt, sent as a present with the words, "I can't believe it but I'm in love with an Italian", imprinted across the chest. That one, I sent to Emanuela. Never to receive a reply, I might add. None of that mattered. Tuesday finally arrived and we prepared for departure the following morning. The floor manager, Joe, had some concerns. My positive and enthusiastic approach to his concerns were met with relief, knowing Will and I would not be leaving until he was satisfied all was well.

Why did you agree to that James? How are we going to figure that camera change? To be able to get the angle he wants is impossible with all the cabling around! Hey Will. It's what we do! And anyway, I've got a plan to overcome this "slight" problem.

Having explained my idea, Will relaxed. "Let's get it done", he said. The set will be ours by four. A visit to Castorama to buy the necessary materials and by six all was ready. Joe, as promised, returned at six thirty to inspect.

"Are you guys free for Wimbledon"? he said with a smile.
"If we can do a deal on Flushing Meadows", was Will's immediate reply.
Never one to miss out on an opportunity. That was Will. "You guys got time for a beer?" Will and I looked at each other. Shrugged our shoulders. Looked around and satisfied with the work I said, "Let's go Joe!" As we took that ten minute walk to the closest bar the sensible me made a decision. I accepted the responsibility as I knew Will would happily drink until the early hours and worry about the six o'clock start at five to six. As it transpired, we had a good time with Joe and were heading back to the hotel at the reasonable time of ten thirty. I called Will at five thirty to ask if he was ready, knowing full well I'd aroused him from his slumber.
I had time to pen a quick message to Anna.
Hi Anna. I went to bed at an acceptable eleven thirty but found sleep eluding me. After what seemed an eternity I must have drifted off, only to be awakened with a rendition of, Castles Made of Sand, in what seemed just a few minutes later. My first thought, (coincidently, my last thought of the night before) and you might find this difficult to accept as the meek and mild you that you are, I thought of you. (Too many you's?) We are leaving in ten minutes. Don't ask why I am potentially upsetting your sleep by sending this message Actually, you can ask why, if the ping of your phone wakes you when I press send.
I got an immediate reply!
So sweet James to be thinking of me just before you leave and as you rightly said, the meek and mild me finds it difficult to accept. Oh to be so! And yes, you did wake me but do not be concerned. I will go back to sleep knowing you care. That's a good feeling. Good Night James. Or should that be Good morning?
We had a ten hour drive ahead dealing with the fantasy world french drivers accept as the norm. When asked what the indicator switch should be used for, most women would nonchalantly say, My handbag? I knew it was an old joke but I sometimes wondered. In any event, did I care? Not in the least! I was seeing Anna this evening but was caught in another of those dilemmas. Was she expecting an immediate response to the why I sent the message at such an ungodly hour or was she now drifting off in the hope I didn't. I had ten minutes before we left so why not create the message and send later. Sometimes James you amaze me with your consideration and perception, I was thinking. Pen a reply and get out of Paris. As was the established custom, I got us out of Paris. Getting out was only superseded by the problem of getting in but it was still a problem. Leaving Roland Garros and five minutes later we were negotiating the Périphérique. Twenty past six and just the right side of total mayhem but one could never assume the driver either side might not, at any moment, decide he or she would prefer to be in our lane. Driving a twenty cube does give one a certain presence. Unfortunately that presence didn't always work with Parisienne drivers. Thirty minutes later and we were heading towards Lyon on

a virtually empty highway. Two hours on. Two hours off, was how we worked it. The familiar first "pit stop" loomed. Time to change drivers. Time enough to visit the toilet, grab a sandwich and cold drink for the route. Coffee on the go as I rolled the first cigarette of the day. Will, while driving, was not one for idle chatter and had adopted a look of concentration as we headed towards Lyon. This suited me just fine as I was given the opportunity to check my, previously unsent, message.

Hi Anna. You asked why I sent my six o'clock message. As long as this doesn't get you giggling I'll tell you. Having had a couple of hours to think of this reply, it is fair to say I became juvenile. A responsible adult would realise, five forty five was not the time to be messaging. I was thinking of you when I slept. I awoke to thoughts of you. Juvenile response? Tell you! Tell you immediately. It has been awhile since such juvenile actions have taken place in my world. I must say, I'm quite enjoying this, devil may care, attitude. Perhaps it's associated with that well know proverb? You are as old as you feel. I left out the bit about, ... the woman ... (Groucho Marx, I think.) While you are trying to work that out Anna I will finish by saying that's a compliment and perhaps it's just one juvenile reaching out to the juvenile that lies within you.

Yes, I was happy with that. So I sent.

Having once again changed drivers, I now had the Lyon decision. The only unknown factor in our journey. There were two possibilities. Take the ring road around Lyon or straight though the centre. I headed for the centre. We knew where the traffic would start queuing if it was to be an easy route through and sure enough, there it was. Out through the other side of Lyon and another four hours to go.

See you at nine James. And yes, I did work it out. In which case you are forty five, (A woman always lies about her age.)

We were on time and should get back to the workshop no later than five thirty. Organise the unloading of the twenty cube and I would be out of there by six. I arrived at Anna's gate at ten to nine and called her.

You're early James. Give me a couple of minutes and I'll open the gate.

I waited for five before the gate opened. At the end of the drive I did a three sixty with ample room to do so and cut the engine. It was a preference of mine. Rather than just park, I preferred to be facing my exit. Perhaps this was a throwback from the time drinking and driving was par for the course and it helped if you were facing the right way when leaving the bar, it was less likely to cause confusion. Reversing from a space after the bar? A manoeuvre I preferred to avoid. I once remembered being stopped by the police and asked to "walk the white line". It was amazing how being confronted by an officer of the law had the tendency to sober one up. I passed that test. Got back in the car and drove home but not before accepting the officers apology for having stopped me which was accompanied by the explanation for having done so. "Of course officer, I understand. We have to make the roads safer and if by doing so, I get stopped on occasion, so be it"! I think he was impressed by that answer. The other occasion that stood out was the time Paul and I left the bar with full pints of beer. It was closing time and there was no way we were leaving full pints at the bar. So we left with them. Paul took it upon himself to spread out on the bonnet of my then, MGBGT. I drove two miles to Paul's place with him on the bonnet as he took the occasional sip of beer. I managed to finish mine quite easily. After all, I was sat in a relatively comfortable seat. Most of his was running down the bonnet.

As I got out, Anna came to great me.

Hello James.

I searched her face for signs of meaning behind that greeting but what was I expecting or more precisely, what was I hoping for? It was a hello for christ sake James. What do you think you're going to surmise from that?

"Hello Anna", I replied. I think my smile had more warmth.

It's so nice to see you James. Come on in. We have some of Marta's meatball's to enjoy.

Whether a reaction to my smile or Anna's natural, perfect hostess taking charge routine, I was not sure. Either way, it mattered not a jot.

"Please, sit James", Anna said, indicating the nearby barstool.

I sat while watching Anna decide on the wine. She selected a favourite, or so I was told. Which had me wondering if she'd have said that no matter which bottle she chose. Forever the cynic? Anna placed the bottle within easy reach and passed the cork screw. She waited attentively, while I did my best to be nonchalant, as I struggled with the foil. I poured the wine and a thought momentarily crosses my mind. Was I not supposed to let the wine breathe before pouring? A well, too late now. Anna didn't seem to notice.

Well James, a toast. To a long overdue reunion.

I smiled.

What?

You want to know why I smiled? ..... As a rhetorical question, I smiled because your actions invoked memories. Memories of enjoying your company. It was a smile of memories.

I really cannot make you out James. To be honest I expected a certain retribution for ignoring your emails and messages but that doesn't seem to be the case. Are you all forgiving? My turn for rhetoric. I did say I would explain my actions and so I will but can we just talk awhile?

She knew I couldn't refuse her. She was an expert at that game. I refilled our glasses and asked when the meatballs would be ready. Anna moved away to prepare. What followed was a convivial hour of conversation during supper. The first bottle was replaced with a second. I helped clear away the remnants of supper and satisfied the Breakfast Bar was clean, Anna joined me around the central island. There passed a moment of silence. The first of the evening. It was a silence I couldn't interrupt. I saw Anna was deep in thought. She lifted her head and reached for eye contact.

I am as you. I know what I need to say but no matter how hard I try I cannot put it into words. Give me a moment James.

I said nothing.

I have battled with my conscience over this, my dilemma. So maybe it would be easier if I explain my dilemma.

That should be interesting. Anna would explain her dilemma. It was a dilemma I thought I understood. Rich Russian Lady meets, relatively poor, Englishman. Who she just happens to like. Delete him from my life and carry on. Go on Anna, surprise me.

On second thought's I won't. To hell with my dilemma. I enjoy your company and I hope you will forgive me for not revealing my fabrication of denials. So James …..

Excuse me for being momentarily assertive Anna but …… What are you doing this Saturday evening? No need to answer as it's a forgone conclusion you will move heaven and earth to reschedule the busy evening already booked to facilitate my request.

I was expecting Anna to reply to that simple question but not Anna.

Kiss me James.

It was not so much the request, more the look she was giving me as she said it. What else could I do? I gratefully accepted her request. I stood and swivelled her stool to face me. Her legs were together which was expected as they were before I swivelled. I gentle parted her legs, to be closer for this expected kiss. If I was going to do this, I was going to do it right. It was not that it was the first time and I knew Anna appreciated my kisses so why not be comfortable when doing so. I took her face in my hands and gently kissed her lips. Anna's response was immediate. I was striving for the, A few gentle kisses and see where it leads, routine. Not happening. Anna was taking control. It was intense. Anna's phone rang. She glanced at her phone mouthing the word, Shit! "I'd better take this. Sorry James". The one-sided conversation I heard, told me enough to know our evening was curtailed.

James! I have to go out. Not even sure I will be back this evening. And I so wanted to …… Let me just say, this woman has ruined my, sorry our, evenings plans. And don't give me that, so innocent look James, you know exactly what I was implying. We have to go.

Before Anna had a chance to dismount the stool I once again took her face in my hands. I kissed her gently and said, "I will hold the passionate thoughts I have in my head until my, sorry our, next meeting".

It worked! Anna started to laugh. I moved away and watched as Anna's thoughts change to, what she needed before leaving. I kissed her cheeks and walked towards the door. "I'll open the gate James", she said in an absent sort of way. "Hope all goes well", I said and left.

Yet another drive home from Anna's, somewhat confused. There was an intimate moment that instantaneously disappeared to be replace with a, matter of fact, attitude. I think what gave me the most concern was the way I was dismissed. Please leave, I have more important matters to attend. I made the decision not to contact Anna but to wait for her to call or message. I felt better. I could now concentrate on reliving those moments of passion. Separating those moments from the rest of Anna was difficult. The ever so proper Anna who whole heartedly immersed herself in the finer points of kissing and took it beyond. That was the Anna I didn't know but surely would like to. The imagination wandered to be shortly replaced by the front gate. I bleeped it open and was about to park when Paul emerged carrying a rubbish sack.

Where have you been to at this time of night, said Paul.

I thought of a sarcastic retort but decided on the truth.

I've been visiting Anna.

Anna? Oh yes. Isn't that the Russian?

Yes Paul. The Russian.

So that's back on? Hey, we are having a BBQ on Saturday. Why don't you invite Anna? There will be about twenty and most you know.

"I'll ask her", I said, as I parked.

"Do that", said Paul as he disappeared up the drive. Rubbish sack in hand. Once indoors the first question I asked myself? What day was it? When was Saturday, became the second question. Ok, it was Wednesday. That gave Anna at least a couple of days to respond. I decided on a coffee and cigarette to assess the possibilities. Possibility one. Anna doesn't respond. Possibility one? Actually that was it. Anna didn't respond. Then what do I do? There was only that possibility that worried me but I needed to be prepared if, strike if, ... when she did. I invited her to the BBQ. That possibility I could deal with. Which might perchance lead to other possibilities thought I, as the mind wandered. Get back on track James. Anna doesn't respond. I finished my coffee and while washing the cup I leapt to the obvious conclusion. If Anna didn't, I enacted plan B. I was consoled by that thought but it had presented me with another thought. What was plan B? That was for tomorrow I decided, as I headed off to bed.

Thursday morning in early June. It was going to be another beautiful day so I decided to take the motorbike to work. My mind was clouded. Not a single inspirational thought the night before. I relied on those moments before sleep but nothing transpired as I drifted off. The traffic was light, which was to be expected when leaving home well before eight. Eight fifteen I was sat in the sunshine, coffee in hand. Another thirty minutes before anyone arrived but rather than precompiling a message in my notes I decided to go straight for the message, thus abandoning the notion of waiting for her to contact me.

Hi Anna, I hope you managed to alleviate your friends concerns. Not knowing what the problem was I cannot get too enthused about the outcome. I'm guessing it was a man or a car as both fall into that category of, not understanding why it's not working. (I do hope it was no worse as my flippant remarks might land me in trouble.) On a lighter note. A most pleasant evening. Is that a typically English response? Or am I a natural in the art of gentlemanly responses? But now for something completely different. (Don't you just love Monty Python!) Paul and Chiara are having a BBQ on Saturday evening and I would like you to be my guest. Other than to say it's from eight onwards, further details can and will be disclosed upon a positive reaction to said BBQ. I could lyric on about the joy this would bring. How having you present would please more than I'm able to articulate but for the moment, suffice it to say, I look forward to a positive response. Are you still in the habit of checking messages at the traffic lights? If so, DON'T! Too late to say, I'm sure.

Anna called, two minutes later.

Hi James. Let me start by saying I was a good girl and did not read your message at the traffic lights. Elena did! You're on speaker phone and I'm dropping Elena at school.

Hello James. I apologise for having read your message intended for Mother but having done so I must say, you do have an unusual way of asking someone out. Am I likely to find similar when I attend university in England? I was being rhetorical James. Like mother like daughter.

I can now hear two girls laughing. By the time the girls got themselves together enough to continue, they had arrived at their destination.

Bye James and the answer is yes. Mother would love to come.

"Good bye dear daughter and by the way. You're walking home tonight", I heard Anna say, who was obviously not about to let Elena off the hook for disclosing her decision regarding Saturday evening.

You will pick her up Anna?

Of course I will but not before a few text messages of apology. I'm not annoyed with her and she knows that but I am slightly surprised she said that. She is normally far more restrained. I have spent seventeen years grooming her to be a lady and she reads one of your messages and all that work, to no avail!

So was it a man or a car?

A man or a ….. oh yes, last evening. Actually it was both! Sarah's husband had an accident and was stuck just outside of Toulon so I was volunteered to pick him up. It must have been close to midnight before Sarah and I arrived and well after two before I was home again. So well done James, on both counts. Have to let you go now but before I do. Yes, as my daughter rightfully pointed out, I'd be pleased to accompany you to the BBQ on Saturday. Big Kiss. Bye for now.

And she was gone.

I walked around the workshop for the first time in a week trying to take in what had been accomplished since I'd left for Roland Garros. Not easy with Anna's Big Kiss remark being analysed from every emotional angle possible.

Hey James. How did it go in Paris?

Morning Ray. Yes good. No problems. Great weather and some good tennis. Couldn't really ask for more. How about the Film Festival montage? Everything ok?

We spent the next few minutes catching up before others arrived. It was the best time of the season. With only us seven full time employees plus two part time, it was all about wrapping up the loose ends before closing for the summer. No real direction needed from me so I concentrated on the outstanding emails and pieces of paper floating around my desk. The day drifted along with little interruptions when, in the late afternoon, I received a message.

Things I need to know James.

How many people. Dress code. Do I bring anything but perhaps most importantly, where do you live? I'm sure there will be more questions to follow but I feel it unfair to avail you of my complete repertoire at this point in our "by a thin thread" relationship. I'm also sure you will have fun with these, my remarks.

Have fun with those remarks. When someone asked the dress code I could become confused. I had two dress codes. Summer code and winter code. Anna on the other hand, I could imagine, would potentially have three or four, in a day. Tennis code. Not too difficult unless as Anna, you had around ten outfits to choose from. Lunch code. That could be more difficult. Knowing the venue would help. Beach restaurant. A flowery frock possibly? Hotel, depending on stars, possibly more formal. Evening code. So many possibilities. How to describe the dress code required at the neighbours BBQ?

I started with the easy one. My address. I closed Notes, deciding the rest could wait until later. I got another message.

Can you buy a NICE bottle of St. Emilion red for me? Oh and a fresh baguette. (From a boulangerie not Carrefour.) I will be bringing a cheese plate with grapes and walnuts. Many thanks.

Did Anna come under that heading of, A high maintenance woman or should I have been more explanatory with my original request? "BBQ on Saturday Anna. Casual dress and don't worry about anything else, all the necessaries to accompany the BBQ will be supplied. It will just need you as you are, to make it complete". I'd never understood the reality of including such but it had left food for thought. I had a few moments so Google St. Emilion wines. Sixty percent Merlot. Thirty percent Cabernet Sauvignon. Ten percent of something else. Even with my basic knowledge of wines I knew it came under the heading of Blended. More interestingly it led me to discover the label on a bottle to be more controlled than the contents within. The wording on the label, controlled to millimetre precision. The wine, on the other hand, often checked by a local taster, well before the wine reached the bottling stage and that same taster might have, shall we say, certain affiliations with the local producers. Reading this gave me a certain solace with rack upon rack. Aisle upon aisle of indistinguishable labels that confront me on a visit to the supermarket. For some reason I would be drawn towards the foreign section. Not for the comprehensive selection available. Quite the contrary. Amongst the thousands of choices available perhaps ten were foreign. No, I am drawn towards the simplicity of the label. It's a Cabernet Sauvignon. It's a Pinot Noir. It's from New Zealand or Chile. Yes, I remembered having that one before. I remembered the red kangaroo. Simple.

Home, at last and a message to compile.

Hi Anna, please find address enclosed. Running forward for a moment, it would be a good idea on Saturday if you call me when you leave. That way I can open the gates in anticipation of your arrival.

I reread that start of my message and wondered why I'd phrased it such? With anyone else it would have followed a somewhat different take. Here's the address. Give me a call when you leave and I'll open the gate. Interesting.

Reference the wine. I usually buy wine in plastic bottles ..... on draft but I will do my best. Baguette? Good point. I'll check with Chiara who will, I'm sure have that on her list. I'm told there will be around twenty people and the dress code will be casual. I will leave you to interpret my usage of the word casual. If I can be of any help in this department don't hesitate to call, particularly if you need help in muddying those waters further. In fact, perhaps you can help me decide on my wardrobe for the evening?

I considered writing more but decided I had covered all the salient points so nothing more to do than press send. Maybe not so surprisingly, I received an instant reply.

So, you're good at delegating tasks James? Le baguette is for the cheese. As well as the wine! And please don't open the bottle before I arrive. I will just ignore "plastic bottle" ...

I most probably shouldn't say this Anna but on reading your message I had an image of you arriving in a waitress uniform complete with short skirt and silver platter full of cheeses etc and an abundance of baguettes. But seriously. I now understand why the baguette. It is to compliment the cheeses and wine. I will therefore endeavour to have an unopened bottle of wine plus baguette awaiting your arrival. (I'll finish the plastic bottle beforehand.) I must say, I am looking forward to you meeting my long time friends and neighbours. I do believe someone once said, Judge a person by the friends they keep. Could be the last time we meet? Have I yet thanked you for accepting the invitation? Thank You Anna, for accepting the invitation.

Should I have mentioned the short skirt? The waitress uniform would have been enough. Hoping she saw through it as a "throw away" remark. It became quiet on the message front. I went too far. I decided to answer a few outstanding emails to occupy the mind. An hour or so passed.

Well James ...... Thank you for thank you. And yes, no problem, I will happily advise you on what you should be wearing. Do you want to go shopping together for a new wardrobe? I'm sure I could find you a cute little skirt with matching top, then you could carry the tray of cheeses. I will continue to ignore any reference to plastic bottle.

And there I was, worried about my throw away comment. This could spiral out of control with the inevitable conclusion of, no date on Saturday.

Is this your subtle way of disclosing your indifference to my style of dress Anna? Either way I will make myself, provisionally available for tomorrow. All hinging on the possibility that it might rain. (Wouldn't want to interrupt the tennis.) I've decided to pass on a thought that just occurred. I say to a girl, "Would you like to come to a BBQ?" She says "Yes." End of discussion. Which has led me to believe I am either ignorant of the decorum associated with such an invitation or, once again in my ignorance, I'm assuming the other party will understand what is necessary? I obviously have a lot to learn, as your questions on the BBQ indicate it to be so.

Bon Nuit Anna. James x

I copy/paste from Notes and sent. It didn't take Anna long to reply.

Raining ...... Unlikely James. So, tennis it will be. Actually I have a tournament tomorrow so wish me luck. Style of dress for you? My advice to you would be, avoid pink. A thought that has occurred to me on reading your thoughts. Don't worry about your lack of decorum James. Honestly, it's ok. Anyway, your decorum is not what interests me. I'm sure that thought will keep you up thinking. Ha. Got you! Good Night James (and yes, an x in return.)

No way could I respond. Good Nights have been said. And yes Anna, it would keep me up thinking. I had thought many times, I'm out of my depth but it seemed Anna didn't see it that way. "..... is not what interests me", she said. I thought back to those first meetings. I felt I did what was necessary and received a positive response in return. And yet, she did disappear for a number of weeks. But she came back! Realised she was on to a good thing. I'd be so lucky. Then why? Why the sudden .... "interest"? I felt. I felt there was something there, between us. It was only ten thirty in England so I decided to FaceTime Tony. I needed some objective thinking.

Hi Tony.

This isn't social, is it James? You have something on your mind to discuss. It's not about finally deciding you want to throw yourself at the feet of the taxman?

Tony, you are so predictable but no, it's not about the taxman. He can wait. It's about Anna. She has just told me, it's not my lack of decorum that interest her. I mentioned in a previous message that I might lack decorum in certain areas.

Don't go there Tony! It's just that after saying that, she said, "That will keep you up thinking." What am I suppose to make of that?

Let's not panic James. My advice to you would be, "Go with the flow." Enjoy the strangeness that surrounds you. You are perfectly capable of rising to the occasion. I do have a reservation. If you are playing a role, which I know you are capable of doing. Could you or would you want to, keep it up? Go with the flow James. Now can I get back to Question Time?

Thanks for that Tony. So sorry to interrupt that political quiz programme. Who's winning anyway? Night Tony, and Thanks.

I went to bed deciding to go to work the next morning, admittedly more thinking about the few glasses of rosé for lunch. In fact I'd just do the morning. Go in search of that bottle of wine in the afternoon. Might even check out the nibbles counter. How to seduce a woman. Nibbles from Carrefour. Mmm.

It was a good lunch. Seven of us present all full of good times ahead. End of the season. Other than Will and myself who were around for a few more days. The downside of Roland Garros. We stayed on at the office purely awaiting the demontage, the rest, finished that day. A longer lunch than was anticipated. Plenty of time tomorrow to buy the wine I thought, as I left the restaurant well after four. Hadn't messaged Anna for almost a day but would have to come up with one for this evening. My phone pinged on the drive home. It could be Anna was the immediate thought that crossed my mind. It would have to wait was the bold reply to myself, as I was driving.

Have you come to any conclusions James? And you know what I mean when I ask that. x

Talk about pressure I was thinking, as I headed for the fridge. I opened Notes and typed a few words. After much deliberating, I deleted. I tried to approach the question in a logical manner. What was it about me that would be of interest to someone like Anna? No luck there. And then it hit me. Forget Notes, this was going direct.

Hi Anna. I must admit I haven't given it much thought on my decorum or lack of it but it seems self evident there can be but only one answer to that question. It's me. It's me you are interested in. So perhaps you can enlighten me, on me and these qualities you feel I possess?

I was tempted to write more but should I? "It was not the first time a woman had found me interesting", could have been included but far to blasé I thought. I pressed send.

Firstly, that's not fair James! You diverted the topic. And secondly, I don't believe you! All day you have been wondering about what interests me in you. Don't deny it. Talking of wondering. Should I wear a dress or trousers and top?

I decided on complete honesty.

You are right Anna. There has hardly been a moment I have not thought about the what and the why. What interests Anna in me and perhaps more importantly, Why? I think trousers and a top. Flat shoes compulsory.
Will she let me get away with that? She would know I'd only admitted to her being right. Good finishing remark I thought, coming back to the, what to wear question.
Yes James, I noticed you've, once again, managed to avoid the topic of conversation but in doing so you might be surprised to know you managed to highlight the reasons for my interest in you. Well, at least one. Back to you James. Let us see if you can figure out what that might be.
I can think of two possibilities Anna. My honesty in accepting you were right or my positive feedback on what you should wear tomorrow.
Let me just say James, it wasn't your honesty, as that has yet to be tested and the day I truly let a man decide what I should wear …
I'm enjoying this James but I have to leave you. Dinner guests will be arriving shortly.
That was what Anna did. She moved from one moment to the next. New moment coming, end the previous. No rundown to the Good Bye. In fact. No rundown, let alone Good Bye. For some odd reason I did find it captivating. At the end of a good book. A good film. It left one wanting more. And Anna certainly knew how to do that. No more correspondence that evening other than a moment of weakness around bedtime.
Hope the evening went well Anna. Looking forward to tomorrow. x
I put the phone on charge and went to bed.
Saturday morning. Another beautiful day I thought. Sat at my favourite cafe in Antibes. Newspaper and coffee purchased. Even the waiter seemed more receptive and convivial than normal. It was not just the blue sky and temperatures in the mid twenties. It was a state of mind. Today was a good day. Which reminded me, I had to buy the wine. I sat back to enjoy the paper. The coffee. The people watching and wondered if they were aware of my inner glow as they strolled past. I put my paper down and wondered about the evening ahead. Paul and Chiara had a diverse group of friends. Admittedly most were associated with boats. (I think I was supposed to call them yachts even though none had sails. A fibreglass shell with a big motor albeit some of those shells were approaching a hundred metres long.) Uniquely amongst their peers, they had an equal cross section of English and French friends and having met most, I had no concern that Anna wouldn't find stimulating conversation within the group. In recent years it had become rare for me to be concerned about the seating arrangement at dinner. I say, became rare. If the truth be known It might have been more on a par with snowfall in Florida. Fortunately there were no seating arrangements to contend with at a BBQ. Having been to the neighbours BBQ's on a few occasions, I knew Anna would enjoy herself. I felt at ease and

sat back to once again, take in my surroundings when a sudden realisation hit me. They are my neighbours. Anna will see my place. We are having drinks. I had an image of Anna arriving fashionably late but insisting I gave her a tour before we went next door. I didn't panic. It was barely ten and I had all day to do some spring cleaning. Accepting that June comes within the bounds of spring.

Good Morning James. And what a beautiful day it is. I didn't return your message last night as the last guest did not leave before two. I am about to leave for the tennis club. An old advisory but very much a dear friend of mine is back in town and we are booked for a knock about game which we both know, will turn into full-on competitiveness. I'll call you when I return home. It is eight to eight thirty this evening, yes?

I thought I should confirm that ETA. Yes Anna, it's eight, ish. I will allow an extra twenty three minutes so anytime before eight forty seven will be fine.

James, my estimated arrival time follows a precise delta of, plus or minus fifty percent. You must know this by now so you will have to take it or leave it and therefore allow more than twenty three minutes.

You take all the time you need Anna. Far be it from me to be putting pressure on one such as you. No sarcasm intended.

You are such an understanding sweetheart James and you still want me to join you. Hope you have bought the wine. Got to go.

Time to leave the bar to face a few hours of precision cleaning but first, that bottle of wine I needed to buy. Wine bought, I headed home. Having a break during cleaning, I decided to take a photo of the bottle.

A picture says a thousand words. If no immediate reply I will assume. 1) You are still playing. 2) Of all types of St Emilion, I have bought the one you don't like or, 3) You are so amazed by my foresight you are rendered speechless.

Nothing like the above James. 1) Match won in two sets with confidence. 2) Bravo! 3) And a fresh crispy baguette from the boulangerie?

Point three has been duly noted Anna and taking into account the necessity of it being fresh, I will buy later. Perhaps you could hold off with that call until you have mentally and physically prepared yourself for the evening. Work it back two hours before arrival time and you never know, you might be early. Point one. Well done!

Nice and lovely accepted but I'm not sure what you are insinuating James? Once I have finished with my days chores, I'll have little time to decide what to wear. I'll just throw something on before walking out of the door and as requested, I will refrain from calling you until that moment arises.

She was playing with me. I could reply with an, ok. Which was all I should do.

I'm sure you will look, just perfect. Expecting a call around eight fifteen.

And that was exactly what Anna did. Did it her way. I got a call around eight thirty to say she was on her way.

Her entrance was initially confusing as Anna insisted on trying a three point turn, prepared to leave. How could I possibly disagree. A girl after my own heart. It was more of an eight point turn. I was anticipating an awkward moment as she exited the car but that was not Anna.

Hello James. Is this where you live? Oh it looks so unusual. So quaint. How are you? Can I have a look? Can we go on the roof?

Somewhere between this foray of words we did the polite kisses. Maybe I felt the moment was almost missed by Anna? Stop being so sensitive James.

"Come on James. Open a bottle and let's take a glass to the roof", said Anna. Almost nine but I didn't worry. Paul and Chiara accepted guests as they arrived, no matter what the time. The view might not be deemed spectacular but the evening, viewed from the roof, as the sun was setting on the distant mountains with the lights of Nice in the foreground, was not bad. Anna seemed appreciative. A perfect moment for some romance I was thinking. If only Anna would stop wandering around. I decided to stay put, in the hope the mountain will eventually come to James.

This is absolutely super James but perhaps we should join the BBQ now. Really don't want to be too late.

So much for romance.

Anna was a great success. Her causal and charming self saw her through conversation after conversation. Asking enough questions to come across as interested but not invasive. Throughout the evening I watched her traverse the guests with such ease and confidence. I didn't for one moment believe I would have to guide her through the initial introductions but seeing the way Anna operated without my assistance did deflate any ego I might have possessed. On the up side. She was with me and that was all that mattered. And then I saw her smoking? Alone for a moment I had to ask.

I didn't know you smoked Anna.

Oh yes, I enjoy the odd cigarette with a glass of wine. Two is usually the limit. Two cigarettes that is, not glasses.

We laughed while I thought of the times I had avoided smoking after a shower. She smoked!

The BBQ was winding down and not wanting to be the last, Anna decided it was time to leave. Having said her goodbyes I walked her to the car, out of sight of the remaining guests, there followed a few moments of generous kissing, only to be interrupted by others leaving. Anna withdrew and after thanking me for a wonderful evening, was gone. I returned to join the remaining few friends and help with some tiding up.

"I do believe you've struck lucky there James. What does she get out of the deal"? Asked Paul.

"Don't start", said Chiara as she saw Paul was eager to pursue that line of conversation. It was another hour before I left. I checked the phone which I had decided to leave at home .

Arrived home safely, in case you are interested James. Goodnight and thanks again for the evening also to Chiara and Paul.

That was a short message? Was I supposed to have already asked if she arrived home safely? Had to say something.

Hi Anna, I was seriously wondering if you made it safely home. In fact I debated asking you to stay. (Just a little concerned about your alcohol intake.) I got involved in tidying away your dirty dishes, hence the lateness of the message. You are by now, fast asleep. While I am thinking....... What a wonderful evening I had with Anna. Was it just the two of us, or were there others present? Untold amounts of kisses, James. Hope this message doesn't wake you.

It's a pity you didn't ask me to stay. Good night James. Big x

I had a tendency to follow my intuition. It was what I'd done all my life. Let intuition be the driving force rather than decision. My intuition was to take Anna by the hand while leading her to my front door. Saying nothing. Having a glass from that opened bottle while hoping beyond hope ..... But I didn't! Once again, Anna's final message of the evening would keep me awake for sometime to come.

Good Morning Anna. I hope you slept well? I am counting twice now, that a good nights sleep has interrupted a not so good nights sleep. Please excuse that thought Anna. It's a morning thing. Oh, btw, I think we should get married. Paul and Chiara like you. And before you comment on that, I am well aware there are other considerations to take into account before marrying. Which side of the bed does she sleep, for one. Well Anna, I'm sure that has given you enough rope. I await your reply with interest. Enjoy the day. James x

No time to answer right now James but one question. Aren't you already married?

A mere technicality Anna.

Chapter Nine

Good Morning James, I've got a friendly match, with a blue eyed blonde, late afternoon so was wondering if it would be alright to visit around eight? Well, eight thirty.

Was there anyway I could say no? Even if I wanted to.

Hello Anna. Enjoy your friendly with the blue eyed blonde. Just remember .... keep the net between you. Look forward to seeing you this evening.

There I was. Complimenting myself on a perfect reply.

Forgot to ask James. Can you make up a fruit salad. I know I'm going to feel hungry but don't want anything heavy. You're a dear.

How quickly that smug feeling of the perfect answer could turn to utter panic! A fruit what? No problem. I'll ask Chiara. Armed with Chiara's "List for a Fruit salad", I headed into Antibes market. One thing I didn't discuss with Chiara, was the amount. I found a very large fruit bowl hidden under the sink but even so, it was spilling over with excessive amounts of fruit which was unfortunate, as I rarely ate fruit. Early afternoon and the salad was chilling in the fridge.

Almost ready James. Red tennis dust washed away so I should be about thirty minutes. See you then. Did you get strawberries and cherries?

Sorry Anna but according to the eleven fruitiers I visited, strawberries are out of season.

Hopeless!

I know.

See you soon James!

Thirty minutes to decide, should it be bowls, dishes or plates? While trying to decide, Anna arrived. She would be a few minutes turning the car giving me a last moment, a last moment to panic. I'll figure out which plates etc., later. Reacquiring my calm exterior I realised I hadn't uncorked the wine but that was easily done I thought, as I unscrewed the top. Why don't French wines have screw tops? Time to greet Anna which was timed to perfection. I open the car door. Anna dressed in a green flowery blouse with bright red trousers that showed her figure without being too obvious …… and flat sandals.

"Hello James", said Anna as she kissed my cheeks. "Gosh, it has been a hectic day". I let Anna describe to me the ups and downs of her day in silence as I poured the wine.

Anyway enough of all of that. How are you James?

I had guessed it right. Anna wasn't looking for response to her narrative of the day. So I adopted my most serious face which was easily accomplished. I only had to think of a particular time stood in front of the headmaster.

Well Anna, your day sounds most interesting but I am somewhat concerned.

What?

Did he stay the other side of the net?

The next hour just disappeared caught up in amusing repartee. Time I thought, to present the fruit salad.

That looks delightful. Do you have a teaspoon? I would like to taste. That is not bad James. In fact that is very good. Where are the dishes? She asked, already opening cupboard doors at random.

I pointed to the cupboard where dishes, plates, bowls and anything else lived, that Anna might decide deemed appropriate for the task. She chose the bowls, obviously. I wasn't sure why but it was a delight to watch Anna eating. Or more to the point, watching her go through the motions. "You need to polish your cutlery James", she said in a teasing manner. So I consciously looked at my spoon, spilling the contents back into the bowl as I turned it.

I must have missed yours, mine looks fine.

You can't see that James, it is covered with juice.

You're right, I can't.

The repartee continued.

Anna was having a question answer moment. These occurred from time to time and it had become par for the course to have these seemingly casual questions thrown out but woe betide me if I slipped up.

Is this your house or do you rent?

This is rented Anna, it's just that I prefer to keep my finances out of France.

I wish I had, or should I say my husband had. You just cannot imagine the on-going fiasco with the Italian and French lawyers and ditto the taxmen, it is a nightmare!

I can imagine. No actually Anna I can't but I can imagine lawyers and taxmen being in the same room would not be my idea of a good time. Let me fill your glass. A toast! To lawyers and taxmen, let judgement be upon them. Did I tell you the joke about what would five hundred lawyers at the bottom of the sea be? …… A good start!

Anna was laughing as she tried to take a sip.

"Yes James you did but it is just as good the second time around. I have to go soon James and don't look at me like that", she said, still laughing.

It is just that I have the builders and electricians arriving at seven thirty. Can I just say, we will have our moment and before you say anything else, could you give me just a drop more wine.

I could make you a coffee if you'd prefer?

A perfect idea James. Can you make it a Noisette?

I could do that. I found the smallest of small milk jugs just the other day. Somewhere under the sink. It seemed to be a place I put things I never used? I'd washed it. Anna was presented with her coffee and a side order of microwaved hot milk. Anna was looking at me in an almost compassionate way.

I like watching you James. You have a way of doing things that intrigue me.

Intrigue as in how Anna?

I'm not sure. You know I'm watching but I don't sense any change in your composure. People tend to react to being watched in many different ways but you don't seem to. It intrigues me.

"Perhaps it's because I feel comfortable in your presence Anna", I said with a slight smile.

Oh Gosh! I am not sure I want you feeling comfortable James. I prefer my men on edge.

I apologise for feeling comfortable and will try to be more, "on edge" in future.

That had Anna laughing with the frustration of knowing I wouldn't be.

You know very well it is not something you are capable of James and anyway …….. I like you the way you are. Perhaps too much? Oh dear. Look at the time, I have to go.

I'd not seen Anna like that before. She'd let her guard down and she knew it. She needed to regain her composure. I understood.

Of course Anna. leave the glasses, I'll clear up later.

I walked her to the car.

I'm really pleased you came over this evening Anna. Thank you.

Anna had opened the door and was about to get in. She changed her mind and stood in front of me.

It's not like me. You have made me not like me but I think I like it. It was a lovely evening James and the salad was superb. And ……

I stopped her talking. I kissed her.

Have a safe journey home Anna.

Good night James.

Having left an appropriate "Hope you got home safe" message, I went to bed. One more day and Will and I depart for Paris. Three days in Paris to do a two hour demontage. I sent Anna two messages during the day. Nothing in return.

Two days passed. I was tempted to message again. To call but didn't. On the third day Anna called.

Hi James I'm sorry I haven't got in touch. I'm in Milan. House business. How are you? Look, I haven't got much time and I called to ask, When do you get back from Paris and when do you go to England?

Did I tell her I was going to Paris, let alone England? I must have but didn't remember doing so.

Hi Anna. I get back from Paris on the evening of the tenth and go to England the following morning.

Oh Gosh. I didn't realise there is just the one evening. I'm in Milan until Saturday. You get back on Sunday. Why don't we invite ourselves to Paul and Chiara's place for early evening drinks and I'll bring something for us to eat later. Can you text me your thoughts? I really do have to go. Hope to see you on Sunday James.

And she was gone.

Could I get Will to agree to leave earlier than early? It would be good to get home by five. That would mean getting up at five thirty! Will was not going to like that.

Having explained my reason for the early start, Will had no problem. So we left Paris at five thirty that Sunday morning. On route I messaged Anna to explain Paul and Chiara eat before nine so could she make it by eight.

I will definitely be there James. In fact, I thought it might be an idea to have a pre drink with you. Expect a call around seven fifteen when I leave home.

I thought of answering, "Right on!" but unlikely to be appreciated by Anna. Once back in Cannes I messaged Anna.

Hi Anna. Back from Paris and just leaving the office so will be home about five. I've preempted next door and they are looking forward to the visit. See you around seven thirty. Did I forget to mention, I am also looking forward?

Anna arrived promptly at seven forty five. She seemed flustered. Agitated. Giving me a half hearted smile and a short hug, Anna headed straight for the bar stool and sat. Shoulders ever so slightly slumped.

Sorry James. I will be alright in a minute. I need a cigarette.

I sat on the adjacent stool and poured Anna a glass.

I didn't mention I have eighteen people at my house. Tanya and her four friends. Elena and her eight friends plus two children aged around four. Wonderful having them here but an absolute nightmare at the same time. Anna paused. *There, I'm feeling more relaxed already.*

I'd said nothing since Anna sat. Perhaps it was my, consoling look of complete understanding of her day? I think the gentle placing of hand on hand might have swung it.

So, how was your trip back from Paris? You must be exhausted?

I felt these were rhetorical questions and was immediately proved right.

Here I am, arriving looking like a somewhat disheveled neurotic woman. Not the entrance you were hoping for I think?
She was giving me a smile that was hard to describe. More than the smile, which was surely there. A smile where only one side of her lips were actually smiling. It was the intense look in her eyes. She was searching for something. She was looking into my eyes as though she was waiting for something. Something she said. Something about hope.
Anna, you are here. What else do I have to hope for? Ok, maybe less neurotic?
Now she smiled a smile.
You and your words James. I am so glad I managed to get away.
Before she could say more, I reached forward and placed her face in my hands. I kissed her and pulled back slightly. Far enough to see her face.
I'm glad you are here, I'm sure Paul and Chiara will be glad when we are there.
She reached forward and kissed me.
Come on then James, we shouldn't keep the neighbours waiting.
Anna was making her way to the door. Laughing as she went. It was nine thirty before we left the neighbours. It could have been later but Paul's tactful remark to Chiara, "I hope they leave soon otherwise it is going to be too late to eat," brought the pre drinks evening to the inevitable conclusion.
Hey Paul, you should have said. I was happy to leave before we got here.
Anna was looking confused.
"Don't think about it Anna", said Chiara, "They do it all the time".
There have been occasions. Many occasions, I've had to explain to unsuspecting friends by saying, Don't worry. They actually like each other. Ignoring them usually works for me.
Surprisingly, Anna seemed to understand. I saw a devilish look in her eyes.
I don't think I told you Chiara but I worked in a Safari park when I was younger. There were enough examples of the posturing male to realise there is very little difference when it comes to the homo sapiens variety.
Paul and I were trying to understand what had just been said. Chiara, on the other hand seemed to have got it.
You've never worked in a safari park have you Anna?
You are right Chiara but if I had, I am sure that would have been the conclusion I would have drawn.
We could see Anna and Chiara were enjoying the moment when in actual fact, it was supposed to be our moment. How did that happen? No chance to think about that. Anna was giving her apologies for keeping them occupied for so long. With something about, "It has been such a wonderful time". And Paul accepting this, became the amicable host who was now regretting our departure. I considered that as Anna and I walked the fifty metres to my front door.

"You have interesting friends James", said Anna as she positioned herself on the bar stool. "Isn't there something about, Judging a person …."

By his friends, is how I believe that ends, Anna.

Be a dear and get me a glass of wine James. Gosh this is the fourth cigarette this evening.

"Get me a glass of wine." Would be an order given to a waiter who one had little regard for. And yet I didn't take it that way. It was the casual, throw-away way she said it. As if she had thought of wanting a glass and having thought it expounded that need in as few words as possible. I didn't take it personally. I poured the wine as Anna talked. Almost without interruption for what must have been fifteen minutes was precisely what I did. She was telling me about the full house. The problems with the lawyers and the taxmen regarding the settlement of the estate. Something about living in France but a lot of the investments were in Italy. The French taxman wanting his share. I think because she was on the topic of money she stopped for a moment then asked, "Do you have a reasonable income James"?

Maybe not quite what you would deem reasonable Anna but I have no financial worries. To the point when buying a tin of Heinz Beans in Carrefour, I don't even look at the price.

I am fairly certain James that was not the answer to the question and stop looking at me like that, I am trying to be serious. Ok, I give up.

She was laughing as she looked around the room.

"I like this room", she was saying but I had stopped listening. I wanted to kiss her.

Anna, would you mind if I kissed you?

She stopped talking and smiled. Why did I say that? Why didn't I just kiss her? Awkward was how I was feeling. That kiss was now expected. How could I possibly approach that casually? In the micro seconds it had taken me to think that? Anna was kissing me!

"You looked like you needed some help James. I hope you don't mind"? she said, drawing a breath.

It wasn't as seen in the movies, where with a swing of his arm he cleared the nearby table of it's encumbrances, laying her down as she wrapped her legs around his body. No, it wasn't like that. Anyway, I didn't have a table to clear. But what passed was passionate none the less. My hands were inside her blouse caressing her back as I lay kisses on her neck. I felt Anna responding. I brought my hand around and slowly massaged Anna's breast. Her mouth searching for mine. Her hand moved between my legs. That was the moment the movie goer wouldn't have expected. Anna the perfect lady, grouping between my legs. I held the thought of laughter in check as Anna pulled away.

Oh James, I so much want to.

I was glad to have kept that humour under control, while waiting for the follow-up of, "but I can't". Not Anna. She just left it hanging.

You must think I'm awful James. I knew this is what was going to happen. It is what I wanted. And now the moment is here, I am unable to follow it through. And you know the most ridiculous part? It's because I like you and I'm getting to like you more. Can you possibly understand?

I understood immediately. When I was going out with, who was to be, my first future ex wife, I was for the only time in my life, seeing two other ladies. I went to bed with those two. The other, I married. What was that phrase? Something worth having was worth waiting for?

I think I understand Anna. We have time and when the time is right, we will both know it. Nothing has to be rushed.

I was devastated of course. So close and yet ..... and yet I did understand and for some strange reason, felt a little smug. Anna was liking me more. I'd just told her I understood and she was looking at me with such warmth in her eyes. She liked me! Strike devastated. I once again took her face in my hands. Kissed her and sat back.

Honestly James I am not sure you can understand fully because I certainly don't. I really want to and I thought this evening was the moment but something inside of me felt ...... felt I wanted more from our first time. Don't ask me to explain in any more depth, I can't but what I can do is take you to the airport tomorrow? What time is your flight?

Twelve thirty.

"I can pick you up at ten. Plenty of time. That is settled then", said Anna with a twinkle in her eye.

Oh another glass. Yes please James and my final cigarette of the evening. That is five. How long are you going for?

Three weeks.

Three weeks! Oh Gosh. Perhaps we should go to bed now? A wicked smile on her face completed the sentence.

I can wait if you can Anna? After all. Anything worth having is worth waiting for. My turn to smile.

What a novel idea James. If I want something, I usually buy it.

"You can't buy love Anna". I said, with as straight a face as I could muster.

Oh I wouldn't say that. I met my husband not because I loved him but because he was rich. I respected him and in the end, grew to love him. So you see James in a round about sort of way, you can buy love.

I concede Anna.

Our farewells at the car were intense to say the least but at some point, sensibility took it's course and she left shortly after, promising to be here before ten the next morning.

Anna was surprisingly early. Early enough in fact for there to be time for coffee and …… before we left. I was certain I still felt the warmth of those kisses hours after landing in Bristol.

Something for us both to remember James. For three long weeks. Hurry back. Was what Anna said.

My flight on time, I boarded at twelve.

For the next three weeks we sent messages. Photos. That photo of Anna walking towards the camera, on court. The look in her eyes. I remembered it well. Most evenings around eleven I would be found outside Tony's flat engrossed in conversation with Anna. The topics forever shifting. "Buy a pair of Tods", I remembered Anna saying. I later asked Tony if he knew what Tods were. "Not sure I do", he replied. Had to Google it. Italian shoes, evidently. I bought a pair on Ebay for forty five pounds. One evening in particular stood out, having recently arrived back from the pub in a, jovial mood, I evidently monopolised the conversation with wit and risqué remarks. Congratulated her on her fiftieth birthday with such gusto it would have put Casanova to shame. Anna told me this the following evening and occasionally made subtle innuendoes on my comments. Could I remember a single word I said! Of course I couldn't. That would stand out as the most memorable conversation I had with Anna. What a pity I couldn't remember it!

Chapter Ten

The day approached. I flew out of Bristol the next day. Looking forward to another three to four weeks of holiday before returning to work early August. Anna had arranged to meet me at one thirty. Drop me off. Giving me sometime to unpack. Or, freshen up, as Anna put it, before arriving at her place for around seven. All went to plan. Anna met me but decided to have a coffee before leaving me to, freshen up. I couldn't remember who held out the longest on that need we both felt. That need to be close. I do remember by the time Anna left she had decided that perhaps five thirty might be a better time. I got a message at four.

James. Come when you are ready. It is ok if it is before five thirty. Btw. We have Marta's meatballs for dinner.

I arrived at four forty five. The gate already open.I parked and watched as Anna approached the car dressed in a pale blue, sleeveless light summer dress that flowed out from the waist. Stopping just short of her knees. She was in her effervescent mood. We entered that vast hallway. She steered me to the Breakfast Bar where an opened bottle awaited.

"A toast James", said Anna. Looking at me.

"Such a list. Such a list", I said. Stalling for time. From nowhere, I said, "To three very, very long weeks that are now behind us and to that that is ahead".

A squeeze of my hand said enough. Anna liked that. No idea where it came from.

Come on James I should show you the rest of the house.

Before doing so Anna, I have a present for you. For your birthday. I'll get it from the car.

It was not elegantly wrapped. A brown cardboard box with an abundance of sellotape holding it together. Packed such to be able to take as hand luggage.

160

Anna ferociously attacked it with a kitchen knife while I tried to point out the delicacy of what lay inside. On seeing the bowl Anna's eyes opened wide.
This is amazing James. It is so beautiful and I know exactly where it belongs. Next to the vase in the hallway perhaps?
You knew. You remembered my vase. Oh James, how thoughtfully original. Thank you so much and it is by far my best birthday present.
I received a warm and extended kiss from Anna.
The rest of the house was the part that wasn't this vast living area. Mainly a study, cinema room and six bedrooms. I got the tour of the bedrooms.
"This one is mine", said Anna as she wandered around the room. "And that is my bed …. for later, she said, as she breezed out. Did I catch that right? It was said in such an off-handed manner, I could have got it wrong? We returned to the wine. Although in an obviously good mood, Anna seemed restless. She was attentive but restless. I understood why with her next remark.
Let's go to bed James.
There was no way any thought but YES was bombarding my senses at that moment but how to deal with it. Screaming Yes at the top of my voice while dragging her by the hand in the hope I remembered the direction of her bedroom, wasn't going to work. I smiled at Anna as I said,
You mean this is that right moment. The moment that wasn't quite right before I left for England. That moment. Is this it Anna?
To hell with that moment James, I want to go to bed!
The look on her face said it all. The corner of her mouth turned up, ever so slightly. Her eyes boring into mine. It was a look of, decision made.
I thought of following up with, You're wish is my command but just in time realised how crass that would have sounded. I followed Anna. Glasses and bottle in hand. It was a large bedroom. I put the glasses on the bedside table and proceed to top up. Anna was closing the shutters. I had a momentary panic attack but decided the best option was to undress. By the time Anna was closing the last and closest shutter, I was already under the covers. She paused and decided not to close the last completely. Allowing a stream of light to fall across the bed. Very romantic, I was thinking. Anna turned to face me as she reached down to the hem of her dress. In one slow continuous movement, Anna had discarded her dress. She was beautiful. She waited for a moment, to allow me the pleasure of watching her. Standing unashamedly in her designer bra and panties, she laughed and slipped under the covers.
In the years following the separation between Josey and myself, I had been fortunate in meeting ladies with a certain know how. I was a quick learner, albeit a late one. It seemed I had a knack and it wasn't long before I'd amassed some meagre knowledge in the art of love making. The key factor I believed was pleasing the lady. If she was pleased, all else followed. The difficult bit was discovering what pleased.

161

I leant over Anna and stroked her hair. I kissed her neck as I felt any tension she might have had, disappear. Somethings had to be slow and easy if one wanted to achieve the desired effect. Anna was responding to my touch. The kissing was now passionate with hardly a chance to take that needed breath. I stopped and sat up. Anna had a look of slight confusion. I took her panties in both hands and pull them slowly down her legs. So much for slow and easy. Anna was no longer confused. She opened her legs and what a beautiful sight awaited me. Anna was completed shaved. I realised, beauty was in the eye of the beholder but never had I seen such as this. This most astounding beauty. No vast cavernous opening. No blemishes surrounded those pouting lips. Those ever so slightly, pouting lips. My intention, if indeed at that moment I could remember my intentions, was purely to alleviate Anna of those pretty panties. But met with the perfection I now viewed, how could I resist? I leant forward and kissed, ever so gently that place that held such mystery. A mystery I intended to solve. Anna had opened her legs to accommodate as I started to unravel those mysteries. There were no outer limits on perfection. Perhaps that should read, no outer lips, I was thinking. I opened that virginal emplacement and expose Anna's pudenda. My tongue searching for that holy of holy spots. Anna's breathing was becoming quicker and more erratic.

I want you to be inside me James when I climax. Not down there.

Her breathing might have increased but Anna was enough in control to know what she wanted. I placed my face to hers. Soft wet kissing as I reached between her legs to guide myself in. Not too far. Slow methodical rhythm while being ever attentive to Anna's response. Anna started to react. I changed my position ever so slightly to allow a deeper penetration. Still slow and methodical I was feeling for the reactions within Anna.

Oh yes James. Just like that.

Anna reverted to Russian. I felt her moment approaching. She raised her hips followed by uncontrollable movements that slowly decreased until she was laid still. I looked in her eyes. I smiled and kiss her.

You are not much of a one for bed-talk James are you? But what you lack in that department you more than make up for. You are amazingly good. It's been a long time since I have felt such ……. tenderness and when accompanied with an ability to know exactly what I need …… Has anyone ever accused you of being perfect?

Stop it Anna. You'll have me blushing. In fact, turn over so you can't see.

Anna turned over and as she did so she was pushing her bottom between my legs. Slowly at first. Back and forth. Anna's face in the pillow as she pushed herself on to me. I took her by the hips and pulled her towards me as I thrusted forward. I took her for all my worth. Anna lifted her head, straining her neck as she lets out a cry of? A cry of ecstasy I supposed would be the name given to moments such as those. She shuddered and collapsed onto the bed. Minutes

162

passed and I felt the need to break the silence. Go for it James. What can you say that surpasses what went before?

"Which side of the bed do you sleep Anna"? I asked. Anna turned to face me. I could see she was willing to play the game. Or maybe intrigued as to what I was thinking.

Why do you want to know that James?

Well. If you sleep on the right hand side, come sleep time we are perfectly suited.

Trust me James when I say. If I slept horizontally across the bed, I don't think we will have problems come sleep time. Not if the last hour or two has anything to say for itself.

Anna reached forward and kissed me.

Come on James the meatballs await. Time to get dressed.

Anna didn't consider her underwear necessary as she tried to zip herself up while leaving the room. When I caught up she had the meatballs reheating in the frying pan and was cutting salad. I placed the wine, untouched in the bedroom, on the central island. Sat myself on a stool to watch. I could see she was doing the, I'm in control bit but there were cracks. Her disheveled hair which was never so. The bow of her dress flapping about, untied. The zip not quiet in place. Her blushing cheeks. I moved around the bar and took up a position behind her. Taking the straps in my hands I tied her bow. She was ignoring my action. I kissed her neck and she swivelled around.

You seem a little flustered Anna. Can I help with anything?

It is you James. You have me flustered but I think I like it. It is me being a little out of control and I like it. Now go and sit down before I drop something.

I remembered keeping Anna amused with tales of my youth leaving out the parts where drugs were relevant to the story. Which at times was difficult. How does one explain why we were steering the world from the hills of Mount Edgecombe one sunny summer Sunday.

Will you stay the night James?

That caught me out. One minute avoiding drug related stories, the next ......

I'd love to Anna.

Giving her a knowing look that was full of humility. Not an easy look to achieve, I might add. Anna's persona seemed to change at that moment. She became affectionate. It was not to say Anna couldn't do affectionate, she could but this was different. It seemed more ..... natural.

I do have a match tomorrow so we need to be up at seven. Is that ok?

That's different. Anna was asking me if it's alright. I looked at my watch.

Seven o'clock it is. In which case it's getting late perhaps we should retire?

James! It's only ten?

You do want to get some sleep tonight Anna. Don't you?

On sheer impulse I put my hand under her dress. Anna did little in response other than to open her legs, just ever so slightly. My hand found that smooth mound. My fingers entered. Anna had her eyes closed.

Anna moved away laughing.

You are right James, it is getting late.

It was difficult getting up the next morning. Places ached were I didn't know I had places. I knew there were moments of sleep. I remembered waking from them. Waking from them with a hard on that would embarrass steel. Anna was forever responsive to this conundrum.

I heard her in the shower. It was just before six forty. As I fought to make sense of my surroundings, I drifted off.

"It is all yours James." I heard Anna say.

I woke. I rolled out of bed trying really hard to put a stride in my step. Anna watching me, naked, which didn't help. I hit my hip on a protruding something. That had Anna laughing.

"There is nothing like a bit of sympathy Anna and that was nothing like a bit of sympathy", I said in the hope of regaining some sort of control over my ineptitude. Anna was still laughing when I left, ten minutes later..

I found myself that morning driving in the direction of work. Why not, I thought. I know Will will be there. Last day, last Friday but Will will be there. Having left Anna's at seven thirty I arrived early. Nothing new there. I made a coffee and sat in the semi gloom of the kitchen. Was that real? That evening and early morning. Or some ..... some dream of such proportions I could but imagine in my wildest dreams. I could see only one downside to this, to this relationship we had. She was rich! I couldn't avoid that dilemma. I thought of Pretty Woman. That ended happily. The phone rang. It was Anna. I only saw her forty minutes ago?

James. Just about to start the match and needed to call you but I have to admit, I have no idea how to translate my feelings of this moment into words. So instead, why don't you just wish me luck.

Good luck Anna. And she was gone.

I spent the morning on and off the forklift. Organising the warehouse as best I could while Will caught up with his outstanding emails. I remembered enjoying those few hours. I rarely got the chance to do anything physical. There is fulfilment in practical work. There is a before and after and in the case of the few hours spent, the difference around the warehouse was, to say the least, dramatic. Pleased with what I'd accomplished and adding to the fact Anna had felt the need to call me. Life was good! In such a euphoric mood it had to be the African to finish the day. I arrived home at four. Euphoric had been compounded with the underlining indulgence of alcohol. I started to put "pen to paper". Just falling short of undying love. It was all there. I relived the evening to Anna. The moments of pure ecstasy. Of tenderness. Of something I refrained from calling love. It was all there, ready to press send. Golden rule. When under the influence of alcohol. Don't! Check it out the next day and if still satisfied send but nine times out of ten, it's a delete. I refrained. Copy/Paste to Notes and grabbed a beer. Phone in hand, I stared at the plant in front of me. It was not difficult to miss. Two metres tall and three metres across. I thought of sending the message but I knew, it had to be a call.

Hi Anna. Now look, far be it for me to jump onto someone else's bandwagon of not being able to translate thoughts into words but ...... let me put it this way. I am speaking words. I understand the words but they have no meaning?

Are you free for lunch tomorrow James?

Thank you Anna.

What are you thanking me for James?

Thank you for allowing me to emerge with some dignity. Tomorrow would be almost perfect.

I know what you are implying James but I can't make it sooner.

Innuendoes. Something that worked or didn't. With Anna and myself. It worked. My friend Tony, a past master at innuendoes but who should steer clear of any "interesting" ladies. The innuendoes could become more of a sexual nature, particularly as the evening wore on. I'd never been a one for such innuendoes but I supposed there was the implication in what I'd said. Either way, Anna was amused. I now strove to be pro active.

I know a nice restaurant in Tourettes sur Loup Anna. I'll see if I can book a table.

What is it called James?

La Cave de Tourettes or something similar. I have the details on my phone.

Ok. Can you make the reservation for one thirty?

I'll see what I can do Anna. Call you later.

I had been to that restaurant the previous summer. It had perhaps ten covers with a choice of three dishes. Delicious food but the pièce de résistance was the small terrace. Just large enough for two small tables. Seating two a table. It was no exaggeration to say this terrace was perched on the side of a cliff with a couple of hundred metres, straight down! The view in all directions was breathtaking. I hadn't manage a terrace table the last time, possibly due to the fact, I didn't know there was one. Half an hour later and I'd secured a table on the terrace. I called Anna.

One thirty it is Anna.

Well done James. (I love the way she said that. As though I had achieved something remarkable.) *I have my friend Jennifer going with me to the garage at twelve. I have to drop off the Mercedes for a service so I should be with you before one.*

Ok Anna. Looking forward to it. I'll open the gate before one.

That was the moment. That moment I could do as Anna and close the conversation down. She beat me to it.

Anna pervaded my thoughts. Distraction was what I needed. I scrolled through the films available on the hard drive. Made a coffee and settled back to watch. To watch anything. Needless to say, sleep once again, evaded me for some time, that night. One thing was for sure. Anna would be late but I thought I had that covered as I'd booked the table for two.

I opened the gate at twelve thirty and waited. Twenty past one and Anna arrived. I was determined not to mention the time which was somewhat irrelevant as the thought slipped my mind seeing Anna arrive in an Aston Martin.

Come on James, we don't want to be too late.

Anna was laughing. Perhaps something to do with the look of astonishment on my face? Standing there in a white dress adorned with large colourful flowers, she looked divine. She programmed the GPS and off we set. Where are those people one knows who should be lining the street, gaping with astonishment as I cruised by with a beautiful lady driving an Aston Martin. I took solace in knowing it wasn't a very long street as I sat back to enjoy the drive. It was explained on the drive. This was her husbands car which she now rarely used. The last time, was at a charity function in Monaco a few months earlier. "It was the only way to arrive", she said. "It's all about the bling my dear".

We arrived in the village finding a space available, that as luck would have it, was in front of the restaurant and a reasonably large space. This was no Mini. How come Anna was lucky to find a space when I knew I would have had to traverse the village more than once to find a spot, and then relieved it was only a two hundred metre walk. It was two exactly as we were being led through that tiny restaurant to the terrace. I could see Anna was impressed with the terrace. See it and hear it. The waitress hovered as Anna went into Anna mode. She was delighted but couldn't decide which view suited. There entailed a lot of shuffling on that rather narrow terrace between the waitress, myself and Anna as she swapped from one chair to the other. Anna, duly satisfied with the seating, we were presented with the day's menu. I checked the wine menu. Anna meanwhile asked the waitress to suggest something. A very good wine I heard her saying. I found it. I could live with that. In fact it was so enjoyed Anna asked if I wouldn't mind getting a bottle to take away.

It was a perfect afternoon. I remembered little of the conversation but I would never forget the time. Those few hours oblivious to all around as we took in the view. A perfect afternoon. Finding a parking ticket on the car when we left did nothing to dampen the mood. Perhaps that was why the space was empty, I thought. Anna came back for coffee. I saw myself lifting that pretty dress above her head.

James, are you gathering wool?

No Anna. I was just thinking of taking your dress off. But I didn't say that.

"A toast James!" Said Anna, as she raised her coffee cup.

Oh christ! Here we go again.

My turn this time James.
I tried to hide my relief.
To a wonderful afternoon with a perfect English Gentleman.
The thought of lifting Anna's dress, slowly disappeared. How could the perfect gentleman do such a thing? Anna stayed for another hour or so when there were moments the dress lifting looked as if it might just happen but the perfect gentleman won out there. But only just. Heavy petting was the order of the day. How I managed to resist the temptation to slide my hand up inside her dress, I will never know. I helped Anna manoeuvre the Aston to face the gate and with a wave of her hand, she was gone.
I seriously needed a distraction. I tried to read but every time I turned a page there was that split second when I wasn't reading. It could have been fifteen minutes that passed before I'd manage to drag my consciousness back to the book at hand. This made for slow reading. I watched three movies, back to back and went to bed around two.
I got a message from Anna around ten the next morning.
Can I call you?
Pro active me, called her. It was engaged. Not expecting that, I looked at the phone and shrugged. Anna would see I called and would phone back when freed up. She didn't call. I sent a few messages. No replies? I tried to call. Always engaged. It was five when Anna finally called.
Oh James, you will never guess. Just after I sent you that message this morning, I dropped my phone in the pool. The day has been a disaster. I had a rendezvous with a restauranteur today about an up and coming dinner party for twenty or so people and I couldn't remember if it was three or four o'clock. I didn't need to remember. It was on my phone! I arrived at three and typical mediterranean French, he was annoyed at my early arrival. (That must have been a first for you Anna, I was thinking.) Meanwhile I have been to Orange three times today and have just managed to get a new phone. Thank goodness my contacts have been saved. Why don't you invite me to the cinema one evening James. I see there is a movie directed by Brad Pitt on in Antibes with George Clooney.
Was that the reason Anna called?
That sounds delightful Anna. We can do that tomorrow. I was wondering. Was there a specific reason you wanted to call this morning?
Yes. Well no. Well yes. I'll tell you some other time James.
I knew it to be pointless to push for an answer, so I didn't.
Ok Anna. I'll let you know the start time of the movie and you can work it back from there.
Wonderful James. See you tomorrow.

No surprise on Anna's immediate departure. So it wasn't the cinema? Then why did she ring? Perhaps I'd never know. I checked on Brad Pitt movies in Antibes. The film started just after eight. Do I give Anna an earlier start time? *Just checked the times Anna. Film starts at eight so if drinks before? See you tomorrow.*

I promised myself I would do some household chores the next day and true to form I'd mopped the entire floor by late morning. Washing on the line with another on the way. Linen basket empty which was almost unheard of. I therefore decided it was time for a well earned break. Picking a book from the shelf at random, I headed for the roof. Next wash load ready in eighty minutes and then the bathroom to conquer. No more than two pages into the book and I got a message.

Hi James. This evening I'll be arriving in Antibes from the direction of Juan-les-Pins. Therefore it would seem logical that we meet in Antibes. Can I meet you at a bar say around seven thirty?

If memory serves me correctly Anna, there is a bar across the road from the cinema. Give me a call as you approach and I can rush into the street waving and shouting. On second thoughts, I'll text you the name of the bar when I arrive.

A few minutes later I received a laughing face in response. I reached for the book. Settled back to the sound of the cigales. One became indifferent to their chirping and it was only when they stopped on mass, did one really notice. It had become a productive day and I was well satisfied with my efforts. It was at the clothes choosing time when I remembered the Tods. That could have created a problem. I now had to decide, from shoes up, what I'd be wearing. Thinking ahead I'd taken the time to shop while in Plymouth where I'd managed to buy clothes I felt would be acceptable. That would be, my idea of acceptable.

Anna arrived just before eight insisting on a glass of wine saying something about there were always twenty minutes of adverts before the film. I did doubt that remark but how could I possibly disagree. We entered the cinema at eight fifteen. The doors to our screening room were closed. An usher arrived. She didn't look happy. Anna proceeded to explain, in her perfect french, the problems I had encountered on my way here. I had encountered? In the time it took for the usher to assimilate said response, Anna had pushed the doors open and was insisting I hurried, or we would miss the film. A sweet smile to the usher and we are in. If it was my choice we would have been seated by seven fifty and getting comfortable well in time for the movie. The movie started at eight twenty. Anna said nothing but I personally, would have preferred avoiding the earlier problems at the door. We watched the film in silence with Anna resting her hand in mine. An occasional glance passed between us indicating we both seemed to have come to the same conclusion about the movie. Once outside the cinema I turned to Anna and said, "Perhaps George should stick to Nespresso ads". She laughed. "But the good news! You don't talk during a film."

Anna hugged my arm.

"Where are you parked Anna"? She pointed in the general direction of the port.

You didn't park in the underground parking, did you?

Yes. It's where I always park when I visit Antibes.

I had to laugh.

What?

It doesn't bother you that there are consequences turning up late at the cinema and yet you don't consider parking closer. You exhibit that of a woman in control but concurrently, you don't like to be outside your comfort zone. I find that endearing and also amusing. You certainly are a multi faceted woman Anna. A jewel that shines forth from every conceivable facet.

And you James have an endearingly annoying ability to cause controversy and still manage to come out smelling of roses. Did you mean that? About a jewel shining?

Saying nothing but giving my most sincere look in a moment of eye contact said more than I could verbalise. Anna accepted this, pulling closer as we headed to the parking. Ticket paid, Anna thought to ask where was I parked.

Oh, I'm parked close to the cinema.

No! Why didn't you say? I will drive you back.

It's ok Anna, I'll enjoy the walk.

Anna was having none of it. I smiled. Kissed her cheeks and said, "I have learnt something this evening Anna. We spent almost two hours without talking and not once did I feel the need to interrupt that silence between us. They are golden moments when the necessity for conversation is unimportant and I truly felt that to be the case. Thank you for that feeling Anna".

I smiled and turned to leave.

James!

I turned expecting Anna to insist on taking me but she placed her arms around my neck and gently but quickly kisses my lips. "Thank you James". It was her turn to smile.

A half an hour had passed. Anna must surely be home by now?

I hope, by writing this "message of the night" I don't ruin our beautiful departure Anna but I have to ask. I didn't think you kissed in public? I can only hazard a guess as to why you did so but that is not important. What is, is the fact you did it. Thank you for breaking out of that comfort zone for me Anna. Good Night and Sweet Dreams. James x

An almost immediate response!

Yes James, I wondered why I did that but having read your message I will take comfort in the why is not important as I did it and enjoyed doing so but don't you get any ideas it might happen again. I am now aware of that possibility and I will be better prepared the next time. It was nice though, wasn't it? Thank you for

the thought of sweet dreams but I am already through my first! Your,
momentarily out of control, Favourite Lady. x
So you've already been dreaming about me Anna?
You James? No, George Clooney of course!
Sorry, my mistake. Don't be jealous James. Your shoulder is much better and
it's available! My shoulder will take that as a compliment. Good Night Anna x
Good Night James x

Chapter Eleven

The quietness of June had long since passed as mid summer approached. I decided to message Anna knowing it to be a Thursday, Tennis day, I sent before nine. I received a message from Anna at the exact same moment.
I received a follow up message.
I think we pressed send at the same moment?
I think we did Anna. What does that mean, I wonder.
Well James, "Coincidence", says my pragmatic self. "Something more", says my romantic soul.
I see your dilemma Anna. Being aware of these but two of the many facets of Anna I would like to think of it as "something more". I like the romantic soul you possess. It is a thing of beauty. Beauty is not skin deep. It is what lies below where the true beauty lies and I think Anna, you have that in abundance. Good Luck with your match today and whatever the outcome, enjoy. Talk later, x
Thank You for the compliment James, so eloquently put but a, "Yes, I agree", might have sufficed.
I was confident in believing Anna would now be laughing.
I'm not sure if I told you James? Maybe not, as I was only made aware two days ago but I have visitors from Moscow for a few days and it will be the first time to the South of France so I will be the tour guide for the time they are here. I believe they leave for Paris on Tuesday morning. Why don't we go to the beach that afternoon? My treat.
I look forward to that Anna. Keep in touch. James. x
I could have added more but didn't know what to say. Was I hoping to see Anna that weekend? Four days. Four and a half days. Don't think about it, I thought. So I decided not to. I had things to do but for the moment it was a good time for the roof. An hour or two, mid morning before the sun started to bake. By the time

I headed inside a gentle breeze prevailed and as the sun had by now moved from the front of the house it was time to open the shutters. I threw the windows open and was met with that gentle, almost cooling breeze. Time for some research. An hour later and I'd chosen our next venue. Horse racing in Cagnes-sur-Mer. Not that I was a racing fan but lunch in the restaurant overlooking the course? I thought Anna would like that.

That afternoon I took the motorbike into Antibes. No point taking the car as there would have been nowhere to park at that time of year. I was fortunate enough to find a table at my favourite bar/cafe and, in the shade. Don't you just love the tourist. Given the choice, a seat in the sun was always the preferred option. I allowed my thoughts to drift when I saw a woman who reminded me of Emanuela. I wondered how she was? Who she was with? Was she happy? Had she forgotten all about me? I had to snap out of that and luckily enough the waiter passed by. Monsieur! Une pression, s'il vous plait. I rolled a cigarette and concentrated on people watching. I was wondering how strange it was, to see people dressed, in almost nothing and yet in a few months, in the same streets, will be people dressed in coats, hats and scarves. My phone pinged.

Showed Valbonne to my visitors. We had "small talk" about this and that and we are now sitting on the terrace, overlooking the pool and drinking rosé. What do I do in between? Think of you. Sometimes. Often. Now.

Anna was making small talk. I liked that. Those messages that might not say anything but it was not about what they said. It was there to let the other person know. Know you were thinking of them. And I was thinking of Emanuela. Well, not really. She entered my thoughts. Can one feel guilty of thought? Possibly. I waited awhile and ordered another beer.

That, I'm assuming comes under the category of, an enjoyable, relaxing day. Mine on the other hand has been relaxing but not necessarily enjoyable. I had a couple of hours on the roof this morning. I surfed the net for porn. (Just checking you're paying attention.) I'm actually sat at my favourite bar in Antibes, sipping a cold beer. Surely enjoyable James, I hear you say. No Anna it's not enjoyable. You are not here! And if that is an admittance of, of something a romantic soul might say. I plead guilty but gain solace in knowing you are thinking of me. x

I liked that. A lot could have said it better but I was not a lot. I was me. I felt challenged or perhaps, at times, overawed by Anna and knowing that I had to up-my-game. I had been in situations, as had we all, when the conversation didn't necessarily revolve around football. One had to up-the-game. No pun intended. Try and draw on any knowledge one might have about the subject at hand. A subject that was forever changing. I usually came away hearing good reports on my presence at this or that function I'd attended. I must have been doing something right. After all. It was just a game but a game I wasn't sure I wanted to play with Anna. How did it go? "We can fool some of the people all the time. All of the people some of the time but not all the people all the time". Anna was all those people. Not actually sure I was fooling her but I was playing my best hand. "Enjoy it while it lasts", came to mind. Should I be that pessimistic? For people who could walk away from a relationship and think no more about it. Well, lucky them. I got hurt. Perhaps I needed to be more realistic? Enjoy it while it lasts would involve enjoying being with someone but don't get too close. How did one do that?

Do you know how happy your words make me James? Which in itself is strange? How can I be happy knowing you are not. I'm happy in the same way I think you are happy James. Happy just knowing someone is thinking of me. I will see if I can get away to a quiet corner this evening and give you a call. Enjoy the rest of your day thinking of me James. x

Time to leave the bustle of Antibes for the quiet of the suburbs. I was forever amazed at the dress code of other bikers. It was thirty something degrees and I was wearing jeans. A bike jacket and gloves. A guy flew past me on a five hundred cc scooter in shorts and flip flops. C'est la vie ici? No point in messaging Anna as she said she would call that evening. I heard Paul outside shouting over the hedge. I got an invitation for a BBQ. Delphine, their twenty something daughter was paying a flying visit.

I'll be there in fifteen minutes Paul. It will be nice to see Delphine. It must be at least a year.

Time enough for a quick message.

Going next door Anna for an early evening BBQ but my phone will not be far away. Hope you get that moment and find a quiet corner. For now x

It was a very pleasant evening and it seemed Paul and I were on our best behaviour. The change in Delphine, having spent the last two years living and working in London, was dramatic to say the least. She'd been brought up in France although Paul and Chiara had always spoken to her in their native tongues but I think Delphine needed the confidence to reply. She had gained that confidence and it was a little strange having that once shy girl talking, with a trans Atlantic accent, throwing out and answering questions in such a self assertive manner. Fluent in three languages. There were times I could barely cope with the one. I drifted away to thoughts of Anna. Russian and speaking the Queens English with her French not that far behind. Was I going to relate everything I heard to that of Anna, I wondered? It was after ten when I wished all a pleasant evening before departing, well aware there was no call from Anna. It wasn't a definite. These were friends she hadn't seen for some time. They were bound to monopolise her, making it difficult to get away. It was eleven thirty before I decided to message Anna.

Ok Anna I've had ninety seven minutes continuously thinking of you. I have decided to take these thoughts to bed in the hope they will prevail my sleep with dreams befitting such thoughts.

I immediately receive a kiss in icon form. Accompanied with the short message of, *Couldn't have my quiet corner. x*

One kiss Anna? Can I interpret that to mean, I so much desire your lips on mine?

It is just an innocent kiss James but why should you worry. I'm not your type anyway. A Big Russian Woman.

Anna was playing games and continued to do so.

I started a phrase. Deleted. Again started. Deleted. I am having trouble expressing myself. I do not know what is appropriate. I will just say Good Night James and two kisses to exclude any suggestions. xx

It's ok, infatuation will do that to you. Good Night Anna. xxx (My apologies for being antagonistic.)

Chapter Twelve

It was beach day. Anna had messaged to say she would be around at twelve thirty and she was!

I thought we would go to Théole James, there is a nice restaurant called The Marco Polo. Have you been there?

I actually had been to that beach. Last summer. Spread my towel on what remained of the part of the beach not taken up by The Marco Polo with a take-away ice drink. I decided not to mention that.

Yes but it's a few years ago. From what I can remember it's a small beach with an equally small carpark.

You worry too much James. I am sure we will find a place to park.

That was a mistake. Full of pessimism. I hadn't meant it that way. I was just stating a fact. It was the week before high season and I knew it to be difficult finding a place in November. I regained my composer and entertained Anna with an amusing tale or two. The last five hundred metres to the car park was nose to tail traffic. Anna seemed oblivious as she pulled into the short drive leading to the parking. Someone was just leaving. Anna waited and reversed in. I grabbed the bag from the boot and we walked the hundred metres to the restaurant. We were greeted at the entrance and Anna immediately spotted a table on the beach that was just being cleared.

"Pourrions-nous avoir ce tableau?" Asked Anna, pointing in the general direction of the table she wanted.

Oui, bien sûr madam.

I think I was in awe, if not that then something similar. I had to ask but first Anna had to decide which seat she would occupy.

Does it invariably happen this way Anna?

What do you mean?

Well. We arrive at a full carpark and someone is, at that precise moment, leaving. We arrive at the restaurant and you manage to procure, not just any old table in a full restaurant but seafront view.
Anna looked bemused. That bemusement answered my question. Yes, that was how it happened for Anna. Diffuse that bemusement before it escalated into having to explain myself with a version of, Some have it. Some don't! I took Anna's hand in mine and reaching across, I kissed the back of her hand. Held out in preparation.
For a woman who never ceases to amaze me.
Very sweet James but do not think, for one moment, I am not aware of your digression. Which wine would you prefer?
She gave me a sideways glance of amusement.
My choice of rosé was accepted and I was about to decide on the salmon until Anna insisted I had the veal. We both had veal and as the coffee was served Anna asked if we could reserve the two loungers adjacent our table. Thus secured we sat back to enjoy the coffee. We moved to the loungers. Adequately shaded by an umbrella, Anna produced a book. Put her glasses on and proceeded to read.
If you catch someones eye James, could you order me an orange with ice.
Ok. Time to upset the apple cart. I ordered an orange, with ice and a Heineken for myself but asked the waiter if he could bring it in ten minutes as we were about to go for a swim.
Oui Monsieur, certainement.
Come on Anna. You can't sit there and read all day. I would feel I have not fulfilled my duties if I was to allow you to spend the afternoon immersed in a book. You might be an amazing woman but I'll not allow you to wallow in that compliment. Let's go for a swim.
"Oh James, as if I would". Anna was up and heading towards the water. "Last one in drives us home!"
And so the afternoon continued. Anna never did get to read that book but true to form, it was Anna's treat. Not that I was curious but I saw Anna didn't receive much in return from three hundred euros. As I drove us homeward. Yes, I lost that bet, Anna mentioned she needed to "pop into" Giant on the way home. A supermarket in Mandelieu. Anna knew what she wanted as she headed for the fish counter. Ordered up a couple of salmon filets and asked if she could collect in ten minutes. Then she turned to me.
You see now why you couldn't have salmon? I'm cooking this for our dinner. Just need to get a few more things.
And with a most delightful smile was off. We are having diner? As we left the supermarket a particular shop frontage stopped Anna in her tracks.
Look James, you should go in and see if they have your size.

Five minutes later I walked out with a new pair of shorts. Anna took over the driving.

"I thought it would be easier if we go straight to my place. I can take you home tomorrow", Anna said with a straight face, adding "I have a spare toothbrush".

How did I answer that? Ok. I saw a way of coming out of this, head held high.

Do you always have a spare toothbrush Anna?

No. I just bought it at the supermarket.

So much for coming out of that head held high! I was back where I started. Anna had made the decision. I was staying the night. It seemed I had nothing to say in the matter. I couldn't just go with the flow. Anna had to realise, two make such decisions. I had to be assertive with my questioning.

So Anna, you've already made the decision. Wouldn't it have been a nice idea to have consulted with me rather than assuming?

You are right James. Would you like to stay tonight?

Fortunately for me, Anna could hold it in no longer. She burst into laughter.

I'm sorry James but once I'd thought of the idea I realised it would be fun to see how far I could take it. You were wonderful I must say.

Ok Anna, let me get this straight. You thought of inviting me but then decided to include a toothbrush into the thought process. You didn't actually buy one?

Yes, that is about right James.

So my question Dear Anna, would be, Have you got a spare toothbrush? Said in a way, with a look that typified that of confusion, had the desired effect. Anna had to pull over. Incapable of continuing. Having composed herself with just the odd snigger to accompany her words she managed to say,

I've always got spare toothbrushes. The amount of times the girls would have friends over. I always have a good stock. Habit I suppose? Anyway it is too late to change your mind. We are well past the point of no return.

I thought one had to have ones mind set on something Anna, in order not to be able to change it?

You are playing with words again James. I've already told you, it is too late.

Anna leant across and gave me a most wonderful but too short a kiss and we were off. Sometime during the last five minutes of the journey, a thought had occurred. I was still back where I started and Anna knew it. I would have to make it up to myself this evening and well before bedtime. While Anna was putting the shopping away I decided on choosing a wine. Not too difficult, there were racks of them in front of me. The cooler. That will be the white and rosé. I concentrate on the racks. In the end I took one at random. Knowing where the corkscrew was kept I felt I was contributing to the evening. I poured the wine. Placed the bottle on the table as Anna simultaneously arrived.

"More of that coincidence"? She said.

I was sure Anna didn't really expect a response. She was looking coy as she seated herself. I was getting used to sitting around on those bar stools. It could become quite intimate, particularly as the stools had wheels. Anna crept towards me.

You are not angry with me, are you James?

You know very well I'm not angry with you but if this is your way of trying to redeem yourself, ……. it's working.

I gave her my kind smile.

I find your take refreshing Anna. I don't think it matters who makes the decision and in this case, a decision we can both readily agree upon helps.

I gave her my wicked smile.

Very good James, now could you please make the decision and kiss me.

Anna returned my wicked smile. I was not sure she'd had a lot of practice of wicked smiles as it resembled a constipated Chinese girl. A cute constipated Chinese girl maybe but it had the undesired effect of having me laughing. Fortunately Anna believed the laughter was a consequence of her previous remark. I got my laughter under control. Looked her in the eyes as I placed my hand behind her neck, drawing her those few inches closer. The kisses were passionate. They were prolonged and then I felt Anna gently pulling away.

I have to have a shower James. I need to wash off the last of the sand and if we are going to eat this evening, I have to do it now. In fact, why don't you join me. You must surely feel the same.

I'm not sure Anna. Feeling the same what exactly?

I am talking about the sand James. We wouldn't want to be finding sand in the bed come morning now would we?

God forbid Anna. Lead on.

Anna casually dropped her beach clothes on the floor and stepped into the shower. Glass surrounded and big enough for four. I stood watching her for a moment and made no move when Anna turned to face me.

Stop looking James and come and join me.

I never considered that situation to be a fantasy of mine but I soon discovered why it was for some. Anna squeezed shower gel into my hands and turned her back to me. I spread the gel over her upper body over her bottom and down her legs. As I slowly reversed the action Anna parted her legs. I ran my hand slowly between her legs and as equally slowly, I withdrew my hand. I massage her buttocks running my hands up her back until I was cupping her breasts in my hands. Pushing my self against her, Anna sighed.

Yes James.

Anna spread her legs that little bit more and placed her hands on the only wall. The entry was slow. Slow with rhythm. I didn't touch Anna. I kept my hands to my side. Slow rhythm nothing more. Anna was pushing onto me. Almost silent up until that moment, Anna became vocal. Not verbal but vocal. Short intermittent moaning. Moments later Anna's moans had turned to what I could only describe as a guttural sobbing. I caught her before she fell to the floor and held her tight. We stayed like that until the overhead shower had infused us with it's gentle petals of rain. Yes, that is how it happened. The poetry of that moment did infuse us with those gentle petals, I felt sure. Anna regained her composure.

As you have already and kindly soaped me down James, I just have one little spot I would like to rewash and I will be out. And don't think I didn't think of soaping you down.

I stood there, waiting for the "but" to arrive as I watch Anna putting far too much gel between her legs but it didn't arrive. Anna left me to soap myself. I found her in the kitchen, preparing the Salmon.

Do you have potatoes Anna?

Yes?

In that case mash potatoes. Where are the potatoes?

Anna was pointing to a cupboard. A chill box of course. For the vegetables.

How long do you need James?

Fifteen minutes from now and they are ready for the table. Do you have any parmesan?

There is fresh parmesan in the fridge.

As I waited for the boiling potatoes to do their thing Anna finished garnishing the fish. I walked up and put my arms around her waist. Anna squirmed in my arms until she was facing me.

You know I talked about soaping you?

No answer was expected.

I knew I couldn't. Maybe not couldn't more ….. incapable of. Or maybe I just wanted to savour the delights of that memory before confusing it with another. Does any of that make sense James?

It makes perfect sense Anna. Petals of rain sense.

What?

Nothing Anna, just a whimsical thought.

She smiled. We kissed and then attended to the cooking. While in the chill box the mange tout had caught my eye. That would do nicely. Anna had set the table on the terrace and I think that moment, as we ate, encapsulated the day. A day on the beach being waited on. Our earlier moments in the Breakfast Bar and later the shower. Even the supermarket. It was all a part of the moment. The moment that would continue on-through the night. Anna was giving me that look. That look which meant, where are you James but before I could open my mouth

Those potatoes were marvellous James. What is your secret?

I have to disappoint you there Anna but at the same time possibly make you the happiest woman in the world. I can't tell you the recipe but I am always available when needed. To cook the mash, I mean.

I gave Anna a moment or two and a millisecond before she thought of what to reply. I managed for maybe the first time, to beat her to it.

I was just thinking of the day Anna. It will always remain a memory I'll cherish. Cherishing the thought of you for making such a day possible.
Anna jumped out of her seat. Around the table in an instant. Grabbed my face and with the ever so slightest sideways movement of her head, kissed me.
I like the way you make me the centre of attention James. I have heard so many versions along a similar vein but when you say it, it is different. And before you ask, I am not at liberty to tell you why. Or I could be honest and tell you I don't know why.
We cleared away the table and I sat watching, while Anna made the coffee. I was feeling good. Be careful James, every time you get that smug, better than thou feeling, it usually ends in tears but no, not this time. I was confident Anna was duly impressed with my assistance. Before, during and after the shower.
Here you are. American as ordered. It has been a wonderful day James ......
Anna seemed to drift off. Not to sleep, just drifted off.
Shall we go to bed James?
After the time in the shower I was thinking of a softer approach for later. Later seemed to be upon me.
As Anna lay there, I ran my hand over her body, gently kissing her neck. I confidently moved my kisses to her nipples. Licking around the aureola. Slowly taking those kisses to her stomach as I moved my hand in a position to open her legs. Anna understood what was happening as she relaxed on the bed. I wondered if I would ever get tired of that sight? It was difficult to image such a time, I was thinking, as I ran my tongue gently over that delicious mound. I believed such things should be enjoyed. One should take ones time. I kissed her inner thighs before returning to more luxurious kissing of that perfect place. It was a time to explore the inner delights. I knew where I needed to be but patience was a virtue. Anna was responding to my tentative first steps. Had I teased her enough when I seemed to discover that spot only to retreat? I do believe Anna was ready. My concentration became intense. Anna was reaching a climax.
"Inside me James". Said Anna as she tried to pull me onto her. I was very quickly inside her. Inside her to coax her back to that climax.
As I awoke that next morning confusion struck. I heard Anna somewhere in the back ground. Well I assumed it to be Anna in the shower. I was in a different bedroom? Ok, I got that. The first time it was a another bedroom. Anna liked to swap rooms? While I ponder that thought Anna emerged wrapped in a towel. Shook her wet hair in my face and asked if I'd like pancakes for breakfast. Complimented with honey of my choice she said, but only if I hurried and got ready. Pancakes and as promised, an assortment of honey, lay before me. They kept coming. I had to say I can't possibly have another, three times before Anna realised.

I have coaching at eleven James so we need to be out in an hour. Come on, help me decide which outfit I should wear today.

Did I heard her correctly? I did hear her correctly. I decided on an all white number as Anna threw her towel aside and went in search of her knickers. Returning, knickers in place. Anna dressed. I remarked on how sexy she looked. And she did! Fifty and sexy. Well done Anna, I thought. We had time for a last decaf before we had to leave which was when I noticed a change in Anna. It crossed my mind she might be getting herself into the, "One hour with the coach" persona. Inevitably, seconds later I wondered which persona was mine? I shouldn't pursue that line of enquiry, I decided. Anna dropped me at the top of my drive but before I could get out, she held my arm, looking at me for what was becoming too long even for a pregnant pause. She kissed me and said, "See you soon James".

What did she mean? "See you soon?" Said not as a throw away remark but with sincerity. I needed to reply.

"Soon Anna", I said, giving my best interpretation of someone who understood. Back home again, pinching myself in the hope I didn't wake up while aimlessly wondering around my living space. We hadn't made any arrangement for our next meeting. It seemed to be the way Anna preferred. Enjoy it while you can, flooded my thoughts. Was that all I should be thinking? It won't last so just enjoy? I thought it was past the point of just enjoy, for me. Now where was I? Occupy the mind James. I decided to wash the cars. A half an hour later and without a seconds thought I grabbed my tobacco, some money and decided to head into town. Now where did I put my bike gloves? Twenty minutes later I was sat, in the empty shaded area, having coffee and reading the Times.

Excuse me. You are English?

Before I had a chance to react I viewed a very attractive lady talking to me.

Could I have your other sugar, if you don't need it? It's just, I dropped mine and really wouldn't like to use it.

"Of course and yes, I am English. Not too difficult to spot", I said, holding up the paper. She laughed.

"Are you on holiday?" I asked.

No, well yes, sort of. I have a house and I rent it out during high season. Normally I would be away but I had to return to sort out some major catastrophe at the house which in reality was very minor. So I suppose I'm back on holiday. My name is Eva, by the way.

James. Nice to meet you Eva. That accent? It's slight but there is one.

Well spotted James and believe it or not, it's an accent I've strived to maintain. Never forget your roots and all that. I was born just outside of Moscow.

The moment she divulged that small detail I wondered if I was unconsciously drawn to Russian ladies or was it them to me? Those eyes, ever so slightly closer together. A tell tale sign. She didn't have Anna's quirky behaviourism that

I found so endearing but there were similarities. She was wearing a pastel blue top and light grey partially pleated skirt with sensible shoes. Her body language signaled her openness for further conversation.

You must have spent some time in England Eva as I can't imagine you to have such a command of the language from a book.

Eva rewarded me with a polite smile.

You do me a kindness James but you are right, I have spent a lot of time living and working around London. And you James. Do you live here?

Yes. I live on the outskirts of Antibes and like you, I'm on holiday. Back to work in a couple of weeks.

You have two weeks holiday and you spend it here?

No, I've been on holiday since early June and have only recently returned to Antibes.

You have eight weeks holiday?

Actually sixteen but yes, eight in the summer and eight in the winter.

The conversation continued. I found out she had never been married. Something about work coming first. Sold her business five years ago and now filled her days enjoying what she liked to do. That sounded familiar? Eva realised it was well past the time for her departure and having thanked me for the conversation, got up and walked away. I raised my paper but I wasn't reading the words. I was thinking positive thoughts and the way positive things happened when doing so. A hand appeared above my paper. It was Eva?

Is this a regular stop for you James?

Yes it was but should I tell you that? Positive thinking should carry a warning notice but what harm was there in telling her?

Yes Eva it is but normally around nine in the morning. Maybe two or three times a week.

She took her hand from my paper and departed.

Having returned home and eventually coming down from that, interesting encounter, I made a coffee and determined to finish my paper, I found a shady area on the terrace and relaxed.

It was about six when I got a message from Anna.

Can I come around?

Of course you can. When?

Now. Well, in half an hour. Is that alright?

See you then.

That was all rather short and to the point. No, Hi James. How was your day. Anna had something on her mind I thought. I cleared away the dishes making sure the Nespresso had a full tank of water and opened a bottle of red. Nibbles! Crash helmet in hand I was wondering what nibbles the local shop might have.

It seemed my concerns were unjustified. Anna was in a glorious mood. Looking very summery in a flowing yellow dress. Reminiscent of the colour on that original photo. The girl in the yellow dress. Congratulating me on the effort I'd made regarding nibbles. She was flirting in a rather open manner. Not like Anna who tended to be more subtle about such things. The early evening flowed with a comfortable feeling of total relaxation. I would like to add, being able to be oneself but that would be a lie. It was not that I lied per se, more of hiding certain traits. It took me twenty years to devoid myself of that Plymouthian accent. Maybe a Russian accent is worth maintaining, I was thinking but definitely not a Plymouthian. Was that hiding traits? I would like to think we all had some skeletons. When dealing with certain work colleagues, swearing was par for the course. It was not something I did when in Anna's company. I'd always upheld the notion, If one surrounds oneself with people, intellectually demanding, it had a tendency to rub off. I used to know a guy during my electrical apprenticeship days. He came across as knowledgable. He knew what was going on in the world. One day when I asked him about this he said, *The Daily Telegraph*. And he was right, I was able to have an opinion about topics that only a few days previously, I knew nothing about. It was a learning curve and I was learning from Anna. After settling herself down on, what was now, her barstool she gave me a look of serious intent.

You haven't asked me why I wanted to come over so early James?

I didn't think that one through when perhaps I should have done. Anna wanting to come over at six thirty, and I don't have an answer. Wing it James.

Oh, I took it for granted you realised you couldn't be without me. You walked around that football sized living room. Strolled out around the pool when it dawned on you. I need to be with James. Did I get that right?

Anna had that look in her eyes with her lips tightly drawn but it didn't last long. She succumbed to laughter.

"You have put me in a difficult position", said Anna, once she was able to compose herself. And she composed herself so well.

If I don't admit to there being some truth in what you have just said, I will be damned. If I admit to there being some truth you will be impossible to be with. Although, thinking about it, that might not be such a bad thing. Just teasing you James. Either way it is not the reason. Elena is visiting tomorrow and is going to be staying a few days. So maybe there is some truth in your statement as I'm not sure if I will be able to see you in the days ahead. This could be our only chance to be together for awhile and I wanted to take it.

I was restocking the nibbles as Anna glided around the breakfast bar to help. I could deal with the absence, no need to get disappointed, after all Anna was very much a free spirit.

I will be moving out of the house next week and moving temporarily to Nice. I am renting the house for a month and I have an empty apartment in Nice. Elena doesn't know it but she will be helping me take some basic necessities to the apartment.

Basic necessities Anna?
Two mattresses. I actually quite enjoy sleeping without a bed. For a short time. Stock the kitchen with cutlery. Plates etc.. Food. Some clothes and shoes. Chairs and a table. Then there is ......
You're hiring a very large truck for this move and maybe half a dozen strong capable helpers?
Don't be silly James. I will have two of my building team deliver the heavy items and I think a couple of trips in the Mercedes should do it.
"Right. Good luck with that one Anna". I said laughing.
Do you have a clothes hanger Anna?
No!
I have one in the cellar. I'll get it before you go.
You have! That will be fantastic. Thank you James. You will have to come and stay. The view over the bay is wonderful. Particularly at night.
Anna was back to being flirtatious and then it all came crashing down.
Actually James could you be a dear and get the hanger. I will have to leave soon.
I did as was asked and at the same time put it the boot of Anna's car. She was sat on the stool, sipping her wine as I entered.
You know I always enjoy our times together James.
Now where did that come from and maybe more to the point, where was it going?
I was in a bad place for months after ..... when someone suggested I try a website. So I did. I have to tell you, you are not the only man I dated from that site. Anyway, to the point. You have helped lift me up James and for that I will be forever grateful. Now I begin to wonder where it will lead.
Why wonder Anna. Take it a day at a time and see where it leads. I am not going off on some philosophical tangent here Anna but isn't that what we do? Take it a day at a time and build on those days.
That is what I will do James. Build on the days. I like that.
I got a kiss which I interpreted as a, Thank you for that thought James but, wrong again.
Allow me to leave with a fond memory of this evening James. Lots of kisses before I have to leave.
Never sure how far one should or could take advantage of a situation such as that. The kissing became serious. The thought of lifting that dress reoccured. Lift and explore? I decided to take her head in my hands and slowly bring the kissing to a level of intensity that enabled the brain to take control. Controlled kissing. Enabling one to bring it to it's rightful close. We stopped as the intensity shifted to the eyes. I kissed her lightly and reluctantly mentioned her need for departure. Anna returned with a smile that would definitely launch those thousand ships.

You never cease to amaze me James. The gentleman under pressure but he is always thinking of the lady first. Do you mind sleeping with just a mattress on the floor? No need to answer that. Of course you don't. It will be with me. Thank you for, ... for another moment when I can be me.

I saw her to the car and waved her away. I got a wave in return. Progress. That didn't alleviate nor affect the feelings I had of days to follow without the possibility of seeing Anna. I decided the best course of action would be to get away for a few days. I called Mike. The next day I was heading for Kitzbuhel.

Chapter Thirteen

Five days in Kitzbuhel. Just what I needed. Mike and I got around, seeing places that weren't on the winter agenda. Within an hours drive in any direction there would be a town, a village, that was having it's annual, whatever. Locally, to avoid competition for such events and in a typically Germanic attitude to such things, these events never coincided. Conclusion? There was always a party somewhere. It was a chance to meet up with people I normally only saw during the winter. It was different. Not so frantic. There was a casual air, particularly where drinking was concerned. I mentioned drinking not to place any emphasis on the subject but .... it was Kitzbuhel. Catching up around a picnic table as opposed to a ski bar did seem less frantic and on reflection, I realised it was the absence of "The Next Run" and more importantly, to some, "Who got to the bottom first". Far less frantic around a picnic table. The time spent was a perfect distraction. There were messages of, I miss you and see you soon, passed between Anna and myself but I didn't feel I was waiting for that next reply. The time in Kitz was exactly what I needed.

Departure morning inevitably arrived. I thanked Mike for an enjoyably and relaxing time and headed for the Austrian border into Italy. Three hours of downhill driving before it flattened out the other side of Trento. I'd just turned left heading towards Milan and the phone rang. I recognised that ring tone. Brown Eyed Girl, it was Anna. I switched to the car phone.

Hello James.

Hi Anna.

I was wondering if you would like to have lunch. I'm about to go to the supermarket and thought it would be a wonderful idea if James could join me on my terrace.

I look at the GPS. ETA Antibes, thirteen twenty.

If one thirty would be acceptable, I'd be only too happy to oblige Anna. Let me rephrase that. Text the address and I'll be there by one thirty.
The rephrasing was all I needed James. You are learning. Lunch at two, giving us time for a glass of wine beforehand. And I have the wine, so just you will be enough. Are you driving?
Yes.
I thought I heard an echo. I will text you the address.
Yes! She was gone.
I estimated Nice was twenty minutes at least before Antibes I was thinking as Anna's text arrived. Twelve fifty two I was told after four attempts at trying to load the address. Why was it necessary to confirm an address? I'd spent five valuable minutes of my life installing the address. Did I do that because I was bored? No! It was because I wanted to go there! I stayed calm throughout that ordeal. Calm but with a certain amount of frustration. Welcome to the ..... to the whatever century we were in. I get cars! I get computers! Brought up on both but it had all changed. It was hard to keep up.
I was told I was two hundred metres from my destination and there was the supermarket Anna mentioned. The gates to the apartment block were open. I found a place to park at the far end, in a semi deserted area. If lucky no one will park next to me thus avoiding that, hard to believe pastime of the local French. Open your car door until it stops. Invariably it stopped when it hit the car parked next to it. Outcome? Multiple dents in the sides of ones car. I returned to my deserted car having forgotten something. Now armed with an appropriate bunch of flowers and a bottle of wine, I walked towards the apartments. I say appropriate but that was my guess on what Anna would deem appropriate. The eye of the beholder and all that.
Anna included the code for the gate and floor of the apartment. All straight forward enough. I stood in the hallway, pressed the button to the fourth floor fifteen minutes early then realised I didn't know which number. I called Anna.
James? You're early. Cross the hallway and veer left where you will find the lift. I'm number twenty eight.
I'd found the lift. I was already in it. I was met at the doorway by Anna who was wearing a huge smile, beige shorts and fashionably co-ordinated blouse.
Oh, flowers. Are they for me?
That left an opening for an untold amount of flippant replies. I couldn't resist.
Yes Anna, for you. I insisted at the florists that the flowers should compliment the beauty of the beholder. Initially she gave me dandelions so I had to ask if she knew you.
Anna was watching me carefully. Only I could ruin a gift of flowers. I corrected myself.
Beautiful flowers for a Beautiful Lady.

Anna smiled and went in search of a vase while I wandered around the almost empty apartment. The view from the terrace was spectacular. Set high on the hills overlooking the bay of Nice. Anna joined me holding two glasses of wine.

Do I have to be prepared for you to always be early James?

Normally speaking Anna, I don't like to be late but I would say my timing having just driven eight hundred kilometres from Kitzbuhel is acceptable. Don't you?

You have just arrived from Kitzbuhel. Did I know you were going? We should go this winter James as I hear it is a top resort, when there is snow. Yes, that is what we will do. Do you know a good hotel?

Hotel? I stayed with Mike. We shopped across the road at the local supermarket as one would when home. My biggest outlay for the time there would be the ski pass. Anna was thinking a "Good" Hotel within easy walking distance of the lifts. The sort of hotel where her Aston Martin would not look out of place.

What do you think of the view James, isn't it fantastic?

Yes, it's special. One could spend some time here taking in the view. Do we have that much wine?

The thought of the hotel had left me. Anna was suggesting she showed me the apartment. I glanced over my shoulder taking in the large living room. Apart from a laptop on a small table in the corner and a sheet draped over something in the centre of the room, it was empty.

Is there more to see than empty rooms Anna?

She held out her hand, which I took and was led around. Empty rooms apart from the bathroom which was inundated with, with product that all girls needed. She opened the door to the last room.

Bohemian style. What do you think James?

There were clothes everywhere. Different piles. I recognised the tennis pile. The dress pile. Shorts and tops and of course, shoes pile. Plus the clothes rail I lent her, full of more clothes. And there in the middle of the room, lay the mattress. Anna was watching me again, presumably waiting for my reaction.

Five star slumming Anna and I think you are enjoying it.

You are right James. I didn't realise how much of my time the house consumes. The apartment has given me a freedom that I am only now starting to appreciate. There is a downside, as when I return to the house there will be weeks of unconsumed time I will have to make up for but let us not think of that. Why don't you go back to the terrace and I will start lunch. You must be ravenous after such a long drive.

"That's true Anna. So can you tell me why we are having lunch"? And I said that with such a straight face combined with a quizzical look. I could see Anna wasn't sure what her reply should be. I helped her out.

Ravenous can wait. Let's have lunch. I'll go back to the terrace.

I think Anna might have been seriously considering postponing the lunch. I had obviously answered too soon. I needed to give Anna a little longer to think through these options once uttered by yours truly. She liked to think propositions through although she could be totally spontaneous, when her idea. I gave Anna a kiss as I headed to the terrace. Ten minutes later, Anna joined me.

It is in the oven and will take about twenty minutes.

What is for lunch?

It is veal I've marinated overnight combined with peppers, onions, potatoes and other vegetables.

Did you say, overnight?

Yes I did.

Anna was now trying her, I've been a naughty girl and I've been caught out, look.

So when did you consider this impromptu lunch?

Yesterday afternoon, when I'd bought all the ingredients.

I leant across and raised my glass. Our glasses touched as I said,

To the woman who fills my life. With her energy. Her intellect. Her humour and her self confessed shallowness but most of all, to you Anna for being You.

Anna was smiling a tight smile but with lips turned upwards. She was thinking. I could tell it was good thoughts.

That was wonderful James and I think you deserve something in return. I have been here a week now. Three days on my own and as I said, with a lot of time on my hands. I've been thinking a lot about you. About us and I must say, I am enjoying what I'm thinking. I liked you from the start. Have I told you that? No, most probably not. I liked you from the beginning and it scared me. I think that was the reason for my "person non grata" pre Roland Garros? Please don't take this the wrong way James but I am used to a different life style. With you I can be natural and relaxed. No competition. With acceptance of weaknesses and without judgement. It is not what I know or at least, not something I am used to. So I would like to say James. I am no longer scared.

There was a ringing from the kitchen.

"Saved by the veal", said Anna as she stood but stopped to take my hand.

Not scared anymore.

Anna just loved her exits. Leaving the conversation hanging as she strolled to the kitchen. The meal was special. Not one to frequent the more expensive restaurants, I could still imagine a customer of such an establishment being more than satisfied with the dish I so heartily consumed. With our conversation touching on political incorrectness surrounding politicians that had recently been a focus of the media to why are snowflakes different from one another and plenty of laughter in between the afternoon on the terrace passed us by.

"Come with me James", said Anna as she stood and held out her hand. She lead me to the cloth covering something sat almost in the centre of the room.

This is for you James. I bought it at the market yesterday and have spent most of the morning cleaning it.

Low and behold. An antique brass lamp that with shade must have stood a metre off the floor. My first thought. Where was I going to put that! Second thought. Not sure I liked it. I needed an instant response before Anna had a chance to see the, shall we say, a look of acute pain.

Wow! And you've spent the whole morning bringing it back to its former glory. It's amazing. Well done you and Thank You Anna. I will treasure it. It will look perfect in my bedroom. Not sure where I will put the bed though?

She laughed. I most definitely got away with that one.

That lamp still sits to this day by my bedside and I wouldn't be without it.

You like it?

Yes.

Then we will have to find somewhere to put your bed.

Now it was my turn to laugh.

Let's go to bed Anna.

She smiled.

I'm going to have to take a quick shower. Nine hours on the road will do that to you.

I will clear the table James so take your time.

When I entered the bedroom I found Anna curled up under the covers. So I slipped in behind her.

Mmmm, I am feeling so relaxed James and it is all your doing.

I curled up close. We were both asleep within minutes.

I awoke to find Anna standing over me.

When I awoke you were in deep sleep. I watched you for awhile and at one point considered possibilities of gentle arousal but decided after such a long drive you needed your sleep.

Anna gave that wicked look. I must tell her one day, how that look brought me close to laughter but not today. It quickly changed to, Miss Sensible.

I left you as long as I could but we need to go shortly. The clients are having a problem with the air conditioning. They tell me it is the whole house. I really don't understand how people with so much money refuse to comprehend the simple workings of a remote control. If we meet at your place later it will not only give you time to fully recover from your journey, there will be another advantage, I will not have to sleep on the floor tonight.

The wicked look returned.

I vaguely remembered on Anna's profile something about, liking to make decisions. No denying that! I had a feeling of being orchestrated. A wave of the hand here. A tap of the baton there. It was not up for discussion. It never was. I then asked myself the question. Could I have done better? Unlikely would be the answer. One had to give it to her, Anna had the knack. It was a moot point when I thought about it, as I was enjoying the experience.

I pass a supermarket on the way so I'll choose something for supper. Do you have any wine James?
I have a dozen bottles of fine Austrian wine in the boot of my car.
We shared a reasonably passionate kiss before leaving the apartment but once outside Anna kissed both cheeks before reminding me to follow close behind when exiting the gate.

With a reasonable amount of tidying up to do before Anna's arrival I set to it. An hour and a half later jobs done. Shower done. Time for some research in a pro-active way. Hippodrome. Canges sur Mer. It opened on Google. I scrolled through the month of August for the fixtures. No races? No races in August! The obvious fact had eluded me. It was hot in August. Not a good time to have horses racing around a track, I supposed. So much for lunch at the races. I wondered if Anna confronts the same problems as I. Was she that spontaneous? Does she think, what shall we do now and an idea takes form? No more time to wonder as I saw Anna had arrived.

"Hello James", said Anna as she once more kissed my cheeks.

I was right. Three men amongst the group and not one of them understood the remote. Do you know what I did? I showed the twelve year old son how it worked. Told the group, very politely, that I have a dinner engagement and perhaps if they have anymore questions, they could ask their son. And further more, to my surprise, they found that highly amusing and wished me a pleasant evening. Can you figure?

Was that my cue? Did it matter, I was taking it.

Perhaps there is something you don't understand Anna and before you say anything, I'll tell you what I think that is. You have a presence Anna. I'm sure you know that but what you might not know, is the effect that presence has on others. Do you want me to continue Anna? I only ask because it might get personal. Personal as in revealing more about myself than needs to be said at this time. That was a stupid thing for me to say. Of course you want me to continue ...... now.

I was expecting Anna to say something with the hope of deviating from the course of that landmine I found myself approaching. But no, she sat there, waiting.

Ok Anna. Now where was I?

Trying to grab vital seconds, that was where I was.

Your presence, but you have to realise this is my take, others might see you differently. Ok, ok, I'm stalling. There are times I'm in awe of you Anna and that could be intimidating. Perhaps it was from that very first time? I'm sorry Anna, I'm going to digress. I remember that first time. Eating pizza and only finding out three quarters of the way through the evening, you'd had a spotlight shining in your face the whole time. Maybe it was you feeling intimidated that time?

That gave me a moments reprise as Anna was laughing, remembering that evening.

I'm not sure at times if it's confidence that gets you through the day or some sort of innocent naivety but you do seem to press the right buttons with people, including me. I therefore wonder, am I falling in love with a presence or a person. And that, my dear is possibly too much information.

Well, I'd said it. Anna remained with her hands in her lap, as they have been for my entire impromptu speech, perched so eloquently on the bar stool. Unusual for Anna? She remained motionless. I'd said too much. No possibility of a retraction. Shit! Then Anna leant forward as she took my arm.

It is me James. It is me you are falling in love with. I have told you before, when I am with you I am me. I know there are variants of me. Dealing with the builders me. Negotiating with Tax Inspectors me. Supermarket me. Tennis me. Oh I do not know how many other me's but there has become one me that I cherish above the rest and that is, the James me. Now possibly we have both given too much information.

I was now in free fall. The emotions were going to come under severe pressure if I didn't act soon but I was frozen. Anna was sitting there, in front of me, proclaiming her .... maybe not undying love but as far as I was concerned, close enough. I raised my glass and that in itself was an almost insurmountable task but I thought, I can do this.

To you being you. To me being me. May you and me long continue being ourselves.

I had absolutely no idea what I'd just said but before Anna had a chance to bring her glass to her lips, I leant forward and kissed her. We raised our glasses. Having sipped her wine Anna reached for and lifted a shopping bag onto the counter.

Are you hungry James? I should have put this in the fridge when I arrived but somehow forgot to do so. I think I must have been distracted. I wonder how that happened?

I'd noticed Anna had managed to steer the conversation away from ...... from giving away anymore secrets. I'd also noticed Anna was pleased with her teasing, last remark. That grin on her face as she turned. Fridge filled, Anna returned to her stool and raided her handbag producing a packet of cigarettes.

You are getting me into bad habits James. Two has been my normal daily intake.

The three best things in life Anna. A cigarette before and a cigarette after. Sorry Anna, I shouldn't have said that, it just came out.

I don't understand?

Oh dear. It's a known fact Anna, if you have to explain a joke, it's not a joke. The clue is in the three things and the cigarettes being two of those. What could the third possibly be?

Anna thought a moment before replying. "In that case, we should hurry up and finish these cigarettes".

Now she was laughing. Laughing at her own joke but with a laugh that said "How about that for a comeback!" It broke the ice. The earlier revelations? The revelations of undying love. Well, that was the way I saw it. We had passed that by. Partially thanks to a really, really old joke. Another missed opportunity perhaps? I had a moment of inspiration, or possibly pro-activeness. Possibly both.

Anna, have you ever played Ludo?

Having explained that it was a board game that didn't involve too much thought and usually lasted about a half an hour, she looked interested. Let the game commence. It took a few minutes to explain the, revised James rules, and we began. Anna didn't pick up on the tactics that first game so the outcome was inevitable. What I hadn't taken into account was Anna's competitiveness. Another game was asked for and then a third. It was now three nil but Anna wanted a fourth which she won. Happy with her win, I took the game away. I noticed an ever so slight change on my return.

Are you hungry James because if not I was thinking of having another cigarette. Only I cannot.

My turn to be momentarily confused.

You said the cigarette was first and third, did you not?

I'm supposed to come up with those lines Anna but far be it from me to contest the analogy.

I slid off my stool. Took Anna's hand and led her to the bedroom.

"We need to do something with those curtains James", said Anna as she unstrapped her shoes.

What was that? I mean, was that the time to be discussing curtains? We both managed to undress almost simultaneously and being a gentlemen, I allowed Anna first choice of the bed. I was not sure if it was an intended manoeuvre of Anna's but she placed herself kneeling at the edge of the bed. As an intended invite? An invite to take her where she was. If it was not an invite I was certainly not going to let that deter me. How often did such a possibility occur? To have had a beautiful naked body kneeling at the edge of the bed in front of me. And such a body as Anna's. I hesitated for just a brief moment then moved my arm to encompass her waist. Stopping her where she was. I was sure I heard a slight intake of breath? I eased Anna's head forward stopping short of burying it in the duvet. I moved my hand slowly around the inside of her legs. Anna was perched, kneeling at the edge of the bed while I stood over her. This was not going to be romantic. This was going to be sex. Pure and simple. Anna's breathing had definitely increased. I told her to open her legs and as she did so. I entered. Anna was quickly reaching a climax. It had only been but ten minutes. She relaxed her body, climax reached and was destined to slowly sink to bed. I had other ideas. With my arm once again around her waist, I pulled her towards me and slowly, ever so slowly entered her again. Anna was not ready for this. It was too soon. She had yet to return from that other place. But I persisted and my persistence paid off, as I thought it might. That competitive spirit within Anna prevailed. "Get back on your knees girl, can't you see you are about to experience the fantasy of a lifetime." At least, that is what I hoped she was thinking. Either way Anna raised herself up to accept and with renewed vigour impaled herself deeply onto what awaited. It became a rerun of the first. Only this time perhaps with more purpose. Within minutes, Anna was shuddering violently and then collapsed onto the bed.

Enough James.

We laid, side by side on the bed and a few minutes passed.

I am not sure I should tell you this James but I recall having a fantasy that was not dissimilar to that.

Before I had a chance to discuss our mutual thoughts, Anna continued.

Which in itself causes me some confusion. You can be so, so domineering in bed and yet so, so different out of it. Have I just dug myself into a hole James?

I didn't answer. I wasn't suppose to.

Let me explain. Knowing you is a wonderful thing and one would never expect what lay beneath and don't you look at me like that, you know what I mean. You are good. Very good, ok? Now I am off to have that third best thing in life before you catch me blushing.

I had maybe five seconds to watch Anna as she left the bedroom in search of her bathrobe. Brought incidentally, the day after we first slept together. Along with a whole bag full of cosmetics that limited my space on the bathroom shelves to crisis point. But what a five seconds and for a woman of fifty? No way, I thought. Not with such a well defined figure such as Anna's.

I found her at the Breakfast Bar making coffee. I opened the fridge to retrieve the Rhum Cocas. When ever I visited Austria I succumbed to the temptation. Ströll rum coated in dark chocolate. Much like Maltesers, only better and perfect with coffee. Anna succumbed. We sat back to enjoy. I took a bet with myself that Anna would notice her bathrobe was slipping. Sitting on the stool with knees slightly apart the robe conformed to gravity revealing at first her knee but it became apparent the inner thigh was not far behind. Three to one Anna notices or should I discreetly mention that if she didn't do something soon the shaved delight would be in full view. I decided to leave it to fate and gave Anna's face my full attention.

I was thinking we could go to the beach tomorrow afternoon James. Lie on the beach with the occasional dip to cool us down.

There was the cue. The perfect opportunity to say something.

If your robe slips any further Anna it might need more than a dip to cool me down.

It took a second for Anna to register what I'd said. She looked down. She pulled the robe between her knees.

That was a test James and you passed with flying colours but I'm not sure how much further I would have let it fall, so you were close.

I had a three to one bet with myself Anna that you would realise and correct.

Were you giving odds on whether or not I would say something?

Not really. It was a pass or fail situation for me.

I don't think you took into account how provocative you were being Anna or the possibility that I might believe you were doing it on purpose. If I assumed the latter it would be fair for me to assume you wanted me to see. I could have assumed you were playing some sort of control game. This can be yours James. Was I assuming too much?

Anna was enjoying this, as was I.

If those are your assumptions James I do not think I need to know your fantasies. Do you see me dressed in leather and high heeled boots. Possibly carry a whip? No. Don't answer that. ……. Maybe tell me tomorrow afternoon. I will have the possibility of cooling down in the sea.

I laughed at that suggestion, although, Anna dressed in ……. Wipe it from the mind James.

This might not be a very good moment to tell you but I will go home tonight. Back to Nice. I have tennis in the morning and if we want to get to the beach by three …..

It's ok Anna. If you think staying tonight will tire you too much for your match tomorrow, I perfectly understand.

You know I was not thinking that James. It was the logistics I was concerned about. You were not being serious, were you?

Not really Anna although I prefer my reasoning to yours.

Do as you are told James and get me a glass of water while I change.

With that remark Anna was off the stool, brazenly allowing her robe to fall open.

Just checking on your control James.

"Your wish is my command Dear Lady", said I laughing while obeying the "request" for water. Anna returned and was hovering. I recognised that body language. Anna's head had already left. Or maybe not? She was in my arms and gentle kissing commenced.

I have to go James.

I was right the first time.

We break apart and Anna headed for the door.

You've forgotten your water Anna.

Oh that, not needed. As I said, I was just testing my control. It seems to work. How fascinating.

I could still hear her laughter, at her own clever reply, as she turned the corner at the top of the drive. I was left with a feeling of contentment. Yes, she went home that evening but I had the feeling she was in two minds as whether to do so or not.

Chapter Fourteen

I was up reasonably early the next morning with the sun already blazing in through the patio windows. I decided to go into Antibes. It would be hours before Anna was due. I needed bread and my favourite boulangerie just happened to be next door to the newsagents, close to my coffee stop. All very convenient. Coffee. Times and first cigarette of the day. And then Eva arrived.

Hello James.

Well Hello Eva. Please ...... as I signal towards the empty seat.

Am I disturbing one of your precious moments?

Not at all Eva. The paper is here for the day. You're not.

And not for much longer James. I am flying to Paris tomorrow and if you want to know the truth, I came here today hoping to find you.

I will take that as a compliment Eva. In fact you have just made my day and my day was pretty much made to start with.

You are flirting with me James.

Oh Dear, could I be getting myself in to trouble. Yes, I could.

I was thinking more along the lines of flattering Eva rather than flirting. Which has to be true as I know flirting has never been a forte of mine. I prefer the direct approach of beating about the bush. A trait well known among the English and much to the infuriation of the rest of the world. Past masters of diplomacy. Never say what you mean but always seem to mean what you say.

So you were flirting with me?

I can see Eva had a sense of humour.

Well, if you put it like that ......

I left the sentence hanging.

We chatted for awhile, then Eva asked if I was busy that afternoon. She was visiting friends and wanted to know if I'd like to join her. Showing my

196

disappointment I had to admit to a previous engagement. She also showed her disappointment.

That is ok James. I completely understand. If I had your number I could have asked you earlier. Hopefully another time.

The conversation resumed but the disappointment in Eva's face was obvious. After what I would have worked out as an appropriate moment to make ones farewells, Eva stood.

I had better go as I have a few things to do before this afternoon. It was really nice to see you again James.

I stood and we kissed politely. I watched Eva until she disappeared amongst the sea of people, ordered another coffee and returned to the paper. A hand came over the paper.

Here is my card James. Call me sometime.

Once again, she disappeared into the sea of people. Perhaps I should get a sign printed. Beautiful, late forties Russian ladies only. Wish I was twenty years younger. Moscow here I come! I was reminded of the analogy between the number twenty seven bus and women. You wait for ages and then two arrive at the same time. Eva was certainly good company and I would have jumped at the chance of an afternoon with her but if nothing else, I am a one woman man. It had become a developed characteristic. Much had changed since my mid thirties. I photographed the card making sure it was in my card app and discarded the original. It wouldn't do if it fell out of my shorts pocket that afternoon. I returned to my thoughts of Anna. It had been six months since we first met. That cold night in March. A lot had happened since and as I contemplated those months, a certain pattern emerged. Most meetings had been decided by Anna. Occasionally not the venue but the "flow of the day", was as good a description I could give to the way Anna manipulated the day. Not in any malicious way, it was just the way she was. She had an idea, one of many and she wanted to carry it through, albeit with spontaneous diversions. We had spent a lot of time together but never two nights in a row with the whole day between. It was a lunch. A dinner. An afternoon. An evening and yes a night, within the combination of those meetings. I put this down to Anna's various distractions that kept her busy. I thought no more about it.

Anna arrived ahead of schedule and we headed for the beach. Should I enjoy always being chauffeured around by Anna? Always her driving? Given the option I had to admit on preferring the Mercedes over my old Renault Scenic. Next time I should suggest driving. The roads were busy and what would take twenty minutes in the winter turned into forty. Never the less we were on the beach by three fifteen. Anna having her charmed life following her all the way to the car park. Straight in. Park. Head for the beach. Simple. Trying to once again point out this charmed life she leads would fall on deaf ears. I didn't. Laid on the beach Anna was talking about the house.

You know James I get almost thirty thousand euros for renting the house in August but it doesn't come close to covering the costs of the upkeep.
It was getting close to what I earn a year, I was thinking.
And soon it will be just Marta and myself once Elena leaves.
"Perhaps you should sell it and buy a place in England", I said. More for something to say rather than adding any positive input.
Where would you suggest James;
Put yourself in the firing line there James. I struggled to think of an ideal place.
How about Bath Anna? A beautiful city and close enough to Bristol or even London in fact. Well known for its many Spas, which were enjoyed by the Celts and the Romans over two thousand years ago.
It sounds perfect James. Run away to Bath. Me and you.
I had to take comments like those with a pinch of salt. Anna might file the idea away but it might not necessarily be me who would be joining her. I was not sure why I'd thought that. Anna and I were seeing more of each other as the weeks passed and I was certain she was growing more attached. For no unexplainable reason, I Love You. You are Perfect, came into my head. Something Emanuela had said only ten months previously ...... and look what happened to that! Never believe the hype James. Well said James. Anna had decided it would be a good time for a dip. Was I incapable of making those simple but obvious decisions in advance of Anna? Anna was a stronger swimmer than I, although that was not saying a lot. My abilities in the water reflected that of the predicament the Blue Whale in Hitch Hikers Guide To The Galaxy found itself in. Floundering! I was brought up by the sea. I spent thirty years living next to the water. My sisters had their swimming certificates in abundance. Cumulating in the much coveted, mile certificate. My father spent his weekends, while dragging the family along to rocky inlets where finding a comfortable spot to lounge about was next to impossible, skindiving. He would spend hours in the water and usually came back with the evenings dinner. All of this made little impact on a skinny kid, ashamed of his own body. It was late in my teens before I filled out to any degree. Swimming was never going to be my thing. Anna was a hundred metres out while I was barely twenty. I turned on my back and played the, enjoying the ambience of the moment, routine. Anna eventually joined me around the fifty metre mark. I decided to try something I knew I would later regret. I dived underneath her grabbing her ankles. Pulling her down and by doing so straighten her legs. Then the piece de resistance. I pushed up. Anna was well over half way out of the water before it was either my strength or Anna's balance that failed but enough was achieved to impress. I had the feeling that was the first time in my life I had tried to impress a woman through physical strength. But hey, it worked. I arrived back at the beach in a respectable close second. As I approached the beach shower Anna was just finishing. She touched my hand as we passed. Nothing more. No conversation. Just that but with a look to

compliment the action. I returned the smile. The afternoon passed, as time with Anna always did. Too quickly. Five hours and it was but a moment.

Do you intend going back to Nice this evening Anna?

I had tested a dozen versions of that sentence. Including. Fancy a bit of sex tonight? One had to introduce these extreme options in order to be able to eliminate them. Once eliminated, what was left had to be the one. Anna turned to face me. There was that wicked look again. I definitely needed to tell her and soon. She had to change that look.

Yes. I mean no. I was thinking, yes I want to stay with James so my answer automatically came out as a yes. Now I am not sure which I am supposed to say.

Stick with yes Anna. I'll understand.

We packed up our belongings and headed for the car. Once at the car Anna realised she didn't have her belt buckle. Evidently one can buy just the buckle? We retraced our steps and while doing so Anna mentioned the value of said piece. That was a weeks wages. For a buckle? Unfortunately it was nowhere to be found. I was devastated. Anna decided it would be a good idea to buy another one soon thus alleviate any pain of losing the first. Couldn't fault that logic! Well I could but what would be the point? I suggested we buy pizzas on the way home which was accepted with enthusiasm. Once home, I didn't hang about. Pizzas getting cold and all that. I'd already decided, we would eat from the box. If Anna had a problem with that ……. I'd let her decide which plates we should be using. No sign of Anna and everything was set to go. I ventured out. Anna was waiting by the car. Door open with seat slid forward.

I've brought these for you but they are too heavy for me.

I didn't believe that for a moment. Anna would have no problem carrying the …… carrying the, whatever it was. It was about manners James. It was what the man was supposed to do James.

No problem my dear. What is it?

You will find out later.

Whatever it was, it was heavier than first thought. It reminded me of something business people carried at airports. Usually containing their suit. Only this felt as if it had a lot more than a suit.

Throw it on the bed James. Where are the plates?

Far left cupboard.

Ok, I will get them.

Take note James on which plates are used. Already got the fruit bowl sorted. It was only a matter of time before I would be able to select a plate with confidence. It was a messy business eating pizza by hand. Anna would always surprise me. I'd supplied knives and forks which would be the elegant way, or so I'd thought but no, Anna was content to grapple with her pizza. "It was too good to bother with cutlery", she said. Why was it that normally mundane tasks, such as eating,

(It's the way I saw it) took on a new meaning when shared. A new meaning that in Anna's case, encompassed every fibre of body and mind? I decided to leave that question open.

Anna said it was time to look at my present.

It was a set of very heavy curtains in a dirty green colour with a satin finish. I held one up as best I could and the decision was made.

They are perfect James. Why don't we hang them.

Fortunately the existing rail was the wrong type or the clips were the wrong type? Either way Anna admitted defeat but would bring the right fixings tomorrow evening.

A day full of splendour and the night ….. the night filled with passion. We awoke the next morning almost simultaneously. Anna started to tease me about how tired she felt. Which considering there was only five hours sleep would not be surprising. I turned over until I rested on her chest. Face to face. My hand between her legs.

"*So I suppose sex is out of the question*", I said with my version of a wicked smile. Before Anna could answer, which was a shame because I had the feeling it would have been a good retort, my phone rang. It was Paul. Would we like to join them at the Cafe Kanter that evening? Anna meanwhile had taken the opportunity to slip out of bed and was now making her way to the bathroom. Paul was talking but I wasn't really listening. I was watching Anna disappear. My first thought, which could be considered rather sexist was, And I've just slept with that! The same could be said if after gazing at the Mona Lisa one said, And I've just seen that! The analogy being, the inability to find words capable of defining what had been seen. I returned my attention to Paul. I made the decision for us and said yes. Absolutely delighted to and thanked him for asking. I could tell Paul was suspicious about my reply. Too formal. Too polite. Was this what I'd become when with Anna? No, it was me, playing with Paul. Anna returned and I explained the reason for the call and our invitation for dinner. She was delighted. She dropped the towel and started to dress.

Is there any possibility you can do that a lot slower?

You are terrible James. I am going to have to start rationing you.

Can we start that next week Anna …… or next year?

Anna was laughing.

Ok, I'll put the coffee on and take a quick shower. You take all the time you want Anna.

We had toast and coffee. I knew Anna would be leaving soon so it came as no surprise when she decided that time had come. I was left with thoughts of the previous night. Things were said. Things that people say to each other when it has gone past the casual relationship stage. The word Love was used. Did she say that in a moment of passion? A moment post climax when the brain was susceptible to suggestion. I sat on the settee accompanied by another coffee and cigarette. I was trying to break it down. Categorise and separate the components. Did she mean what she said? It took me awhile to climb out of that whirlpool of thought.

Anna arrived at seven forty in plenty of time to join Paul and Chiara on their terrace. It was rare for Anna and I to be involved with others. I was interested in discovering Anna's compatibility within this small group of four. She shone as I expected her to do. Never monopolising the conversation but very capable of guiding it. Chiara was being politely inquisitive about Anna's background and admittedly asking questions that I should've had the foresight to have already asked. Make a mental note James. Ask about life living in Moscow during those times. Also find out when those times were. Ideally before showing ones ignorance about Moscow in the seventies, Google it. Time for the restaurant and we piled into Chiara's Panda thus allowing Paul to indulge in the odd drink.

We had a good table with room for six. It helped knowing Paul was friendly with the owner. In their selective restaurants Paul and Chiara made sure they were known. Dinner was an undeniable success. The meals superb. The situation. The ambience. It all came together on that warm August evening. Malcolm joined us for drinks after dinner. He only lived a few minutes away. If one was looking for the epitome of an English Gentleman then look no further than Malcolm. His easy way with the ladies kept the evening on a high note. We ended with Irish Coffees all round. Strangely enough, Anna had never tried Irish Coffee but was now hooked. I would always remember that evening as one of the highlights of the summer. It was hard to describe but going out with another couple made one feel part of a couple. Anna and I were a couple. There were moments through the evening when Anna was defending me against a throw away comment by Paul. It was the two of us against the world. That's how I felt.

We left the restaurant arriving home in the same jubilant mood. Invited next door for coffee, Anna graciously declined, feigning tiredness and maybe just a little to much alcohol. It was approaching midnight as I closed the door and Anna who didn't exactly look tired, insisted on making Irish Coffee. I had the ingredients and thought, why not. It was difficult showing Anna how to do something. She was a, hands on, pupil. I stepped back giving instructions as Anna, duly enthused, made the coffee with confidence. I don't think I made another Irish Coffee. That became Anna's thing. The first attempt wasn't bad only let down with the inconsistency of the cream but it sure tasted good. It was enjoyable watching Anna. She did throw in the occasional, What? but I think the alcohol had taken it's course as she had become accepting of my gaze. The way she laughed. The way she talked with such expression on her face. Her body language. All used to emphasise those endearing qualities.

Come on James, it is bedtime. That was a wonderful evening. Why not extend it a little.

That Irish coffee was having some effect. Anna had a gay abandonment about her. Standing in her bra and briefs Anna had decided to undress me. I thought at my age I would have previous experience of this situation. At least once if not on several occasions. Nope. Never before. I found it a little unnerving.

"Lie down James", said Anna having relieved me of my clothing.

I did say Anna was a, hands on, sort of woman. It was interesting, the thoughts that were going through my head. The dignified, elegant, classy lady was going down on me! It did stop short of any climax which maybe was a good thing, I was not sure I could ever have looked at Anna in the same way if that occurred. Although I did consider the possibility. I wondered what she would have done. She decided to sit on me. Her breasts moving to the rhythm of her movements. It was a beautiful sight. A sight not easily forgotten.

"I was thinking of getting implants. maybe a little bigger". Said in a manner as to encourage a response.

Anna's breasts are not large. I liked small breasts so I was biased.

Your breasts are beautiful Anna but if ever the day occurs you feel the need to have implants, don't make them bigger. They are just perfect!

I then admitted to being biased. Anna laughed. She stopped laughing and looked at me beneath her. I would be lying to myself if I didn't believe it to be a look of ...... of love.

Time slowed down. Every movement was felt. Every movement accentuated to accommodate the other. This was an emotional rollercoaster of sexual closeness. We knew when to kiss. When to caress. When to heighten the ecstasy Anna was having to deal with between her legs. As though I read her mind. Able to anticipate. To control. To slow down until the inevitable sequence of events started to fall into place. I was conducting the outcome and outcome it was.

If I die tomorrow James, I die a happy woman.

Go to sleep my dear, you are emotional and there is a very good chance the next words you utter will be something like, Do you know how much I love you James? I get the, Do you know how much bit but, ... Anna started laughing. She wasn't going to finish that sentence.

Chapter Fifteen

It was change-over-day for Anna so we were up reasonably earlier although perhaps thirty minutes later than Anna hoped for but she didn't complain. She was cuddly affectionate over coffee and left very relaxed and considering her day ahead Anna had time enough to thank me for the wonderful time she'd had. *Can one have too much of a good thing James? When I have a chance I will buy a diary. I know, rather an old fashioned idea but I would prefer these thoughts hand written. I think it is more personal and these hours have been very personal. Thank you James.*

A big kiss followed which surprised me a little as we were outside. Not quite in public domain as there was an eighty metre drive separating us from the, very infrequently used, main road but all the same, outside. Before releasing her I said, "If you have any problems through the day, don't hesitate to call. I mean that. Don't hesitate".

I think I should get another boyfriend James. Nothing permanent you understand. Just long enough to remind me how wonderful you are. I was watching you at dinner last night. Actually intense scrutiny would be closer to the truth and you came through the scrutinising. I am still confused about the reasons why I like you so much but I have come to the conclusion, it does not matter.

And with that, she was gone. It was now down to Anna to say farewell to the departing guests then she and Marta had seven hours to prepare the house for the next arrivals. When you had six bedrooms. Seven bathrooms. Three separate toilets. Immense living area, kitchen and Breakfast Bar. A sauna room and pool area which needed all the appropriate linen to be replaced. That was going to be a killer. I had to hand it to Anna, she was not afraid of work. Two hours later, I got a call from Anna.

They have just left! He was insisting on a five hundred euro reduction because of the air conditioning not working properly. Can you imagine the nerve! He couldn't work the bloody remote control and he wanted me to pay for his ignorance.

That was the first time I'd heard Anna come close to swearing.

It is a difficult position to be in James, as guests are encouraged to comment on their stay. A bad comment can sway future clients into choosing another house. I was trying very hard to remain calm under this barrage of ridiculous excuses for his ineptitude until his friend came to the rescue. I have a solution, he said. As this seems to have drawn to a stalemate position and our flight looms ever closer, give Anna the money less five hundred and I will gladly pay the difference. I've had a most enjoyable and pleasurable experience staying in your beautiful house Anna. And so it was solved. He took me aside before they left saying, You will get a good write up from me which should shame my friend into agreement. That helped but I am still fuming. Marta, bless her, has been hard at work during my absence so I think time is still on our side.

Anna, it's ok. As you say, time is on your side. One step at a time while avoiding the whole picture and before you know, you and Marta will be having a glass of wine cursing the arrivals for not being early.

Thank you James. I knew it was a good idea to call you. I am already feeling more relaxed.

I'd done nothing. Anna just wanted to vent her frustrations but it did present an opportunity.

You just needed someone to feel your pain Anna. Someone who you feel close to. There is no need to thank me. It should be me thanking you for thinking to call me.

Was that perhaps just a tad too sickening? But before I could ….

Now you are getting creepy James. Well, that is what I would have thought if I didn't know you better but definitely a little over the top, even for you. Don't you think?

There was that giggle again. Don't you just love her!

You have restored my equilibrium James and for that I thank you. Now I must go before Marta goes on strike. Call you later.

And she was gone!

I was fine with that. It was a sunny Saturday afternoon and the world was a wonderful place. I took the Figaro into Antibes, managing to park in a standardly accepted illegal spot. It was late August in Antibes and it was full! Full of tourists trying to figure out what to do with their day and in doing so, inhibiting ones progress. I was lucky, there was a copy of The Times still available at the Tabac but sold out of The Mail, I'd noticed. That perhaps said something about the tourists that picked a holiday in Antibes? I turned the corner and managed to secure a place in the shade to order a coffee. I realised I was just filling in time while waiting for Anna to ring but that was not going to happen for a few hours so I opened The Times to check on how the world was doing. Not looking good. Nothing new there. The waiter approached with my, à longé. "*Excusez-moi monsieur, est votre nom James"?* I nodded with a slight suspicion. "*Oui? Alhors, c'est pour vous".* He handed me an envelope with James boldly written on the front. Interesting? I looked around for the candid camera but nothing obvious was in sight. It was from Eva.

This is a rather bold approach which is totally out of character and therefore has me wondering why. Why would I be writing a letter to an almost total stranger? Not only that but delivering it in such a way. I can only think of one possibility and that being, you made an impression. You could be happily married with three wonderful children that you adore. In which case, I apologise. I don't wish to create problems for you and if the family is reality then please, don't read on but if you insist on doing so, (I certainly would!) then do so just for curiosities sake before throwing the letter in the bin.

I am a woman lacking for little in my life. I come and go as I please with only regard for the few commitments that cannot be ignored and one of those commitments is imminent. In fact it will be a very time consuming commitment. All business but the outcome will be more freedom. I am trying to tell you I will not return to Antibes for some months. You have my number so if you are free to do so, I would like to hear from you.

For now,

Eva

I had to admit, that letter was far more interesting than anything I was reading in The Times. Eva? What to do about Eva? Was that a song? I would have to call her. It was the least I could do. Eva took the effort to reach out and made herself vulnerable in doing so. Maybe a message will suffice? I opened Notes. Selected a new message and thought about my opening line.

*Hello Eva, (*Good start.)

Your letter first filled me with a feeling of humility. I wondered why I deserved such boldness. Another thought then emerged, once your words had filtered their way to those places in the brain that deal with such matters. There was a connection.

(That sounded familiar?)

I do not have a family. What I do have are two ex wives and a similar amount of grown up and flown the nest, children. I will not lie to you Eva, I do have a casual acquaintance who may or may not be around in another two months. I understand how callous that may sound (wanting my cake and eat it) but it was not intentional. It was just truthfully put.

May I suggest we keep in touch. Why? The connection we made and your boldness that was the catalyst.

Hope to hear from you Eva, James

205

After untold corrections, I copied and sent. Was it something about being single where the pendulum seemed to swing from one extreme to the other? One got the highs but in the last ten years of being single they were inevitable and unfortunately, closely followed by the lows. Married life, from what I can remember was about dealing with irrelevant arguments. Ok. Maybe a little too cynical? Talking about remembering, Josey and I spent sixteen years together before we married. Two years later and it was over. I accepted the idea I had a biased view on marriage. I reminded myself it was a beautiful day so turned the page on that thought and continued with The Times. After a second coffee, I folded The Times and headed for the car. Roof down and The Eels cd playing, I decide on a whim, to drive into Nice. Lane cutting with no indication didn't upset me. I was beyond that. It was an hour later I found myself on the Promenade des Anglais. A journey that would normally take twenty five minutes. I decided to do a U turn and head back. My day was made when sat at a crossing with a Porsche beside me. People crossing and ninety percent were looking at the Figaro. Smiles on their faces and giving the odd wave. Mr Porsche looked over and when the crossing was free, waved me on with a big smile. I was considering asking him if he'd liked to swap but resisted the temptation.

It was almost seven before I got home. Anna should be dealing with the arrivals about now so I resisted the temptation to message her. Anna called about thirty minutes later.

Hello James. Well, the good news. We were ready to receive by five thirty which was a good half hour before the clients were expected. The bad news? They called about five minutes ago to say the flight has been delayed and they are not expecting to be here before ten! I am devastated as I was assuming I would be relaxing at your place by eight. So here is the really bad news. It will be ten thirty at least, before I leave here and have decided the best option will be for me to go into Nice.

I needed to think, fast. If I wanted to give the unexpected answer. It wasn't difficult. She wasn't staying the night. I can perhaps turn this around?

No problem Anna. I'll come to you about ten thirty tomorrow and cook you an English breakfast.

Are you for real James? Firstly there is your understanding way. There are some who would take it as a personal insult. "What, you are turning me down for this evening"? Not you James. And then there is the offer of breakfast. Now you have, caring for my wellbeing, added to understanding. I can do no other but take you up on your kind offer but perhaps I should hold off on congratulating you for your consideration of my wellbeing until after breakfast.

I didn't know why I found Anna's rebuffs refreshing. Perhaps it was the accompanying giggles? That time, I was on the pedestal only to have my legs cut from beneath me the very next moment. I wasn't surprised the evening would be sans Anna. I was getting to know her well therefore my initial reply was easy.

206

It was how Anna threw out compliments only to later enforce the underlying, unsaid understanding that I think I was supposed to get but I didn't. I made a decision based on a milliseconds thought, Anna was insecure or being very cautious. No chance to continue that thread. It would only have me wondering why Anna who is so, so very much in control, would have any insecurities with me? I decided on impulse to invite myself over.

I have a really good bottle of Chilean red. A box of M&S cheesy biscuits. I'll be around in fifteen minutes and disappear about ten.

A pregnant pause.

The glasses will be waiting. And James, Thank You.

Sitting on Anna's terrace, I avoided asking myself the obvious question. Why me? Anna was delighted to see me. I could see she was tired but she hid it well. An hour passed as though a minute.

Why do I feel our time together slips away James?

Previous experience alerted, I gave her a knowing smile as Anna continued, not expecting an answer.

I enjoy being with you so perhaps that is the reason. Things we enjoy doing always end too soon.

Is this your buildup to, It's been nice knowing you James but .....

I regretted saying that the moment the words were out of my mouth. Not because it might have been the wrong thing to say, that wasn't the problem, as affirmed by Anna's laughter. No, I distracted her. I knew there was more to follow but unable to resist the temptation of an amusing comment, it had disappeared. Lost because of my distraction. It was approaching ten and I had promised to leave about that time.

I should leave Anna. Your guests will be arriving shortly.

Anna's shoulders visibly dropped. I didn't think she'd realised the time. I remembered a thought occurring. For someone having so many social engagements where timing is essentially the key issue, it didn't seem to work for us.

Oh gosh, you are right James. Oh gosh!

We stood and Anna hugged me? She hugged me, not held me. There was a difference. Slightly bemused Anna pulled away resting her hands on my waist.

This was an awful day James filled with hard work and frustration. Then you arrived.

Anna was looking deep into my eyes. I knew that was a good thing but unsettling all the same. I said nothing. I was not going to ruin the moment a second time. She smiled and kissed me. Not a deep passionate kiss but a kiss of affection and perhaps something else?

Thank you James.

That wicked smile returned.

Anyway, the sooner I get rid of you James, the sooner breakfast is served.

207

I was close to laughter. Anna noticed.

What? I am being ridiculous aren't I? Say something James and help me climb out.

I didn't think it was the appropriate moment to mention anything about that, wicked smile.

I'm sure Einstein had a theory that made perfect sense of what you said. I also think the best way of helping you out of the hole you find yourself in would be to take your hand and lead you to my car.

Anna said nothing, she took my hand and lead the way to the car. The sun was casting it's last rays on the upper most branches. The air was still and it was a comfortable twenty eight degrees. It could have been said, a romantic setting. The mood of that moment did not go amiss. If it wasn't for Anna's phone ringing ....

They have just reached Biot so they will be here in ten minutes. I so look forward to breakfast but for now ..... Good Night James.

Anna had regained her composure which was still full of warmth but drifting towards the oncoming arrival. I gave her a last kiss. Tapped her bottom which got a reaction of amusing disapproval as I got into the car. Anna said she would message me on her arrival in Nice. That message arrived at ten past midnight. I returned with a, "Glad you got back safely. Get a good nights sleep, you deserve it. See you at eleven. I think you might be grateful of that extra half hour in bed". "Eleven", came the response, with a kiss. I went to bed.

I was up early the next morning boiling potatoes that I'd mash with finely chopped onion, egg yolks and once cooled formed into rissoles which I left in the fridge until departure. Heinz Beans, back bacon, eggs and Cumberland sausages completed the breakfast list. It was nine thirty. Anna should be well rested so I decided to message her but she beat me to it.

Good Morning James. I hope you like Buck's Fizz as I've just laboured up the hill from the supermarket with the necessary ingredients.

If you don't mind Anna and considering the time of day, could you make mine a Mimosa? As it's a Sunday and the traffic should be light I'll be early, if you have no objections? Ten thirty?

For a person who doesn't really drink champagne, how come you know what a Mimosa is? You can explain at ten thirty. x

Anna had left the door open and was waiting on the terrace. She wore light khaki shorts that stopped just above the knee but what almost drew me to a halt was the cream top. Anna turned to greet me and on doing so the cream top seemed to disappear, silhouetted against the bright sunlight. To say it was a captivating sight was an understatement. The outline that took in those perfectly rounded small breasts that firmly hung above the precipice that became Anna's well defined stomach was something to behold. Anna was watching me.

What?

I needed to distract Anna for just a few moments longer. That was an image I wanted to imprint on my memory. I tried the obvious.

"Don't move Anna". I said, taking up what I believed would have been a photographers stance.

Actually can you move just a little to the left.

Amazingly, she did.

Perfect. Now can you lift up your hair.

I stood and watched trying hard not to focus on her breasts but instead cast a disparaging eye to encompass all.

I firmly believed Anna had no idea what was happening but she knew I was playing some game.

Ok James. What is going on?

You're not aware of the effect sunlight is having, are you Anna? Obviously not, seeing the bemused look on your face.

Anna's phone was on the table. I opened the camera.

Return to that pose Anna with your hands on your head.

I took the photo and passed Anna the phone. It took barely a second before realisation hit. Expecting a disparaging rebuke for such, I was surprised by Anna's response.

I can't believe that is me. I really like it. Take more James.

The next ten minutes were filled with Anna recreating from memory, she told me, of poses in Vogue. And she did it so well. Every pose accentuating her delicious curves. While Anna was uploading the photos to her laptop, I started preparing breakfast. All was ready to go when Anna called me to the living room. I stood behind her. There were about twenty photos and Anna ran through them slowly passing comments on each and every one. Occasionally asking which I preferred. Finally organised by preference Anna sent me her first choice.

I do not imagine anyone else will ever see this so please keep that one safe James.

Thank you Anna and thank you for trusting me. Although I don't think you would have to worry if others saw it. After all, the question on everyone's lips would be, I didn't know Anna was on the cover of Vogue? You are in charge of the Mimosa while I cook.

I left Anna with a look of bemusement on her face. English breakfast was always a challenge but not a mathematical impossibility. Four ingredients to fry so start with the one that took longest. Lighting up the beans somewhere in the middle. Anna started to hover.

Go away Anna. If you enjoy this, the only time you will ever eat it again, is if it's cooked by me.

Drinking certainly more champagne than orange juice we demolished breakfast.

"Two hundred and forty at least", said Anna.

My turn to look bemused.

As much as I enjoyed your breakfast James, I couldn't possibly have more than one a month, hence two hundred and forty.

Before I had a chance to answer my phone rang. It was a London number but not Kat's? But close. It was Tim. We chatted about nothing in particular until Tim popped the question, asking for Kat's hand in marriage. Tim is old school. Well brought up and this is how it was done. I thought of saying, Good Luck with that one but held back. It wasn't such a surprise as Kat had warned me of the possibility a few days earlier. Welcome to the family Tim and congratulations. Anna was sat open mouthed as Tim and I said our goodbyes. Her exuberance on hearing of the engagement was contagious. "You should call Kat and ask her how many carats". I gave her a look of disbelief. "What"? I said. Never did get back to the topic of two hundred and forty.

We cleared away the dishes and Anna disappeared. I heard her calling from the bedroom. She was sat on the mattress, silhouetted by the floor lamp and naked but for the cream top that was doing it's best to disappear under the glare of lighting.

I couldn't have possibly thought of anything more inviting. You never cease to amaze me, you are definitely the most alluring creature it has ever been my pleasure to visualise and here you are, a vision beyond any image the mind is capable of conceiving.

Why don't you just stop talking James.

My first thought was to turn her over. Undo my trousers and take her. Worry about undressing later but Anna was in seductive mode. I undressed as Anna watched. I knew what she wanted to see if her antics produced the desired result. She had little need to worry on that score, arousal was complete, seconds after I'd walked into the bedroom. It was an odd thought perhaps but I preferred the arousal to be part of the preamble to sex. Standing fully erect in front of Anna was a little disconcerting. Anna pulled back the duvet inviting me to join her. Time seemed to stand still. Every touch. Every kiss, as gentle streams, flowing sedately, until converging into a wider river. Picking up speed as it rushed towards that inevitable waterfall. And our streams had joined, reaching that waterfall simultaneously. It was rare for me to reach that combined climax. It was a sensation, a feeling of closeness, a realisation that surpasses anything. Nothing else out there allowed two people to express without a word spoken, the togetherness felt at that moment. The tenderness lingered on but unfortunately the erection didn't. I moved onto my side allowing Anna the chance to breathe. With my arm across her breasts, we fell asleep. Anna woke me as she tried to reach for the water. We shared the bottle. Anna was the first to break the silence.

Was that a dream within a dream James? Please tell me I didn't dream it.

I was believing Anna expected a sweet adorable response. I'd decided not to give such a response.

Now don't take this the wrong way Anna but I've not thought of you as sexy. It is not the way you portray yourself or would like others to perceive you so I think that comes as no surprise but this afternoon, you were like a bitch on heat. Did I just say that? I don't suppose anybody has ever referred to you as a bitch on heat before? No, didn't think so. Take it as a compliment and tuck it away somewhere in the hope it might reoccur. But to answer your question. No, you didn't dream it.

Anna's expression had started with what could have been described as, A look of horror. I expected that. By the time I had got to the, No, I didn't think so, said with such pathos, Anna had melted and the thought of her retaining, A bitch on heat as some sort of memento, really got to her. Anna had told me earlier she would have to return to the house. She'd given the clients a brief explanation on the workings, promising to return that afternoon. I reminded her of this, seeing it was past three.

You are right James, I should be going it is just that I can't stop thinking about something you said.

Anna had her hand between my legs.

Bitch on heat.

We left shortly after four thirty.

I got home deciding to arrange some furniture on the roof. I wasn't sure why as there was little chance of being there this evening. Maybe I just needed something to occupy my mind? Parasol. Table and two chairs. Table cloth and cushions ready to be brought up. Satisfied with my labours I prepared a coffee. I climbed the stairs. Switched on the computer. Plugged in the phone and searched for a backdrop. I found a backdrop. A sunny beach with a prominent palm tree. With the help of Photoshop Anna's background changed from that terrace in Nice to that of Vogue model on deserted beach. I sent it to Anna. It was a couple of hours before I had a response.

Hi James. I love it! I'll call you when I am through dealing with a very nice but needy group. Hope to see you around nine for Ludo and Irish. ps I have the cream. x

I'm glad you like it Anna. It's the backdrop on my computer. The problem is, I switch on my computer and immediately forget why I did so. Very distracting! Just joking. It has joined my other Anna photos in a locked folder. See you around nine and give me a call when you leave. No kisses from me. You get a warm passionate hug on your arrival.

Anna called at eight fifteen! The coffee and the game were afoot well before nine. The conversation flowed between sips of Irish but most of all it was Anna's competitive spirit that took the starring role. Anna played to win. Physically I was no match but Ludo. Anna made tactical errors. Playing by rules that differ from the norm. Set up when Josey and I use to play. Two people. Two colours each. Admittedly the game did rely on the throw of a dice but a bad throw could be tilted in ones favour. If you knew what you were doing. It was rare for us to contemplate serious conversation on Ludo evenings so it was light and humorous. Anna was at ease and it showed. With the score standing at two each Anna decided on a second Irish coffee. To see the transformation in Anna was rewarding in itself. The carefree attitude she had adopted over the past hour or so was tinged with an underlying excitement, an excitement one would have expected from that giggling school girl. I watched her prepare the coffee accompanied by non stop chatter. She returned to her seat.

This is so much fun James. I know you think I am too competitive at times and I am, but I must say, I would almost, not mind losing.

A bold statement Anna, perhaps I should find other such games, completely irrelevant to life, the universe and everything, knowing as I now do, you don't mind losing, occasionally?

We have our own game James which is not irrelevant at all.

I had noticed Anna would make those remarks when she was most relaxed. Were they just, throw away, remarks? Before I'd thought that through Anna was following up her remark, leaning forward and giving me a very affectionate kiss. Followed by a big smile. Having distracted me, she started to roll her dice. To start the game you threw your dice as many times as you could. No, taking it in turn. The first to roll a six, started. Anna had already rolled a half a dozen times before I found my dice which had been hidden while distracted by that kiss. Definitely competitive, I was thinking. Although she took it very well when I'd won the fifth game.

Well done James but you know I will win one day.

Looking forward to that day Anna.

With a sweet kiss from Anna she wondered off saying something about needing a shower and time to freshen up. I thought the two were the same? I think it was the second or third visit that Anna arrived with a bag full of items that adorn the bathroom shelves. I only had one shelf left, or at least I did have, as she had brought more. While waiting I went in search of my music hard drive as I'd promised to give Anna a copy. Anna emerged from the bathroom in her bathrobe with her hair down. She has a tendency to wear a ponytail and when out during the day, combined with a baseball cap. I always thought that to be incongruous to her style. A style of designer clothes and baseball cap? What did I know.

What?

She had caught me watching her entry. This was one of the few occasions "What", required an answer.

I realised, it's not often I see you with your hair down. My next thought? I like it. It could almost be another You. Now that's an interesting thought. Would you like a coffee Anna?

I'm not going to get caught up in that thought. Coffee? Yes, why not if you don't mind rearrange the, Three Best Things In Life? I was thinking of 1,3,2. I'm sure 2 won't mind being last Anna.

Anna gave me that wicked smile.

I was thinking while having my shower ....

I wondered why it took you so long.

No. It took so long, as you put it James because I was making myself beautiful for you.

So I was right Anna. It took all that time to think. ...... because you were already beautiful when you entered the bathroom.

I was wondering who was going to win this little, oneupmanship game we now found ourselves in.

Thank you James but it takes a lot of time to maintain this naturally beautiful complection. Give me a kiss.

I was going to play, hard to get. I placed the coffees on the counter and walked around. Instead of walking up to her, I sat opposite.

I'm sorry Anna, have I got that wrong? It's just that I thought you wanted to give ME a kiss, so I sat down to wait for said kiss.

Anna slowly stood and stepped that half metre that separated us, saying nothing. She kissed me and sat back on her stool, smiling.

I asked you to give me a kiss James and on this occasion, I was willing to come to you. Unfortunately this means you lose out. When you sat down, I realised the game you were playing and made an instant decision. I will come to you but not tell you what I was thinking. I really do hope that kiss was worth it James?

Isn't it said, A kiss is worth a thousand words? If it isn't, it should be. So I am content Anna.

You are saying you are not curious James? I was in the bathroom for an awful long time. Lots of thinking was possible and you say you are content? I don't believe you.

Anna, you said you won't tell me. My assumption is you aren't telling me because you don't want to. Maybe giving away too much about your feelings for me. Possibly it would make you feel vulnerable. What ever the reason, I can but surmise which it might be, so I am content.

So you are content because you believe it to be one of those reasons? What if I was to tell you it was none of the above?

Then I would think of another reason which would make me equally content.

I'm going to call a halt to these proceedings, not because you are infuriating me James. Actually you are infuriating me but not in an annoying way. In an intellectual way. I have always enjoyed being challenged over my political views. Equality of the sexes. Racism. I think you get the idea but I don't get challenged about myself. You have this way of putting me on the spot, not directly, oh no. You remind me of the sheep dog herding the sheep into a pen. Going this way

213

and that. Picking up on those loose ends. Sitting. Waiting. Until finally the last awkward sheep is ushered in. You skirt around James. You pick at it in such a surreptitious way and before I realise what I have done, I've told you more than I should have but I love it. Now perhaps I've said more than I should have done?
Anna then surprised me again. This was a lady who spoke Queens English. A lady who attended functions. A lady who organised functions. Was a perfect host when entertaining .... Anna stood. Pulled the cord on her bathrobe and just for a second, revealed enough of that beautiful body to have me trying to defy gravity as I toppled forward on the stool. Meanwhile Anna had pulled her robe around herself as she turned.

I'm going to bed James.
We had managed three Irish coffees, none of which were short on the Irish. Anna was not a drinker so I was wondering if she would regret the impulsive robe opening tomorrow.

I'll clear away the dishes and join you soon.
Anna was sat in bed, surrounded by pillows. The duvet around her waist.

You are going to sit there and watch me undress?
"Yes", said Anna.
Needless to say, seeing Anna sat there with such a demure innocent look on her face and yet naked from waist up, once again placed me in that situation of disrobing with a full erection. I undressed and stood in front of Anna, my erection in easy reach. Anna pulled back the duvet with one hand and the other, firmly clamped around my erection, drew me into bed as she parted her legs. It never would cease to amaze me, that beautiful sight. She placed me at her entrance and removed her hand. What followed was, different. It was always different. From the very moment I entered her it was obvious. Anna was wet. Anna wanted sex. Not slow caresses that built and built. No, Anna wanted sex. So that was what I gave her. All the way in. Hard, thrusting, plunging to the depths with every stroke. She responded, raising her hips. There was no conversation. This was not a time for conversation. The sweat was building on me. Me, a person who rarely sweats. This was physical. Anna exploded and for some unknown reason which was not particularly, a conscious thought, I turned her over. Knowing Anna enjoyed it thus so and although having just experienced her moment of ecstasy, she couldn't resist the calling. No quarter given. None expected should have been the inevitable outcome, and yet, I resisted the temptation. I tried to lock myself into feeling Anna's emotions. Listening. Feeling. For those subtle changes that took place within her. Moments when penetration was but rubbing those outer lips. Moments of slow, deep penetration. Moments when I held myself within her. Unmoving. Before we fell asleep in each others arms, Anna took my face in her hands saying, "I feel so close to you James". It didn't need an answer.

I was the first up the next morning allowing Anna to doze. Grabbing her bathrobe I went to make coffee which I felt was the least I could have done after waking her at four o'clock because I had awoken needing her and her being, oh so compliant. It was the least I could have done. I changed my mind. I threw some clothes on. Grabbed my helmet. The bike started first time and I headed for the local shop returning with fresh croissants, oranges and some cheeses with ham cut from the bone. I had just managed to clear up the mess of ten oranges, squeezed with a hand held device that barely managed to contain the orange when Anna appeared in the bathrobe.

Mmmmm, breakfast.

I handed her a just made, à longé. Breakfast was spread before her. Anna cut open a croissant, buttered it and had half eaten it before saying a word.

I have heard sex can make one hungry. I'm starving! Good Morning James.

She was looking around for something?

Do you have any serviettes?

Shit! Forgot that one. I got Anna a serviette. She wiped her mouth and kissed me.

Just because you buttered me up last night James, it doesn't mean I should get butter all over you this morning.

Still the affectionate Anna, I was pleased to see.

What shall we do today James?

We are going into Antibes to catch the market before twelve. We are then going to return for a picnic on the roof.

Now if that didn't come under the title of pre-organised, I wouldn't know what did!

We could stop off for a beverage on the way back Anna as I can't see us being hungry for awhile. That's what I thought we could do.

I like that idea James. We can finish breakfast and be in Antibes by eleven.

Anna finished her croissant, took a sip of orange and slid off the stool to change.

I'm coming back for more James so don't clear away.

We finished breakfast. Headed into Antibes and had an enjoyable time buying far too much for a picnic.

Do you really think we need three baguettes Anna?

We stopped for a glass of Rosé before heading to the car park. Anna drove of course and as usual used the underground parking. I didn't dare mention that parking on the street was free on Sundays.

I'd only ever used the roof for sunbathing with a book and coffee so I had to admit the whole layout seemed incongruous but in being so, added to the pleasure. We had spent an hour in preparation and sat at that table with the spread played out before us, it was well worth the effort. Sunbathing. Eating. Moderate drinking and even some reading all to be accompanied with sporadic humour. The only blip in the whole day was Anna telling me she would be going

215

to Nice tonight. Something about a match in Monaco at a prestigious club who's name alluded me. Up bright and early hoping to win.

"The sacrifices one has to make for ones art". I said.

I knew Anna enjoyed the sex but she kept it in perspective. Prioritisation as if, simultaneously she lived now and twelve hours in the future. Always on the look out for what might effect that next day. On that occasion, it was me. We left the roof around six and with everything cleared away, sat on our usual stools at the breakfast bar. Until Anna came into my life I had rarely used those stools but more often than not, this was where we sat. I was not sure how the topic came into being but we were discussing marijuana.

It is something I have never tried, not that I have tried anything remotely similar but I hear it is relatively harmless.

After some to-ing and fro-ing I said it might be possible for me to obtain a joint. That seemed to both excite and terrify her. We left it at that. Twenty minutes later Anna was gone in a flurry of such organisation it bewildered me. She had items spread around. Her phone on the coffee table. Her notebook was beside me. The ham in the fridge she wanted to take. God knows what was in the bathroom but in seconds Anna had combined all into her functional handbag. Was there a thought process that proceeded that?

Chapter Sixteen

I didn't see Anna that next day, Monday. Although we did correspond via messages. She lost the match but was magnanimous in defeat as she felt her opponent was far superior and definitely in the wrong league. It was Tuesday, late afternoon. Anna had invited me for a surprise evening. No mention of staying overnight but that wasn't unusual. It was to be assumed. Assumed as in, Anna will decide sometime during the evening. The surprise turned out to be an hour in the jacuzzi which was only the second time Anna had used it. The first being with Elena, a week before. If nothing else, I would always be that first lover to join her. Enjoy it while you can James. I think one had to experience that time to appreciate the bling. That ex pool room measuring some forty square metres with separate changing rooms, showers and toilet. Underfloor heating, an obvious must, was magnificent. The subtle changing of lighting which seemed to cycle through five or six colours before repeating.

Laying on the soothing bubble bath while jets of water rippled up and down my back, Anna asked if I'd like some more wine and not waiting for my reply reached out for the bottle. She had to stand and bend over. Her perfect Pudenda came into focus between her legs. A vision like no Playboy photo could ever portray.

"Were you looking at my behind James"? said Anna as she sat down.

I felt I should go defensive in my reply but the devil in me got there first.

Actually Anna, that was only part of it.

Anna passed my glass with a knowing smile on her face but did not pass comment. I'd always thought it would have been a wonderful environment for sexual adventure but soon realised hot water like cold, had a detrimental effect. Well, it did on me. Fortunately I didn't think it was on Anna's list as she was perfectly happy enjoying the pool, wine and conversation, so no harm done. With the wine bottle empty it was an appropriate time to call a halt to the proceedings which was fortunate for me. Our physical closeness over the last five minutes gave me thought to consider maybe Anna had changed her mind. It could have been embarrassing. Anna was first out and as she walked towards the shower room, turned to say,

I am going to take a shower James. Please, don't join me and don't look at me like that. I told Marta we will have dinner at nine so we don't have the time, and anyway, it is going to be a cold shower for me.

I heard her minutes later in the shower, still laughing at her remarks. Marta was no where to be seen when we entered the house just after nine but there was a pot on the stove bubbling gently, the subtle aromas, captivated the senses. The terrace table was set. Anna was taking dishes from the fridge. I asked if I could help.

Can you take the pan outside? There are oven gloves next to the tea towels.

I did as asked and by the time I'd opened the wine the dishes were on the table. It was chicken and an abundance of vegetables in the pan, cooked using Marta's recipe. The salads were prepared by Anna before I arrived. Anna had forgotten something and while she was away I had, once again, the chance to take in my surroundings. Surroundings surrounded by silence. It would have been easy to have been overcome by what I viewed. The sheer luxury. Every detail thought through. I could only guess at the renovation costs involved in bringing this house into the twenty first century. Anna returned.

Anna, do you have any, before renovations of the house, photos?

I have a whole album James. I will show you later if you like.

Yes, I'd like that. It's a pity I couldn't have seen the photos before I came here. It's a bit like reading the end of a book and then turning to the first page to get the story. I just made that up. Did it make any sense?

You make me laugh James and perhaps that is the only sense I need. Have you finished because if so we can clear away and I will find that album.

Anna found the albums in the study. Yes, albums. Five in total and very thick. The first album was professional photos. Taken from all exterior angles which continued through the house. After came Anna's photos of the progress and the progress was time framed. Photos taken from the same spot. In one photo a wall. In the next a pile of rubble where the wall used to be and so it went on. Evidently a tip the photographer gave her. We had just completed the third and I brought up a previous conversation.

Do you remember the other evening Anna, when we spoke about smoking a joint? Well, I made some enquiries and this was the outcome.

I produced a well tailored joint. Anna's eyes lit up. Followed by a look of concern.

If you would rather not Anna, I can give it back tomorrow. (Not much chance of that, I was thinking.) Anna's curiosity overcame her trepidation.

"Let's do it," she said.

Isn't that suppose to be, Just Do It?
I lit the joint while Anna's concentration doubled. She wasn't going to miss a beat of this illicit moment. I passed the joint to her. She gave me a look as if her life depended on the outcome. I pretended to withdraw the offer, wondering what would happen next.
Gimme!
Was all Anna said, with a look of fascination mixed with a devil may care look in her eyes. I reached for the forth album while explaining to Anna the need to hold her breath. Count to five before you breath out. The joint passed between us without further ado. I found the transformation of this tired sixties style dwelling to be compelling viewing. Anna was filling me in with a running commentary as I turned the pages. Anna told me she felt no different. I explained that it was not uncommon. perhaps it was something to do with the expectation. The unknown entity. What were you expecting? Certainly not flying pink elephants. Expectations set too high? It wasn't long after her statement, I noticed more commentary with each photo, sometimes veering off on a tangent of, "I'd forgotten all about that day. We were expecting a delivery which was crucial to the schedule and it was late." And so it continued. It took another hour before the fifth was completed. No effect Anna? Ok then! Then she hit a wall. Whatever metaphorical wall that was, it had the effect of indecisiveness and that was confusing for Anna. A woman who, if nothing else, was decisive. Having been there myself, I understood that feeling. Guidance was what she needed. Someone to decide what was to happen next. I was enjoying the terrace and equally enjoying Anna's dilemma. I stood and said I'd get another bottle. I could say I took advantage but only in so much in the hope Anna might reveal more than she would normally and another glass of wine might just tip the balance. I returned with the wine and poured her a glass. Anna was sat quietly .... Listening? Thinking? Just looking? I wasn't sure what to think or do so I sat and once again, took in the silence. I don't think I was envious of Anna's good fortune it was more, glad to have the opportunity of experiencing such wealth. How the other half live. I decided to break the silence as I stood.
I'm going for a swim. Come on Anna why don't you join me.
Ok. I think I have a bikini in the sauna room?
Well, I haven't got one. Not a bikini, I mean. Which is fortunate. I'm sure you would be laughing your head off as you called for security to show me off the premises. So it's skinny dipping for me, I'm afraid.
Anna forwent the Sauna room and joined me. The backdrop of a beautifully laid out garden surrounded by mature trees of all descriptions with subtle lighting highlighting particular plants. The house towering over us. What a setting! Anna entered the water. I thought, if this was a movie it certainly wouldn't be me here but it could very well be Anna. The envy of any lighting engineer, Anna was enveloped in a flood of light. I wondered if Anna was knowingly playing a part?

219

Was she playing a part in this, this vision that was Anna? Perhaps she was but who cared. She looked radiant and I told her so. We swam about five or six lengths. Well, Anna did. We returned wrapped in towels to the terrace deciding on a decaf before bed.

I think there might have been a slight effect James.

I said nothing.

Having tried it once, I am not sure I see the value in it. I will continue with my few glasses of wine and two cigarettes a day with an abundance of exercise. Talking of which, isn't it time for bed?

That was supposed to be my line Anna. You had the advantage of knowing what you were going to say and beat me to it.

We walked arm in arm to the main ensuite bathroom. I knew it not to be uncommon but having the, His and Her basins was a first for me. I liked it. Synchronised teeth cleaning. Me with my, two minutes electric brush cycle staring into one mirror with Anna scrubbing away at the other. Occasionally catching each other in the mirror. I liked it.

You go ahead James, I will be right behind you.

I was lying down in bed.Then I was sitting up. I tried to decide on which I should be doing. Sitting up won out. Now what should I do with the duvet cover? I experimented. Slightly higher up. Slightly lower down. I settled for throwing the duvet up and where it landed was where it would stay. It was awhile before Anna entered by which time I must have changed my position and duvet, many times. She stood at the head of the bed, still wrapped in her towel. Having my undivided attention and said,

I bought these today. Do you like?

She dropped her towel. She was wearing what can only described as the cutest bra and briefs set I had ever seen. She moved around to the side and posed with one knee in front of the other with slightly slopping shoulders. It was time to say something. Anna won't hold that pose for long.

This is ridiculous Anna. I can't formulate my words. Ok. My first thought was how cute you looked but your body language distracted me. Cute and yet dangerous. You stand before me and if I believed in God I would be thanking him. Thanking him for bringing us together. To be able to enjoy everything I see before me. Thank you God. (I became a believer.) This Anna, is why I feel at a loss. There aren't words in my vocabulary that enables me to describe my thoughts. How about very cute and sexy and I promise to scour the depths of my mind for those missing words. You most certainly look cute though.

Anna slid under the duvet with a smirk on her face. She pushed up her pillows and sat next to me. I lent forward slightly and looked in the obvious direction of her breasts held in a natural position by the light grey bra having small splashes of black surrounded with puckered white lace.

Exquisite Anna. Not only in looks but also in agony. The exquisite agony that accompanies one when faced with such a dilemma. The dilemma of not wanting to alter perfection while at the same time knowing I must. The need to see what lies beneath this perfect ensemble.

Anna gave me the sweetest of smiles. Was it because I felt a little uncomfortable? Having already forgotten what I'd said I wasn't sure how I was supposed to react. I wasn't sure? If in doubt James do the usual and manage to ruin the moment.

They do say, you can't make an omelette without breaking eggs.

Amazingly that worked. Anna's sweet smile became serious but only for a second.

Then you had better break some eggs James.

I pulled back the duvet revealing Anna. Anna in her entirety. Anna looking so serene and relaxed. She was happy to see where this led. I moved down the bed until level with her legs. Kneeling there I took in the view before me. A part of me didn't want to remove those oh so beautiful panties but I eagerly did so. For no reason I could understand, Anna had the giggles. This could have been somewhat disconcerting. There I was about to ravage this beauty before me and she was giggling. Ok, forget ravage. Fun is what it was going to be. I kissed her stomach just above her navel. It had a reaction in Anna. It was as if I had discovered an erogenous zone. She was still giggling but intermixed with short outbursts of what was obvious pleasure. The giggling subsided. I moved from her stomach to her mouth. Anna put her arm around my neck to pull me closer. It was intense. One moment Anna seemed engrossed in that particular kiss, the next she was raining kisses on my lips. My hand slid between her legs, coinciding with a particularly engrossing kiss. It was slow. It was passionate. I could still visualise Anna beneath me, still wearing her, ever so cute bra which I was sure went some way in establishing my mood of that night. I almost felt I was making love to a different woman. Perhaps that was it. We were making love. Not having sex. We kept it simple. I had straddled Anna's legs bringing them together. It was not going to be Anna beneath me, legs wide apart. I was in no hurry and I could tell Anna felt the same way. We lay for moments at a time motionless while my erection lay deep inside her. Time no longer relevant. Our soft existence wrapped in a cocoon of togetherness. We flowed with the tide. No need for conversation. No need for thinking. There was that inner awareness that two people shared. It was making love for the first time and being lucky enough to get it right. Maybe never again to achieve. The explosion within our bodies happened simultaneously. Neither wanted to be released from that moment. It was some time before we managed to separate. Laying side by side, Anna was whispering in my ear.

That was wonderful James. I'm not sure why but it felt different.

I could have told her why. Well, my interpretation of why.

We were amazing were we not James? And do you realise, I've never done that before, I mean kept my legs together.
Anna gave me a smile that said more but held back from putting it into words.
I'm going to sleep now. I want to dream wonderful dreams. Dreams of love. Good Night James.
A final kiss and Anna turned.
"Dreams of love"? I wasn't going to go there. I listened to the sounds of Anna. The sounds of that almost silent breathing. Sleep was fortunately, soon upon me. Over coffee in the morning I wondered whether to discuss the night before. What to say? That was the most amazing sex I have ever had? I think we moved mountains? Or possibly, Anna, I love you. I let the moment pass as Anna pondered her day.
I need to go shopping for Marta and then I have lunch with the girls. Have you ever watched 24 hours? I'll bring the series with me this evening to your house and we can watch it, after I beat you playing Ludo.
I had nothing on my agenda just a week full of spaces I'd hoped to fill with Anna. What I did have was a large pot of white paint. Anna had casually asked when I had last painted the place. A while ago, I could have said but thought better of it. I hadn't in the nine years I'd lived there so remained silent. I had seven possibly eight hours to make a transformation.
Anytime after eight will be ok for me Anna as I have a busy day ahead.
Oh, what are you doing James?
"I'll tell you tonight," I said. Anna didn't push it. I waved her good bye. Once inside, I set upon the task ahead. Cleared the furniture from half the room. Laid a plastic sheet and started on the ceiling. By six I had finished the ceiling and two walls. One of which I had decided on a very pale yellow. Enough time to change out the hidden fluorescents and replace with an led strip. Mission accomplished. Everything back in it's place with plenty of time to relax before showering. Anna called.
I am just leaving Nice, would it be alright if I arrive in half an hour?
I'll open the gates in twenty minutes. See you soon.
But she was already gone. I decided on a quick beer and cigarette to compensate for the lost relax time, prior to shower. Anna noticed the change immediately on entering.
Wow James. That makes an incredible difference.
A difference I should have made years ago, I was thinking.
I do like the yellow. I was thinking of getting one of the bedrooms repainted and I would like to use that colour. Do you have the reference?
The reference? A big tub of white paint. Seven blobs of yellow and stir furiously until mixed.
Anna just looked at me, and then said, "In that case you will have to come around to mix it. Are you painting the kitchen?"

222

After explaining my colour scheme for the kitchen. Basically, yellow and or white. Anna seemed satisfied congratulating me once more on my efforts. I poured the wine and produced a cheese plate accompanied by dishes of nuts. Once again, Anna just looked at me and then smiled.

You've forgotten the Ludo James or are you worried I'll win and are stalling for time?

I said nothing but smiled in return. I came around the bar and moved to kiss her. The kiss was warmly accepted. It became lingering.

You are worried aren't you James but if it is a choice between you losing Ludo or kisses, I'll choose kisses every time.

"In that case, I accept defeat", said I, as I took the back of her head and brought my lips to hers.

Get the Ludo James.

Ok.

Three one. Would she ever learn? We settled back to watch 24, a program I'd never seen and am now watching Series Six. We watched the first four parts deciding the rest could wait until another time. Anna disappeared to the bathroom and I tidied up. Obviously making herself beautiful I thought, as I laid in bed. Anna reappeared. Kicked off her sandals and pulled her dress over her head. It had the desired effect. The sight of another set of beautifully crafted underwear was enough and Anna knew it. I thought on our first two or three occasions Anna was a little shy but no longer. I had told her often enough about my admiration of her nakedness. We had discussed her breasts and her thoughts on implants. I do believe I had convinced her it was not necessary, certainly not in the near future. Yes, they were not the breasts of a twenty year old, not that my memory allowed me that luxury of that thought. No they were not but they maintained a firmness that was gratifying to the touch. Anna was still standing. A minute might have passed when she said,

Pull back the duvet James.

I did as was asked revealing a very firm erection. Anna pushed her panties to her knees and let them drop. Stepping out of them she came to the bed. Kneeling forward she held my erection.

Have I told you, your size is a perfect fit? Smaller and I wouldn't be satisfied and if larger I think it might be too much. Mmmmm

Anna's grip tightened as she moved her hand in long slow strokes. All the time watching me. I don't know why I reacted as I did but I had the feeling she was waiting. Waiting to see what I would do. So I did something. I sat up and hand behind her head guided her towards the task at hand. The temptation to lie back and enjoy was there but why stop now. I kept my hand behind Anna's head, following the movement for awhile. I applied a slight pressure on her next downward stroke. Anna understood what I was attempting, when she withdrew ever so slightly all the while feeling the pressure of my hand resisting. Both

223

hands behind her head I guided her forward. I did believe Anna was as interested as I to discover just how deep she could go? She stopped but after withdrawing for a moment continued until once again she stopped with a big smile on her face as she crawled up the bed.

You deserve an award for such "depth" of character Anna. In fact I would have found that difficult to swallow if I hadn't seen it with my own eyes. Well done. Now turn over. Get on your knees and be ready to receive your award.

Full of those, almost giggles, Anna obliged. Why wouldn't she. It was a favourite position but it required stamina if one was to follow ones natural desires when finding oneself in this position. So I didn't! No rampant excessive energy used. Holding onto my erection I allowed but a few centimetres to penetrate Anna's most sacred place. With a perfect view of that slightly protruding pudenda. Her, mons veneris with the temptation to plunge myself into her being almost irresistible but I continued restricting Anna to those few centimetres. Withdrawing completely before entering again. She wanted more. I resisted. Until Anna said, "Take me James". So I did. I took my hand away and allowed myself to slowly enter. That first stroke went deep. Anna shuddered. The strokes were gaining momentum. Anna dropped her shoulders to the bed. At the end of a full stroke I waited a brief moment before pushing those few extra millimetres and withdrawing. Every stroke became a double stroke. The latter gaining but those few vital millimetres. Anna dropped and I went with her. She laid there with me, still inside her. I gave her the briefest of time before reawakening her desires. Not sure she was quite ready for more, I made some tentative, explorative movements while my brain was still trying to understand how come no one had informed it of those "going-ons" because if they had it would have put a stop to it long ago. Anna's response was partially of reluctance but like me, her brain was well and truly excluded. She recovered beautifully and was rewarded with yet another pleasurable time of pure joy, in her favourite position. No way were we going for a third. My body was not playing tricks. No way was I going for a third. Evidently I got that wrong. Getting too old for this, thought I.

I laid back. Thoughts in my head as Anna drifted off to sleep. It was those times in bed when we were equal and as such I was at ease taking control. Anna was compliant. She approved of my decisions knowing full well they were the right ones. And yet, for the rest, it was different. Anna managed our day time activities. What did she write on that web site? Something about being proactive in life, often taking the initiative. I had been warned.

Today was tennis day. We were up at seven and Anna was ready to leave by eight, looking oh so cute, in her tennis outfit. It was always going to be difficult imagining Anna in a mini skirt but there she was showing off her well shaped legs and perhaps just a little too much, I thought, watching her check the back seat of the car, to confirm she had two rackets while saying something about needing to have one re stringed. Tennis outfit. Short skirt. Stretching across the back seats. I waved Anna goodbye quietly thanking her for that vision, at the same time, realising we'd made no plans for our next rendezvous. Perhaps before she left I could have said something. I didn't. Another beautiful day in the South of France I thought, as I headed for the roof. Anna called around three.

James, we didn't make any plans for today! My mind was so much on the tennis. Why didn't you say something? I feel so bad!

I didn't say anything as I didn't see the need Anna. I knew your mind was on the tennis and once the adrenaline had receded we would be having this conversation.

"No you didn't James", said Anna, laughing.

You would have to be devious to consider that possibility and my dear sweet James is not capable of being devious.

You only have yourself to blame Anna. To accommodate your intellect, one has to avoid blandness. One strives to entertain. Particularly in situations when one finds oneself incapable of an intelligent retort. Do you think I am over doing the usage of "one"?

I'm not getting into this James.

Anna was still laughing.

I have some shopping to do James so I can be with you around five.

Have you eaten Anna?

Yes, I had lunch at the club so don't worry. Anyway I can pick something up at the supermarket.

And she was gone. Five, she said. Going shopping, she said. I didn't really expect her before six. It was quarter to seven when she rang to ask me to open the gates.

There are some bags in the boot. In fact everything needs to come in. If you can manage that, I'll bring the food in.

I placed the contents of the boot on the sofa while Anna filled the fridge. There was, in plain sight, a frying pan on my sofa, nestled between two carrier bags and what looked like, soft furnishings but definitely a frying pan. I picked it up. Top quality frying pan still in its wrappings but what was it doing here?

You said you needed a new frying pan James. Hope you like it. Don't touch anything else just give me a second.

Did I say I need a new frying pan? Anna had arrived with a yellow "throw over" and flowery patterned yellow cushion covers. Yellows that perfectly complimented the, just painted walls.

Thank you Anna, it was kind of you and in such a thoughtful way. I most definitely like the additions. It is a pity I couldn't afford you as my interior designer.

"One more addition James", said Anna as she handed me another present. It was a cashmere jumper. Anna insisted I tried it on. It was the most comfortable item I had ever worn. Anna was running her hands over the jumper as she walked around me. How could I possible deny her. She was enjoying herself.

I was wondering Anna. Do you think kissing someone wearing a cashmere jumper heightens the senses?

Good question James.

The obvious conclusion. We embraced. I could have sworn, it heightened my senses. The feel of Anna's hands wondering across my back as we kissed was close to erotic. We separated.

What do you think Anna? Personally, I'm not sure. Perhaps if we could repeat the procedure?

You are not sure James? I suggest you switch your brain on and take note because I think you are sure.

As Anna spoke she lowered her eyes. She was right of course. When one is wearing linen trousers and no underwear, my thoughts of erotica were plain to see.

I don't think there is any way I'm talking my way out of the obvious is there. I guess that's a no for a repeat then?

We played Ludo. Maybe one day she would win. Having eaten only a small proportion of the delicacies Anna had brought we were now ensconced on the sofa, 24 hours. Series 6. Fifth, or sixth episode? Did it matter? Four, or five episodes and another Irish later, we called it a night.

I laid beside her and with no preamble, kissed her. My hand already between her legs. How long before she wanted me inside her. For the time being she was enjoying lying, legs slightly open while I found that spot. Finding that spot was never too difficult it was the manipulation, once found, that was the key. Not being too eager. Manoeuvring ones fingertips, ever so delicately. Anna's hand reached for my erection. It won't be long now, I thought.

Oh James.

I took that as my key and moved onto her. It wasn't long before Anna was giving forth her silent rapture. I slowed but continued my movements. Anna, just for a moment, fought against me, wanting me to stop but only for a moment. She rode that wave beautifully and was looking for the next.

The following morning I showered. Leaving Anna to slumber I checked out the remnants of the previous evenings meal, managing to rescue a very presentable brunch. I took Anna an orange juice. She was awake but not quite awake. The lack of cover exposing her breasts gave me that clue. Once awake, Anna soon realised her situation but rather than feign embarrassment, she reached for the juice.

You look beautiful my dear.

I leant forward. Kissed her cheek and left her to it. While waiting for the coffee I was thinking that same thought. We had seen each other everyday that last week before I started back to work. Sometimes the afternoon. Sometimes afternoon and evening. Sometimes evening and night but only once in the months I'd known Anna had we spent a continuous twenty four hours together. My thoughts broke off as Anna entered.

I thought I'd smelt coffee. Oh food and I'm starving.

Exercise will do that for you Anna, so perhaps you can imagine just how hungry I am.

What are you trying to say James.

And so our day started. Anna picked up on my off hand remark and wasn't going to let it go. One could not afford to let ones guard down with Anna.

Do you really want me to go there Anna? Do I need to explain while you were lying there absorbing the pleasure, what I was doing to facilitate such? It's not all about lying there thinking of …….. what were you thinking by the way?

Don't try and change the subject James.

Why is that Anna? Too revealing an answer might be forthcoming?

Anyway, while you were there thinking, My Goodness James is fantastic, I expelled more calories in the first five minutes than you did in the entire three hours. Or was it two? What were you thinking?

You will never know.

So it wasn't thoughts of how fantastic I was then?

You were wonderful James, now lets eat!

Half way through brunch Anna explained her need to be in Milan, again. Leaving on Sunday to be ready for a Monday morning meeting. Tanya will be joining her on Tuesday, giving the girls a days shopping in Milan. Hardly enough time between shops to put the credit card away methought. Then home on Thursday. I thought, well, it did take the pressure off fitting Anna into what will be a heavy work schedule. On top of that news it was Saturday. Her clients would be leaving. Anna had to be home by one, before they departed and then there was the clearing up. Anna did say she would only be concerned about her bedroom. I thought, but which was that, we'd slept in three? I said nothing. "Why don't we go to the Cafe Kanter this evening", I said. Anna was delighted at the possibility. "Just the two of us". Which was met with a kiss and a look of ……. ? Of fondness. Hey, possibly it was love but one should never assume. One could but hope. There is a line in the Shawshank Redemption went something like, Hope is a commodity we can't afford. I therefore accepted, "of fondness". It was coming up to twelve thirty when Anna shifted into, going home mode.

Must leave James. Now where did I put my undies? Oh yes, they are, in my handbag.

Yes, there they were. You couldn't miss that lacy fabric, cascading from the bag.

"It's a good job you're not wearing your tennis outfit. If you were, you wouldn't be leaving now. In fact, not for some time," I said with a straight face.

You say such sweet things James.

Said with a touch of sarcasm, I noted.

I think I should go James before you have any other ideas.

Now she was laughing. Anna was in the car and gone but not before some lingering moments. Saturday! After almost two months off, this was to be my last weekend before that inevitable Monday reared it's ugly head. I was having thoughts of work! Although I had to admit, in some way, I was looking forward to another slow build up where that inevitable ticking clock replaced the sedate pace with organised chaos. Knowing before I started back, there were two new builds and a possible third. Hundreds of pieces being manufactured. Some for one client and some for another. Having established the client. What finish. Laminate? Paint? Fabric. Which colour? The list goes on. Oh joy! But that was for Monday.

I contacted Paul, who knowing the owner of the Cafe Kanter, could reserve us a table. Ideally a table on the terrace. After a short bout of, "What I do for you", Paul obliged. Ten minutes later he confirmed a table for two at eight thirty on the terrace. I bowed and scraped in the most humble manner as I thanked him most graciously. "Oh piss off", he said.

Ok Paul, see you later.

Yes! Well done Paul. One would never try to make a reservation for the coming evening and certainly not on a Saturday. I texted Anna. Table booked for eight. Thinking we might just make eight thirty on Anna Time. We did. Eight twenty five which included circling the block three times to find parking. For once Anna's, swing into a convenient parking space, let us down. I recognised the owner from the few occasions I'd been before. He liked to greet his guests.

"Bonsoir James," he said as he shook my hand. He didn't know me from a bar of soap. Paul had obviously asked the owner to play this game. Anna, not being shy in coming forward was now introducing herself.

J'ai su que James a eu une belle dame mais ....

Finished off with a shrug of the shoulders that in French meant, "But your beauty was understated". Or something very similar. Certainly that was the way Anna took it. Accepting the compliment with gracious ease, we were shown to our table. The table was well placed. Off to the side and not surrounded by others. An observant fellow such as I would have noticed the tables had been reorganised. Shifted slightly further onto the pavement. Why? To allow for this extra table. I was a great believer in, It's not what you know but who you know. Well done Paul. Anna had decided where she would like to sit. I remembered that evening took a few conversational turns. Turns infused with humorous anecdotes. I know I said the right things at the time but it wasn't until a few days later that I caught the under current of Anna's conversation. There were some topics she wanted to cover. Serious topics. Us topics. It hadn't taken long. Aperitifs ordered, Anna was ready to discuss.

You know you take up a lot of the thoughts in my day James. I am not talking about when we are together. I'm talking about the time apart. When I am busy it is okay but as soon as I relax, it is you I am thinking of.
If it is any consolation Anna, I find myself in a similar position.
I said no more, believing it was Anna who wanted the floor.
What is it you think James?
She'd turned it around. It was me on the floor. I was awaiting revelations from Anna and she sat there waiting for my response. Well done James. You just blew it!
What do I think about? I think about your nuances. The way you talk with every word perfectly pronounced. The way you say What, when I'm looking at you. The devilish look that occasionally crosses your face. Your schoolgirl laughter. And then there is you. You the person. I have to be careful here. I know you appreciate flattery but to avoid any disappointment, I tell you now, I will be holding back from divulging the full truth.
Anna was already looking disappointed.
You capture my thoughts Anna. You are fun to be with. You are a challenge to my intellect. Although, maybe not such a challenge?
Those humorous anecdotes. Where would I be without them.
I spend my time thinking of being with you. To hold your hand. To hold you.
Anna was no longer looking disappointed.
…….. and that, coincidently, brings me to the part about great sex. I'll stop now. But, before I do, I have to apologise for my inadequate description of my thoughts. All I can say in my defence is how does one describe perfection.
My turn to sit back but before Anna could reply the first course had arrived. We hadn't ordered it and I didn't know if it was normal when all one had done was order a main meal but that was only the second time I had been there without Paul and on both of those occasions, Paul had made the reservations. The first, I remembered, was with Emanuela. Fortunately Anna distracted my thoughts.
Thank you for those sweet words James. Much appreciated the "great" bit. Holding back the full truth and yet you describe me as perfection. I can't wait to hear the full version. This is delicious James. You should try the salmon.
I happened to have my mouth full of some sort of stuffed pastry when Anna said that. I thought of perhaps spitting it out to free myself up for the, to die for salmon. I thought better of that idea. I replied with a closed mouth, Mmm Huh! Followed up with a closed mouth conversation about why I couldn't try the salmon at the moment as my mouth was full. I had her laughing. She was off guard.
So what about your thoughts Anna?
My thoughts are confused. Confused because I am not supposed to like you.
My turn for a look of disappointment. Anna noticed this and laughed.
Maybe I should explain myself. My late husband was an Italian industrialist with important connections. We had dinner parties for twenty or more people. Some

were invited as friends while others for business. There was always business. In fact we had an online diary that either could update. Mine was tennis. Lunch with friends. A reminder the pool electrician arrives on Wednesday at three. His? New York Monday through Wednesday. Thursday, lunch in Milan at one for Anna and I. Home for the weekend. That was the life I knew. That has changed. It is amazing how couples we knew no longer invite me. A good friend of mine who also happens to be "single", laughed when I told her. Oh Anna, you are single. You are a threat. You see what you are doing to me James? No, because I am digressing!

Anna enjoyed that thought and continued.

Back to the point. Why am I so attracted to you? I have asked myself that question so many times. The obvious. You are attractive. Intelligent. Definitely humorous. Courteous. Attentive and I am sure it is only your modesty that prevents you from adding more.

I laughed at that.

And then there is the other obvious. Our lives are, different, as I am sure you will agree. We both understand those differences without the need to express the obvious. And that James, is the conflict that rages in my head.

As we had finished our main meal and without that conversation concluded, we were interrupted, to our surprise, with a plate of cheeses and glasses of brandy. Not ordered. Compliments of the management. Well done Paul, I thought. That interruption accompanied by an added distraction of street acrobats diffused the moment. They toured the area in the summer months. When you've seen it once …… Five minutes it was all over with clapping from the restaurant. Quickly followed up with the man with the bag. Passing expertly between the tables, graciously accepting the donations given. By the time things had settled back into an evening of restaurant goers enjoying their evening meal, our conversation had drifted. "A conflict that rages in her head", was the thought raging through mine. Twenty minutes later and Anna was ordering Irish coffees. It was eleven thirty before we left the restaurant. I opened the front door. Anna made a bee line for the fridge. Ten minutes later and we were sat, Irish coffee's simmering, as our eyes met.

You have been thinking about what I said earlier, haven't you James?

What could I do but smile?

A conflict that rages? May I make a suggestion Anna. Why don't we enjoy this time and see where it leads. Maybe it's a dead end. Maybe it's the start of a beautiful friendship that in years to come we can look back upon. Hopefully still sipping our coffees, albeit from a wheelchair. Don't worry about it Anna. One day you will know what you want to do but for right now? Hopefully you will agree with me and accept what we have. What we have right now.

You are right of course James, I shouldn't let it concern me but that is the problem. I do! Normally I wouldn't have to follow your advice. I am quite capable of making decisions on such matters. Yes. No. Easy!

I understand Anna.

I said that with my very best serious and understanding look.

You would like to get rid of me but you can't bring yourself to do it or, you want to keep me but the problems that incurs prevents you from doing so. I think I've just talked my way out of a beautiful relationship?

I waited to see Anna's reaction. She burst into laughter.

Let's go to bed James.

Chapter Seventeen

We had an early breakfast on the terrace. Fresh baguette with a choice of jams and marmalades. Coffee for Anna. Tea for me.
"Perhaps it is the sex"? Said Anna, who was obviously just thinking aloud. I awaited an explanation of that remark. None was forthcoming. I let it pass. It was decided I would take Anna to the airport around one. Anna left with assurances from me to be at her house by one. It was a pleasant journey to the airport. Anna was looking forward to seeing Tanya and was in her effervescent mood. Very much, touchy feely.
You will pick me up on Thursday won't you James? Seeing you when I land would be just wonderful.
I wasn't sure if Anna meant that or was securing her lift home but I liked it anyway.
Of course I will. Text me the flight details and I'll be here.
Here being the airport. We had arrived at the, "Kiss and Fly". A few moments to retrieve Anna's bag. Kisses on the cheeks and not a backwards glance as she disappeared through the glass doors. I headed home with mixed feelings. Anna was away that coming week. I knew I'd miss her but at the same time it allowed me to concentrate on ……. work. Oh what joy distractions bring, I thought. Hence the mixed feelings. What could I do Yes, work occupied my mind but not seeing Anna? I received an, "Arrived safely message", to which I responded but it was now Tuesday and nothing since? It didn't matter, I told myself. Work was all consuming. It was Wednesday. Late morning and I received a text.
Have we been playing, "Who is going to send the first message game", James?
That was it! That was all she said! I was confused and at the same time dogmatic. Dogmatic in the sense of not willing to play Anna's game. I didn't reply.

Three hours later, I received a photo of Anna and Tanya, sitting at a fountain. Mother and daughter taken by a passing tourist. I could not but reply.

You got me Anna. How could one refuse but to comment on such a photo. You need to save that one. It's a photo, taken by a complete stranger that, in my eyes, exemplifies the natural love between mother and daughter. Definitely save that one. Get it framed. Digressing but on the same tangent ..... I'm missing you.

I could have added more, which normally I might have but I was struggling to maintain that aura of "Interesting and Windswept". Withhold information. No matter how trivial I thought it to be. Withhold. Was I playing a game of banter or of intellect? I hoped banter but maybe Anna's insecurities played a part? Why do we have to complicate our lives this way? I received a reply.

I am confused James. I do not hear from you for two days and then a loving response to a photo?

Anna was not a needy person. She was a person in control of her emotions. She had put me on the spot, again! I could only perceive myself as being the guilty person. Why did I not text her on the Monday morning? Perhaps wishing her, Good Luck with the lawyers. Too late for that analogy.

Don't give me a hard time Anna. You know I miss you. In fact, almost as much as you miss me!

That was directed at diffusing the situation but I needed to add more.

Forget, I Miss You as we've already established, you miss me more. How about, I Need You! My life is but a straw in the wind. A drop in the ocean. Time, irrelevant if not in your arms. Nothing can compare to a brief moment in your company. .... How am I doing?

Redeeming yourself James.

I was right. I was conceived as being the guilty party. I couldn't let that go without some defence and as we all know, the best form of defence ....

Redeeming myself? I consider myself redeemed. Adulation poured from my lips not from a feeling of guilt but from feelings that have been restrained for these past two days. Thoughts held back. Held back wondering when Anna will have the time to chat. I was not being evasive but considerate when allowing you space to deal with matters at hand. It was perhaps foolish of me to believe you could survive for two days without me but I was wrong. So for that, I apologise and will, in future, be more understanding to your needs. Totally my fault. Can you help it if you are inexplicably drawn towards me? I'm in trouble, aren't I? And I was doing so well!

No James, you are not in trouble and you are still doing well. Perhaps you are right. I am inexplicably drawn towards you. Or perhaps I am just drawn towards these shallow conversations because they alleviate my real world. How am I doing James?

You are doing very well Anna, I thought but I didn't give her the satisfaction of knowing so. At least not just yet. An indignant response? The little boy hurt? Confused? Or Oneupmanship?

What is real Anna? Tennis is real. Your swimming pool is real. The man in the street is real but all, mere distractions. Real are the people you interact with. Be it a quiet conversation with a close friend. A riotous party. A small dinner gathering or making love. These things are real Anna. Welcome to our real world! Long may it alleviate your other, self professed world. May I also add. You were doing very well Anna. To change the subject completely before you have a chance of admitting to your deep attraction for me ...... Any success regarding lawyers?

Ok James, I will let that one pass as your rambling amuses me so. Unfortunately it is not the same with the lawyers. There are moments, all be them brief. Very brief. I feel like walking away from it all. My stepdaughter is being a particular bitch. She wants me to pay the taxes on her inheritance. Why would I do that? Can we get back to amusing ramblings? I like that world. Sorry, our world.

A sexist joke about obesity coming up Anna!

After years of stuffing her face, my wife finally took it too far and fell into a deep diabetic coma. After two weeks of no improvement, her doctor took me to one side. "I'm sorry, but all our tests indicate no sign of her ever recovering." He told me soberly, "It might be time to take away her life support." Suddenly, my wife's eyes sprung wide open as she sat bolt upright in bed. "Did someone mention takeaway?"

Aren't you supposed to be shopping with Tanya? And if so, how can you possibly have any time to message me. I have an image of you sitting on a most uncomfortable chair outside the changing room, for possibly not the first time today, while Tanya tries on yet another outfit. How does it work? Is it time divided or do you take it in turns? Or is it, First to the changing room wins. Now there is a possible SAS derivative in the making. Have I mentioned how much you are looking forward to seeing me? I have a solution to that uncomfortable chair. Tell Tanya it's lunchtime. That should do it. Happy shopping!

Now I know you have a spy in my camp James. Only it was not a chair, more like a pouffe that was designed for a person with perfect equilibrium. No matter how I tried it was impossible not to fall sideways. We are already at lunch. Well, I am. Tanya, who thought it a good idea to drop her shopping off at the hotel before joining me, has still to arrive. It is ok. I'm sat with a glass of Perrier, ice and lemon, watching the other world go by. Talking of worlds and our world in particular, I have another meeting on Friday so will not be flying back until Saturday. I do hope you can be there to meet me? Tanya has arrived so I wish you a pleasant day and yes, I am missing you. x

Not back until Saturday. The thoughts I had of taking the Friday off disappeared. Perhaps Monday, albeit after tennis. I felt a frustration building. September was the month to enjoy what the Riviera had to offer. The tourists had left. Normality returned. The beaches. The restaurants. The bars. The scenic areas. All were available without effort. It was approaching mid September and my possibilities of having any days off, including weekends, diminished as October approached. I will pick her up on Saturday, sometime. Do we spend the day together? Unlikely. Anna would be tired. A lot of things to catch up on in her absence. Was it an evening flight? Drop her off with a promise of Sunday? Maybe just a call on Sunday to say, "Can we see each other on Monday James?" That would be after tennis, I could have heard her say. I do remember hedging my bets by informing all that I felt necessary to know, I had a dental appointment on Monday so won't be around in the morning. The next few days revolved around Anna's arrival. I sent her a few messages of encouragement during those days.

Thank you James, for your messages of encouragement and I do apologise for not getting back. The last two days have been beyond belief. It is almost twelve months since Christophe died and it seems no one cares about that but me. It is all about, "Whats in it for me"? I am so depressed. You will have that burden of depression meeting you at the airport. All I can say is ….. I am so pleased it will be you. I so much want our world right now. The flight arrives about six thirty. Marta will prepare dinner for us. I will message you the flight details later but right now I'm taking a nap before the dinner with all parties concerned in this debacle. So looking forward to seeing you tomorrow. x

Marta was to prepare dinner? Was I staying over? For the last two days I'd been sending messages with no response and now I discover I was to greet a depressed woman who expected miracles from me. No pressure there then, I thought. Anna sent me the details on Saturday morning. Six thirty five, arriving from Milan. I filled my day weeding the patio. Scrubbing algae from the steps while noticing the first of the winter leaves. Too early. Surely, too early?

Arriving at Terminal two, I sat and waited. There was no missing her. A carry on bag and loaded down with shopping. Breezing through as if the concourse was empty. A huge smile greeted me. How did she manage to get those extra bags on an Easyjet flight?

Oh James. So kind of you. Can you take a couple of bags? I've missed you. I really have.

As she kissed me on both cheeks. I could but smile. Anna was back. We made it to the motorway heading for the Villenueve Loubet exit. Anna's chatter was hyphenated only by the occasional breath. Excited Anna. "I've so missed you James". No depression there. It was hard to define but Anna's chatter alone elevated my day. Not to mention the thought of dinner and ……

Was my life so void of interest that listening to Anna, being with Anna, was all encompassing? The thought did disturb me but not for long. Dropping her bag at the door Anna made her way to the Breakfast Bar.

Can you choose a wine James? We should have dinner under the pergola but a glass of wine first. Please?

While Anna busied herself in the kitchen, presumably checking all was prepared, I choose a bottle at random and set off across the patio.

Wine is with me Anna. On the terrace.

Instantly realising my mistake I corrected myself.

I'll drop it off and return to help. I can carry better than I can cook so I'll lay the table.

You know James, most men wouldn't even consider the thought of helping. You've considered it and that is enough. I will join you in a minute, just pour me a glass and relax.

Relax. That was debatable. Sat in those lavish surroundings with a woman outside my understanding of how women behave. Only aware that farting would not be deemed amusing. Not that it was one of my party pieces but all the same …. I knew where I was. Surrounded by opulence, that was where I was. Just relax James. Easier said than done, I thought, as Anna joined me. She sat and smiled.

I love this time of evening but this evening is different. I've returned from Milan too many times to remember and have sat here hoping to forget the days spent with those awful people but to no avail and I hate myself for feeling so. For ruining what was a beautiful evening. An evening to be enjoyed, and I was unable to do so. This evening is different James. The evening is ours. Thank you for being here.

I wasn't expecting such an outburst of appreciation. Did Anna really mean my presence meant so much to her? Her body language dictated my next move. I leant forward placing my hand under her chin. Drawing her towards me.

If my presence helps you enjoy an evening such as this then I can only but in all humility, be overjoyed that I contribute to your well-being. Perhaps that should have been a toast rather than an excuse to kiss you?

I did manage to kiss her. Once she had stopped laughing.

Anna was a perfect host. I barely noticed her departures. It was only through realising dishes came and went. And there were but the two of us. Call me slow to realise but maybe I was, finally relaxed. Either way I was completely enrapt with a desert to die for. Marta's recipe, I was told. To put that evening into words would be impossible. It was a living, breathing time. Full of idle chatter with the clinking of glasses and a time I knew, I had rarely before encountered. Those times come and go in our lives but are not often remembered. I would remember the exact day. Month. Year. The memory would never be diluted. That was one of those days. Clearing away the dishes to make way for coffee. Laughing when the automatic sprinkler system kicked in, catching us unawares. We dwelled over coffee under the cover of darkness. The air was still but not humid. The stars, clear in the sky. All helped to capture the atmosphere of two people seemingly alone in the world and not caring if we were.

You know James, please correct me if I'm wrong but I do not believe we have spent an entire twenty four hours together.

That was the way I saw it but I didn't answer.

Why don't we get up late and go to the beach. I know a good restaurant on the front at Cap-d'Ail. We can spend the day and as long as you don't leave me before seven on Sunday evening, et voila. Thirty six hours!

So, it looked like I was spending the night with the added bonus of another twenty four hours. Anna rose and picking up my empty cup said, "Bedtime"?

It had been a perfect evening. The electricity between us had been far from static which still persisted even as we were cleaning teeth at adjoining sinks. Anna was first to the bedroom and when I joined her, she had her back to me?

From behind James. Slowly. Ever so slowly.

This was a position we more than occasionally found ourselves enjoying. Please the woman James and all else follows. And so it was. I had a time, around three in the morning when, for some unknown reason, I would wake to a hot rod that needed to go somewhere and didn't need wheels to do so, Anna was always obliging. There was not the need to satisfy that which had no brain. But I digress.That was, as requested, very slow even to the point of stopping while embedded far within. An ever so slight movement was all that was needed. Managing to caress her breast while kissing her neck, Anna, I felt sure became unaware of her surroundings. Unaware possibly of me. She was reaching down to depths only she understood. I had no idea how long we remained like that but it was a blissful eternity for me. For Anna, maybe more? I felt the first tremors from deep within. She exploded from those depths like a cork from a bottle almost shaking loose from our connection. I thought I rode it well.

Stay inside me James. I want you there while I drift off to sleep.

I came to the next morning with Anna facing me. Watching me. She smiled.

Thank you James. For last night.

I saw, even with only one eye open, Anna had more to say.

Can we do it again?

It was amazing to find how quickly ones dormant faculties were capable of responding to such a request.

We can do it again Anna but not like last night.

I was turning Anna over as I spoke. With my arm around her waist, I eased her to her knees. Spanning her legs with mine, I entered slowly but not for long. It was unlike the night before. This was sex. My tip on her shaved pudenda and all before me vanished. Consumed by a fire that must have been stirring in Anna while I slept. It was not long. Anna was soon to collapse onto the bed, followed closely by me and managing to remain within as she sank, I took advantage of the situation. There was a moment that Anna might have objected but it soon passed. This time softer, more aware of Anna's current needs. She had already received what she needed but I believed there was always room for icing on the cake.

Anna's first words after five minutes of silence as she recovered from her second and possibly more intense "occasion" of the morning.

If this keeps up I might have to give up tennis.

I laughed.

Why don't I take a shower Anna and you can follow on while I prepare coffee.

Anna looked at me. Gave me a big wet kiss and laughed.

Great sex and he can make coffee. What more could I ask for?

I gave her my best smile and headed for the shower. Left in charge of the Nespresso machine I placed cups, saucers and capsules nearby. With certainly twenty minutes before Anna was likely to surface, I decided to take a walk around the gardens. Six thousand square metres of garden? Just enjoy the walk James, I thought. Don't dwell on the incidentals. There was a path that led away from the pool, through a neatly arranged wooded area with the almost inevitable hidden pagoda. Placed perfectly where the wooded area receded and a wild garden started. It was late September. The sun was casting it's rays across the grasses. Showcasing the dynamic reds, yellows and oranges. The grasses catching the morning sun. I must say, it took my breath away. Perhaps something to do with my present state of mind but I saw myself enjoying that place of tranquility. I stood rooted to the spot, not wishing to break the mood. Anna did.

James, there is no coffee? Ten out of ten for placement but it's that last procedure you seem to have overlooked.

She was laughing as she approached, putting her arm through mine. She looked stunning. A light grey dress that could have only been made to measure. You didn't get anything like that in Primark, I thought. It fitted everywhere and ended just above the knee, accessorised with an amazing wide brimmed white bonnet adorned with a grey silk band and bow.

It is beautiful, isn't it? I often come here and when I couldn't find you something told me I'd find you here.

The spell was broken. Not that I was complaining. Anna's presence took my thoughts in another direction. Wonderful times here, with Anna. I kissed her.

Let me make you that coffee Anna.

We walked arm in arm around the back of the house past the vegetable garden which was Marta's domain apart from a row of radishes that Anna insisted she planted, plus, she added, the rose bushes that surrounded the garden. I made coffee.

It was approaching midday when we left for the restaurant, already pre booked by Anna. We drove in silence for some time. I say "we drove". I had no objection. Who wouldn't mind being driven around in a convertible Mercedes with top down? The silence was comforting. I do believe Anna was also comfortable with that silence. Threading our way through the back streets of Nice a street dweller decided it was an opportune moment to cross the road, pushing his shopping trolley that only had three wheels. It seemed almost inevitable. He saw us approaching and panicked. The trolley soon lay on it's side. There was plenty of room to go around him but Anna stopped. Hazard lights on and she was out of the car.

We have to help him James!

It took maybe ten minutes to get his trolley and all it's luggage back upright to the annoyance of many motorists who were by now forming a not too happy queue behind Anna's car. To her credit, she ignored the occasional honking of horns. Job done we returned to the car. I was the first to break our, in-car-silence.

That was very gracious of you Anna and to be honest, unexpected.

Surely you would have done the same James and I think you know I am susceptible to needy causes.

Said as she glanced in my direction.

So you think I am in need Anna?

Of course James. You more than most.

Once Anna had finished giggling, she placed her hand on my leg and continued.

You need me! James.

More giggles as Anna found a parking place. Once parked she turned to me.

..... but I need you to James.

Before I could respond, Anna was out of the car.

Come on James, we don't want to be late for lunch.

I wasn't sure whether she was embarrassed by her admittance and covering it or just happy with the day. By the time I caught up she had her sandals in hand and had started the short walk across the beach to the restaurant. I didn't feel it was the time to quiz her on the remark as Anna was considering her entrée as we walked. Having been there many times before, she knew them by heart.

Which will you have James?

I had no idea. I am not fluent French, not by a long way but I could have conversations in French and I could certainly understand menus but that required a menu to be present. I didn't have a menu present as we strolled across the beach! Anna released her mistake.

The chefs salad is rather good. Mainly cheese, corn, chicken and salad but the vinaigrette is to die for.

It was going to be one of those lunches. I could feel it. I wasn't disappointed.

Monsieur. Madame. S'il vous plait.

It was maybe twenty five degrees and here was a guy in suit and tie. His shirt looked as if it had just been pressed and I meant, just. He was immaculate. It was a beach restaurant! Or at least that was what I was led to believe. Wrong

239

James. It was not just a beach restaurant. There was no terrace. The whole restaurant was the terrace. One might have imagined a Hawaiian setting. All gnarled timbers lashed together. Surrounded by bamboo trees. Not this place. Stainless steel and mauve drapes. White tablecloths with dark purple napkins. Complimented by white chairs and yes, purple cushion covers. The cutlery was so perfectly placed and gleaming in the sunshine, and that was the moment my hunch was confirmed. It was going to be one of those lunches. The type of lunch where I felt uneasy. The waiter came to the same conclusion. Most probably while I was still walking across the beach. He tried not to show it or maybe he was trying to show me he knew it. Either way it was not a good start. Anna meanwhile was oblivious to the conclusions that had just taken place. That embarrassing evaluation was mine to endure.

Marco, it is so good to see you. How are the girls?
Oh great. Anna knew the waiter.
Madame, it is a pleasure to see you, as always. The girls, are young ladies now. Monic has just started in law school and Annette is studying Chinese in her last year at school.
Good for them Marco. I'm sure they will do well.
We had been steered, ever so gently, to a table. Certainly a good choice Marco, I thought. And then he made his mistake. He offered Anna a chair.
"I think you'll find Anna prefers to decide on where she sits Marco". I said. Perhaps I was implying, no I was certain of it. I was making Marco aware of something. Yes Marco I might be out of my depth but I know Anna. And guess what Marco, you just blew it.
Actually Marco, James is right, I would prefer to sit over here.
Anna sat herself down. I was still standing. Marco glanced my way. I smiled and sat. Marco and I came to an understanding from that moment. Nothing was said but throughout lunch he went out of his way to subtly guide me in the etiquette necessary to accomplish the mountainous task ahead. Anna was charming throughout and that was something I noticed. Charming. One of Anna's many facets. Blending into her surroundings with ease. Those surroundings required a charming front. I found myself becoming equally charming. That wasn't perhaps as difficult as I first thought. I had the chefs salad followed by Dorade. Always safe with Dorade. A piece of Cod, usually with potatoes of some description and vegetables. I was right but the presentation got me. A very large plate and in the centre, surrounded by emptiness, was a small tower of food. Mash potato. Ok, but with vegetables and a piece of fish balancing precariously on the top? A swirl of sauce snaking around the empty space. It was delicious. The day was delicious. Marco had reserved our loungers on the beach where the day drifted by under an ambience of pampered luxury.
We returned to Anna's around six.
Let's go for a swim James.

You mean splash around trying to make it to the other side of the pool. Yes the other side, as the far end of the twenty metre pool seemed so, so far away. Although I had to admit it was a good idea. A refreshing plunge after a day on the beach with toes still full of sand. I was sure Anna's filtration system had it within its capabilities to deal with a few grains of sand. Evidently I was wrong. As I discovered on arriving at the pool edge.

We should shower first James, we don't want sand in the pool.

My reply was going to be of my previous thought. Surely the filtration system ……. but why go there. It was Anna's pool.

Lead on my dear. Do we shower together?

I don't think so James as it's in a direct line of the house.

The shower was at the end of the pool. Set in it's own, beautifully tiled arena. I wasn't serious about the showering together. Anna's laughing response was a clear indication she knew. I managed three to Anna's seven laps. Dually refreshed we changed by the pool. This area was covered from the house. I watched Anna change. There was no embarrassment on Anna's part. It was not that she flaunted herself in front of me, more a case of ignoring my presence. That was how she did when here alone. It wasn't until we got to the house did she make a remark.

Was that acceptable for you James.

Here we go, I thought. Anna and her devilish mood.

Anna, if I was to emulate my thoughts into words, you wouldn't believe me, so perhaps it's best I don't try. Don't you agree?

No I don't James. You are not getting away with this one. No digressions. No changing the subject. You are on the spot. Explain yourself.

Anna was enjoying herself, particularly as she felt she had me at a disadvantage. No escaping this one was obviously the way she saw it. Ok, why not. Anna wanted my thoughts so I should give them to her. The only problem I foresaw was giving her a story she would believe, although I felt somewhat confident I could deliver.

Ok. Seeing you naked presented me with a variety of thoughts. Some sexual. Some, believe or not, approached with an artistic eye and some, having me pinch myself to prove I wasn't dreaming.

Artistic first.

I looked at Anna. She was definitely enjoying this. I continued.

You were towelling yourself off, with your back to me and the setting sun was positioned to perfection. You raised the towel to dry your shoulders revealing a naked Anna from waist down. The light cascading through your open legs. It was a sight to behold and as you turned towards me the effect of the cooling breeze and the water on your breasts was obvious to see. That sideways position you held for but a moment, accentuating your breasts against an amazingly flat stomach. If only I could upload those images I am sure you would

241

see the artistic value. What I saw defies my ability to describe more adequately so I can but say, in my own humble way, that vision before me will never leave my subconscious. For years to come I will be able to recall that moment in vivid colour. Anytime I pinch myself.

That had Anna laughing. What I said had the right impact. Anna's body language had changed during the telling. It had started with a triumphant attitude due to her having cornered me. The change was subtle. She became, interested in what I said. I most definitely saw that as a compliment. All going well so far.

Now what was that other category of thought?

I paused but Anna was quick to remind me. Knowing full well, I hadn't forgotten.

Some sexual?

Ah yes, that was the one. Thank you Anna for reminding me.

I got a big but impatient smile for that.

I wondered, when I was young, if I would ever be lucky enough to make love to a Playboy Centrefold. Those thoughts came back the moment I saw you take off your bikini. To digress for a moment. Don't worry Anna, I will return.

I must have been fifteen or sixteen but I still remember those thoughts. Well, a variation. She was perfect. Perfect skin. Perfect smile. Perfect hair. Perfect proportions, standing with one leg discretely placed in front of the other to hide any possibility of blatant sex. I was in lust. Such portrayed innocence only helped to compound my thoughts that swayed between the need to have her and the need to protect her. And there you were. Your innocent awareness of my presence with no idea what the sight of you naked was doing to me. I could have taken you there and then. Hands against the rocks with your legs spread and don't tell me that's what you were imagining because if you were it might upset me in two ways. Firstly, there goes that innocent perception and secondly, I really don't want to know that.

That last remark got Anna. She tried to hold a poise of indignant behaviour but couldn't manage it for long.

Of course that's what I wanted James. Why do you think I spent so long drying myself. Oh! If only James.

Now that really had Anna laughing. I left her laughing to select a bottle of wine. I poured the wine and Anna decided on a toast. She liked toasts or maybe it was something she was used to doing? She glanced at the clock.

To twenty four hours and the certainty it has been the best twenty four hours in a long time. Thank You James.

To the next twenty four and no Anna, it is for me to thank you.

We clinked glasses.

Maybe not the moment James but do you want the good news or the bad first? Don't answer that. I'll give you the bad news first. I'm going to Milan on Tuesday and I'll be gone for the week, returning Saturday morning but I hope I can see you on Saturday evening. The good news? Thirty six hours?

242

Let me think about that Anna.
I raised my glass.
To thirty six hours!
Lets watch a film James. Someone gave me one called Idiocracy. It is set in the future and is suppose to be very funny. Now where did I put my cigarettes?
Anna found her cigarettes. Exactly where she'd left them the evening before. We smoked, drank wine and chatted. Half an hour later we were in the cinema room enjoying what was turning out to be a very amusing film during which Anna changed her position a few times but settled on placing her head on my shoulder and linking arms. I moved to compensate and we settled back.
I really enjoyed that James. Imagine watering crops with coca cola but not only that. Not understanding why the crops failed. Very funny but also poignant. To think, it could happen. We assume our intelligence as a race will forever increase, not decrease.
I was thinking along the same lines Anna. Breeding out intelligence. If only we were younger. We could have helped maintain that intelligence in the world. Do you think it's too late?
I wonder why I bother watching comedies when you are around James. Oh, I've upset you, ... Said with sarcastic intent ..... *It's one of your most endearing qualities James. So in saying so and before we retire to the Breakfast Bar, give me a kiss.*
So much for making babies. I duly did as was requested. It took time. Anna was the one who finally broke away. I picked up on the moment.
Another glass of wine in the Breakfast Bar methinks. Would you like to join me Anna?
Anna was collecting her composure. She smiled.
As I said. A man of many qualities.
I reached out my hand to assist her standing.
You can now add gallantry to that list if you'd like Anna.
Having returned to the Breakfast Bar, via the vast unused area, I topped up the glasses with the remainder of the bottle. I asked Anna about the times of her youth living in Moscow.
We all lived in high rise blocks and went to school in grey overalls James.
I knew it! It wasn't propaganda. Poor you!
I had called her bluff and Anna knew it.
Actually, we lived on the outskirts of Moscow. In fact on the outskirts of a small village, on the outskirts of Moscow. My father owned a greengrocers and also sold wholesale in Moscow. We were not what "Westerners" would have considered, well off but we were comfortable enough. Our needs were not excessive. I enjoyed those years and from what I've seen, with a child's eye, no different from the children here in France. We played. We were mischievous and life was good. I seem to remember being outdoors most of the time but that of

course, couldn't be so. Moscow has severe weather but I'll stick with my version if you don't mind. My schooling from the age of twelve was in the centre of Moscow. I had an auntie living there so I stayed with her during the week, only going home at weekends and holidays. Those were good holidays. Having friends from school come and stay. And yes most of them did live in tenements so to come to the countryside was a treat in itself.

Anna seemed to drift off.

Would you like a coffee Anna?

Yes please. Decaf as it's getting late. Talking of late, ……..

I knew that look.

I didn't tell you the other bad news. I have tennis tomorrow therefore up at six I'm afraid.

That's fine Anna. It will mean I get to work on time.

I wasn't sure if that was actually going to be possible as I had to go via home to get changed. What I did care about was being with Anna until morning. I put the cups and glasses in the dishwasher as Anna cleaned surfaces. We walked to the bedroom, hand in hand. If I ever have the chance I'll have a bathroom with two sinks, I thought. Watching Anna watching me while cleaning teeth was, and I don't know why, the start. Not in the cinema room. Not drinking the wine and later the coffee. No. It started here. Cleaning teeth and watching Anna, I was sure she was thinking something similar. It was only the bedroom from here. This was the preamble. Who would have thought, cleaning ones teeth was the moment that the sexual tension of things to come, really took hold. I must discuss that with Anna one day, I thought. Or maybe a psychiatrist?

Either I was very perceptive or Anna's body language was up there in neon lighting. Or should that now read, LED? Whatever it was I was quickly in tune with Anna's desires for the night. And then I thought, yes, it was me making the decisions. It was I who decided whether it should start soft and gentle with kisses and caresses. Or turn her over and take her from behind. It started soft and gentle. I felt the mood required it. Anna responded in a very positive manner. We kissed and caressed for some time with no desire to take it further. Until Anna's caresses became more intimate. I followed suit and ran my hand over her breasts. Her stomach. Between her open legs. Don't rush this James was upper most in my mind even though another part of me had other ideas. Was this becoming a match of wills? Anna was obviously excited but continued her methodical stroke, grasping that who's only desire was to get inside her. I couldn't take this much longer, I thought.

Inside me James. Now.

Well done Anna! It was not said in a commanding way more in a pleading way. Anna had reached that point. It was going to be an easy ride. Not really intended as a pun but never the less, true. Sure enough within five minutes, Anna was arching her back. Keep that rhythm James. Don't be tempted to speed up. It

244

paid off. Anna was content. I played no active part for the next few minutes other than kept a secure hold within her. Slowly, I started again. Anna quickly responded. There was to be no kissing and caressing. I straddled Anna's legs, keeping them together. Full insertion while pressing with rhythm, using those remaining few millimetres to the best of my ability. Anna pushed forward to meet my every stroke. Anna wanted it this way. There was no mistaking that zone she was now in.

Take me James. Take me to that place.

No mistaking it. She found that place and I slowly withdrew. As we lay close, I watched her. She didn't want to move. Didn't want to break the spell. I understood that. I waited. She looked so beautiful, laid there. Fully naked with one leg straight out and the other thrown over. I so much wanted to kiss her. She moved her hand towards me. Not looking, just reaching. I took her hand, lowering it over her stomach. We adopted our, Oh so familiar, spoon position. Sans penetration. We fell asleep.

I awoke, as usual around three or four o'clock with an obvious physical desire. Why always so hard at that time? Anna's arousal from sleep seemed to follow automatically when I made that first, tentative movement towards her. It never lasted long. It was always from behind. Maybe ten minutes at the most but more likely five and then, everything that was mine, was now within Anna. We stayed in that position with me inside her and once more, fell back to sleep.

The alarm woke us at six.

Go back to sleep James. I will wake you with coffee.

True to her word, maybe thirty minutes later, Anna woke me.

You should decide which outfit I wear today James so come on, choose.

Still barely awake and naked, I followed Anna to the walk in wardrobe. I chose an outfit. I sat on the bed while Anna threw her dressing-gown aside. I watched her dress.

You forgot to choose my knickers James!

If I did then I am glad I did so. Why don't you give me a twirl.

And she did. Not just once but three times. Delightfully reminding me of that seventies poster of the girl seemingly scratching her bottom while advancing towards the net. Only Anna had no knickers. It was a fleeting moment amongst many but I remember there was an understanding that passed between us. It wasn't anything that could be put into words. It was a knowing mixed with feelings. Two people in harmony. I gave Anna my tenderest of smiles.

Come here, please.

Anna walked over to face me.

You know, you forever amaze me. You're repertoire seems to be never ending. If I had to describe your character to someone, I would first ask them how much time they had. From frivolous to someone with purposeful intent. From giggling like a school girl to someone who can deal at the highest level. From ignorantly oblivious to her surroundings and yet capable of enthralling present company. You are a conundrum Anna and long may you remain so. Now go and put some knickers on.

Before she had a chance to respond, I kissed her. She smiled a smile that reached deep within me and then removed herself in search of her knickers. She returned from the wardrobe now wearing white spandex shorts under the skirt.

You knew that's what you'd be wearing, didn't you Anna. Which leads me to wonder why you originally appeared without them?

To be honest James, I'm not sure. Why don't we just say, a tribute to our last thirty six hours together. It felt right, particularly knowing you would appreciate the gesture. And you did, didn't you James?

You look gorgeous Anna. With and without the knickers. A word of advice. While you're playing the game this morning, remember, you are wearing knickers. I'd hate for you to be distracted. My thoughts now digress to the scenario of no knickers and just how many people might end up watching that match.

You are terrible James. As if I would. Do you think we could advertise the up and coming event and sell tickets?

If we did, I don't think there's a stadium large enough to accommodate such an event Anna.

Terrible and sweet James. Now go and take a shower while I make us another coffee.

My cue to hurry up and get dressed. Anna was sitting at the breakfast bar when I arrived. We drank our coffee in a cocoon of silence only to be broken by Marta's entrance. I smiled and said hello not believing Marta knew that greeting. She smiled back and I made a move for the hallway. Anna came with me. I opened the car door and turned expecting Anna to be a few paces away. She wasn't. She held my face in her hands. Gave me a passionate kiss and thanked me for our time together.

Thank you James. This has become one of my treasured moments and when the lawyers and stepdaughter are becoming too much I can think of this time and realise there are more important things in life than ...... things. See you on Saturday?

Dressed as you are? Yes please! Sorry Anna, I couldn't resist that. Most certainly. I will be looking forward to Saturday.

Driving from Anna's place that Monday morning, I was full of ...... Full of Joy that was clouded by the knowledge I won't be seeing Anna for a week! It was going to be a long week, I thought.

246

Chapter Eighteen

Yes, the week was long and arduous. The thoughts of the two months summer holiday had been replaced with thoughts of getting through this. This our busiest period of the year. One show up and running at The Palais des Festival with another buildup starting this weekend. Busy would have been an understatement. The trucks were loaded for the weekend montage at the Grimaldi Forum in Monaco. Three other trucks loaded with empties awaiting the demontage in Cannes that weekend. The warehouse was almost empty. Four stands, taking up a fraction of the space, ready to be sent out for Tax Free in Cannes starting the following Monday, were the only evidence we were involved in the business of exhibitions at all. I doubted I would have had the time or energy to have seen Anna that week. I did not believe how quickly the days all but disappeared. It was Friday evening, already! Five days gone! The first day of the demontage in Cannes over. Saturday we should be finished around seven. Plenty of time to be home and changed by eight, no matter how tired I felt, I knew it would disperse once Anna arrived.

As I walked to my door around seven fifteen the first splatters of rain fell. Anna had called me earlier and said she will be over around eight. Read eight thirty as the earliest possibility of Anna's arrival. The rain was torrential by eight when Anna rang to say she was leaving. As much as I wanted her with me, I did question her about the rain. "It will be fine James, see you soon." Was her reply. The rain was no longer a torrent, it was now a waterfall! Anna called.

I'm stuck James! I'm at the lights in Biot and the police are turning everybody back. Evidently the Golf course is underwater.

Not the time to say, I told you so.

Go back Anna but please, be careful.

I will call you when I get home. I so much wanted to see you this evening. By the way, I was right. Things didn't get to me in Milan, thanks to you.

She was gone. I was worried. Rain in the South of France could be heavy but I'd never in all my time of living here, seen anything like that. It was frightening. Anna texted thirty minutes later.

I'm cut off from home …. All the roads are flooded. I'm totally encircled. Waiting along with other cars on the hill until the rain hopefully lessens. Fortunately I have the Irish coffee ingredients in the car, plus homemade cakes. I'll survive. And you?

Me? I'm fine apart from the minor problem of a waterfall cascading down my stairs. It's you I'm worried about. I don't suppose you have a flask of hot water for the coffee?

I'm feeling okay actually. Luckily the fuel tank is full. Cannot heat coffee but can easily drink the other ingredients. It's just boring, thinking I might have to spend the night in the car.

A few minutes passed.

Some cars are moving across the flooded roundabout. I'm going to try. Wish me luck.

I was wishing her luck. The rain was not letting up. Anna texted about twenty minutes later.

I'm home James. All our area is in blackout. I so much wish I'd bought some cigarettes!

It's the same here. The electricity died about an hour ago. Phone has a fifteen percent charge and I'm running out of candles but I do have cigarettes. I'm glad you are safe.

I didn't see Anna that week as she had decided to visit Tanya for a few days. Maybe just as well as my days were still hectic and tiring. It was a week of work, sleep, work. All over come Saturday as mid October loomed. Anna was unaccustomedly quiet that week. I was receiving maybe one reply for every three messages I sent. Then late Thursday afternoon I got a message.

Hi James. Sorry I haven't been so responsive this week. We'll talk when I get back. We need to talk. Can we have dinner tomorrow evening?

"We need to talk". Should I respond to that? No, it can wait until tomorrow. That decided, I replied.

*Tomorrow evening is fine for me. I'll book a table at that Italian, just above the covered market. Eight thirty? Do you want me to pick you up. (*That was my way of saying, Will you be picking me up. After all, she passed close by my house on the way into Antibes.)

I will be in Juan les Pins James, visiting a particularly awful woman who unfortunately needs my attention so it would be better if I meet you at the restaurant at eight thirty. My granddaughter is now demanding my attention so, see you tomorrow.

It didn't sound right. Anna was almost formal. I put it down to being surrounded by family and away from her usual surroundings. It was forgotten by the morning as we prepared for Saturday's demontage. Talking of forgotten, I remembered a few years ago when the ladders were forgotten. Not easy taking something apart that was approaching three metres in height, without ladders. I managed to get away by six and was showered, shaved, changed and at the restaurant by eight twenty five. No need to be too early as Anna had her reputation to keep up. Reserved our table and sat outside with beer and cigarette. I saw her approaching as I sipped the last of my beer. Only fifteen minutes late. Almost a first. I stood when she was sufficiently close. Saying nothing, I looked into her face.

I just wanted to make sure it was you. It's been awhile.

Anna smiled when normally, I think she would have laughed.

Hello James. Have you been waiting long?

All said as we did the cheek kissing thing.

No, not long at all. Shall we go in.

I held the door open for Anna and pointed in the direction of our table. There was an edge to Anna's conduct that was passed onto me. I refrained from the usual triviality that would have had Anna laughing. Fortunately the waitress appeared at our table distracting my thoughts. I ordered the wine as Anna glanced at the menu.

Why don't we share a starter Anna?

Yes, that sounds fine and I'll have the Fettuccine Alfredo to follow. I'll have the Arrabbiata.

We made small talk about her visit to Geneva and my crazy busy week. The wine had been served and we were, unenthusiastically, picking at the variety of meats spread out before us. Our eyes met and for a brief moment, nothing was said.

I think you know what I want to say James?

Until that moment, I hadn't but if pushed, I could have guessed.

Maybe I do, maybe I don't Anna but either way I think it would be better coming from you.

This sounds awful. I do like you James but I cannot continue with our relationship. I'm sorry.

I can't say it was a surprise. Anna had been withdrawn from the moment we met. All the same it hit me. It hit me hard! For the briefest of moments I thought of countering her revelation but only for a moment. I'm intelligent enough to acknowledge the inevitable. Anna has thought long and hard about her decision and it could not have been easy for her. Typical me. Anna had just told me it was over and I was defending her position. How do I reply? As the gentleman Anna assumed me to be.

249

Anna, there is no need to apologise for your feelings. These situations are never easy but I don't intend making it difficult for you. Of course, it is not what I want but it can't work unless there are two in agreement. I have to accept you don't wish to continue no matter how hard that might be.

Anna then tried to soften the blow.

I hope we can still be friends?

How often has that line been used? Of course you wanted to be my friend. As long as we didn't actually see each other again. The main course had been in front of us for maybe ten minutes. I hadn't touched mine. I noticed Anna had also lost her appetite.

I think we should leave Anna.

After assuring the waitress it was not the fault of the meal, I paid and we left. We walked side by side down the hill while Anna recited all my positive virtues. Possibly something she thought might help alleviate my pain. I listen, gracefully, until she had finished by which time we'd reached the entrance of the underground parking. It was my last chance to say something before I never saw Anna again. But what could I say? "Please change your mind Anna?" "It's been great!" No, best to keep it civilised. Others had arrived and were trying to find change amongst themselves to feed the machine. Anna was distracted by the recent arrivals. Hardly the ideal background for such a parting. I took her hand and she turned towards me. I looked her in the eyes giving my best, considering the situation, consoling smile. I squeezed her hand and let it go.

Good bye Anna.

I turned and walked away not looking back. On the way to my car I caught Anna in my peripheral vision, slowly driving by. I resisted the temptation to look as the rear of her Mercedes disappeared around the corner. Alone on the street. Oh there were people around but unnoticed by me. I drove home concentrating on the drive. Pushing my feelings to that place that helped separate the truth from reality. I was just going home. Nothing unusual in that. Concentrate on the driving James.

To say that was a restless night, didn't come close to explaining the thoughts that spun around my head. Not helped knowing I had to be up at five thirty. Finally I must have dozed off but the alarm seemed to wake me moments later. I had volunteered myself for that early truck start knowing the guys had enough to do concentrating on taking the stands apart. A physical day that I was not involved in. Logistics was my role. I arrived at the truck pool at six fifteen. The ninth twenty cube inline for the Palais. That was good. I would be parked up well before our truck arrived to disgorge the many empty crates, pallets, pump trucks and those once forgotten ladders. There were the badges to collect for the team and while stood in the queue a Polish guy started a conversation. I remembered him being immediately likeable. His casual banter with a command of English that amazed me. It passed the time as a pleasant distraction, helping very

250

slightly, to alleviate the pain I felt. The guys arrived ready to go and the truck arrived, shortly after. It had always fascinated me, why a group of intelligent workers, needed to be told what to do. Not only in that situation but generally. My role as Logistics Manager encompassed many other duties and if decisions had to be made, no matter how minor, it was left to me. Switch off the brain and let someone else decide was the way. Inevitably I fell into the trap. That time was no different. I organised the forklift to unload the pump trucks first. "Ok, you guys take that crate." Pointing to the first off the truck. "It's your furniture crate and by the time you have it filled I'll have the next inline". Slowly but surely the truck was unloaded and the guys disappeared to their various stands. The first two full crates soon appeared from the depths of the Palais. I had to organise a forklift to put them into my small truck. Knowing I'd have to do three such deliveries back to the shop as the seventy cube didn't have the capacity for everything. Back at the shop I'd unloaded the crates and decided to have a coffee before returning. I think, in retrospect, that was a bad move. I should have left immediately. Sat with my coffee, alone, I had the chance to think. And think I did. It was depressing. You've got a demontage to deal with. Concentrate on that James, I told myself. I locked up the warehouse and climbed into the cab. I got a message. It was Anna?

Hello James. How are you? I couldn't sleep all night.

"How are you?" "You couldn't sleep?" How was I suppose to answer that! I decided not to. An hour later I got a call. It was Anna. I ignored it. She left no message. She called three more times during that day, leaving no messages. Until at around four she called and did leave a message.

Call me James. Please, please, call me.

There was a part of me that wanted to ignore that message. That message that was said in such a ..... such a pious manner. I couldn't ignore it. I found a quiet corner that was almost impossible to do during a demontage. I sent her a message.

I'm in the middle of a demontage Anna. I'll call you when I'm home which should be around seven.

Straight to the point but also giving Anna a reason why I'd not taken her calls. It also gave me good reason to make sure we were out of there by six. I was home by six fifteen. Time for that beer and what must have been the tenth cigarette of the day. At quarter to seven I received a message.

Are you home yet?

Are you home yet? Not how Anna would normally phrase such a question. I wasn't sure how I thought she would have phrased it but the thought had occurred. I left it another nine, excruciating minutes before calling her.

Hi Anna. I'm home.

I'd made the decision not to expand on those few words. The ball was in Anna's court. She instigated this call. Not so much a hard line, more I didn't know what else to say. I didn't have to worry, Anna was already talking.

James, I've made a terrible mistake and I don't know if you will forgive me. I told you I didn't sleep last night. What I didn't tell you, was why. On my drive home I had La Traviata, full volume. It was supposed to drown out my thoughts. It didn't manage to do that. By the time I was home, all I wanted to do was fall to the floor. I thought a coffee and cigarette might help. I sat at the breakfast bar for most of the night trying to figure out how I had come to the conclusion I wanted to end something that was very dear to me.

Can I interrupt you Anna?

Without waiting for a reply, I continued.

The message you left me earlier had me thinking. Why does Anna want me to call her? There could be only one reason. She's made a mistake but I couldn't allow myself to think that way. There had to be another reason and now I find to my confused but elated self, I was right. So yes Anna, I can most certainly forgive you but I am very confused.

Can you come over this evening James?

As much as I'd like to Anna, I'm tired. It's been a hard day and I think tomorrow would be a better idea, when I'm more ..... compos mentis.

Ok James, I understand. I have tennis in the early afternoon but should be free anytime after five. Can I call you when I know?

Ok Anna. Let's talk tomorrow.

Good night James, sleep well my dear.

Good night Anna ....

She'd gone.

Sunday. My first day off, in what seemed like forever. I had the alarm set for eight. With temperatures still in the mid twenties, I intended taking advantage by spending the day on the roof. Minus the three hours of midday sun. Which fell neatly around the time "the neighbours" had invited me over for lunch. I hadn't seen them for some time and I knew Chiara would want the latest update on my personal life. I was walking out the door. Beer in hand, heading for the neighbours when I receive a message.

My Dear Proud James, tennis is cancelled today. So I am free anytime after two.

I put the beer down, debating whether I should return it to the fridge. This could take awhile. Actually, no it didn't need to. I replied.

Hi Anna, I can be with you around three. Three thirty at the latest. I'll text you when I leave.

I could have added more. I wanted to add more but held back. I was the injured party after all. .... I should have added more, I thought.

Ok James, see you soon. Do you have any Irish whisky?

How did she do that? Plain simple English and yet why do I feel those simple words had turned me from injured party to casual observer who felt he should have been paying attention.

"I do believe I have", I text back.

Leaving the beer, I found the whisky and placed it next to my car keys. No forgetting that. I locked up and went next door. Paul and Chiara were sat, reading newspapers.

Good afternoon, Mr. and Mrs. boring.

Paul responded.

Just because you lack the intellect for anything that doesn't contain a picture to describe the event, it is ill advised too for you to presume others are of the same ilk.

"Stop it, you two", said Chiara. "I want to hear the gossip. Well! ..... What's happening?"

It's no less than I expected but I hadn't even sat.

Give me a break Chiara. All in good time.

I would have been a fool to have expected that time to be very long. I was right but at least I'd managed to sit.

Have an M&S Cheese Stick James.

Thanks Paul.

Alright Chiara, what do you want to know?

Everything! How is Anna?

Anna is fine but the boiler in my ensuite has decided to pack up.

"Nicely said James", said Paul. "Now, can we start the BBQ?"

We left Chiara, metaphorically, open mouthed.

Later, I could contain myself no longer but was determined to get the timing right.

Oh, a bit of updated news. Anna dumped me on Friday night.

I gave them the run up to but left out the aftermath of that evening. Both were surprised but cynical Chiara did add in her, oh so subtle way, something about being out of her league. I answered questions for the next five minutes, looked at my watch and said I had to leave. "Going somewhere James", asked Chiara.

Yes, I'm off to Anna's place but that's another story. It can wait until the next time.

But I thought you said, she dumped you?

She did but you know me Chiara, ladies can't resist, no matter how hard they might try.

I got up laughing, leaving two, metaphorical mouths open.

I had a half an hour to compose myself before leaving for Anna's. I was careful as to the amount of wine I'd consumed earlier so felt fairly level headed. What greeting should I expect? What was Anna going to say? Equally important, how should I respond? I thought back through my life. Had that happened before.

Been dumped and reinstated. Nope. Never happened. That was no help then and even if there was such a time, what similarity would any other relationship have in common with Anna. No one in my life was like Anna. Decision made. Wing it James. Time to change. BBQ wear was not Anna wear. Where did I put those Tiffs or Tods. Who cared what they were called. Where were they? Blue, short sleeved cotton shirt. Cream trousers and Tods. Very acceptable James I thought, staring at my reflection. Satisfied I text Anna. "On my way".

It was a nervous drive. Those fifteen minutes, not seeming long enough, as I approached Anna's gates. They opened before I could get out to press the bell. Looking out for me, I realised. Was that a good sign? At the top of the drive I turned and parked. Anna appeared from the side of the house where the patio was a continuation of the front terrace. Dressed in a sarong of enchanting colours giving the occasional glimpse of her bikini underneath as the light filtered through the garment. I let her approach the car and when, within metres of me, I reached into the car to produce a bottle of wine.

Oh James ..... but surely, it should be me giving presents, not you.

I'd thought about that Anna. When two people have a disagreement, it just takes one to say sorry. Not necessarily the one who is wrong. It doesn't matter. Very often it will burst the bubble of any previous conversation. Put it in perspective and soon to be realised, it was all about nothing. But don't think you are getting off lightly Anna. You have a lot of making up to do.

She hadn't decided whether I was joking or serious. I came up beside her, kissed her gently on the cheek and said, "Hello, my name is James", and smiled. Anna took the wine putting her arm through mine.

You are right James, I have a lot of making up to do. Why don't you sit by the pool while I get some glasses. Do you have your swimming attire?

No Anna, I don't. (Swimming Attire?)

Not to worry, I am sure I can find something.

No skinny dipping this time I noted. Anna returned with the glasses, corkscrew, a plate full of nibbles and carrying my attire. Nibbles resembling those seen on movies when there was a formal gathering and waiters discreetly hovered, plates full of indescribable but desirable delicacies. Did she buy these with purpose intent? You wouldn't get this at Carrefour. In fact I had no idea where you would have got them. I tried one which had recognisable salmon embedded in the top. It was, as an understatement, delicious. Anna threw the shorts in my direction. I almost dropped the remaining savoury delight. I proceeded to undress. Anna removed her sarong and sat, upright, on the lounger. Not necessarily watching me but aware. I was sat on the adjacent lounger facing Anna.

I've rehearsed this James. Exactly what I was going to say but now it all seems so .... false.

Anna was going to wing it. This should be interesting, I thought. But before she could continue, I opened my mouth. Will I never learn?

Perhaps I could help with the direction of this conversation. When you finished with me on Friday, that was it. I was upset naturally but given time I would have gotten over it. But you came back. The next day! So I would ask the question, What were your reasons for ending it? Reasons that so conflicted with the way you felt that very next day.

They were misguided reasons James. I had barely seen you in the last three weeks. Mostly my fault I know, being away as I was. Thoughts crept into my head. To not put too fine a point on it, thoughts about our differences. So I had bowed to those thoughts and decided the best way forward was to end our relationship.

I started to mildly interrupt but Anna was having none of it. (Still not learning.)

Sorry James, let me finish. Before we met on Friday I was convinced I was doing the right thing. So I carried the process through to it's preset conclusion. As I was driving away, I saw you, on the other side of the road and wondered what the hell it was I had just done and why. La Traviata at full volume all the way home and feeling so depressed. I couldn't sleep that night, not because of what I'd done but why. Around and around in my head trying to understand. Finally I came to a conclusion. Seeing you on Friday gave me no doubt about my feelings for you that swept aside any thoughts I might have previously had. But too late did I realise this. Like a mechanical doll. Wound up and ready to go. I said what was preordained. Does any of this make sense James.

Anna was being serious and expected a serious answer.

Let me see if I've got this right. What you are saying is, Love conquers all.

She relaxed instantly, having held herself in an almost regimental sitting position for the last five minutes. She smiled.

You are right James. It must be love. ..... I love the way you relieve me of my guilt.

Anna laughed for the first time that afternoon. She leant forward, her arm wrapping around my neck.

Serious for a moment if I may. You must have something James. Something so strong it forced me to realise my mistake. It must be love. ... Kiss me.

She was doing it again. It was not that she was being devious or calculating. It was Anna. I kissed her and she was forgiven. That was how it worked. I kissed her. It was a well defined kiss. Two people who had reached an understanding. From here on in, it was not that it was forgotten but the memory of that Friday night could recede. Given time it would become a distant and irrelevant memory.

We need to expend some energy James. Five laps of the pool?

I'm all for that Anna. You carry on and I'll join you on the forth.

To make the point, as Anna stood, I raised my glass and sat back. I joined Anna in the pool. I don't know why, or perhaps I did? Either way I dived. I saw

255

Anna above me. Why choose a bikini consisting solely of black and grey, I had earlier thought? Not colours one would have associated with beach wear. Answer? She looked gorgeous. A total understatement that suited her figure. I broke surface face to face. A good idea but not thought through. Laughing, Anna swam over me. Spluttering and gasping for air, I headed for the "shore". By the time Anna had emerged from the pool I had regained my composure. I greeted her with a glass of wine and feigning the humble servant, her towel over my arm. An afternoon spent with an amazing woman. There was conversation. Drinking. Eating and yes, the inevitable, "Dip in the Water". Another idyllic afternoon with Anna. I wasn't able to analyse the last thirty six hours, which was what I'd have liked to have done but there wasn't the chance. We were so involved in us. It must have been seven or maybe eight by the time we were seated at the terrace. Anna had changed into the white dress with large and colourful flower imprints. Marta had performed her magic once again while Anna and I were by the pool. An amazing salad with potatoes fried in a way and with what? I had no idea! I stole the odd moment of thought that enabled me to wonder at my presence there, with Anna. Twenty four hours previously, my life was over. And now .... In the company of someone .... someone so ..... so alive! Surrounded once again by her company. I would have been kidding myself if I hadn't thought it somewhat strange.

It's Monday tomorrow Anna. Tennis? We will have to be up early?
I'd said that knowing what I was implying.
Yes James, it is tennis day but I don't have to be there before ten thirty and it's only ...... nine fifteen. More than twelve hours away, so I am going to make our favourite coffee.
It seemed I was staying the night. I think Anna already knew that. Long before I thought of the idea. Most likely, before I arrived.
I'll clear the table while you make the coffee.
I picked up some dishes and headed for the kitchen. Five minutes was all it took and we were sat on the terrace sipping hot Irish coffee. The peace. The pool lit up. The silhouette of trees against the star studded background and Anna in a jubilant mood. A "pinch myself" moment if ever there was one.
You know Anna, that is one of my favourite dresses. You always look so radiant when wearing it.
OMG. Have I worn this before!
She was laughing out loud.
And I hope you continue to wear it. Throw away your wardrobe and buy another six the same. One for each day.
Certainly James. I'll rent a large van. Two strong men who will spend the day filling it with my wardrobe of clothes and send it off to the Charity Shop. That should help stabilise their finances for some time to come.

Very amusing Anna, I thought. We sat back sipping our coffees. The silence was almost deafening. October was a beautiful month. Warm from sunrise to sunset with temperates around eighteen through the night. The tourists had departed and the hectic days of work behind me. I could think of no one I'd rather be with and given the surroundings, no place I'd rather be. Tony's words came to mind. "Enjoy the moment". Having just re established contact after our brief separation, those words seemed more poignant somehow. Anna rose.

I have to go and change. I will only be a minute.

She smiled and touched my shoulder as she passed. Going to change? Was it something I said? My reference to that beautiful flower printed dress? Or perhaps she will emerge in high heels and black lace? Calm down James, just enjoy the serenity. Anna reappeared wearing the same dress? The same sandals? Anna could see my confusion and was thus enjoying the moment.

What did you expect James? Black lace?

Actually, high heels, and black lace, did enter my head but I certainly didn't expect you to reappear in the same dress.

"Poor confused James", said Anna, giving her best interpretation of being sympathetic. "Let us finish the coffee and go to bed".

I looked at my glass which was still half full. Looked back at Anna.

I've finished.

Anna's glass? Also more full than empty ......

"Me too" she said, and we both laughed.

Anna's ability to spend unnecessary time in the bathroom, had to be waited on to be believed. So inevitably, I was first in bed. Anna came in and asked if I could unzip her. She stood at the side of the bed and dropped her dress.

I went shopping in Cannes on Saturday. What else is a girl to do when she is feeling down? New underwear James and do you know, when I was trying it on I was wondering if the person I bought it for would ever see it.

Another masterpiece of provocative innocence. All the more alluring by the pose Anna had adopted. One knee in front of the other, made possible by raising her heel off the floor. Her hips set just slightly off centre. her shoulders sloping the other way. Adorned with that sweet mischievous smile. She looked sensational. Had she been looking at old Playboy editions?

Were you really thinking that Anna? I was wondering earlier, at what point during the day you knew we would be here. Here in your bedroom. The only certainty I had was knowing you knew a long time before I did.

I laughed and diverted the topic of the previous remark.

"You know the phrase, Too good to eat, Anna? This is a moment too good to spoil. How long can you hold that pose?" I said with a slight smile. "Come here". I said with more compassion.

Anna slipped under the covers. In the movies it happens exactly as predicted. In reality there was always that, Where do we start? How do we start? But not

with Anna. It was exactly as the movies show it. I felt in control and I could do that because it was Anna .... I ran my hand over that delicate framework of lace that perfectly accentuating what lay beneath. Good start James, I thought, as Anna responded. I wanted to leave her underwear intact for as long as I could manage. Anna had returned. After a brief interlude and that interlude was my incentive to make this perfect. Show her what she potentially could have denied herself. Casanova, I am not but I sought to make this night, a night for her to remember. Anna had made no secret of our connection when kissing. It seemed, I was good at it? I gave her mouth my full attention. My hand wandered from that delicate framework to her panties. Expensive underwear had a certain feel to it. Such a delicate fabric that allowed me to feel all beneath. The kissing continued. It might sound repugnant but our faces were awash with saliva. The excitement was intense but still I held back. Anna could take it no longer. She brought her legs up and took off those beautiful panties.
Please James.
I do believe, that was my cue. The cue I'd been waiting for. I could now, take that control. Control is an emotive word. It always took two. Two that understood that separation of sex from reality. I found it unusual for a woman to discuss what happened, "The Night Before", the following morning. Anna was no exception, or maybe it was me? Either way, sex was separate and I felt in control, or maybe it was the role I was given. "Hey James, I deal with everything else. You have my permission to take control in bed." I didn't see it that way. Anna didn't see it that way. It was just a thought. I slipped gently inside her. She was expecting me. I raised myself up to take in all that was possible. My rhythm remained slow and penetrating. We managed eye contact but for a brief moment. I glanced down. Her breasts still encapsulated within that framework of fine lace. Her stomach, held in as her breathing became more intense. My sex disappearing into .... into, the jewel in Anna's crown. I felt myself losing control. Think of something else James! I reestablished eye contact. What was happening below became abstract. I concentrated on Anna's face. Our eyes said it all. We moved in unison. Anna was with me, it was special. Anna and I were back. As we lay side by side, conversation was unnecessary, the eye contact still worked, only interrupted by the occasional kisses. The minutes ticked by.
Can we do that again James?
I smiled. More eye contact. Anna turned her back to me. Once again, I entered her. I had the perfect opportunity to undo her bra. It came away with such ease. No fiddling with multitudes of hooks. It came away at my touch. Is this what money buys? I thought. I moved my hand to her breast. Small but perfectly proportioned. I kissed her neck. Anna sighed. Slipping my left hand under her hip and in doing so, pulled her towards me. Unable to move forward Anna could do little but accept my rhythm. She didn't hesitate, in fact, understanding what I

was doing she pressed herself against me to match the rhythm. She was reaching her climax. I could feel it. I could hear it. Which was fortunate for me as one's stamina was no longer that of a thirty year old.

We fell asleep in that position and the next morning I was quietly woken with a hot coffee. I still hadn't told Anna, I preferred tea as my choice of first drink in the morning. Too many occasions had passed to be so churlish as to mention it now. I accepted gracefully. We parted company on a roundabout somewhere in Sophia Antipolis around seven thirty. Me, heading home to change. Anna, shopping before going to the courts.

I didn't see Anna until the following Thursday evening. Messages and calls had transpired through those missing days with apologies from Anna as to her unavailability. I was not concerned or at least those were the feelings I portrayed.

We ate out on Thursday evening, somewhere inland from Villeneuve Loubet. I say somewhere as Anna had booked and Anna was driving. I doubt if I could have retraced the steps if I'd wanted to. It's a strange thing, or maybe not but I found if I drove, I remembered for years to come the route taken. Maybe not as a whole but travelling towards that destination I became aware of which exit on the roundabout. Left or right at intersections and et voila, destination reached.. It was a beautiful setting. I don't know why but I decided on taking a short cut. Avoiding the footbridge, the shorter route was via the river. I had reached the other side, hopping from one rock to another and turned to watch Anna. The sun, reflecting off the water. Catching Anna mid flight. The next moment, Anna poised, preparing to launch herself onto the last but one rock. Maybe "launch" and "mid flight" came under that category of, Poetic License and she but stepped from one rock to the other. Anna holding her white sun hat out, awkwardly maintaining her balance. Not so easy in a pencil skirt. I did point out that possible dilemma she might face before entertaining the crossing. Anna took challenges in her stride. Albeit on that occasion, very small strides. She refrained from pulling her skirt up to facilitate longer strides. She was that beautiful setting.

Anna had been before and from what I could gather, on numerous occasions. I hoped it wasn't going to be a repeat of, knowing the waiter. I needn't have worried. We sat at a table with a view of the river. Looking far more innocent than in the earlier crossing. It wasn't deep. Barely covering the large pebbles of the basin in most places. A few sandy outcrops that created deeper pools were spread along the banks. A slow moving river that perhaps went someway to establishing our earlier mood of that evening. I was unaccustomedly quiet. Anna was pensive, but the need to talk was absent. It felt good. Aperitifs already chosen we checked out the menu. I felt the need to say something but didn't want to intervene. Didn't want to break that silence but knowing that if I didn't, the waiter surely would. I put the menu down. Anna saw me and followed suit. I slid my hand across the table, resting it on hers. I broke the silence.

I've missed you Anna.

259

I wasn't sure what I was going to say next but I needn't have feared. Anna placed her free hand on mine, while turning her hand underneath. She now held my hand in hers, and smiled. It was a smile that mirrored my thoughts. No one spoke. There was no need. Actually that was not quite true. The waiter spoke, who had surreptitiously arrived without notice. "Are we ready to choose?" He asked, in English. Are we ready to choose? This was the South of France and even I knew, that was not something the average waiter in England would consider asking. "You ready to order". "So, what do you want?" These were phrases I was used to. Was that a collective noun? It didn't matter. The spell was broken. I retrieved my hand and we ordered. We talked. We talked about our days. Mine being mostly prefabricated hoping to achieve that, "Windswept and Interesting" status. Intermittent humour helped. I can remember a friend many years ago, having a group of us enthralled, telling about a day, out of his many repetitious days, of the walk to the bus stop. Picking out moments. Freezing them and seeing something funny where others didn't. Billy Connelly once said, on a visit to Australia, he saw a sign on a beach. "BEWARE, STINGERS". Now that, he mused, might work for Australians but for a Scotsman, it certainly didn't. Stingers? "Do they arrive in taxis"? "What the fuck are stingers"? Amusement from a seemingly benign but informative notice. Anna's days had highlights. Tennis. Lunches. Friends to enjoy a few hours around the pool. Dinner with so and so. It was becoming apparent the reason or reasons, Anna was too busy to see me. Know your place James, came to mind. I wasn't convinced my place in Anna's busy scheduling was to my liking.

I have a remembrance day on Saturday James. It's been a year since ..... There will be about forty people at my place from two until about six or seven. To be honest, although I organised it, I'm not sure I am going to enjoy it. Maybe not the appropriate word but I'm sure you understand my meaning. The question is. Can I come over after? I think I will need some ...... some of what only you can give. No James not that. I mean just being with you. Is that alright?

Of course Anna. You know you are always welcome and it pleases me to know I can give what you need.

Anna smiled one of her, You are so understanding James, smiles. Followed with, "Give me our world".

We left the restaurant around nine thirty and headed back to mine. An obvious choice as Anna was driving. Was she going to stay?

Do you think we have time for a game, or two, of Ludo?

Time before what Anna?

The moment I discovered if Anna was staying.

She laughed.

Before bedtime of course James.

Would that be, your bedtime. My bedtime, or our bedtime Anna?

My turn to laugh.

Maybe that depends on whether I win James.

We both laughed.

Two nil but it was close on the second game leaving Anna frustrated and wanting a third. She had such intriguing ways when on the losing side. Her competitiveness almost denying the possibility of the loss. Anna liked to win. Enjoyed the game but liked to win. We played a third. Two one. She was satisfied with that.

I was thinking James, you've mentioned Kitzbuhel. Why don't we take a week and go there, early December.

Wonderful idea Anna. I like to go there about the tenth because if the snow is good it's amazing. There is literally no one on the slopes. It's pre season and doesn't get busy until Xmas week.

That is decided then James. Which airport do we use?

Actually Anna, I drive. It takes about eight hours. If not it would be Munich airport which is about two hours by car from Kitz but I'm not sure there is a direct flight. I'll check on it.

I will look into hotels. Is the location important James?

As near to the Hahnenkamm lift as possible. Two hundred metres is about as far as I like to walk in ski boots. How about you?

The Hahnenkamm it is. ..... How do you spell that James?

Show your ignorance James, I thought. I know there are an abundance of "h", "n" and "m"s but in what order?

Perhaps it's best if you Google it Anna. You'll have a map of the area. If you like, I can send you a link.

Quick thinking on my part, I thought.

"Do it now. Do it now", said Anna in an excited and demandingly childish voice. It always cracked me up. She knew, I knew, it was part of the game. Anna wanted something and she wanted it now and the way she got it .... well that depended. She had many bullets in her gun and I was sure more than I knew of but she knew this one worked. I opened Google. Pressed the microphone icon. *Hahnenkamm. Kitzbuhel,* I said.

Seeing the word, it became instantly recognisable, as it always did. Ask me two minutes later and I would have told you it had a number of repetitive letters. Spell it? I sent the link to Anna. Satisfied she had received it, we went to bed.

It was a beautiful, slumbering, sensual night infused with humour. There was the moment we found ourselves entwined in the duvet, unable to make contact. I remember we were still laughing as I entered her. Sex with Anna was ..... natural. Played out without taboos. If we wanted to laugh, we did. The oneupmanship was alive and kicking therefore our conversations, brief as they were, could have been regarded, by some, as confrontational. Some might have thought, Off Putting. Not us! I'm sure it could have been said, the humour added to our enjoyment of the sex. It really did depend on our mood at the time. We

261

could do sensual. Actually we had built up quite a repertoire of possible bedtime scenarios. We never tired of change. We slept soundly that night.

Anna seemed nervous the next morning over coffee. Why didn't I have tea? Irrelevant, I thought. Anna was edgy. Why? I had to ask.

Are you ok?

Sorry James, it is the organisation for tomorrow. It has just hit me. Perhaps one day you can explain to me why, when I am with you, my other world disappears. I definitely have two realities. You and that other one. Unfortunately that other one has to be accepted on occasion. It is of concern. It is not the amount of people it's ..... it's the reason they are there.

Anna. Stop! You have been arranging this memorial for some time no doubt? You have dotted the "i'''s and crossed the "t'''s, I feel sure, it's the last minute nerves that have you feeling this way. Everything will work out. You will be the perfect host, on this, the first anniversary. People will look upon you in awe, wondering how you manage to be such a magnificent host and yet be able to carry the burden of loss with such dignity. You will shine for all to see.

Anna had been facing me as I said that. I was trying to work out what I'd said. She leant across. She kissed me. It was a unique moment, so brief it could have been missed but I thought as she pulled away she had more to say. She didn't. Our eyes had said it all. Well, Anna's eyes had told mine. It was enough.

I should go James.

Of course you should.

I held her hand and smiled.

I'll open the gate.

We walked to her car. She put her arms around me.

"Thank you James, Don't you ever disappear from my life. You promise?" She said, giving me the briefest of kisses.

I promise I won't ever disappear from your life.

I walked on ahead to open the gate and stood in the road as Anna roared away with hand waving from the open window.

Friday was a good day. Started by sending Anna a don't stress message. Just let it flow over and around you, I said. Achieved more than expected at work and had a five thirty rendezvous with a few of the boys at the Quays in Cannes to look forward to. I must have received ten messages from Anna through the day. All relating to some minor disaster or another.

I have just visited the caterers who are suppling the bulk of the food for tomorrow. I had given them the list weeks ago and have just found out they have changed the menu. We agreed on my requirements and they change it! Ok, it is nothing serious but as the client you think they might have thought of discussing it with me first.

The chairs and tables arrived. Four large tables. Good. Thirty five chairs. Not so good. I showed them the rental agreement. Forty chairs. Sorry, he said. I'm just the delivery man you will have to take that up with the office.
The electrician arrived to replace a faulty outside light. I now have NO outside lights. Aggggh
And so it went on. My responses were commiserate without the light touches of humour. Not, I felt, what Anna needed.

Finally the Quays. There were five of us. It soon settled into, tell Mike and Steve about your woman James. Ten minutes of cross examination that mostly revolved around, what would a seemingly intelligent, beautiful rich woman see in you James. I managed to stay the round and changed the subject. Five minutes passed and now Stuart had become the target. I helped to "stoke the fire", happy that I had survived my grilling. And then the phone rang. Brown Eyed Girl, Anna's ring tone and Stuart knew it. Looked like the ball was firmly back in his court.

"Off you go James. Answer the call. Can't keep her waiting", he said.

That feeling of, What goes around comes around, entered my head and I do believe Stuartathan was taking great pleasure in reminding me. I slipped away leaving my beer on the terrace table and aimlessly walked along the wide pavement.

Hi Anna. Everything ok?

Yes James, everything is ok. I know you are with your friends so I won't keep you long. I just wanted to .... to thank you for your support today and ....
Oh I don't know what to say. It has been a long stressful day but made lighter because you were there in the background. It gave me strength knowing I was not alone. I hope that makes sense James?

Actually Anna, it does. Why don't you take advantage of that Jacuzzi for an hour or so. A glass of wine and unwind.

That is a good idea James. I will, as soon as I decide which bottle of wine to take with me. Enjoy your time with your friends. I will message you later. Now which wine? Bye James and .... Kiss.

No point in answering as experience had taught me, Anna would be gone before I could do so. I walked back to the table prepared for the guys reaction. I had decided to just smile and take it. It worked. They were soon bored. As I arrived home that evening, around eight, I received a message from Anna.

Can you call me when you are home? I so need to talk to you. Nothing specific, just talk.

I decided to give it an hour before calling. Didn't want Anna thinking my evenings ended early. Who was I kidding. Nine o'clock is not exactly late.

Hello Anna. Bad day I guess?

It was but I took your advice and relaxed in the Jacuzzi. Not much left of my bottle of wine which had the effect of making me somewhat melancholy.

263

Understandable I thought but a strange feeling. The reason for tomorrows gathering was in my thoughts but also what has happened since. I found myself, unfairly, placing you alongside my dear departed. One moment wondering if he would be happy for me. The next how I feel about you. Imagine how confused I became.

Actually I was more hoping for an expansion of, How I felt about you. I settled for confused.

Hopefully you've managed to separate those thoughts?

Yes James. Now feeling mellow. Emotions in check and have decided on positive thinking for tomorrow. It's a time of sorrow but also a reflection of good times shared with most that will be present. How was your evening? Did I create a problem for you when I rang?

The couple of hours with the guys was fun, as usual and no, no problems. I'm metaphorically used to being hung, drawn, quartered and dropped into a vat of boiling oil.

Oh sorry James.

Is it customary to laugh when apologising? You are not sorry at all and if you must know, you monopolised the conversation this evening for the best part of twenty minutes.

Did I? What did you say?

I said they were all jealous of my good fortune of having met someone as amazing as yourself. I even mention your moustache was acceptable as no one is truly perfect.

You should remind me to shave James. You know I am always forgetting.

The conversation continued awhile along the same vein until I felt it time to call a halt.

How are you feeling Anna?

Exactly how I imagined feeling after talking with you James. Relaxed and happy. I have some people to call about tomorrow so I have to leave you but I promise, when I stop laughing about your dilemma this evening, I will take a moment to sympathise.

That might have sounded more sincere if you weren't still laughing as you said that Anna. I'm sure you will have some happy reflections tomorrow and on that note I wish you a successful day. As long as you accept the emotional moments for what they are. Moments of the past that brought joy, it will be a successful day.

I waited a brief second or two for the inevitable, line terminated tone but to my surprise .....

Perhaps I shouldn't be saying this but what will help me get through the day will be knowing I am seeing you in the evening. Love you.

"Opening up too much James?" She said laughing. *See you tomorrow.*

Line terminated.

"Love you?" What was I supposed to make of that? Particularly when followed up with laughter. Sleep didn't come easy.

Saturday and a trip to Carrefour at opening time. I was not expecting Anna to be hungry with food available all day but one never knew with Anna. Thirty minutes later and I had that covered. Back home by nine thirty to face a few hours of housework but before that, why not a couple of hours on the roof. It was now approaching midday. I'd just plugged the hoover into the socket and about to press go when I heard that familiar ping.

Watching four of my male guests, who volunteered an early arrival to place furniture for me. I wonder if they would be so helpful if they knew I was taken? It is an amusing thought. I'm actually feeling quite relaxed considering but got to go. x

The "x" had not gone unnoticed neither had mentioning, being taken. I pondered a reply but decided on some hoovering. Although I'd pondered, I couldn't think of a reply that would suit Anna's mood, hence the hoovering. Five minutes later I switched off the hoover, ready with a reply.

You are terrible Anna. I can almost see you asking those particular volunteers, knowing full well what their answer would be. Although I must say I'm flattered to know you've chosen me above all others. Albeit the others amount to but four. Go with the flow Anna and be the woman doing what comes naturally. A perfect host.

Satisfied, I headed for the bathroom. With the back broken on the cleaning front there was time for a visit into Antibes. I did intend a coffee and The Times but found myself sat at the edge of the recently created, open area, around the port. People watching with my mind in free fall. I'm taken, she thought. What did that mean? Anna and I forever? Or an off hand remark without fore thought? Then for no unexplainable reason, I thought of Eva. When did she say she was returning? It was enough of a distraction. I watched the day go by. Or more precisely, I watched people, watching their day go by. Anna called. It was four thirty.

Hello James. What are you doing?

I wasn't expected to answer.

I've managed to slip away from the guests for the sole purpose of calling you. Everyone started on their best behaviour, voicing their own personal message. It was very sweet but I felt, a little contrived. I did wonder if I'd ever noticed this before and if I didn't, why am I noticing it now. I blame you and your spontaneity James.

How can it possibly be my fault? I'm just people watching Anna.

What?

Sorry but you did start by asking me what I was doing.

Anna laughed.

But seriously, everything is going well?

265

It is perfect James. There must be half that are here that I haven't seen since ...... well, at least a year. All promising not to leave it so long the next time. The ambience is reminiscent of times gone by. Good times. Saying that, I do hope they start leaving around six. Got to go, I can hear my name being called. I will message you when people are leaving. Big kiss.

And she was gone.

Time to make my way home and prepare for Anna being late. Perhaps that was a little unfair as no exact time had been mentioned. It was before seven and I received Anna's message.

Just the last few remaining and strangely enough three that helped in the furniture arrangement are amongst them. I had a plan. I saw a few were clearing away the remnants on the tables. I told them thank you for the help but it's not necessary, as the caterers will be along shortly to do that. I also added that I hope they come soon as I have a rendezvous this evening. Three men disappeared within five minutes of me announcing my plans for the evening. I had to smile at that obvious departure. All things being said, I am hoping to leave around seven thirty. I am not going to change beforehand as I thought you might like to see me as I am. I will call you when I leave. I want to play Ludo and drink Irish. Can we do that?

I could reply with a, Yes of course we can do that. It would have been enough I was sure but it wasn't in my nature to be so precise.

We can do that. You know, I do believe I've been on the receiving end of the situation you describe. Perhaps many times? Being one of the bees around the honey pot. Not being told no, per se but having the lid firmly screwed down, all the same. I wish you and I could have had this conversation thirty years ago, it would have saved me a lot of backbreaking furniture arrangement.

I promise never to ask you to volunteer for furniture duty. You are so funny James. Talk soon.

Funny? I was being truthful but then the truth can often be funny. One has to be able to demean oneself for the sake of humour and I'd discovered, women tend to appreciate a man who didn't, at times, believe himself to be above personal ridicule. The truth. A useful tool. I must have drifted off into thought, again, when Anna called.

I gave the last guest five minutes and left. I am on my way. See you in ten minutes James.

I ate my words. Anna was going to be early. All was prepared so I gave it five minutes and strolled to the gate deciding on waiting for her at the entrance. I was sat on the low wall as Anna's Mercedes came around the corner, a hundred metres away. She flashed her lights and drove past, down the drive. I beeped the gates closed and walked down to meet her. Anna was waiting for me. She looked sensational. I first noticed the hat. Black straw with a wide brim and a white lace band tied in a bow at the side. Light grey pencil dress with a thin line

266

of black around the neck line. She stood taller than I. That would have been the black high heels that finished off the outfit. She had made an impression and knew it. I needed to choose my words carefully or the whole evening could end right here.

Asked to move furniture? Right now Anna if you ask me to move heaven and earth .... I would try. You look sensational my dear.

It was enough. Anna's smile said it all. I decided not to push it. I followed Anna into the house. She put her bag on the sofa. Took a quick glance around, maybe expecting changes, I was not sure. Smiled at me and took my face in her hands. Thirty seconds of being unable to breathe and Anna released me but not before placing one more short but equally delicious kiss upon my lips. She sat on her bar stool and managed to drop her shoes to the floor.

You know today was an important day for me James but there came a time when I just wanted it to end and yes, be here with you. Now are you going to offer me a glass of wine?

Anna had a way of asking questions such as these. "Can you bring the cushions in"? "Be a dear and get my scarf. I think I left it on the table". They were commands yes but disguised as a request. It was the tone in her voice. Her body language. She had been doing it for years no doubt. I loved it. To me, it was part of the game and depended on an instantaneous decision, made all the more difficult as the possibilities for a provocative answer, were endless. Without formulating my words prior to replying, I decided on the, humble servant approach.

Of course my dear. You have had a very busy and emotionally stressful day. You keep that pretty bottom exactly where it is and I will excel in delivering on your every whim.

Stop it James. Remember, I am getting to know you. Whatever my reply you will turn it around to suit your devilish mood. I would like to drink some wine. Play Ludo and smoke the odd cigarette.

I saw Anna was intent on retrieving her handbag but before she could descend from the stool I was around the bar, bag in hand and at her side.

This is not me excelling. This is me being helpful.

She loved it. Anna most definitely liked to be pampered but with a character that had so much to give, how could one possibly refuse. I brought the Ludo to the bar. As the evening unfolded I had come to the conclusion, Anna needed this distraction. Something to take her mind off the day. Anna would momentarily drift off, with a pensive look on her face, only to recover the very next instance. Not often but noticeable all the same. It was a good evening. Full of idle chatter. Laughter and indisposed with interludes of hand holding while we gazed into each others eyes. We called a halt to the evening after Anna obtained a two one victory. I remember it not being easy to throw that third game but Anna's delight in winning was worth it. I felt it would be inappropriate, considering the circumstances, to indulge in any form of sex that night. All the more so, having witnessed Anna's pensive moments. We fell asleep in each others arms.

I don't know why as I am usually out like a light until the alarm woke me in the morning but I found myself slowly coming to and finding Anna sat on the edge of the bed.

I haven't been able to sleep James. Thoughts that are going around in my head have prevented it. I think it would be better if I go home.

I was now fully awake.

Anna, whatever you think is best. Are you sure I can't help? Sometimes just talking can help and I am a very good listener.

You are sweet James but I think it's better if I go home. It is not you, it's me.

Where had I heard that before? I started to get dressed while Anna tried to insist I shouldn't disturb myself. Disturb myself? It was three in the bloody morning and I'd just found out Anna was leaving! I wasn't sure I could be more disturbed.

It's ok Anna, I'm awake now and anyway, someone has to open the gates.

With the light on I could see Anna was distressed and very tired. We were both dressed by now as Anna tried to smile. I moved forward and held her.

Come on. Let's get you to your car.

Apart from Anna saying, "I'll call you", just before she drove away, no more was said.

Chapter Nineteen

Anna called. On Tuesday afternoon.
I am sorry I haven't been in touch James. It took me a couple of days to come to terms with my ...... my dilemma. In the end it was easy. I realised it was the past overlapping the present and that doesn't work. So I put the past where it belonged and went shopping. Can I see you tomorrow evening? Why don't you come to me. We can watch a film and drink Irish. Say about eight?
I could have said no. It would have been ...... churlish? But possibly self gratifying.
Ok Anna. See you about eight.
Ok
End of conversation.
As I drove to Anna's that Wednesday evening I wondered if I should ask her about the dilemma but thought better of it. Whatever it was, she seemed to have recovered, judging by the phone call. I arrived promptly at eight. The gates opened almost immediately. A good sign? I was right. Anna was waiting and as I turned the car she approached.
James, so lovely to see you.
I was barely out of the car and Anna kissed me.
Hopefully it will be lovely seeing me all evening Anna.
"Don't forget the night James". Anna said with laughter in her voice.
I hadn't even begun to consider the possibilities of the next few hours, let alone the night. No matter, plenty of time to think about that. I had brought a bottle of red which I retrieved from the car.
It's South African Anna, it will make a change from French. I hope you like.
I am sure I will James. Shall we go inside?

That wasn't really a question. More of a statement in disguise. Following Anna through to the breakfast bar I chose the right drawer and retrieved the corkscrew. While Anna was searching the fridge, I unscrewed the top and put the corkscrew back unused, figuring Anna would prefer a bottle with a cork. I threw the screw top in the bin and poured.

This is a very acceptable wine James. Is it a Chardonnay?

Well done Anna. Yes a Chardonnay from Aldi. Two euros ninety five.

I wasn't going to mention the where or the price but that devil looking for controversy got the better of me. It didn't work. Anna's reply was not expected.

That is amazing James. I will have to visit Aldi in the near future.

Anna was taking the cling film off the bowls as she talked.

I have a movie borrowed from a friend. Now what was the name? Oh yes. Cowboys & Aliens with Daniel Craig. You like science fiction and I like Daniel Craig. Et voilà!

Having removed the cling film Anna handed me a bowl.

This is a Polish Dill Pickle. It's a Gazpacho. I hope you like it.

Not really being a one for cold soup I was wary but hopefully it didn't show. It was actually very good and with sliced baguette that was pre buttered with "the most expensive butter in the world", Well, that's what Anna told me. It was delicious. Supper finished, Anna reached under the bar.

I have a present for you. I told you I went shopping. What I didn't say, I was shopping for you.

You went shopping for me? Oh Anna, how thoughtfully sweet.

I received an, eyes momentarily raised to the ceiling for that remark.

I unwrapped the present. There was a jumper and something I can only describe as a long sleeved polo shirt. Both with embedded logos. Neither of which registered to me.

Try them on James. Come on. Come on!

Anna was showing more excitement than I. She was enjoying her excitement, of a somewhat childish but still under control manner. Watching her was present enough and I told her so.

That is all very well James but I want you to put them on.

How did she do that! Condescending some might say but it wasn't. It never was. Not the way Anna said it. I changed. First the long sleeved polo shirt. I would never have bought it. Not my style I would have thought. Looking into the full length mirror, I had to admit, I liked it. The feel on the skin was not that of any polo shirt I'd ever worn. And then the jumper. Bottle green, which complimented the shirt collar. The remainder of the shirt was mostly a sort of insipid brown. Needless to say, the combination worked.

Oh, it's perfect James. I thought they would be ideal for Apres ski.

Thank you Anna and may I add, when in the future I am shopping for clothes, you will accompany me. Your taste in my clothing is far better than I can manage. Thank you.

You are very welcome James and yes, I think I should accompany you.

She laughed. I took the jumper off but decided to continue wearing the shirt.

If you could pour another glass James, I will set up the DVD.

The cinema room was a comfortable place to be. A wall full of books that surrounded the fireplace. Pictures hung around the two remaining walls encompassed by large gold edged frames. A small bureau in one corner, adorned with framed photos that were not quite, quilt edged, they were more conservative. More than likely, just solid silver. Thick drawn curtains closed off the remaining windowed wall. A large rug covered most of the wooden flooring, which I might add, was the only untiled room in the house. A large cottage style settee was the seating in the room. Large but cosy. Having pulled the coffee table closer, the only other piece of furniture to be seen, Anna placed the glasses. It was her cigarette time. So I joined her. We settled back to watch the movie. Neither spoke from beginning to end. So gratifying, being with someone who didn't talk through movies. Entertaining from start to finish. It was not the sort of movie one snuggled up to, noticed when Anna grabbed my arm, during the scary parts. Evidently, there were quite a few as I remembered. We carried the empty bottle and glasses through the vast lounge. While passing an area that one would describe as "The Lounge" I asked Anna if she ever sat there. She thought for a moment before replying.

No, I don't think I do.

Onward to the kitchen. I placed the bottle with the other empties while Anna opened the dishwasher.

I thought I would have a last cigarette and coffee on the terrace Anna.

What a good idea. You go and I'll make the decaf after I've finished here.

I strolled out onto the terrace. It was early November and eleven thirty and yet it wasn't cold. Maybe the long sleeved polo shirt had some hidden qualities I mused, or maybe it just wasn't cold? I walked to the edge of the terrace and looked down on the pool and as if orchestrated, the pool and garden lights came on. Enjoy it while you can James, but my thoughts were interrupted by Anna's arrival. She placed the coffees on one of the raised plinths that lit the slated steps to the pool. Having second thoughts, she took her coffee and sat on the opposite plinth to mine. The steps separating us. She sat looking at me until a slight smile appeared on her face.

I enjoy being out here at this time of year James. There is a peaceful spirit that prevails. So I have a rule. I only allow good thoughts.

She walked over to me and said,

Welcome to my sanctuary, good thought.

She kissed me and returned to her coffee.

I smiled but said nothing. I glanced to the heavens before returning my attention to Anna. Still nothing was said. For maybe fifteen minutes we remained in silence until Anna spoke.

Shall we go to bed James.

It had been a wonderful evening, full of variety and the moment that surpassed all others was the time on the terrace. In silence. And so it continued in the bedroom. Nothing said while we undressed. The silence broken when I whispered in Anna's ear, "I think the peaceful spirit lingers on".

The mood was set. We took our time. Gentle caresses. Soft kisses. Making contact with Anna as I did that night. We were two as one. It was more than sex. Time was unimportant. Time was irrelevant. This was making love. A deserved love. To make love to that one person who deserved that love was one of the few absolute rewards of being human. To make love to the right person made up for a lot of the mistakes we make. We laid, propped up in the pillows, arm in arm.

You know you said earlier about being your last cigarette James? Why not make it the last but one and I'll make more coffee.

Anna handed me a bath robe and I headed for the terrace. Anna approached me from behind. Put her arms around me, coffee in each hand.

This is a beautiful moment James. I feel …. I don't know ….. different. That is you James. You did this to me this evening.

I took the cups from her hands. Placed them on the pedestal and turned to face her.

I don't think I have ever felt more content than at this moment Anna.

I reached forward and gently kissed her. Conversation was once again, unnecessary.

Shall we retire to the bedroom Anna and see if we can utilise that other function the bed provides? Sleeping.

Anna laughed. Picked up her cup and headed for the house. Following her in I happened to glance at the clock. It was almost four! Unsurprisingly, sleep was almost instantaneous. Much like the alarm two and a half hours later. By seven thirty there were kisses at the door and I was on my way to work. Fortunately I had preempted the possibility by bringing along some clothes for work. The guys would have laughed seeing me in Tods. Plenty of time to change I thought and then the phone rang.

Hi Anna. Surely you are not missing me already?

You wish! No, I rang to invite you over on Friday evening. We can spend Saturday lazing around the house, after a morning visit to Carrefour. Can you make it for eight?

But Carrefour doesn't open until eight forty five.

You know James, I still think about what I am going to say before I call you. I don't know why as I know your answer will not be what I expect. Not Carrefour, my house on Friday evening. There, I've said the obvious. Now are you happy.
My happiness is unimportant Anna but having left the "peaceful spirit" behind I find myself reverting back to one of devilment. I would be most delighted to take up your kind offer. Shall we say eight?
What a good idea James.
I heard Anna laughing as she disconnected.

The days were relatively untaxing. We had a stand at the ILTM show but that was weeks away and anyway, it was ready to go. Time was mostly taken up with the inventory of stands for up and coming shows. This was fortunate as I was never particularly radiant after only a couple of hours sleep. It was noticed. It was remarked upon. I ignored the, "Up late last night, were we", jibes and hoped coffee would see me through. I received a message from Anna around twelve. She had gone back to bed and now felt fine. Was off to lunch somewhere and would call me later. The idle rich came to mind but knowing Anna, I felt guilty of that thought. She was anything but idle. Sorry Anna. Thinking of lunchtime, not long to go. Wouldn't it be nice, not to be restricted by time. Start time. Break time. Lunchtime. Home time. By the time I had that luxury it would be retired time. By which time I wouldn't need to go back to bed as I'd only be capable of the one function the bed provided. Does tiredness bring on depression? Back to work James. Snap out of it. Anna rang just before six.

Hello James. How are you? I haven't been back long. Marta and I went shopping after lunch and now I'm exhausted. I'm going to have a light salad and retire early.

Well that just about covered it, I thought. Had lunch. Went shopping and before you ask, I'm too tired to see you this evening.

I'm fine Anna. Glad you managed to fit in shopping before exhaustion hit. I'm going to have a coffee. What's left of a half bar of chocolate and do the same. You know, I think we should live together. I understand it could be weeks, possibly months before we settled into an acceptable rhythm of less sleepless nights but don't you think the sacrifice would be worth it?
If that was true James I would say move in tomorrow but you are lying to yourself. It would be years before that acceptable rhythm took hold. Knowing that, I think more thought is necessary before we rush headlong into it. It's a nice thought though. See you tomorrow James. Sweet dreams.

I didn't reply. At least I'd got a good nights sleep. Nine hours. Couldn't remember the last time I did that. I sent Anna a Good Morning message around ten. Lunch soon came around. Usually on a Friday when all was quiet, lunch had a tendency to creep beyond the allotted hour. It had the added bonus of home time following shortly after. That Friday wasn't the exception. Arriving home I knew I had two hours before I needed to leave for Anna's. Cigarette and beer was first on the agenda while I decided what to wear. Something to go with the new blue suede shoes. Start from bottom up. It was going to be all blue. I wondered how long it had been since I'd worn my Converse All Stars? Outfit decided I took another beer from the fridge and rolled a cigarette. Couldn't smoke after the shower. Did not want to arrive stinking of cigarettes. That had me thinking. Stinking. Smelling. Aftershave that Anna gave me. Must remember that. I decided to put the bottle in the bathroom sink. That way I would see it after the shower.

On my way. Toiletries bag, clean shirt and light jacket in attendance. The forecast for the next day looked good. Hitting the early twenties with a blue sky day. Unsurprisingly Anna had the evening planned. Wine ready for me to open on the counter which allowed me to feign forgetfulness.

That reminds me Anna, I have wine in the car. I'll get it.

I returned with four bottles of Aldi special and a pretty little purple plant, bought on an impromptu stop at the florists on the way. Anna placed the wine on the table and took my hand, heading in the direction of the bedrooms, plant in hand. I had never been much of a "flowers" man. I understood the idea but for me, it seemed a little too contrived. "Here love, I just spent eleven euros fifty as an expression of my love for you." Call me cynical if you must. It was just the way I saw it. I preferred spending time creating something that would please. A couple of hours Photoshopping out the terrace to replace with a palm tree background. Or knowing she would be late home from the office. Cook dinner. Candle lit room with her favourite relaxing music playing in the background as she entered. Washing up and clearing away while she settled on the couch. No thanks needed. None expected. It was done for love. If only it could be added to the water ..... but I digress. In tow and heading for the bedrooms I thought, make a note James, must buy more plants ..... and it was less than eleven euros fifty. Anna swung into her massive on-suite bathroom.

There James. It will sit here, in full view and remind me of you whenever I bathe.

Do you bathe that often Anna?

She laughed.

Let's go and drink some of that wine. I have pre dinner nibbles that we can take to the jacuzzi.

I did say Anna had the evening planned it was only now that I had become privy to those plans. Wine with nibbles and the jacuzzi. It was what Anna did. Make plans that sounded like good plans. I led on. Anna had, I thought, deliberately left the pool and garden lights off allowing the glow of the sauna room below, to guide our way.

"Nice effect Anna", I said

It is all about the bling James.

It was one thing having a naked woman in the bedroom but for me, in an obscenely over the top, glorified bathroom, albeit a very large bath, it was something I needed to get use to. Anna had claimed the water jet massage bed that lay just beneath the surface of the water.

Can you give me a top up James?

I stood to reach for the wine.

And no James. I am not looking at your behind but I would love a photo.

She had turned the tables. The roles were reversed. It was Anna reaching for the wine that first time. What could I have done?

I'm sure this wine is further away than the last time. It might take me awhile to retrieve it.

Playing the, "I can play that game as well", card.

Take as long as you like James.

Now what could I do? She had called my bluff. I turned to face her.

That is the problem with the temperature of this water, I'm afraid Anna. All good things come in small packages. So rather than disappoint you further .... would you like that top up?

After you give me a kiss.

Always, so easy with Anna. I was not sure how long we spent in the jacuzzi. Sometimes separated. Sometimes entwined in ways only possible in water. Sipping at the wine with such scrumptious nibbles. No idea what they were. Watching Anna towel herself down after a shower knowing I'd seen a woman getting dressed before but at that moment, for the life of me, I couldn't remember any. Standing before me. Naked and seemingly at ease. The bra and then the panties. I sat, fascinated, when at long last, she came over to sit next to me. Now fully clothed.

That was a first for me James. I did wonder if I could do it. Stand naked in front of you, that is.

I was thinking something similar Anna. The first time for me, that is. All I can say, as a first for me, please feel free to repeat anytime you like. You are very watchable Anna.

Anna was looking at me. I'm not sure she was convinced ..... and then she smiled.

Thank you James.

She kissed me so I suppose if it wasn't exactly what she wanted to hear, it was close enough.

Let's go and eat. I've prepared a light chicken salad as I knew it would be late before we ate.

It was nine thirty. We ate and I opened a second bottle. Anna, who rarely drank more than her two glasses, was well into her third. My mother would have called it, frisky. I would have to agree. Anna was delightfully captivating. She was talking but I wasn't listening. I didn't need to. I think the expressions on my face said it all. She was the centre of attention. She knew it and was revelling in it. And then she asked me about previous girlfriends. For me, it was a no no, to talk about previous relationships. It was not what one's girlfriend usually wanted to hear. Or so I believed.

Previous girlfriends? In alphabetical or chronological order? Once having established which you prefer, is there anything specific you would like to know?

Chronological, starting with the last.

Emanuela.

I waited.

Oh come on James. That is not fair. I expected a little more detail. Not just a name.

She is forty seven years old.

I waited.

And!

She is Italian. She lives in Torino. She has a daughter and a dog. Her parents live nearby. She drives an Opel.

You are playing with me James. You know that is not what I am talking about.

Actually, I didn't know what she was talking about, exactly. Until she said that. Why should I have been surprised when my first thought was, Did she mean sex? I'm a man and I had recently seen Anna naked in front of me. That had to focus the mind. If I was right an appropriate response was needed. But what if I was wrong? I was going to play it safe.

I do now. At least I know I'm not giving the information you require. Perhaps you could help me out here Anna. Name a topic and I will talk about it.

Hoping I was radiating a, I know what you want to talk about but you're going to have to say it, sort of radiance, I waited for Anna's response.

Sex James and if you want me to be more specific, was it good sex?

Ok, I was right but how to respond?

Why do I get the feeling of being under the microscope? Can I rephrase your question and answer accordingly?

I didn't wait for an answer.

You're asking me where you come in the pecking order of those that have come before. Please excuse the pun.

Anna picked up on that. Trying to maintain her nonplus expression intact she replied.

You are right James, that is what I am asking so I am wondering why I didn't? There is a part of you that still remains a mystery to me. I am very good at assessing someones character and can adjust, if necessary, my questions accordingly. So why do I feel sometimes I am in uncharted waters when I am with you? Still the man of mystery and in case you are wondering, I like it.

Second, said I.

"What!" Said Anna.

I've put you second. Forever to wonder who is first. I could have been honest and said first but where would that leave the man of mystery?

I decided to digress.

I had sex with an eighteen year old once. ….. I was twenty at the time.

Anna laughed at that.

It didn't work. We didn't really know what we were doing. One gains experience or not. One needs a receptive and innovative partner in order to gain that experience. Over the years since I have been lucky, I suppose.

Anna was looking confused at my digression.

The, Wham, Bam, Thank You Mam, days were over. I was shown how to please a woman. I have looked back on those days prior to that realisation and physically cringed at my past actions. Please the woman and the rest follows. With you, the rest that follows has always been a union between two people. No pretence needed. The mask is lowered to allow the union to blossom. To blossom slowly as the petals unfold that are eventually rewarded with the warmth of sunlight or as a volcano that waits and waits until it can repress the eruption no longer. Wherever our individual desires wish to roam they are absorbed by a stronger mutual desire as we are brought harmoniously together. So to hell with the man of mystery thesis, you have your own pedestal Anna, way way above all others. Have I adequately answered those unspoken questions?

Anna remained unmoved giving me her thoughtful face. And then she started to smile.

Yes you have James and I couldn't have put those answers to unspoken questions anywhere near as eloquently as you.

I knew she was thinking of more to say but before the topic tumbled into diversity I had to ask.

So, having answered your questions to the best of my ability, would you like to share your thoughts on the subject with me?

What are you asking James?

Here we go, I thought. Anna still wanted to play. Expecting a question that was as near the truth as I dare go. A question that knowingly would result in another from Anna, I decided to disappoint and try the direct approach.

I'm asking you where I appear in your list of top ten sexual partners. If I appear outside of that list then lie.

You should know better than to ask a lady such a question James. Shame on you.

She still wanted to play.

Got it. A Lady can ask such a question but is not expected to answer a question of similar merit. You realise your avoidance of my question puts me outside the top one hundred. At least that is the way I see it.

If you say so James, I would not want to delude or deceive you into believing it was otherwise.

I wasn't going to get a straight answer on this one so play the game.

I would willingly put myself outside the top one hundred Anna but in doing so .... it would mean you've had an awful lot more lovers than I hitherto realised. For the sake of your dignity I will place myself at number eleven.
Ok James, you are in the top three. Happy now?
"Yes", was my instant response.
You do realise I will, at times, wonder where I am in the top three but to be honest Anna, I don't really care. At this moment in time it's just about you and me. Don't you agree?
Let's go to bed James.
I'll take that as an agreement.
We both laughed and headed for the en suite.
I was not sure if it was the wine or the conversation that put Anna in such an excitable mood. Anna was being proactive but it seemed to me, she couldn't make up her mind on which position to adopt. This had to stop. I managed to manoeuvre her into the classic man on woman position.
Anna, relax and enjoy.
Later it had me wondering if there was a record out there waiting to be broken. The, We didn't stop for what seemed like hours, record. The, How many positions can be obtained in a given period, record. Modesty would normally prevent me from including the next record but .... The, How many times can you bring your partner to that moment of pure joy, record. I saw myself in line for that one. Although, most probably not. It was enough for me knowing Anna had said she was amazed and didn't think it was possible to have so many moments of ecstasy. Ecstasy was the word she used. I was pleased. More than pleased. I was quietly elated.
We slept late the next morning. Unconscious would have been a closer call to my condition. Orange juice and coffee with Anna leaning over me, was my first recollection of that morning.
Hello sleepy head. Take your time but breakfast in half an hour. Oh, and you were marvellous last night.
She kissed me on the forehead and left.
I was marvellous. That thought was as an alarm clock. An alarm clock that one didn't want to switch off. I was out of bed in a flash. Orange juice in hand I headed for the shower. I closed the door. I opened it, looking for somewhere to put the orange juice. I was marvellous!
"Hello Marta", I said, accompanied with my most ingratiating smile, as I opened the dishwasher, carefully placing the empty glass. She smiled and said hello in Russian, an improvement, I thought.
Put your coffee cup in James, I have a clean one on the patio.
Marta disappeared shortly after, leaving Anna and myself to enjoy the silence around us as we ate breakfast.

We don't have to talk James. I'm sorry, that is not what I meant. We don't need conversation all the time. I'm happy just sitting with you. Being in your presence comforted by the thought, conversation is not always necessary. You see what I've done James? I've broken the silence to say, Isn't silence a sometimes wonderful thing.

I took her hand and said,

I will never tire of listening to you Anna and in this particular case, you enhance the silence with your beautiful melodic voice. After all, it is not completely silent at this time of day. The insects buzzing from flower to flower. The gentle breeze. The rustle of leaves as the foxes meander through the trees. Even the flapping of the blinds add to the soothing, silent noise of the morning and of course my entry into this silent noise, adds a rather pleasing dulcet tone. Don't you think?

I love the way you talk James, particularly when I think I've got it. I think I have understood what you are saying and then, moments later, wonder what it was you just said. What did you just say James?

I said your voice would never break the silence, it would merely enhance it.

You are sweet James and as a reward for such sweetness, you can sit there while I clear away.

As Anna stood I started to rise.

Sit there James and enjoy the coffee I am about to get for you.

With that, Anna collected plates, cups, an abundance of miscellaneous items in her hands. I looked on in awe.

Darling, one has to be prepared to step in if the staff are not doing their job.

She winked at me. Held in her laughter and marched off to the kitchen. Was I expected to believe that? Unable to answer that question I allowed my mind to drift. That didn't work. Full of too many questions. I felt a hand on my neck as the coffee was placed in front of me. Anna silently collected the remainder of breakfast and slipped away only to return moments later with a fresh cup for herself.

James.

I recognised that tone.

Do you want the good news or the bad first?

I looked at Anna.

You tell me in the order you think it might be best to hear Anna.

Ok. Good news. Give me a minute.

She left and returned with a large carrier bag.

Actually this is the good news and the bad news rolled into one. These are your birthday presents and I'm giving them to you now because I won't be here for the day. I leave for Milan tomorrow and will not return until Thursday afternoon.

I gave Anna my understanding but slightly hurt smile.

Hey Anna, I understand, Time and the Italian courts, wait for no man so now, right now, today is my birthday. May I?

279

Anna handed me the bag. There were three parcels, wrapped professionally and complemented with satin bows.

That one first James.

I thought I should delicately take them apart as it would be criminal to tear into such beautifully wrapped gifts indiscriminately. So I slowly tried to disengage the ribbon from the first parcel. This wasn't going fast enough for Anna. She was excited and wanted to know if I liked my presents. She produced a pair of scissors.

Just cut the ribbon James and rip the paper away.

This could have turned into another game but I felt Anna's frustration was somewhere close to breaking point. I ripped the paper. A ski jacket. A ski jacket in lime green. A very nice ski jacket. A very expensive ski jacket but ……. lime green!

Do you like it? Try it on.

I tried it on. There was little doubt of the quality. The fit was perfect.

*It's perfect Anna. You know I've have had my ski jacket, my now previous ski jacket, for fifteen years. This is something else. (*No lie there. It was something else. It was lime green!)

Next present James.

A jumper of Merino wool and another long sleeved polo shirt completed the trio of presents.

Something more to wear for apres ski? You've made my birthday with your uncanny ability of knowing what I need. Even before I knew I needed it. Thank you my dear for such thoughtfulness.

"I don't know why", said Anna. "As I never do during the day but I would like a cigarette"?

You get your cigarettes Anna and I'll make another coffee.

"I am so glad you like your presents James", said Anna on her return.

You know Anna, you are a perfect example of someone who epitomises the saying, For it is in the giving that we receive. Francis of Assisi, I think?

What?

I had to laugh.

You get great pleasure in the giving. Perhaps somewhat too enthusiastically but nevertheless, with great pleasure. It is another of a long list of endearing qualities you posses.

She was looking at me with half closed eyes. I think she was trying to decide if she should kiss me or hit me. I felt sure it wasn't the latter but it was quite a look.

You like me, don't you James?

I more than like you Anna. Why do you ask?

I asked in the hope of getting the right response so don't look so worried James. You passed. I more than like you? Mmmm, I must try that when I meet someone I like.

Anna's turn to laugh.

Let's have lunch on the beach James. It is a beautiful day. Perfect for a beach lunch.

Beaulieu-sur-Mer. Café del Mare was the destination as I found out on our arrival. Of course there was a parking space directly outside the restaurant. Anna seemed not to notice the convenience. Billy Connelly once wondered if the Queen thought the world smelt of paint. On a visit, there would be a painter just ahead frantically finishing off the last fence or rusty pole. I think Anna viewed the world similarly. If she needed to park her car, a space would appear. Perhaps this was the way it worked for some?

This is my birthday treat James. Be prepared to consume some champagne.

Could I ever be capable of tiring of Anna? We were engrossed in conversation of a frivolous nature. We were silently eating. We people watched while passing the occasional comment. We knocked feet. We both apologised. We both laughed at the absurdity of it. Like an old married couple used to each other and yet every day, a new day. I had to admit, I could never have considered for one moment being with someone like Anna. What was your type James? Anna would not have been listed and yet there I was, with someone not my type. Had I always excluded women like Anna? If that were true, I realised many an opportunity could have passed me by. But not this time. Never too late to learn from ones mistakes.

What are you thinking James and don't say you're not as I now know that far off look.

I was thinking how fortunate I am. How fortunate I didn't consider type when I met you.

What?

You are not my type Anna. At least that is what I've always believed. You fall way outside my criteria. Then I thought, How special must Anna be when she is able to break forty years of my stubbornly held beliefs.

I smiled.

You know James, earlier on today, I wasn't sure if I was going to kiss you or hit you.

So I was right!

I have that same feeling now. Most of me wants to kiss you but there is a small nagging need, call it an itch, that needs to be scratched. You say such wonderful things with such meaning but when I asked you what you were thinking why didn't you just say, Thinking of you. I have to wait until the very last line to know what you were thinking.

Anna's turn to smile.

…… but I wouldn't have it any other way. I must derive some sort of pleasure, frustratingly waiting for that concluding line. "Is there a name for that"? Said more to herself than to me.

I'm not sure there is Anna but if you were to include the words, hit, pleasure, kiss and need into a Google search, it might be interesting to see what came forth. Please excuse the reoccurring pun. Unless you'd like me to add that to the search?

It took Anna a few seconds to understand what I was suggesting.

She laughed, which was badly timed, as a lady passing by had just dropped her bag, spilling half the contents under table and chair and now believing Anna was laughing at her predicament. Anna looked at me. Looked at the lady. Looked at the well spread contents of her bag and got to her feet. Sprang into action might have been a closer definition. She was almost on hands and knees, seeking out the far removed items and handing them over. Mission accomplished, Anna congratulated the lady on her fine choice of perfume. One of the last items recovered. The lady smiled and said, "I apologise for my initial thoughts. Thank you so much for helping to alleviate me of my own stupidity. I could but sit back as if watching a movie. A comedy, where the heroine turned potential disaster to her advantage and came out smelling of those roses. Anna came to rest.

What are you smiling about James, and try to fit the answer somewhere near the beginning.

You're amazing.

Well done James. I was expecting a little more but well done.

I just smiled.

The waiter arrived with a bottle of champagne. I thought it was ordered by Anna but no. It was a complimentary bottle given in recognition of Anna's help earlier. Evidently the lady, was a Lady. Been coming for years. Valued customer and all that. That forestalled our possible departure for another hour or so. Out on the terrace on a warm sunny November day. We were in no hurry to leave.

It was late afternoon before we returned to Anna's place. It had been mentioned in the car about a possible "dip" in the pool. I was hoping that, outwardly spoken thought, was just that. A thought.

Skinny dipping with Anna had it's benefits but those benefits rapidly disappeared as one became engulfed in eighteen degrees of water.

Ten laps James?

No it wasn't just a thought. I could barely see the end of the pool and I'd entered via the steps that came to a stop about midway down the pool. Ten laps! No way!

Anna?

Not waiting for a response.

I was brought up swimming in the Atlantic. Summer temperatures barely hit twenty, mid summer. I moved to the South of France to avoid such temperatures. Therefore I'm going to say two laps. You will reply with something

above five until we finally agree on four. As you have already done two, I'll
expect an Irish waiting for me on the completion of my laps.
Anna smiled as we crossed on her third lap. I finished my laps as Anna arrived
from the direction of the house with coffee's. Having had the time to change. A
pale blue dress. Wide straps over the shoulders. It was a flimsy material that
somehow seemed to accentuate Anna's subliminal contours. I snapped out of
my thoughts as Anna handed me a very comfortable, apres pool robe.
Happy Birthday James!
Thank you Anna. You know what I'm going to do? I'm going to cancel the forty
or so people that were coming to celebrate my birthday next week. Why?
Because today is my birthday and I don't want anything to spoil that.
That had her thinking.
I don't know what to say James? Should I hit you for lying about the birthday
celebrations or should I kiss you for lying in such a wonderful way? Why don't
you just kiss me.
She said but didn't wait for me to respond. She kissed me and didn't stop. It
became, if it wasn't already, a heated exchange. I only had a loosely tied robe.
Not much of a defence. Not that I was looking for one. My hand was on her
behind, inside her dress. Everything became surreal. Five minutes of thought
flashed through my head. Summarised it went something like. I've got my hand
on the ass of an amazing woman. A woman who is surrounded by luxury. A
woman who lunches. Who stands around being praised for some thing or
another. Who lives in a different world. I've got my hand on her ass. What do I
do next? Do I take her, here on the terrace? Do I drag her to the bedroom?
Perhaps on the Italian marble floor?
I think the coffee might be going cold Anna.
I realise now, I might have lost that moment. That moment on the tiles. I couldn't
do it! There was something preventing me. I realise now, Anna was a women.
She had her needs. At that moment her needs might have been the tiles. I had
no way of knowing the truth then but I now believe Anna might have succumbed
to the possibility. Ah well! I decided on the gentleman's approach and suggested
we should possibly consider the coffee. Anna's reaction wasn't what I expected.
The look was one of idolisation. Something I said?
I ..... I ..... think you are .... amazing, James. I would have been on those tiles
in a second and I know you felt the same way but you saved me. You saved me
the post sex embarrassment. You saw that. So unbelievably considerate. So
unbelievable. Men normally aren't considering the consequences. The
aftermath.
If I was the sort that collected points, that just threw me way ahead. She slowly
removed her hands from inside my robe. I was a man who learnt. Mostly I'd
forgotten what I'd learnt but when it came to women, it was filed. I wasn't trying
to manipulate the situation. I just felt uncomfortable and tried to redirect the ....

283

the almost unbearably impossibility that was Anna on the tiles. Panties already discarded. Her invitation to join her. To this day I don't know why I stood back but it felt right. I had to say something.

You want the truth Anna. It was something about respect. You are right, I could have taken you on the tiles and maybe one day …. but only when I know it's ok to do so. It's a balance Anna. Sex verses respect and with you, respect will always win through. So you see my dear, you can congratulate yourself on your impeccable ways. Ways that allow me to marvel at your being. Ways that prevent me from approaching you with anything less than total respect.

Not sure if Anna got that.

So what you are saying James is, You would have loved to take me on the tiles. I like how that sounds. Take me on the tiles. ……. Unfortunately you were incapable of doing so because of respect for me. Is that right?

No need to answer. Just a nod of acknowledgement sufficed.

Therefore in conclusion I would say you have just missed out through respect.

I couldn't be sure if she meant that but it didn't matter. We both found it amusing.

I don't think I missed out Anna. In fact I would say I saved the day. If it wasn't for my well timed interruption, we would have been drinking cold coffee.

It worked. Anna laughed as she stood. I'm not sure what possessed me at that moment but I stood to face her. I kissed her and continued to do so. I put my hand under her dress and between her legs. Immediately finding that spot, my finger moved to a slow rhythm, matching that of Anna's who was surprisingly responsive at such short notice.

I'm not sure where you think you were going a moment or two ago Anna but right now you're going to the bedroom.

She immediately disengaged and turned towards the bedrooms. I loved it when she did as she was told.

It was around six thirty when we returned to the Breakfast Bar. I mused as to why with the mass of living space in front of us, the barstools seemed the right place to be. I was pondering that thought when Anna spoke.

Are you hungry?

Surprisingly no.

Then why don't we go to the cinema this evening?

Good idea Anna, I said as we both reached for our phones. I got there first.

Spectra is in Antibes. A James Bond movie or there is a romcom. Which do you prefer. Good choice, I said without waiting. *James Bond it is!*

Yes James. Remember, I have a thing for Daniel Craig so it suits me.

You know my name is James?

That is nice James but it doesn't start with Daniel and neither does it end in Craig. It is ok James. I have a thing for you to.

She found that amusing.

What time does it start?

284

I checked the times.

We have one hour and forty five minutes. Think you, sorry we, can make it?

I definitely can James but I can't speak for you.

We enjoyed the movie and decided on a cocktail before leaving Antibes. Latinos it was. I chose the one second from the top. Choosing from the list that was purely based on the last time, the very first time I had drunk a cocktail, which coincidently was in this very bar with Paul advising me. I remember it contained an awful lot of gin and was second from the top. Anna had the same. It was eleven thirty and decidedly chilly by the time we'd returned to our barstools. Anna was raiding the fridge. Toast. Foie Gras and cheeses were laid out.

Can you take me to the airport tomorrow James?

Of course. What time is the flight?

Anna checked the details.

Four fifteen.

Sleep in. Followed by a late breakfast/lunch somewhere on route and get you to the airport by three.

Lovely idea James. More Foie Gras?

By the time we went to bed the hit from that cocktail had receded. It had been a long and very memorable day. A memorable day that started the day before and won't finish until around three tomorrow. Actually that was three today as it was then a couple of hours past midnight. A long memorable and tiring day. I awoke with daylight seeping in through the partially open shutters. It was nine thirty and Anna was sleeping. I remembered we both collapsed into an almost instant slumber when our heads hit the pillows the night before. I wondered if Anna wanted to make up for that loss. She was on her side with her back to me. I ran my hand over that oh so flat stomach. Occasionally venturing close but not too close to that area of arousal. Anna was drowsily acknowledging my advances. It wasn't long before Anna, without turning, made it all too clear what she wanted. I don't know why it was but I had always found the morning not to be the time for self control. I wasn't disappointed.

Spooning, as in spoon fed. I said almost to myself as I fed Anna what lay inside me.

What?

Nothing Anna. I was just thinking of the time I said, "Giving has it's own rewards".

It was after eleven before we'd managed that first coffee. I remembered a restaurant on the seafront heading out of Antibes. Booked a table for twelve thirty and told Anna. Anna dressed in light brown mohair trousers? Sensible shoes that were fortunately flat. A pale green jumper that hid, to the large part, the cream blouse below. Gathering up her oiled jacket I couldn't resist the temptation.

Are the shotguns in the car?

It took Anna a millisecond.

Yes James and if you don't hurry up I might use one on you.

I said nothing about being ready for the last forty minutes. That would have been childish, not to mention potentially ruining Anna's enjoyment of her response.

"Coming my dear", I said, in a non committal way that had Anna laughing all the way to the car.

We arrived at a quarter to one. Not bad! The thirteenth of November and we were bathed in sunshine sat on the terrace of that small family run Italian restaurant. The warmth of that winter sun encapsulated the way I'd felt the entire weekend. Don't get carried away with that thought James. You might say more than intended. Keep it light.

Did I tell you what happened at the cash point the other day Anna?

No?

I was at a cash point when a little old lady asked if I could check her balance, so I pushed her over.

That one took Anna by surprise. A fraction longer than normal before the realisation of it being a joke hit her.

I shouldn't be laughing at that! That is horrible James! Did she break anything?

Anna looked at me seriously and then once again, broke into laughter.

I am as bad as you James. Imagining that poor old lady falling and us creating humour from the incident. As you said it, I had a vision of a very surprised old lady falling to the ground. Oh gosh. Do you have any more?

Do you know what Lollypop Ladies are?

Yes?

I could see Anna was confused.

If there is one thing that make me cross. It's Lollypop Ladies!

I waited.

She laughed so much, with the sweep of an arm, almost dislodging the wine from the clutching hands of the waiter.

"Oh! Desole monsieur". Said Anna, trying to control herself. It wasn't long before I was thinking the mood was right. I could succumb to earlier thoughts. The warmth of the sun. The warmth of the weekend. The warmth of Anna. Right now, as she sat opposite me. It was a good moment. Anna beat me to it. Why wouldn't she?

James, I've been thinking.

You know I hate it when you do that Anna.

And that, is a part of what I've been thinking about. Your humour is a part but not just that. Your very pleasing ways. I can expand on that later if you wish.

A big smile from Anna.

…….. In a nutshell James. I so much enjoy being with you.

Anna was being serious without being too revealing. Still wanting to play her cards close to the chest.

In that case Anna, I propose a toast! To two people. Two people who will hopefully never be confronted with the obvious as the obvious can seemingly be confusing. As your Jerome K Jerome once said, "What I am looking for is a blessing not in disguise".

You read me well James. To two people.

I purposely remained silent as we returned our glasses to the table. Anna watched me watching her.

What?

I thought I'd remain silent Anna, waiting for the expansion of my pleasing ways.

I said later James. This is not later. This is now.

Another toast. To later than now.

Which I said with a hopeful smile while looking deeply into Anna's eyes.

And with a lot more laters to follow James.

We had time for coffee before the need to be airport bound. During coffee Anna related the problems she perceived on meeting her stepdaughter once again. I could only suggest she didn't allow herself to be undermined but stick determinedly to what she thought was a fair compromise particularly remembering the concessions she had already made.

You are right James, I have made concessions and she needs to be made to see, there are no more forthcoming possibilities. I think the problem is, she doesn't get it.

I could see Anna was drifting away. Thinking of up and coming events. I had to distract her. I didn't want our parting to be filled with thoughts of the coming few days. I caught the eye of the waiter.

L'addition s'il vous plait monsieur.

Before he returned, I held Anna's hands.

Whatever happens in the next few days Anna just remember these last days.

I could feel myself succumbing.

If these days have meant as much to you as they have to me ……. they will see you through anything the Italian has to throw at you. Think happy thoughts and she will never penetrate your inner calm.

Anna now held my hands.

I will do that James, I will be filled with those happy thoughts. Bring her on!

Anna laughed at the thought of that. I paid and we left. Twenty minutes later and we are at the Kiss and Fly. Terminal Two. As I was about to get out, Anna pulled my arm. An ever so quick kiss on the lips followed. Anna doesn't do that in public?

You know I don't kiss in public James but I wanted to thank you and it seemed the best way for you to understand how much I thank you.

Once Anna had been reunited with her suitcase she said,

Will Thursday evening about seven be ok? I know, with all that has happened over the weekend I forgot to ask you if you can. Pick me up that is, or did I? Send me the details Anna. I'll be here.

A big smile. Kisses on the cheeks and she was gone, disappearing through the glass doors fifty metre away. It was going to be a quiet few days. I sent Anna a, Hope you arrived safely etc., message around eleven and went to bed.

I checked my messages prior to the morning shower. Nothing from Anna. It was ten past eight when I sat down in the empty warehouse that Monday morning. I thought of sending Anna a message but resisted. I recalled the weekend instead and that was where I stayed for as much of the day as I could. It was the slowdown to, End of Term, only interrupted by Mapic where our involvement was minimal. One small client. Montage Tuesday Wednesday. Three day show. Take it out on Sunday. Everything was prepared. We had adopted a five o'clock finish for the remainder of the month and therefore I found myself home by five thirty. It was already going dark as I sat hovering over my phone.

Thinking about you and hoping your day went well my dear. How ever it was, get yourself dressed up and head for a favourite restaurant but please, try to avoid instructors, of any kind. James x

I was happy sending that. It could have been worse certainly.

"Anna, I haven't heard from you. I hope everything is ok. Please let me know. Don't worry how late it might be, I'll wait up". I could have sent that. No I couldn't have done that but thinking it, allowed one to reject it. It was nine thirty when I heard from Anna.

Hello James. Sorry not to have messaged sooner, it's all been rather hectic. The day went well but tomorrow is the meeting with the stepdaughter. I always thought it was the stepmother who, as the stories tell, received the bad press? I've taken your advice and am enjoying the company of a local financier at a rather nice restaurant but don't you worry. I have thoughts of last weekend to keep me safe. I'll let you know how tomorrow turns out. Big Kiss, Anna

Now what was I supposed to make of that. Was Anna with some banker? Perhaps she was but she told me? Why tell me if she was? Was she teasing me to see my reaction?

I'm glad you took my advice Anna. Enjoy your evening. Catch up tomorrow. Big Kiss, James

If she was expecting a reaction, I wasn't going to give it to her and anyway, she was her own woman. If she was with some banker I hardly saw myself flying to Milan to confront him. Mainly because it was easy to work out, I'd arrive too late. Assuming I was even contemplating such a ludicrous idea. Anna came back.

You are such a spoilsport James. You know you are supposed to at least try to emulate jealously. It is good for a woman's soul. It enables us to feel wanted.

I'm on my way to the airport as I speak Anna. Flight to Milan in forty three minutes. I can't have you talking to strange men. I'll be at the restaurant in under two hours. I am so upset!

I sent it and then followed up with another.

Uhm you couldn't perhaps tell me the name of the restaurant?

You're not on your way to the airport are you James?

You're not having dinner with a financier, are you?

Actually James I am having the most amazing salmon salad ...... in my hotel room.

That's good news. Airport parking can be so difficult to find at this time of the evening. I'll turn around and go home.

Ok James, while you drive home I will finish my salmon and go to bed. I wouldn't wish to be the reason for your lack of concentration on the road.

A laughing face with tears concluded that message.

Good Night Anna. Sweet Dreams.

Mine was an icon blowing a kiss.

Chapter Twenty

It was late morning before the guys were ready to set off. The twenty cube loaded down with stand and build materials. The warehouse fell silent. I decided to stop off in the electric room on my way to the office. A morning message for Anna that I'd hoped to compile sooner but was forestalled by the guys early arrival.

Good morning Anna. Hope you slept well and are now ready to face the evil stepdaughter. You always have the option of walking out. In the end she has to come to you. You, as is said, hold the purse strings. I'm sure she is intelligent enough to realise a stalemate is not in her interests. I would wish you good luck but I've always believed wishing someone good luck infers they need it. You don't! Enjoy the day Anna. x

Now I could concentrate on my day. I headed for the office ready to face some long overdue reports. An extended lunch with John and Will shortened the day considerably so it wasn't long before I found myself at home. I had decided to finish those reports at home. A message from Anna. I ignored it, focussing on finishing those damn reports. Twenty minutes later, I read Anna's message.

You will never believe it James but I walked out! I read your message while waiting for my solicitor just before the meeting started. Then she arrived. Before she had sat down, her body language had already betrayed her mood but I was calm. Within an hour she was standing shouting her demands. So unladylike, I thought. Anyway, I collected my papers together and said to my solicitor, "When she is ready to talk rather than shout, you will find me at my hotel, having lunch". And I walked out James. That was just before twelve. He called at three saying she had calmed down and promised to be civil. I said I was at the airport ready to depart but would return to my hotel for another meeting tomorrow as it will be far too late to reconvene today. He relayed the message and another meeting is set for ten tomorrow. That was your idea to walk out James and not the only one. Your joking yesterday evening about being at the airport played it's part in todays events. And do you know what James, I felt so infused with a sense of …. I'm not sure ….. achievement, gratification of the moment ………... I went shopping. I am now about to go down for dinner. Thank you for that message James, it really did help to turnaround my day. You are so understated. Do you realise that? I think perhaps you don't, but that of course is why I love you. Hope your day was full of me. Bon appetit.

"I love you" did not go unnoticed. That was a long message but having read it a little more than, once or twice, I came to the conclusion I had given Anna the options and she had reacted. In a positive way. She had taken my verbalising and turned it to her advantage. It was a strange moment. A feeling of humility. Anna had reacted to my message by acting on it. How many thoughts did I have, never to act upon? Was what I said so enlightening? Did I understate my true potential? My head started to veer towards self assessment. I was never comfortable with the idea but this was a positive. Anna, the woman with all the ideas. Where we should go today. What we should do, had taken my, throw-away words, as something more. …… That unthought of, points system, reared it's head once again. I concentrated on my reply.

To answer your one and only question Anna. Yes, I realise you love me.
I have to admit, when I suggested you walked out, I envisage Micheal Douglas turning his back on The Board. I never imagined, for one moment, you would do it. Bravo You! Other than having the pleasure of watching you play tennis, being a "Fly on the wall" to that moment would have made my …..day/week/month/year. Enjoy your well earned dinner my dear and hopefully tomorrow is the beginning of the end of your worries for the future. Bon appetit.

I was not expecting a reply. (To expect was to be disappointed.) I had more important concerns. It was nineteen degrees in the house. The oil fired heater was doing it's best. The electric radiator, now on twenty four hours a day, wasn't really contributing. It was shower time giving me enough body heat to see me through the next hour or so. I was in bed by eleven. Deep in sleep a noise distracted my subconscious. Anna's message tone. I woke. I wasn't sure if I heard right but I had to check. Sure enough a message from Anna.

I have been so tired James. In my room for the past two hours waiting for midnight. It is midnight James and I have renewed energy. It is your Birthday and I am excited for you. I wanted to be the first. The first to wish you A HAPPY BIRTHDAY ……. Your first and hopefully last birthday without me. I will say no more …. certainly not after almost three glasses of wine. Happy Birthday James.

That was worth waking for. I returned to bed.

Every year it was the same thing. It was James's birthday but almost half of the team were at the Palais? Every year, we would go to Cannes around lunchtime to celebrate my birthday. On this occasion, seven people present. Three would return to the Palais. Fortunately the one driving the truck, didn't drink. It was three thirty before we dispersed. No way anybody was going to be responsible for anything constructive that afternoon. Morrisons was suggested as an after work birthday drink. In two hours time. Three pints of Kilkenny and it was now nine o'clock. I had to go. "Hey James, I hear it's your birthday. What do you want?" I tried to steer the conversation away from "What do you want"? Sometimes it worked, sometimes it didn't. I was on my fifth pint when I heard someone was going to Antibes. It took another fifteen minutes to unentangle myself from the birthday wishes before the fresh air was upon me. Twenty minutes later, I was home. I sat, oblivious to the room temperature, staring at my phone. No follow up from Anna. It was ten thirty. At least that's what my watch said. Once I was able concentrated on the hands. The phone rang. Brown Eyed Girl! It was Anna.

Happy Birthday James! Have you enjoyed the day?

I really did want to say something at that moment but for some reason my mind couldn't focus on the words. It didn't matter. I wasn't supposed to answer.

Where have you been?

In a bar, getting drunk, was a possible answer but once again, an answer wasn't expected.

Are you home?

Yes, just got in.

I had a chance to say that.

I've actually enjoyed maybe one or two too many birthday drinks Anna. Maybe you should talk about your day and I can grunt accordingly.

Anna thought that amusing.

In my present state I am likely to say something I won't remember in the morning but you will.

What sort of thing would that be James?

Not falling for that but I will say one thing. Luv yu Annu.

Said in what I thought was the epitome of a drunken person. It hadn't taken much effort to adopt the role.

I know I'm going to say that at some point Anna so I thought I would say it to clear the way for discussions on a Spring or Autumn wedding.

Let's make it Autumn James. It will give you more time to save for the wedding and honeymoon. Perhaps no more than one hundred and fifty guests for lunch. Honeymooning in the Far East for a few weeks, or so.

So how was your day Anna.

She laughed.

My day was ..... purposeful James and I do believe we are close to settling most of the important issues on the agenda. In fact there is no need for me to wait around until Thursday as there is little more to discuss until our next meeting. Could you pick me up at the same time on Wednesday?

Of course Anna. Once you send me the original flight details I am certainly capable of subtracting twenty four hours. Thursday read Wednesday.

Sorry James, I forgot. I would have remembered once I was focused on the flight home.

The flight details appeared in my message box.

Ok Anna. Got that and if you don't mind I think I'll take a couple of Ibuprofen and avail myself of the bed that is calling.

It has been a long day for both of us. A good nights sleep will leave us refreshed for tomorrow evening. Good night James. Sweet dreams.

I expected an immediate disconnection but no.

Aren't you going to say Good Night, James?

Under normal circumstances, yes but you rarely give me the opportunity Anna.

You are right James. I am so used to ending business discussions that way. I'm going to have to try harder to give you time to respond.

And she was gone! A minute later I received a multitude of tearfully laughing icons. I just knew she was feeling so pleased with herself at that moment. Now where did I put the Ibuprofen?

Collecting Anna from the airport. Sitting waiting outside arrivals I thought of the first time we met here. Anna collecting me those many months ago. The day that started the magical adventure. Anna was stood over me and I hadn't noticed. How long had she been there?

Sorry Anna I was miles away.

"I had noticed", she said with a smile.

I stood. Kissed her cheeks and we were gone. As her plane was delayed for an hour, it was after eight before we arrived at her place. I'd brought a bottle. Anna said she was going to make a light tuna salad after dumping her suitcase. I opened the wine as Anna returned. With a carrier bag?

I told you I went shopping James and as I know how much you like blue, I couldn't resist.

Anna raised her glass.

Happy Belated Birthday James. Sorry, I had no chance to wrap it.

A casual shirt in very light blue. It certainly was eye catching but not flamboyant. Anna had too much taste for that to be a possibility.

Thank you Anna. I love it. The colour is so unusual or possibly it's the fabric that makes it seem so? Either way, Thank you again.

Will you stay tonight James.

I thought Anna's mood had changed. Her casual manner had an edge of …… of needing. What Anna needed. Anna got.

Of course my dear as long as I don't die of hunger first.

Are you that hungry James?

No Anna, I was attempting to divert the answer, once already given, away from that particular topic.

293

Such a gentleman James. Tuna salad coming up.
It was a few hours of Anna at her best. She could barely sit still. After our light supper Anna became frivolous. How one becomes frivolous during an attempt at putting dishes in the washer, I had no idea but Anna managed it. There seemed to be a bombardment of kisses intermixed with the noise of plate stacking and Anna's cheerful voice. I made coffee as Anna went in search of her cigarettes. Something about not remembering where she'd left them before leaving for Milan. I rolled mine. I suggested we go to the terrace. It was cold but acceptable for the brief time we were there. Anna was still .... In my day as a young hippie, I would have said, ... Speeding. She had the characteristics, well almost. There remained that iron clad control, admittedly slipping but still present. Stood watching Anna walking back and forth, turning on the spot. One moment facing out towards the distant sea. The next, inches from my face with a smile. Lips that were spread but not open. It was not the smile that captured my heart it was what accompanied that smile. The look in her eyes. Focused. Looking for that connection between us. Waiting for that place. That place that appeared and enveloped. It enveloped me. I could do nothing but accept those feelings that passed between us.
Let's go to bed James.
It was a night of passion. A night of hilarious moments. Anna did not relent. She was possessed. It was all I could do to keep pace.
I would like another cigarette. Come on James.
Anna wrapped the bathrobe around herself but before doing so, allowing me very intimate glances of what lay beneath. I followed her out but stopped when I reached the kitchen to make coffee. Can't smoke without beer or coffee. I took the coffee to the terrace only to find Anna's mood had changed. She was pensive. I didn't disturb her. Placing the coffee on the table, I lit a cigarette. And so we stood. No one speaking.
I like you James. You know that. I like you a lot, ok, more than a lot and yet I am confused. Confused about my feelings and what that entails. Don't worry James. It's me, not you. Where have I heard that before? *I just need to convince some very small part of me about my feelings for you.*
She had said all she was going to say on that subject as was obvious by her next remark.
Isn't it a beautiful night? What time is it? Forget that, I don't want to know.
Anna talked for awhile and then we returned to bed. We made love. I say love as it was so far removed from earlier events. This was .... capturing movements as they happened. The slightest change in position was registered and reacted on. We moved together in sublime ecstasy. The climax was mutual. We laid side by side for some time. Anna was the first to move. Reaching forward to give me the most soft and succulent kiss.
Good Night My .... My Ever-so Dear James.

Anna turned away. I set my alarm for seven thirty. As I laid down I decided not to relive the evening. Not that it mattered, I was soon asleep.

Breakfast consisted of porridge and coffee. I didn't complain. I liked porridge although I do believe, mine had less lumps. Anna seemed sleepy. Not surprising. It was three fifteen when I set my alarm.

James I wanted to tell you last night. I am unavailable for the next couple of days and I have some Russian friends staying this weekend so I won't be able to see you until next week. I think they leave on Tuesday morning.

I gave her my serious look.

A kiss, a very long kiss, might just see me through until next week.

Anna came close and yes, it was a very long kiss.

Will that see you through James?

No.

No?

No amount of kisses will make up for time spent apart.

Anna was now looking at me with such affection.

Although ……. having had my hands inside your bathrobe for the last five minutes, that might just see me through.

Look of affection disappeared. To be replaced with a smiling sideways movement of the head.

Sometimes James you are too honest for your own good. Kiss me and go, and keep your hands from under the bathrobe as you do.

It was a good parting. That feeling of being enveloped still permeated. It lasted for the twenty minute drive to work. Four days of work and a weekend in-between. I was sure I would survive. A BBQ at the neighbours on Saturday. An inevitably long lunch on the Sunday, yes, I'd survive. I'd sent Anna a couple of amusing messages on the Thursday. It was Friday afternoon before I received a response.

Hi James. Waiting at the airport for the weekend guests. It all became rather hectic yesterday morning when the A/C decided to fail on me. Again! I contacted the company who are, as I write, scratching their heads and muttering in unrecognisable french dialect about the problems they foresee. At least that is what I think they are muttering. Meanwhile another company is fitting a, Stand alone system for the living area. Enough of my woes. Miss you.

That was Anna's message. A triage of air conditioning problems and a, miss you. Perhaps she was thinking I might have been able to solve the problem? No, this was just Anna wanting to say, I Miss You but didn't wish to be too obvious. Wrap it up with air conditioning. Less of an impact. I decided not to send an immediate response. It was well into the evening before I did.

Hi Anna. I haven't replied sooner, hoping, your A/C worries are now over. Also ……. it gave you more time to miss me. By now everybody has settled in. Large glasses of vodka being hastily drunk. Cossack music blaring in the background

and someone giving their best but embarrassing rendition of the Hopak. I
therefore wish you a pleasant evening but advise two ibuprofen before bedtime.
Miss You Too.

I received a reply fifteen minutes later.

Oh James. I had to show your message to my guests. They agreed I had two
choices. Get rid of you immediately if that is your opinion of Russian people. Or
.... marry you immediately based purely on your sense of humour. The A/C
is still problematic but the back up is working a treat. You will have to excuse
me now. I have to get another crate of vodka.

I could hear her laughing as she sent that.

Saturday morning and things to buy at the English shop. I decided to
incorporate a breakfast into the bargain as I won't be eating again until evening.
As I walked through town the sun was shining down on my cafe. The food and
breakfast could wait. I ordered a café. It was ten thirty before I sat down for
breakfast. Washed down with a pint of Kilkenny was not my norm for this time
of day but hey, why not. Once home my day seemed to be filled with, stuff to do.
A quick message to Anna before going next door.

Hi Anna. Hope you're not suffering the aftereffects. You should know it's wise
to stop after one crate. Going next door for one of their BBQ's, sans Anna
therefore unlikely to be any interesting tales to tell come the morrow. Although I
did hear there was a chance of a group turning up. Something about a twelve
women yachting team. A Swedish yachting team I believe. Most probably ski
instructors in the winter. Anyway, don't get up to any mischief and I'll let you
know tomorrow how my evening went.

That will get a reaction but I had no idea what form it would take. I did not have
too long to wait.

I will have you know James, I was up at seven hosing down the patio. The
groceries for the weekend arrived at eight. Coffee and croissants with the quests
at nine. By ten thirty we were visiting apartments for sale in Cannes that I had
prearranged. One thirty and back for lunch which yes, I had also prearranged.
Admittedly with a little help from Marta. Four o'clock at the golf club so the guys
could check out their swing and now back preparing dinner. Such an all
consuming day and when your message arrived and I hoped for some light relief,
even possible encouragement from you but what do I get? Accusations of
alcoholism and an interest in Swedish girls. I am so upset!

Ok. Not quite what I expected. And then another message arrived.

Or I could tell the truth by thanking you for advising the Ibuprofen. (Too much
wine. Not vodka.) When I awoke at ten I had but a slight headache. We've had
an enjoyable lounge about day. They have gone for a walk which has left me
with the dinner preparations. That bit is true. I got you, didn't I James. That will
teach you for throwing imaginary Swedish women in my direction. Have a lovely
evening with Paul and Chiara and give them my best.

Yes, she got me.

Yes, you got me. I promise never again to provoke your wrath. For my sake more than your own. Enjoy your evening Anna.

Time for the BBQ. It was roughly the same crowd I'd seen the last time, with Anna. If I was to hear, Where's Anna? Anna not with you? Or derivatives of, just one more time ...... but it didn't persist. A most enjoyable evening but not wishing to be the last, I wished my good nights to the remaining few, around one.

The sunshine persisted and although a chilly morning it was time to get the roof down on the Figaro. I headed for Nice. Something I rarely did but parking at that time of a Sunday morning wouldn't be a problem. I parked on the Promenade des Anglais. Maybe a twenty minute walk to the harbour but first, a coffee. There was a boulangerie nearby that briefly held my attention with a steady flow of people to interest me. Bread bought daily. Perhaps even twice or three times. The sacrifice made for preservative and additive free bread. The baguette didn't stay fresh long.

It was three hours before I returned to the car, now carrying the light jacket I was wearing earlier. I was going to take the long way home, I remembered thinking. Via the harbour I'd left an hour previously. One hundred and eighty degrees in the wrong direction. Stuck in traffic, works well in the Figaro. People see it. People wave and smile. If given the chance, would ask me about it. Driving a Figaro one was surrounded by happy people. Well, that was the way it felt. It was late afternoon as I drove into my road with the shadows growing rapidly longer. It was a little like a horror movie. Be home before dark. There was some truth in that statement. It got cold, very quickly in the South of France as late afternoon approached. What was eighteen degrees only an hour or so before, will be ten very shortly. Get in. Put the heating on and batten down the hatches. Anna called.

Hello James. How are you? We've just been to Nice.

Me too! I thought.

We walked along the promenade and had coffee.

Me too! I thought.

It was a glorious day. While we were there Anton managed to get tickets for a show this evening.

I didn't do that.

How was the BBQ? Did anyone ask after me?

Now were those questions about the BBQ or Anna? No much doubt, I thought, which it was.

The BBQ was missing but one element for a complete success and yes, everybody asked why that element wasn't present.

Really James?

Now why I wonder, do you ask a question Anna, when you already know the answer.

Oh come on James. Tell me. Tell me.

She was in one of her devilish moods. Childishly devilish.

So much was the interest in you I reached a point where I insisted on everybody's attention and said, If just one more person asks me about Anna I will not be held responsible for my actions.

You didn't?

No I didn't but I think I could have. You were the star of the show Anna. Albeit an absent one, it was far more than the fifteen minutes Andy Warhol accredited us. How was your evening?

Relaxing, after the evening before. Less wine helped. I am in the bedroom at the moment about to have an hour or so of sleep. Oh before I forget, can we see each other on Tuesday evening. I could come to you. I'm missing ...... our Ludo time and Irish coffee.

Of course Anna but don't feel afraid of expressing your true feelings. To say you miss me, is ok. At the usual time?

We have a usual time?

So, Anna was going to ignore the gist of that remark.

Usually you suggest a time Anna, that's what I call the usual time which invariably turns out not to be the time you suggested.

In that case James, see you at the usual time. Did I miss something?

She was laughing as she hung up.

The next two days could not come soon enough. I received a photo and brief note from Anna around two on Monday. Anna and her friends having lunch. Anna blowing a kiss with a glass of champagne in her hand. A glass of champagne in hand. Now that brought back memories.

The kiss is for you James. Don't work too hard!

Little chance of that. The days had become more coffee breaks than work. Less than three weeks and Kitzbuhel here we come. I concentrated on that and sent Anna a message.

You look divine my dear, wearing one of my favourite dresses. Enjoy lunch but try to keep them off the vodka.

Mentioning what she was wearing was a moment of inspiration. To some it might come naturally to compliment a woman on her dress sense. Not quite so natural for me.

Oh James how is it possible you can be so thoughtful and yet so political incorrect. And how is it possible your political incorrectness has my friends laughing. We raise a glass (champagne) to you. I'll call this evening.

My moment of inspiration was deemed thoughtful. Take note James. The rest, had the desired effect of creating humour. The day flew by, aided by reactive action to emails from New York and thoughts of ..... Thoughts of Anna.

Hello James, sorry to be so late. It is the first chance I've had to get away.
It was ten forty five and I could already hear the gaiety in Anna's voice.
I do love them dearly but I will be glad when they leave. My liver needs recuperation but after tomorrow evening. I am not sure how many glasses of wine I have drunk this evening.
And so Anna continued. I had very little to say. Not that I didn't have something to say. Just no chance. Some of what she said didn't really make sense. It didn't matter. Anna in that mood was a joy to the ear.
Am I making any sense James? I'm not, am I? I should go. Love you James.
She was gone. It didn't really matter. Love you James. That's what mattered! I knew I shouldn't have paid too much attention to those words. Anna was definitely under the influence which was not her norm. It was just words used to finish the conversation. And yet she said them and not for the first time. Sleep didn't come easy that night.
I was tired the next day. It was late morning before all cylinders were firing and not for the first time today, I contemplated calling Anna. At least a message, only I was unsure of the content. Hi Anna, nice to know you love me. Love you too! No need to worry. Anna messaged me.
Good morning James. This is the second hangover I've had this year. The other was the day before yesterday. I remember calling you later than I wanted and as it turned out I was right. I should have made it earlier then I would have remembered what I said. I do remember talking a lot, sorry. They are slowly getting their belongings together while Marta is preparing a light lunch. I have the second coffee in front of me but still finding it difficult to do anything but stare, glassy eyed at nothing in particular. I will have time for a couple of hours sleep this afternoon. Need to be at my best this evening. See you soon. x (What did I say?)
Don't worry Anna, I can replay the recording I made last night. Have a restful few hours and yes, see you soon. x
I couldn't resist it. I wasn't really expecting a response from Anna. I wasn't disappointed. I was home at six after visiting the supermarket. An hour later a tuna pasta with gorgonzola sauce was ready for the oven. It was a last minute thought, imagining Anna hadn't eaten since her light lunchtime salad. I decided to message her.
Hi Anna, I'm not sure if you've eaten since lunchtime. If not you will be pleased to know dinner is prepared. See you sooner.
Perfect timing James. I've just woken up and as I'm feeling hungry I shall shower and go. Expect me in an hour.
That would make it about eight thirty, I thought. I'll open the gate just before nine. Anna arrived promptly at nine fifteen. She was wearing the dress from the day before.

Divine does not encompass the reality Anna and I struggle finding words that do you justice.

A kiss would be a good start James.

The flattery, that came so easily, worked. Anna loved compliments and was happy to express her gratitude but we were outside so the gratitude was brief. I followed Anna into the house. Her light grey dress, cut in at the waist and hugging her hips had me wishing the front door was a lot further away.

You are watching me, aren't you James.

It is not for no reason, I've declared this dress one of my favourites Anna.

She turned to face me.

And from the front James?

That was an invitation, the way I saw it, allowing me to scrutinise Anna from top to bottom. I took my time. Anna took up a few dignified poses. Anna never appeared or acted in a manner that one would associate with sexy. And yet ……. Was it possible to maintain a seriously composed but sexy manner without defining the latter?

From the front, I have a dilemma Anna. You look so readably gorgeous I waver between wanting you and taking you but in doing either would remove the vision I now see before me. I suggest we start with a glass of wine. At the very least that would prevent your dress from being crumpled in a heap the moment we were inside.

So you like the dress James?

We both laughed.

What are we having for dinner James? Let me see.

I produced the Pyrex dish from the fridge. It might have just been a tuna pasta dish but the chopped red peppers and celery dotted around gave it colour and hopefully a more interesting appeal. Anna sniffed the contents of the bowl.

What can I smell James. Oregano I think. Garlic with a pungent cheese sauce. It smells delicious. Can we eat soon?

"It will take twenty minutes in the oven Anna". I said, opening the oven door.

We sipped our wine as Anna recalled her last few days. I still wasn't sure if Anna told a good story or it was in the telling that I enjoyed so much. To watch her, full of confidence and utilising her own adorable characteristics. Her voice rising and falling in sync with every facial and bodily expression she made. It was an art form. Anna's very own art form. Pasta on the plate was the only thing that slowed her.

That was delicious James. Can I have the recipe?

"No", said I, as I cleared away the dishes. "But I'll cook it for you".

I have just realised Anna. I have dinner and breakfast covered. …… It reminds me of the, cigarette before scenario.

That had Anna laughing as she prepared the Irish coffee while I set up the Ludo. Being such an easy game to play there wasn't the restriction on conversation as found in other games although that wasn't going to distract Anna from concentrating. Still trying to understand the complexities of a game where none lay. She liked to win and you're not going to do that without concentrating. She would start a conversation and then realise it was her move. Silence. Threw the dice, looking left across the field of play. I followed her eyes as they slowly shifted right. Finally deciding on a move that was apparent from the outset. So I am a Master of a game who could most likely be beaten by a ten year old. If a ten year old could be bothered. But for Anna ...... maybe it was just too logical? Too simplistic? It ended three to one not that Anna was disheartened.

One day James I will beat you again.

I look forward to that day Anna.

It's still early James. Let's watch the final episodes of 24. I will make more coffee.

That left me to set up the DVD. It was something I thought unusual. Anna with her home theatre yet everything was on DVD. Not a hard drive to be seen. I opened the box set and found the relevant DVD. As the DVD booted up Anna suggested I got the bed blanket. I got her dressing gown. You don't want that dress creased, I said, then went in search of the blanket. When I returned Anna was stood, in her underwear. Her dress neatly folded on the chair.

I thought you would like to see before I wrap myself in the dressing gown.

I slowly walked over to face her. Placing my hands around her bare hips I kissed her. Not passionately. Small kisses around her mouth. Anna sighed as I drew away.

Now may I suggest you cover yourself up because it is doubtful, if you don't, we will see the concluding episodes.

Anna reached for the dressing down.

Spoilsport James. I was hoping you would drag me to the floor and ravage me.

Well, that is what you were considering, wasn't it?

Now I am Anna.

The next hour and a half were spent snuggled up under that comfort blanket. It took some time to drag my thoughts away from Anna. Anna, who stood in a light blue ensemble with pretty yellow flowers adorning both bra and panties. That was not sexy. That was an insatiable appetite viewed by a hungry me. Looking sexy didn't even figure in the equation. The way Anna looked at me. "I know you want to take me James. Here I am but you know you can't touch. You also know I want you. Isn't it delicious?" Her eyes said that and more. How difficult it was to concentrate on those flashing pictures and nonsensical words on the screen. Not made any the easier with Anna, head laid on my chest and our arms entwined around her waist. That bare waist. That flat stomach. I had just about received clarity from brain to television when the episode ended. No problem. Find the remote and choose, next. I had to leave that to Anna as it was buried beneath the blanket. Anywhere I might have put my hands would've jeopardised the partnership recently agreed between my brain and that television. Remote recovered we faced the ultimate episode.

While the credits rolled I managed to untangle myself from both Anna and the blanket. Time to clear up before bed. Dishes away, I looked from the sink to the settee only to find, no Anna. Just blanket. I turned off the television and the lights and made my way to the dimly lit bedroom.

I think you need to get an electric blanket James. It is definitely not warm under here.

If you're referring to the temperature you're most likely correct. If you are referring to you. Definitely incorrect. You had my temperature rising by some degrees earlier and I don't think much has changed. Perhaps a smoke alarm rather than an electric blanket would be a wiser choice?

Very funny James now can you please come and warm me up.

Anna was still in her underwear as I slipped in to lie next to her. I decided to not to waste any time. I kissed her as my hand foraged below. The fabric of her panties was so soft to the touch, my fingers were able to trace the outline of those lips that lay beneath. Anna reacted to my touch as our kisses became more intense. Together we managed to discard that fabric and no sooner done, Anna opened her legs to receive me. From that very first time, one Sunday afternoon in July, there had been a sexual connection. Discovering Anna and she me, came as naturally as breathing. We had no misgivings. We held nothing back. For me it was about pleasing Anna and that was so incredibly easy to do. For Anna? I do believe she felt the same way. Please me James and you will discover how wonderful it can be. Ephemeral was never the way between us. Occasionally I might have wished it was. None of us were getting any younger but with Anna time was of little importance. Anna's last words to me that night?

Mmmm, Good Night James.

I was the first to wake. I tried to exit the bedroom quietly but Anna stirred.

"Orange juice and coffee coming up," I said.

I returned with the drinks as Anna was sitting up. I thought it sweet and amusing, the way she pulled the duvet up to cover her breasts.

Thank you James and thank you for the coffee and juice.

I knew what she was referring to, particularly as it was accompanied by her wicked smile.

If anybody deserves a thank you it would have to be given to another, not me. Either I dreamt it or I spent the night with Venus. She is the one who deserves my thanks. You wouldn't happen to have her number?

You do have this annoyingly wonderful way of disguising your compliments James. You'll find her under Anna in your contacts.

Touché. I let it be known yesterday at work, not to expect me in too early so how about English breakfast? I don't know about you but I'm famished and the Hopstore opens in fifteen minutes.

I am hungry, maybe not quite famished. Perhaps it is a calorie thing? Maybe you've burnt off more than I?

Before I could think of a retort, Anna was out of bed but finding it difficult to untangle her underwear. Laughing will do that.

We decided to take both cars as we would be heading in opposite directions after breakfast. Twice around the block and I managed to secure a place to park. Anna was waiting for me when I arrived. The advantage of using underground parking.

You are late James.

And you are infuriatingly correct. Shall we sit my dear?

Anna laughingly sat. Every day was a sunshine day, I thought. Yes, the sun was shining and for the next hour or so, that winter sunshine, shone on us but that was only a part of it. The sun on Anna's face as she looked at me.

A penny for your thoughts James.

I was comparing.

That is not your thoughts James, that is what you were doing with your thoughts.

Comparing you to sunshine.

Who won?

You did!

Would you like to expand on that?

No.

Anna was slightly taken aback but soon recovered.

In that case, I will not tell you what I was thinking.

Of course, Anna expected me to crumble. Divulge every detail of my thoughts.

But Anna, I already know what you were thinking. You were thinking, What else does James have to disclose.

And so the time passed with a mixture of humour, small talk and a lot of hand holding.

James, I am going away on Saturday afternoon, for a week, to stay with Tanya. She is in need of some love and sympathy. Can you finish work early on Friday? Come and stay the night and we can have lunch before I leave. On the terrace if the sun is still shining.

She did that. Mixed the high points while disguising the implications of the low. Friday afternoon? I was sure I could leave at lunchtime. Twenty four hours with Anna. Not until Friday? Ok, it's only this evening ...... and Thursday. It still felt like a long time to me. We finished with coffee. I paid followed by kisses on the cheeks.

That is three now James.

I looked confused.

Three Thank You's for today.

She walked away, laughing.

I arrived in the office just before midday thinking, it would be ideal if this was the norm. Fitting work around social, rather than the other way around. I concentrated on working out the electrical consumption of a potential new stand. Times are a changing in electrical consumption. It was only a few years ago I would have been estimating twenty or thirty kilowatts, now it would be under five. I emailed my findings to those concerned and went for lunch.

A chance to text my favourite girl. (I'm so glad I got her number this morning.) How is my goddess? Now I will try to be serious. I thought you'd like to know, I can be with you around two thirty on Friday.

Perhaps you could start with a dip in the pool James. I think you need to cool off! See you then. x

The kiss did not go unnoticed. It certainly saw me through the rest of that day and drinks and dinner with the neighbours was the perfect closure.

Thursday was uneventful other than being a day in the way of Friday. Will and I did manage to disappear for a few hours, hunting a specific style of sofa. After about fifteen emails describing the colour, the size, the materials with the client. Why they couldn't have just sent a photo along the lines of their thoughts, I'd never know. We could build a stand with less information. What the client wants, the client gets.

I must have spent an hour that evening, admittedly it did incorporate two beers and as many cigarettes, trying to decide what to wear the following day. I would have time to come home, shower, change and go, if I was to get to Anna's by two thirty. A Friday afternoon, plus evening and the following morning. I didn't want to take a change of clothing and then it hit me. My apres ski birthday presents. That was the shirt and jumper taken care of. The trousers and shoes were easier. I had a limited choice. A light jacket in case lunch happens on the terrace. I was just settling down for the evening when Anna called.

Such a crazy day. I knew it would be which is why I reluctantly thought it better we didn't meet this evening. I spent all morning at the Hotel de Ville, smiling, cajoling, basically doing what ever it took to get a few documents accepted. On top of that I had been told there could be a small crack in the pool and if so it would have to be emptied to be fixed. There were three workmen wondering back and forth with various instruments for two hours. The conclusion. There was no leak. The first man was wrong. I also had to take Marta to the doctors. Nothing serious. A slight ear infection. Then shopping. As I am going away for a week we needed to get food in for her. A pile of paperwork that had to be sorted through. Those were things I had to do today but not what I wanted to do. What is it like to be wanted James? Sorry James but I do feel better now. Thank you for listening to the woes of my day. How are you? How was your day?

I considered saying she didn't need to thank me as I didn't exactly have a choice in the matter but rightly so, decided against it.

My day? Three hours shopping for a sofa. Followed by lunch and I think that about sums up my day.

You are buying a new sofa? You should have asked me to help you choose.

No Anna, it was for a client with specific requirements. No taste required above and beyond their needs. I know this because it took them an awful lot of emails to get this far.

Before I forget James, can you pick up a couple of baguettes on your way tomorrow and a bottle of Irish whisky. I only noticed when I got back that we are almost out.

Anna was tired. There wasn't the usual lively tone in her voice.

Of course I can and if you think of anything else before twelve tomorrow you can text me.

Thank you James and now if you don't mind I think I will find a book and go to bed. You know, I've hardly read a thing since I've known you. I wonder if that means anything?

Possibly because there is nothing like the real thing Anna? Good night James.

Chapter Twenty One

I bought the whisky on the way to work the next morning at a local Carrefour, that was surprisingly open at eight o'clock. I would get the baguettes at my corner shop before driving to Anna's. A quick message before the guys arrive.

Good morning sleepy head. Hope you are feeling refreshed. It was perhaps a good reason you decided on taking a book to bed last night. I'm sure the book didn't keep you up half the night.

Anna's response was a call around eleven.

Yes James, totally refreshed but the book does not give the afterglow I am used to when you are around.

I could almost see her trying to hold a straight face as she said that. Desperate to keep her words neutral.

A light lunch at three giving us plenty of time for the jacuzzi later. What do you think James?

About the afterglow? I'd like to hear more.

No James. Not the afterglow, the lunch and sauna, as you well know. You are so incorrigible. Never change. Promise me you will never change.

I promise but can I have the occasional shower?

See you at two thirty James.

Anna wore a dress I'd never seen before. It reminded me of the flock curtains that were all the rage many years ago. A very thick fabric. The background black although little showed as it was covered with pale pink roses in full bloom. Splashes of greens and greys. A figure hugging dress that finished just below the knee. Long sleeves and round neck completed the look. The look was outstandingly chic. Glossy magazine chic. My face must have said it all.

Such a wonderfully understated compliment James.

They say a picture is worth a thousand words Anna. Pick the words you most like from my face and they won't come close to defining the elegance and grace I see before me. You look stunning my dear.

Why thank you kind sir. Actually I held back on the make up knowing the sauna was up and coming. Normally I would wear a black eye shadow with this dress, as it compliments the dark undertones of the fabric. I like your shirt and top. Someone with taste bought those I think?

Yes Anna, someone with taste.

Anna gave a generous smile and led me through the house to the terrace.

They say it is going to rain on Monday. Perhaps our last chance to take advantage of this prolonged Indian summer.

There was a bottle of red already opened on the table. I poured.

To the end of a beautiful Indian summer Anna. A summer that will live forever in our hearts.

Oh James. Lets drink to that.

Lightly grilled salmon with green leaves, was lunch. Tatsoi, I was later to discover, was the preferred name for the green leaves. We cleared away the remains of lunch. I managed to find the right button that closed the wall of glass.

"Can you help me James", said Anna as she disappeared in the direction of the bedrooms, "I need help to unzip this dress. The sauna is calling".

I entered the bedroom as Anna turned her back to me.

There is a little clasp at the top. Yes that is it, now can you please pull the zip down, until it stops.

This was sexual. In her bedroom and being asked to ..... to undress her. I wasn't prepared for this moment. Watching Anna expertly slip the dress from her shoulders. It fell to her waist. She still had her back to me as she manoeuvred the thick fabric over her hips and let it drop to the floor. Naked bar panties and bra. She turned to face me.

Your bathrobe is over there James.

I turned to face the direction Anna was pointing. Pointing with an expression that read, Later James. Later. I took my clothes off, trying really hard not to stare. Anna saw me staring.

I make no excuses Anna. You have to be the only person I've seen naked, that no matter how many times, I deem myself fortunate. Fortunate but knowing it will never be enough. Never will I tire of seeing you undress. Of seeing you naked.

Anna looked across at me as she, slowly, wrapped her robe around her.

You always say the sweetest things James. If you were saying that twenty years ago I would have accepted it without merit. That was twenty years ago.

She walked over and kissed me. Acknowledgement of some imperfection I overlooked perhaps? There was no imperfection. As we kissed I took the back of her head in my hand. I forced my kisses on her. I withdrew fractionally to allow her a breath.

Anna, what I said was true. I will never tire of seeing you naked as I will never tire of seeing you. Of being with you. Of our hands touching across a table. Of seeing you smile. Of hearing your voice. It is all part of the Anna that I could never tire of.

"Let's go to the sauna James and you can tell me more of those beautiful lies". Said Anna with that wicked smile on her face.

I picked up the glasses and an almost full bottle of red on the way to the sauna. We were outside on the terrace. It was maybe ten degrees and there we were, heading for the sauna in bathrobes and slippers. All so surreal. Watching Anna throw aside her robe as she climbed the steps into the sauna added to that surrealism.

Do you know James, this is only the third time I have been here and twice with a naked man. I will let you work out with whom that might be. I honestly wasn't thinking when I had this sauna built, I would be naked with a man. Well, maybe a little fantasy. It is sublimely sexual don't you think?

You want me to answer that Anna?

Yes! Well, I do now.

I feel myself caught. Caught with a longing to embrace your body. Adorn you with kisses. Hold you close. Surround you in the fluidity at our disposal and yet, because of the temperature , I am left with a realisation. A realisation of the final act being outside the range of sublimeness for me. What I can offer is a glass of wine and a toast. .... "Sublime is no substitute for the reality we have".

Is sublimeness a word James?

I doubt it but that wasn't the point.

And the point was?

Why want for greatness when what we have is all we need.

Beautifully put James.

Anna raised her glass. "To what we have".

Yes Anna, I thought, To what we have. Sitting in this vast transition of a pool house to jacuzzi with Anna floating opposite. Her breasts just above the water line. What more could I possibly ask for. We touched glasses.

You do present me with a conundrum Anna.

Anna waited.

I am here in an oh so hot tub with physical feelings that are beyond my capabilities of understanding. I am sure, in fact, I'm certain, you know that. You know I ...... I think of your physique as perfection personified. It has become obvious to me over the last months that your attitude to your own nakedness in my presence has changed. You now flaunt your nakedness . Why? You know you have an appreciative audience. You are happy in your own body knowing

someone ..... ok, me, will always .... always pay homage regardless of any imperfections, if any.
So which parts do you think as imperfect James?
The moment imperfections was out of my mouth, I regretted saying it. Now Anna is asking me to quantify her imperfections.
I didn't say you have imperfections. I said .... IF you have any, they would be irrelevant. I put my glass down. I approach you. I kiss you. I move my hands around your body.
We kissed as I continued talking.
This gap between your legs. The slight shudder that corresponds with that touch. I move my hand to encompass your breast. I find no fault Anna. You have none. Regardless of the personality that dwells within, no matter it's beyond a mere mortal as myself to fully appreciate, ... to be allowed to view your body, is reward enough.
This reminds me of a picture you text me James. Do you remember? There was a woman sat facing a man having a drink. He said, "You are beautiful". She said, "You are only saying that in the hope I let you fuck me". He said, "Intelligent too!". Is that what you are doing James?
The devil in Anna spoke. She wanted me to admit to the bullshit I had just verbalised.
I hadn't thought of it that way. It could be true to some extent but you have failed to see the obvious. I have no need to compliment you in this way if I didn't mean it. You've already let me fuck you!
Anna almost dropped her glass. She was laughing so much. Once she had regained her composure .....
You are right James, I have allowed you. Is that my hold over you? Is my body such a temple? Do you idolise my every naked movement? Am I revered?
And so speaks the intelligent woman Anna. Always trying to quantify their sexuality.
I took Anna's glass from her. I placed mine next to hers. I lightly held her neck in my hands.
Ok Anna, we've had enough times together in bed, to recognise our compatibility. When I watch you naked. When I watch you grilling the salmon. When I watch you on the phone talking to ..... who knows who, in Russian. When I watch you exit the car. When I watch you. .... I am not thinking of the intelligent woman I am fortunate enough to be lying next to. I am thinking Anna. That's you Anna. You who I hold between my hands.
Kiss me James.
I did. We excelled in kissing. Does one learn such a thing? Does experience count? Are there classes? How does one achieve such a report through kissing? Take skiing. I spent two seasons in the mountains. Had one lesson at the beginning of my ski career. The rest I picked up following on the tail end of ski

schools. Until I got kicked off. Hence, self taught skier. Am I a good skier? No. So how come kissing, self taught, can be any different? It didn't matter. For some people sport comes naturally. Some, solving problems. Others, a gift for being a people person. Me? I could kiss. And we did.

Our departure from the jacuzzi was less intoxicating than previous visits. It was a practical application. We showered, put our robes back on and headed for the house. Possibly Anna came to the same conclusion as I? There was only two possibilities post jacuzzi. One would have us rolling on the heated tiled floor which would have been the natural conclusion to our heated embraces post jacuzzi. The other? Let's be sensible and be grown up about this. Why take the tiled floor when the bed is far more comfortable. We might have come to the same conclusion but perhaps not the one I was secretly hoping for. Although Anna had the potential for mischief it would not be at the risk of her values. She was, above all else, a Lady and Ladies should not be seen rolling around on the floor and certainly not naked in the arms of another. Back to the house it was. Anna had preprepared a variety of vegetables and chicken, cut and sliced appropriately.

If you can open another bottle James I will try and find the wok. Marta never uses it and me rarely, so it will gradually get pushed to the back. Ah, there it is!

We hadn't spoken during Anna's cooking time. She was concentrating. I was happy to watch. We spoke during dinner about Kitzbuhel being only two weeks away. This led Anna to ask me about my time as a barman. Which led me to lie. No I didn't get drunk every night and if it was true about barmen and their exploits with women, I never saw it. Might not be believed, so I was on safer ground telling her about the endless blue skies. Knowing where best to go to avoid the crowds. The crazy things we did on the slopes.

You liked it James? The dinner.

It was delicious Anna.

She was about to say more.

Stop it Anna. It was delicious! As are you.

I put my hands on her bare knees. Leant forward and kissed her. I topped up her glass.

Don't you move. Stay right where you are while I clear away.

Anna didn't move. Now I could feel her watching me.

A coffee to finish?

Yes James. Shall I make it?

Did I ask you to make it? I distinctly remember asking you not to move.

We sat with the coffees between us not speaking. I ran the back of my hand down her face. She moved her head to her shoulder while closing her eyes and trapping my hand between shoulder and face. She slowly and gently ran her face against the back of my hand. She opened her eyes, and looking straight into mine she smiled. I couldn't break away from that look. I wanted to remember it. Serene. Tender. Fragile innocence. Acceptance. A look of love? It was Anna who first moved. Lifting her head from my hand. Kissing me, then whispering in my ear.

Time for bed James?

Anna was closing the shutters as I entered the room. I walked to the last shutters. I moved aside to let Anna complete her task. Shutters closed Anna was about to turn but she met with resistance. I was behind her with my arms now firmly around her waist. She waited. I untied her robe as I kissed the back of her neck. She rolled her head in response. A slight murmur in her throat. I ran my hands over her breasts. Those small, firm breasts. Her bathrobe open from top to bottom. It was not difficult to slide it off her shoulders. Naked in front of me, with my hands on her hips, Anna stood still. It was a sensual feeling.

I'm yours James, be gentle.

I turned her to face me, to be greeted by a look that confirmed the words just spoken. We kissed. We kissed, my hands around her neck. Her hands concentrating on relieving me of my bathrobe. Anna stood back. With a final look in my direction she pulled back the duvet and laid down. Laying on her back, she opened her legs, just ever so slightly.

I want you inside me James. I want what I know only you can give me. I want tender love James.

I was as certain as one could be, those next few hours were nothing if not tender. I anticipated Anna's every move. Slowly, so ever so slowly, bringing her to a climax. Before she could fully recover, returning her to that place. Anna could take no more as I attempted the third.

No more James. Just stay inside me.

With her back to me, I stayed inside. That time, I waited for Anna to speak. It was some minutes before she did.

I now understand when it is said, "You can have too much of a good thing". There was a good chance I would have passed out if we continued.

That broke the silence. Anna was laughing. The inevitable consequence of Anna's laughter? She inadvertently pushed me out. Realising this, Anna turned to face me.

You are amazing James. Or maybe I should say, you never cease to amaze me. You know exactly what I want in fact you seem to know it before I do!

That had Anna laughing again. When she had stopped, she put her hands to my face. Kissed me and said,

Pleasant dreams James. Mine most certainly will be.

Anna turned away. I lay there listening to her breathing as she slowly descended into sleep.

Chapter Twenty Two

Let's go for a walk James.
I opened my eyes to see Anna, fully dressed, standing over me with a coffee.
I thought I'd achieved my quota of exercise last night Anna?
It is a beautiful day James and we need baguettes. Come and get me when you've showered, I will be in the study. And don't take too long.
I gave her an endearing smile. Anna put the coffee on the table and threw back the duvet.
See you soon.
And she was gone. I was going to pay her back for what she thought was funny. I sipped the coffee. Took a shower and went in search of Anna, naked. She was sat at her desk as I entered.
James!
I gave my most confused look.
Didn't you say, after I'd showered, to come and take you and get long?
Anna almost fell off her chair.
"Guess I got that wrong?" I said, continuing my confused look compounded by an equally confused manner as I turned and walked out. Anna's laughter still ringing in my ears.
When I returned, now fully clothed, Anna hadn't moved but was shaking her head with a huge smile on her face.
You did that on purpose didn't you James.
Yes.
I know why I am in such an effervescent mood James, after last night it would be impossible to be any other way. But that, that was the icing on the cake. Don't ever change James, no matter what. Never change. You promise me?

I promise. Now, shall we get those baguettes?
It was a ten minute walk to the shops just off the roundabout. Anna didn't stop talking the whole way. Occasionally apologising for talking too much. We walked hand in hand. From the moment we left the house, Anna couldn't settle on what she wanted. Arm around waists. Arm on shoulder. Holding hands. She was trying to express her mood in actions. She wanted to be close. We entered the boulangerie. Anna seemed to take great delight in investigating all on show. A child in a sweet shop came to mind.
Anna?
Yes James?
Bread? We are here to buy bread?
Such a spoilsport James.
Anna spotted the pain de campagne.
I am going to treat you to the best bread topping in the world James.
We bought two baguettes and the loaf. Next stop the greengrocers opposite. Anna picked up some Italian tomatoes and we headed back.
Would you like to help James?
Sure. What would you like me to do?
Anna found the cheese grater.
Can you grate the tomatoes.
I had never grated tomatoes. It was not an easy task but fortunately the tomatoes were firm, which helped. A pile of tomato pulp lay on the chopping board. The remainder covering my hands. Anna meanwhile had four large slices of bread cut. Olive oil. Garlic and some herbs from the garden standing by.
Well done James. Now if you can clean up the mess you've made and make us a coffee, I will finish up.
We had coffee on the terrace. I guessed at about fifteen degrees but with the warmth of the morning sun reaching it's apex, it was pleasant enough. Anna took a call from Tanya. How different she seemed, talking in Russian. Was it the Russian or the context of the conversation that made it seem so? I wasn't to know but once the call had finished Anna did say Tanya was wondering why it will be so late before her arrival.
I don't think she is happy knowing I haven't left. She thought I was leaving in the morning and would be there by three. I told her. I am having an early lunch with you and will be there around seven. Talking of which, if you can prepare the table I will organise the food.
Fifteen minutes and we were tucking into a mackerel salad with a side dish of Pan con Tomate.
I think it must be thirty five years ,when visiting friends living near Barcelona, that I tasted such as this. It's delicious Anna. You were right. The best tasting topping in the world! Well done. .... Is everything ok? You seem a bit withdrawn.

Sorry James, I'm allowing Tanya's annoyance to filter through.
It's ok Anna. Would you prefer to leave sooner? After all, I don't want to come
between you and your daughter. And anyway, if I tried, I think I would lose.
Anna managed an acknowledge smile.
I don't want to ..... but maybe I should.
It's ok Anna. We can clear away and you can be on your way in thirty minutes.
Anna looked at me, taking a moment to reply.
Actually I've told Tanya I will be in Geneva around seven. If I leave in thirty
minutes ..... I will be there about six.
She had a wicked look in her eye. I decided to check if I read that right.
Clear everything away in ten minutes gives you time to change Anna. You will
need help, obviously.
Obviously.
I read that right. We almost ran to the bedroom. Nothing sensual about this
one. Anna was naked before I could undo my shoelaces. Anna was patient. ....
To a point.
Just take me James.
I struggled with the laces for another microsecond before I was able, with all
the natural laws of physics against me, to discard the shoes. Anna was knelt at
the edge of the bed. Head buried in the duvet. Knees apart and waiting. Naked
from waist down, I entered her. I was never forceful no matter what the situation.
Call it an inbuilt desire to please. I entered, slowly. I reserved the thrust even
when believing that was what Anna wanted. But she did! So who was I to deny
her. It was a few minutes before Anna was burrowing her face in the duvet, not
wanting her sound to travel. I lost control about the same time. I collapsed upon
her. There was something to be said for the, "Wham Bam Thank You Mam",
strategy. ..... with reservation. If it's what is wanted. ..... at the time ..... and one
happened to be so inclined, then who was one to refuse such an offer. I didn't.
Hence, there I was, laying on top of Anna. One moment clearing away the
dishes, the next ..... it was all too much. We lay there, exhausted. Maybe fifteen
minutes had past and we were lying there. Both our desires fulfilled.
You know we have my daughter to thank for this James? If it wasn't for her we
would have taken our time over lunch and wished each other a fond goodbye.
"Thank you Tanya", I said.
We still hadn't moved.
If you don't mind James, I will not be passing on your considerations to Tanya.
If for no other reason than I am not sure how I might do so.
How about. James says thank you and if it wasn't for you, your mother and I
wouldn't have been laid here, physically exhausted by the aftermath of an
excessive sexual liaison. I'm sure she'll understand.
I am sure she would .... if it had been excessive.

What Anna wanted, Anna got. It was some time before we left but enough time for Anna to make it to Geneva by seven. Well, seven thirty. We parted at the Peage with a wave and toot of horns.

Anna text me on her arrival saying all was well. Talk to you tomorrow. I replied with, Kisses from me. Watched a film and went to bed.

I was used to my space but every time I returned from Anna's, all was strange. The wide open space was now curtailed. My living room was not a hundred and eighty square metres of unused space. It was maybe thirty. All used! I needed to adjust. Mostly mentally as the physical confines were obvious. The neighbours came to the rescue, mostly unknowingly, but that was the way it worked with friends. Sunday afternoon BBQ that concluded around bedtime. I did manage to send a short message before retiring. I thought short was the best approach after my alcohol consumption. It was Tuesday before I received a reply.

Hello James. My granddaughter has kept me busy during the days and Tanya through the evenings. I am not used to such full days of interaction. Hope all is well with you.

Three days of nothing and then? "Hope all is well." Ok, so she was busy. I could understand that but .....

Hello Anna, I will read busy as, having fun. Particularly knowing how much you enjoy your granddaughter's presence. You will feel lost without their company on your return so I suggest you immerse yourself now and like any good grandparent run away when it all becomes too much. Enjoy!

No reply on Tuesday. Nothing on Wednesday. Thursday morning I sent a message.

Is everything ok Anna? I haven't heard from you. Too much immersion perhaps? Get back when you can.

I got a reply later that day.

Immersion could not be nearer the truth. It is difficult for me at the moment. Sorry to be so evasive. I will message you at the weekend James.

It was two months ago. A Saturday evening. A week before we flew to Munich and on to Kitzbuhel. I received what was to be that weekend message. Anna's last message.

I'm sorry James but it's not working for me. I cannot give you reasons. Maybe one day we can be friends. Somewhere, somehow but that would be another story. Needless to say, it would be inappropriate for us to go to Kitzbuhel together. Please don't contact me in the near future as it is all too distressing for me at this time.

I wish you all the happiness in the world. Anna

Epilogue

It has finally decided to rain. People running for cover as a sea of umbrellas appear. I take a glance at the remains of my coffee and fold The Times. I head for the car wishing I could avoid the repetition of my thoughts that were in my every waking moment. Wishing I had thought to bring an umbrella. Wishing the car was closer. Wishing I had never seen that epiphany in a yellow dress. Wishing I could turn back the clock and go out on that Friday night. ....
A Year Ago Today.

TIME

Time is irrelevant, a meaningless pirouette
With life surrounding their silhouette
Two together with time to spare
A brave new world, if only they dare

Dare they did, removed from all fear
Butterflies ignoring the winds they hear
Full of optimism for what the future might bring
Until the fat lady did, inevitably sing

And sing she must in this, a sad tale
Of two lovers who were destined to fail
So part they did as falling leaves in season
With no rhyme nor no reason

But to those who love, I give you hope
For the memories, they will never fade
And no one can deny those times you had
No one can deny, no matter how sad.

To not understand nor really know why
As time passes on, as time passes by
The thought of those memories will set you free
Those thoughts, with time, will Let It Be.

#0038 - 031018 - C0 - 210/148/21 - PB - 9781784566005